D1063947

DEAN C. BARNLUND

FRANKLYN S. HAIMAN

THE DYNAMICS

I am the stronger because only my civilization possesses the power to bind into its unity all diversity without depriving any element of its individuality.

Antoine de Saint-Exupéry

SAN FRANCISCO STATE COLLEGE

NORTHWESTERN UNIVERSITY

OF DISCUSSION

HOUGHTON MIFFLIN COMPANY · BOSTON

The Riverside Press Cambridge

The Riverside Press
CAMBRIDGE, MASSACHUSETTS
PRINTED IN THE U.S.A.

To Jean

PREFACE

THIS IS A BOOK about group discussion. The writing of it has itself been an experiment by the authors in collaborative learning and decision-making. From conception to final proofreading we have attempted to work in accord with the philosophy and methods set forth in the pages we were producing. Not only was the over-all organization of the book jointly planned, but detailed outlines for each chapter, including all the ideas and even many of the illustrations, were developed in conference. Labor was divided only for the writing of original drafts of the chapters. These manuscripts were reviewed and edited in further conferences, and were regarded as fair game for the red pencil of either writer. The order in which the names of the authors appear on the final product was determined by the toss of a coin.

The purpose of the book is to analyze the processes of group discussion. Part I, The Setting of Discussion, describes the place of discussion in our society, the varied forms it takes, and the goals of those who engage in it. In Part II, Group Thinking, the content of discussion is analyzed — the kinds of problems dealt with, the methods by which these problems may be explored, the raw materials of discussion, and the rational aspects of conflict. Part III, Interpersonal Relations, is primarily concerned with the human element — the ways in which interpersonal relationships develop and become stabilized, and the attendant problems of apathy, emotional conflict, and communication. The line dividing the topics dealt with in Parts II and III is an artificial one, created for purposes of analysis and explanation. The two areas are, in real-life situations, inextricably interwoven and interdependent, and must be dealt with simultaneously. The authors could just as sensibly have reversed the order of presentation of these two parts of the book, and some who read and use it may prefer to do so.

The question of leadership is dealt with in Part IV — the various functions of discussion leadership, the locus and the styles of leadership, and the all-pervading problem of control versus freedom. Although we have chosen to postpone formal consideration of leadership until this point in the book, it is our view that actually we have treated that topic throughout all of Parts II and III. For we see leadership as any significant influence which a participant brings to bear upon a group, and presumably the reader of Parts II and III will be equipped to do better at guiding a discussion at that point than he was before. Hence, in Part IV we seek to make explicit what has already been implicit and to place it in the more familiar context of the usual language of leadership. In Part V we consider some of the uses and abuses of discussion, as well as some changes taking place in the modern world that will influence the future of democratic processes — the impact of the mass media of communication, the increased specialization of knowledge and skills, and the growth of centralized government and large-scale business organizations.

An explanation for the inclusion of an appendix on methods of training may serve to acquaint the reader with one of the principles which have guided the authors in writing these pages. We believe that if people are to learn to improve their communication processes they must participate in and help shape their own course of instruction. Any program of teaching and learning is in itself a process of discussion between, and among, teacher and students. Since one of the primary methods of teaching people to improve their skills is to make them more sensitive to what is happening to themselves and others when they engage in group communication, it would not only be wasteful, but somewhat sterile, to pretend that discussion is something that happens only in "real life" outside of the classroom. To avoid analysis of the interpersonal relationships among teacher and students in the classroom itself, either because of squeamishness or simple failure to see the opportunity, is to miss one of the richest, most vivid, and most immediate sources of material available to the members of a group. The methods by which a student can learn about discussion should not, therefore, be secretly filed away in an instructor's manual or supplement. Self-consciousness about the *way* in which one is learning is, in our view, an integral part of *what* is being learned.

Speaking of learning, we would at this point like to express our indebtedness to the following persons whose works and teachings have been so influential in our thinking about discussion: Robert F. Bales, Kenneth D. Benne, John Dewey, Harrison Elliott, Mary P. Follett, Erich Fromm, George C. Homans, Irving J. Lee, Kurt Lewin, Eduard Lindeman, and James H. McBurney.

Finally, to Louise, for supporting our writers' conferences with levity, an excellent cuisine, and a third point of view, and to Mark, for not being quite old enough to get his hands on the manuscript, our deep appreciation.

DEAN C. BARNLUND
Associate Professor of Group Communication
Northwestern University

FRANKLYN S. HAIMAN
Associate Professor of Group Communication
Northwestern University

August 15, 1959

CONTENTS

PART FOUR • Leadership

PART FIVE • Discussion in the Modern World

APPENDICES • Learning to Discuss

INTRODUCTION

Of all the qualities one thinks of as being uniquely human there are two which are surely of the utmost importance — the ability to communicate with others through the medium of speech, and the ability to observe and evaluate the results of our behavior in order to act more effectively in the future. There is little doubt that man has utilized the first of these abilities from the beginning of his evolution, engaging with his fellow men in the processes of group communication. As for the second of these abilities, observing reactions and learning from them, there seems still much room for development. True, man has learned a great deal about himself in the centuries of his existence and has been able to improve his life in a multitude of material ways — through medical science, industry, government, etc. It is only in relatively recent times, however, that he has begun to achieve sufficient objectivity to study and improve those aspects of living in which he is the most personally and deeply involved, namely his own human relationships. So it is that the social sciences — psychology, sociology, and the study of communication — have achieved major stature only in the past half century.

It is true, of course, that great thinkers of the more distant past did concern themselves with these problems and wrote treatises which reveal important, albeit limited, insights. Aristotle's *Rhetoric* and his other works, for example, show a high degree of sensitivity in the fields of human behavior and interpersonal relationships, as do the works of such men as St. Augustine, Machiavelli, Francis Bacon, and Thomas Jefferson, to mention but a few. But only in the late nineteenth and twentieth century has the study of human behavior and social processes achieved the stature of a science — a label accorded only to the rigorous systematizing of insight. Whether we have in fact even attained that degree of development is questioned by the "pure" scientists. Nevertheless, it must be conceded that at least a great effort has been started and that we know much more in these fields than we ever did before.

The study of individual behavior has, in the past fifty years, received much attention and is therefore widely known. Less well known, probably because less has been accomplished, is the development of knowledge about group communication, a field which has only begun to come to the fore in the past ten years. There has, however, been considerable activity in this area ever since the end of World War I, flowing through two rather different channels. It is out of the confluence of these two streams of thought and experimentation that the material presented in this book has come.

The first of these channels stems primarily from the thinking of John Dewey and his associates. Their interest in group participation as the basic activity of a democratic society led not only to numerous books on the subject, but to serious efforts to promote group discussion in the United States. The organization of the Inquiry of the 1920's, the Great Books movement, the growth of college courses in discussion in speech departments throughout the country, the interest of religious leaders and social workers in group thinking processes, the increased use of discussion in the classroom as a tool of progressive educators, may all be regarded as flowing generally from the same source. The names of Eduard Lindeman, Mary Follett, Harrison Elliott, Grace Coyle, Harry Overstreet, Lyman Bryson, James McBurney, and Kenneth Hance come to mind in association with this development. These people were applied rather than pure social scientists, and their concern was primarily with the way in which *ideas* are generated and communicated in the context of American political and social life.

The second and perhaps more widely publicized stream of developing interest in the discussion process is *psychological* in its emphasis and issues primarily from the work of Kurt Lewin in the late 1930's and early 1940's. Lewin gathered around him, first at the University of Iowa and later at Massachusetts Institute of Technology, a group of students who were extremely productive, and together with them established the Research Center for Group Dynamics which is now located at the University of Michigan. Out of this center have come such active social psychologists as Dorwin Cartwright, John R. P. French, Ronald Lippitt, Leon Festinger, and Alvin Zander, to mention some of the prominent figures.

But Lewin and his colleagues did not long remain alone in this enterprise. They were soon joined by psychotherapists who began to see the central importance of communication in their work. Men like Harry Stack Sullivan, who originated the interpersonal school of psychiatry, J. L. Moreno, Carl Rogers, Jurgen Reusch, and finally the leaders of the group-therapy movement, such as W. R. Bion, have all contributed significantly to our understanding of the psychology of small group behavior. Add to this the insights coming from leaders in the "Human Relations in Industry" school, for example Elton Mayo and F. J. Roethlisberger, from sociologists like George Homans and Robert F. Bales, and from adult educators such as Leland Bradford, Kenneth Benne, and Herbert Thelen, and the stream becomes a veritable river of activity. Here again, as in the first case, the leaders have for the most part been applied as well as pure social scientists, although empirical and experimental research have played a much larger role in their work. Some have even rejected entirely the notion of "action research" propounded by the Lewinians, preferring the pure air of the laboratory which is presumably less contaminated by unscientific value judgments. Among all of these men, however, whether in the laboratory or in the field, the major focus of interest has been on the human element in discussion rather than on the thinking process *per se*.

The authors of this book have experienced, have been influenced by, and have been a part of both of these two major approaches to discussion. In teaching more than one hundred courses in discussion over the past ten years, in the college classroom, in the industrial world, and in the community, we have drawn strength from both. It is our belief and hope that the influence of each upon the other is now being felt in many places, and that the time is ripe for an integration of the two. That, essentially, is the intent of this volume.

In addition to providing the foregoing background, it may be helpful to the reader if we clarify some of the assumptions upon which we have operated in writing this book. One of our basic premises has been that discussion is a dynamic, ever-changing process — hence our choice of the title, *The Dynamics of Discussion*. It is therefore impossible to formulate any laws, principles, or pieces of advice which will hold good under any and all circumstances. This is not a subject that lends itself to formulae or final answers. There are no six easy lessons. We assume that the best we can do in training a person for more effective group communication is to help him learn how to solve problems rather than to give him answers. This involves essentially three steps:

(1) He must learn to become infinitely more sensitive than most of us now are to what is going on in any given discussion. He must learn why people behave in their interpersonal relationships as they do and must be aware of as many of the factors operating in the situation as he can possibly discover. A large share of the information presented in this book is intended to fulfill these needs.

(2) He must develop a basic set of criteria or values by which he can judge and choose among the many possible courses of action he may take in a given situation. In other words, he must have some goals clearly in mind before he can decide what to say or not say, what to do or not do. More will be said about this shortly.

(3) He should know about many different ways of dealing with situations, so that when he is faced with a concrete problem of interpersonal communication he will have a variety of alternatives to draw upon, and can choose among them in accordance with the requirements of the particular situation and in line with the values by which he is operating. Again, this book will try to acquaint him with many possible alternatives.

In short, the approach we propound is essentially experimental. It is our conviction that education is not the giving of answers, but rather the providing of a framework and a stimulus for problem-solving by the student himself. In view of this philosophy some may wonder at our occasional use of the word "training," a concept which may imply to some a process of drilling certain skills or techniques into a person, much as one thinks of training a dog. We wish to make clear that we disavow such connotations when we use the term in this book. We feel it is possible to think of the word as being synonymous with "education," and it is in this sense that we make use of it. In fact, we take an extremely dim view of any process — be it labeled training or education — in this field where the aim is primarily or exclusively that of teaching people a set of skills and techniques. We do not wish entirely to exclude such practices from our teaching, but we do feel that these are the more superficial matters. We have observed too many people who are master craftsmen in the techniques of discussion, and yet miss completely the real meaning of human communication, to feel that this is the goal toward which we are striving. At the other extreme we have known people with a lively sense of interpersonal communication who appeared on the surface to be awkward, unfriendly, dominating, or dogmatic. Education in discussion must be more than word-deep.

The remaining basic premises upon which this book is built have to do with the kinds of criteria or values which are recommended to the student as he faces and solves the problems of discussion which he encounters. It is obviously impossible to write a book designed to help people learn to do something better unless some judgments about what is better have been made by the authors. In short, we cannot avoid ultimate value judgments, and it is better to make them explicit than to pretend that they do not exist. It is difficult to sum up, in a few sentences, the values which have operated in our writing. We hope they will have been made completely clear by the end of the book. Suffice it to say at this point that we assume that the ultimate purpose of discussion is to bring about greater understanding among men, so that they may think and act together effectively in dealing with the problems which confront them, and so that they may satisfy their needs for human companionship.

We assume that when men act in concert it is because they feel they can achieve goals for themselves with the help of others that they cannot attain alone. In other words, group action is a means for achieving the ends of those individuals who participate in it, and should never become an end in itself. Although there may be times when the problems which a group confronts may be so taxing that individuals must subordinate their personal interests to those of the other members of the group, we take these to be temporary conditions which are tolerated only because they redound eventually to the benefit of the members. In short, the ultimate value is the development of the individual.

We further assume that men engage in discussion because they are basically rational beings who believe that observation, reason, and reality-testing can be trusted to yield solutions to problems that are superior to those reached by unconscious motivation, personal intuition, mystical revelation, authoritarian decree, or other non-discussable, non-rational means of problem-solving. We do not assume that all men are always reasonable, but only that most of them are capable of being so most of the time. To the extent that their behavior is unconscious or non-rational it is essentially non-discussable. We believe that as men grow in maturity they develop in understanding both of themselves and of the world around them — that this, in fact, is their highest goal. We know it is ours. We assume that the ability to communicate with others is intended to serve this end; that, therefore, any process of communication which aids directly or indirectly in the development of objective knowledge and of self-awareness is good, and that any process of communication which is a deterrent to these ends is bad. Again, the ultimate value is the growth of the individual. In presenting our views on discussion, therefore, we will tend to favor freedom over restriction, and equality of opportunity over privilege and status.

A few words need also to be said about the scope of this book. What do we mean when we speak of discussion? We have attempted to regard this phenomenon as broadly and realistically as possible. We feel it is discussion when a group of friends get together for a "bull session" or when a sub-committee of the United Nations meets to talk about disarmament. It is discussion when two people explore some personal problem together, and when twenty-five business people hold a staff meeting to solve some question of production. We are interested in all kinds of situations where people come together and talk — with two major exceptions. First, we exclude casual, social conversation (as distinct from concentrated bull sessions or gripe sessions) — not because it is not discussion but rather because its purposes are so diffuse and because, frankly, we have so little scientific information about it. Second, we exclude for the most part those kinds of meetings where many diverse little items of business are dealt with — announcements, pep talks, assignments, etc. — or where parliamentary procedures govern a sequence of speeches or debates. We are interested in such meetings only insofar as they may dwell on one topic for a significant amount of time, and where there is a relatively unrestrained flow of ideas on that topic among the participants. We refer those readers who are interested in learning how best to organize, in an over-all way, the items of business of a meeting, and how to conduct parliamentary procedures, to the many excellent books which have been written on those subjects. We confine our interest here to the process of discussion itself.

Part One

THE SETTING OF DISCUSSION

Chapter One

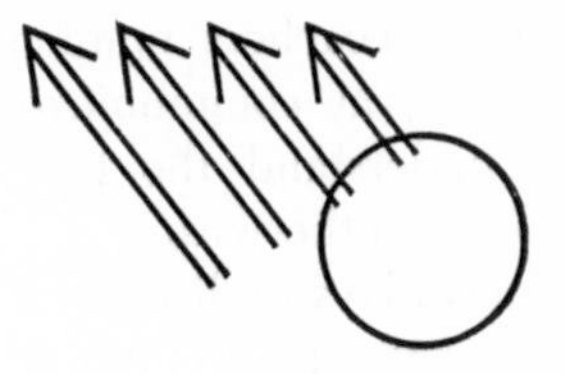

Discussion and Democracy

HISTORIANS AND SOCIAL SCIENTISTS are fond of coining phrases designed to capture the essence of the times with which they are dealing. The Age of Reason, The Age of Anxiety, The Atomic Age, The Space Age — these are but a few examples of their efforts. Had we been similarly inclined we might have entitled this book The Age of Communication, for surely ours is a time when people, perhaps more than ever before in history, are engaging in talk with their fellow men. Barriers to the flow of discussion are crumbling on every side — among governments, among races, among employers and their workers, among teachers and their students, and even within the family.

To anyone familiar with modern business and industry it hardly seems necessary to point out the amazing amounts of time that are spent in meetings. So conference-conscious has American industry become that voices are already being raised against the "group-think" and conformity which it is feared the "Age of Communication" is bringing in its wake.[1]

Likewise in the schoolroom the era of discussion has arrived.

[1] See, for example, David Riesman, *The Lonely Crowd* (Yale University Press, 1950); William H. Whyte, *The Organization Man* (Simon & Schuster, 1956); and Sloan Wilson, *The Man in the Gray Flannel Suit* (Simon & Schuster, 1955).

Although some of the more extreme aspects of the progressive education movement have been mellowed with time, and in some places a reaction has even set in, we can be certain that the American school system will never again be the teacher-dominated institution it was before John Dewey and the progressive educationists came upon the scene. Teachers' opinions are now open to question, with much more two-way communication taking place in the classroom. Those who understand the true nature of the learning process would not want it otherwise.

It is rare nowadays to discover a family which still operates under the old philosophy that children are to be seen and not heard. Although there are undoubtedly moments when harassed parents might wish for a return to the good old days, upon reflection they would not really want it so. The average family in our society has accustomed itself to the idea that all need not fall into unquestioning silence after father or mother has made a pronouncement, and that indeed such a state of affairs would not only be unnatural but unhealthy. Rather, the typical dinner table is likely to be a place for active conversation by all members of the family, and parental opinions on almost any subject are virtually certain to be examined and debated.

In practically every local community across the country groups of citizens with common interests and purposes are coming together to talk and, hopefully, to act. As social problems arise — from water fluoridation to school desegregation — increasing numbers of groups develop to discuss these questions and to advance the interests of their members. At both the national and international level, where there has always been much talk, the number of conferences and councils has constantly been increasing. Wherever we look we find people meeting and talking together with more frequency and intensity than ever before. Just as atomic energy and missiles are here to stay, just as we must learn to live with them and manage them in ways that will be helpful rather than harmful to us, so must we accept the growth of discussion in the modern world and develop our understanding of the process so that we, as individuals, can be its masters rather than its servants.

The Parallel Between Discussion and Democracy

What has brought about this tremendous expansion in the amount of time and effort devoted to discussion? To find the answer to this question we must first recognize that the phenomenon we have observed is not simply a matter of an increase in the number of words and sounds that are being passed between human beings. What we are actually witnessing is an increase in the extent to which democratic processes are coming to govern the lives of men. For to discuss means to behave democratically.

The fact that discussion and democracy are parallel, if not synonymous, concepts can best be seen by looking at what happens in societies or institutions that are not governed democratically. The most common alternative to democracy — whether in nations, businesses, or families — is rule by one man or by a small group. Here decisions are made at the top by those with the power to enforce them, and are handed down autocratically to those who must obey. Although on occasion the holders of power may consult other people before making their decisions, once a conclusion has been reached by the leaders there is no further room for discussion. In fact most autocrats regard discussion as a threat to their position; they not only refuse to be drawn into it themselves but frequently make deliberate efforts to suppress it among others, or at least to prevent its culminating in any sort of action. It is typical for dictatorial governments not only to abolish opposition political parties and to maintain careful control of radio, television, and the press, but also to discourage all kinds of familial, educational, religious, and professional associations where a critical examination of government policies might occur. Discussion presumes the possibility of mutual influence, and where influence is meant to flow in only one direction there is no place for discussion. Talk between autocratic leaders and their followers takes the form of giving and clarifying orders and instructions. To the extent that any exchange of views is allowed to take place, some degree of mutual influence, or democracy, has been admitted into the relationship.

It is actually a rare situation where influence is entirely one-way and discussion *completely* nonexistent. Even in the most authoritarian institutions there is frequently a good deal of two-way communication, hence democracy, within the circle of the leaders themselves, as for example, the so-called "collective leadership" of the Soviet Union and the high-level policy-making conferences of our own military commands. Even the most tyrannical of dictators is not able to suppress or ignore entirely the grumblings of his people. The significant point, however, is that to the extent that discussion takes place and leaders are influenced by their followers, the democratic process has achieved an entering wedge. When we observe a growth of discussion in our times what we are really seeing, then, is a spreading of the democratic process — into our homes, schools, industries, religious institutions, and body politic. Thus, when we ask why the amount of discussion is increasing we are actually seeking to understand the reasons for an expansion of democracy.

Causes of the Growth of Discussion

Some rather obvious explanations immediately come to mind when we begin to analyze the causes of the developments we have described. It has already been suggested that our society and its problems are more complex than they ever were in the past, that our institutions have grown in size, and that nearly every field of knowledge has become more specialized. Hence one can no longer be a rugged individualist in the frontier sense of the word; he cannot know and do everything for himself. He rubs shoulders constantly with his fellow men who have different, and often conflicting, desires or ideas; and he needs these people in order to sustain his own life. The old-fashioned business tycoon who was familiar with every detail of his company and could make decisions singlehandedly must now turn to his lawyer or accountant to help him with tax problems, his engineers to help him with automation, and his psychological consultants to advise him on personnel matters.

Increased size and complexity are also evident in the government. The establishment of the National Security Council is an illustration of the result of these forces. So many different departments and agencies of the federal government have become involved in the national security, and are so interdependent, that some kind of coordinating body had to be created where information and viewpoints could be exchanged and mutual problems thrashed out together.

Although these new factors of size and complexity would seem to account for much of the discussion that now takes place, they do not by themselves explain the extent to which it has been carried. For leaders and coordinators could still collect the information they needed from the specialists in written or oral reports and make the final decisions themselves. This is, in fact, done in many instances.

There would seem to be still other reasons why statesmen, business men, teachers, and organization leaders have moved so strongly in the direction of discussion.

Another cause appears to be the growing realization that, as a result of having the opportunity to participate in discussion and thus to exert their influence, the members of a group or society are better informed and more loyal than if they have not had a share in the decision-making process. In the case of educational groups, participation in discussion not only seems to increase the student's interest in learning but also enables him to assimilate the material more thoroughly. In the case of groups whose purpose is to make policies it has been found that discussion increases the member's willingness to implement whatever actions are agreed upon. In both instances, discussion leads to a greater sense of identification with the group and intensified attraction to its goals.

But these facts have been known by wise men for centuries; so that although the realization of them may be spreading, it is difficult to believe that this factor alone would be sufficient to account for a large share of the growth of discussion. As far back as the Renaissance, a political philosopher, Marsiglio of Padua, wrote:

> A law is useless if not obeyed. . . . Since that law is better observed by any one of the citizens which he seems to have imposed upon himself, the best law is made by the deliberation and command of the multitude of citizens. . . . This cannot be if a single man or a few make law by their own authority. . . . In such case the remainder of the citizens, perhaps the majority, would endure such a law, however good, with impatience or not at all, and bearing contempt toward the law would contend that not having been invited to share in its creation they would in no wise observe it. On the other hand, any citizen will endure and obey a law however irksome, that is made from the deliberation and consent of the whole multitude, because he himself seems to have imposed it upon himself and, therefore, cannot complain against it.[2]

We may find a fuller explanation for the increasing acceptance and utilization of democratic processes if we examine four other trends in twentieth-century civilization which have a vital bearing on whether or not discussion can take place.

[2] Marsiglio of Padua, "Defensor Pacis," in Francis William Coker (ed.), *Readings in Political Philosophy* (Macmillan, 1938), pp. 250–251.

Distribution of Knowledge

The first of these is the ever-increasing spread or distribution of knowledge to all strata of society. Not only has the level of basic literacy across the earth been rising, but, in our country particularly, there has been a tremendous growth in the percentage of our population receiving an education and in the number of years of schooling they complete. Information not only on political issues, but on scientific and psychological subjects, is widely disseminated; and organized efforts to distribute knowledge on such matters as medical care, mental hygiene, and world affairs abound. As the gap between those people who know a great deal and those who know practically nothing is narrowed, we would expect to find an increase in discussion and democracy. For discussion and the mutual influence it involves are virtually impossible in relationships where one party possesses all the knowledge and the other is ignorant. Only as the competence of people becomes relatively equal is discussion made possible.

In fact, it is then made necessary. Each individual now possesses information which the other may not have. He draws conclusions from that information which are affected by his own personal needs and are likely to vary from the conclusions drawn by others. Certainly we have all observed that when people know something about a subject they are much more likely to demand a hearing than if they are ignorant. This may be one of the reasons why children have more to say nowadays than formerly in family councils. They simply know more than their parents did at the same age. This is also the reason why individuals and groups who are seeking to exert influence on their superiors recognize that before they can achieve a more effective bargaining position they must gain possession of vital information. Employees, for instance, must find out about the financial position of their employers if they are to negotiate intelligently about their wages; and frequently employers who do not wish to engage in a democratic process with their workers will attempt to make such data inaccessible. Numerous topics which in former days were considered taboo in many circles — sexual problems, mental illnesses, physical handicaps, race relations — are now discussed with a directness and honesty which suggest that many of our ignorance-based fears have been dissipated.

Advances in Scientific Method

Along with the spread of knowledge there has come a second change in our society that leads to a greater degree of discussion and democracy. This is the advancing acceptance of the scientific method for dealing with problems. Although scientific ways of obtaining knowledge and solving problems have existed since the earliest days of mankind and have achieved high peaks of popularity during the height of Greek civilization and the Renaissance, there has probably never been the truly widespread support and understanding of them that has developed during the past several decades. Whether we look at the advance from witchcraft to modern medicine, from torture of prisoners to rehabilitation centers, from sun worship to flood control and irrigation, from economic panic to unemployment compensation and bank insurance, from slavery to desegregation, in almost any field one can think of we find a general trend away from authoritarianism and mysticism to science and reason.

And what has this to do with discussion? The relationship is direct and immediate. So long as a field is governed by an authoritarian philosophy there is no need to discuss questions which may arise. The answers given by the authorities, whether they be the church fathers, the tribal chiefs, the great books of the past, or the customs and traditions of the society, are accepted without dispute. To the extent that mysticism is the prevailing philosophy, there is again no room for discussion. Beliefs which one has derived from hearing "inner voices" or seeing visions cannot very well be verified by others. Such beliefs can only be asserted, and then accepted or rejected on the basis of the credibility of the speaker. Although probably all of us at one time or another operate, and justifiably so, on the basis of intuition — "I don't know why; I just feel it" — most of us nowadays would agree that a more reliable method of understanding is preferable in most circumstances.

When one bases his approach to problems on the philosophies of empiricism, rationalism, and pragmatism — that is, on carefully controlled observation, on rigorous logical deduction, and on testing out possible solutions in action, in short, on scientific methods — one is virtually compelled to engage in discussion with others. For a scientific observer is aware that as a human being his own perception of objects and events is influenced by his biases; that try as he may to be relatively objective, the process of perceiving is a selective activity governed by his own needs and experiences. Hence he will have to check and discuss his observations with others, in order to arrive at a more complete and accurate picture of the situation. Likewise the processes of logical deduction are often too intricate and tricky for a man to place exclusive trust in his own reasoning powers. He will want to expose his chain of logic to others whose minds he respects in order to discover any fallacies he may have committed or any other ways of interpreting the data which he may have overlooked. Finally, in the testing-out phase of problem-solving, scientifically minded people are eager to exchange experiences; to find out how a particular hypothesis, solution, or course of action worked out when tried by others; to compare notes on their successes and failures. It is through processes such as these — essentially democratic in the mutual influence they exhibit — that modern medicine has replaced witchcraft, irrigation and conservation have supplanted worship of the weather gods, and economic controls have superseded the myth of the "free" market. To be sure, in all these areas we still have far to go. We still practice some methods of medical and psychiatric care which are not far removed from witchery, and we are a long way from having become completely rational about our economic and international affairs. But there can be little doubt that the trend is constantly in that direction, and that as it continues discussion will increase with it.

The Dignity of the Individual

In addition to the wider distribution of knowledge and the growing acceptance of scientific methods of problem-solving, there is a further change which has taken place in our society. It is, perhaps, simply a result of other forces we are noting in this chapter, but nevertheless it appears to be exerting an independent influence on the increase in discussion. We refer to a growing adherence to the concept of the dignity of the human personality. Once such a philosophy is embraced it follows logically that more discussion and democracy will ensue, for along with a recognition of man's dignity comes a respect for his individual needs and opinions and a willingness to include him in the decision-making process. Hence in the family more discussion has come about as there has been an increased acceptance of the idea that "children are people too" with individuality and rights of their own. In education, more discussion has resulted when it has been realized that each child is a unique personality with interests and potentialities that are different from those of every other child. In business, particularly in places where labor has not attained a significantly greater degree of power than it formerly held, the fact that the worker's rights and interests are often recognized and respected would indicate that humane as well as economic motives may be operating.

In international affairs, the emphasis increasingly being given to helping former colonial peoples of the so-called backward countries to achieve self-government cannot be explained entirely by factors of economic self-interest. It is undoubtedly motivated in part by a recognition that they are human beings like ourselves who deserve something better than disease and starvation. True, the impulse to help others rise above their misery has probably always been present in people who were better off, but it has often been coupled in the past with a paternalistic attitude which, while recognizing an obligation to help others achieve a higher material standard of living, did not carry with it a recognition of the rights of others to political, social, and psychological equality. Although this is still the pattern of help, unhappily, in too many instances, it is clear that this attitude is changing, and that along with the desire to see others become more prosperous there is a growing recognition that they may and should also become more independent and eventually achieve a position from which they can exert influence on those upon whom they once depended. The givers of aid, though aware of this likely outcome, continue to be generous because they realize that a growth in the power and influence of others does not necessarily mean a reduction of their own strength. Rather they are aware that often it can redound to their benefit, for they can gain in both knowledge and comfort from the contribution that the newly emancipated people can return to them as they begin to express their own creativity.

It may be, as some observers of the social scene have suggested, that the increased recognition of human rights is a result of the fact that we can better afford it these days. In business, for example, the technical problems of production have become so well mastered that management has time to concern itself with the human element. Families, communities, and nations which have attained high standards of living possess the leisure to analyze and improve their human relations. All this means more discussion; whereas in those societies which are still struggling with the basic problems of obtaining adequate food, clothing, and shelter, there is less time for the luxury of democracy. Whether or not this observation is a valid one, it cannot be denied that the philosophy of individual dignity, whatever its causes, is by no means universal. But, to the extent that it is present in a given society discussion is more likely to occur.

Equalization of Power

A fourth major change that has been occurring in our society, and which may be either cause or effect of the first three but is in any case a potent force in promoting discussion and democracy, is the increased equalization of power, both physical and economic. When one person or a few people in a group or society possess all the guns, muscles, or money, and the others are relatively weak and helpless, optimum conditions do not exist for discussion, mutual influence, and democracy. Discussion in such circumstances occurs only at the sufferance of the powerful; and generous as these persons may sometimes be, they are not likely voluntarily to abdicate their power when vital interests are at stake. To be sure, one can cite innumerable instances in which powerful individuals or groups have seen that it was in their enlightened self-interest to accept influence freely from others who were in no position to force it upon them. A number of benevolent dictators in history have, on their own initiative, attempted to institute democratic processes in their countries long before revolutionists had to come along and fight for them. Many enlightened businessmen provided decent wages and working conditions for their employees before unions came upon the scene. But these are tenuous grounds upon which to base democracy, for the fact of life remains that the biggest boys in the gang can bring discussion to a screeching halt the moment they take a notion to do so. "A democracy can be such in fact," said Theodore Roosevelt, "only if . . . we are all of about the same size."

The most solid and enduring basis for democracy exists when the participants possess relative equality of power. Discussion is assured only when those desiring discussion — usually those who are dissatisfied with the present state of affairs — have sufficient power to make those in control of the situation listen to them. For example, it is the feeling of many political observers that the Negro in America will never be able firmly to secure his other rights until he has gained full and free access to the schools and the voting booths. The biggest hurdle which advocates of change usually confront is to gain the concession from those in power that a topic is at least discussable. Although the advocates of racial desegregation may at times become impatient and discouraged, they might well take comfort in the fact that, even where the walls of resistance seem impenetrable, talk about the subject is going on. Admitting a subject to discussion is admitting the *possibility* of change.

The correlation between power and democracy can be seen clearly in the family. As children grow older and gain the physical strength — and sometimes financial independence — with which to fight back, their parents are forced to become less arbitrary with them and to discuss issues that may arise, relying on reason and persuasion rather than coercion. But, it may be asked, children have always grown older and gained this kind of power; why, then, is there more democracy in the home today than formerly? In the first place, as we saw earlier, children seem to be smarter than they used to be, and knowledge is in itself a form of power. But in addition to this there are more opportunities, earlier in life, for a youngster to earn enough money to pay for some of the things he may want but of which his parents disapprove. With the age of the automobile young people have become more mobile — they can escape farther and faster from parental supervision. They also spend more of their time in activities outside the home, thus lessening the influence of parents and increasing that of their peer-groups.

In the field of labor-management relationships the shifting balance of power and the resultant growth of discussion and democracy is even clearer. In those industries where unionization has been most successful, labor has attained a tremendous increase in strength and has, as a result, been able to demand a larger share of the profits as well as many other benefits. Bosses are now forced to discuss questions which they used to regard as no one else's business. In addition to better organization, other factors have contributed to giving labor a greater voice. (The expression, "a greater voice," is in itself an indication of the close relationship between power and discussion.) Labor has become a more precious commodity, and it is no longer so easy for an employer to say, "If you don't like it here, we'll get someone to replace you." (This, of course, varies with business conditions.) Labor, too, has become more mobile — workers are willing and able to move to another town to find more attractive jobs.

Within management itself there has also been a greater equalization of power. The ownership of stock is spread among larger segments of the population and is less concentrated in the hands of a few. This means that more people have a right to participate in important managerial decisions and that those company presidents who formerly, as a result of owning the lion's share of the stock themselves, could make relatively arbitrary decisions, are now forced to consider the views of many other people. One is sometimes amazed in talking to people in high positions in modern business and industry at the feeling of powerlessness which they express and the degree to which they feel hemmed in by outside pressures.

Likewise in national affairs we discover that individuals who are usually thought of as having great authority — such as a cabinet chief or even the President himself — must constantly be sensitive to all sorts of interests, and must confer and consult with many others before making a decision. And surely this is more true of a country such as ours, or other Western democracies, where the distribution of wealth is fairly widespread, than in countries like those of the Middle East, where the wealth that exists is still concentrated in the hands of a few. It is no accident that those nations which we think of as having the most purely democratic forms of government — Switzerland, Sweden, Denmark, and Holland — are also the countries that have attained the greatest equality in distribution of wealth; whereas those nations with a highly unequal distribution of wealth — such as in South America, the Middle East, and the Soviet orbit — are the most authoritarian. It is interesting also to note that in West Germany, for example, the development of democratic processes since World War II has come hand in hand with a rise in economic status among the lower classes.

Perhaps the clearest example of the relationship between power and discussion is seen in the international field. Now that the nations of the world have become so interdependent that none is strong enough to "go it alone," the necessity for working problems out through discussion has become evident. Even though the United States is clearly the dominant power among the Western nations we apparently are not so powerful that we can act unilaterally on matters of foreign policy. Hence, even before writing a reply to a note from the Soviet prime minister our State Department feels obliged to discuss the matter with our NATO allies. In the same way, both the United States and the Soviet Union, much as they may feel frustrated by the endless and seemingly futile discussions in the United Nations and at other international conferences, realize that there simply is no other alternative short of war — for neither has the power to impose its will upon the other, and both are therefore forced into discussion.

In summary, then, we find that in order for discussion to flourish in a society or institution certain conditions must be present. There must be a reasonable spread of information and knowledge among all members of the group. The people involved must be committed to scientific methods of problem-solving, rather than to reliance on authorities or intuition. Power, both physical and economic, must be relatively equal; and to the degree that it is not there must be a compensating attitude on the part of those who hold the advantage that it is in their ultimate interest to respect the dignity of others and to share the decision-making processes with them. The fact that the people of the world, and particularly of our own country, seem to be moving more and more in the direction of these conditions would seem to explain the growing uses of discussion. To those who wish to promote even further the methods of democracy it should be apparent that there must at the same time be an increase in the distribution of knowledge, strength, and wealth; a development of respect for scientific methods; and a growth in the humanistic philosophy of life. With the attainment of these conditions the foundations for democratic living are laid, and we are then free to turn our attention to the improvement of discussion itself.

RECOMMENDED READINGS

Fromm, Erich. *Escape from Freedom.* Rinehart & Company, Inc., 1941.

Mills, C. Wright. *The Power Elite.* Oxford University Press, 1957.

Riesman, David, Nathan Glazer, and Reuel Denney. *The Lonely Crowd.* Doubleday and Company, Inc., 1953.

Smith, T. V., and Eduard C. Lindeman. *The Democratic Way of Life.* New American Library, 1951.

Spiro, Herbert J. *The Politics of German Codetermination.* Harvard University Press, 1958.

Chapter Two

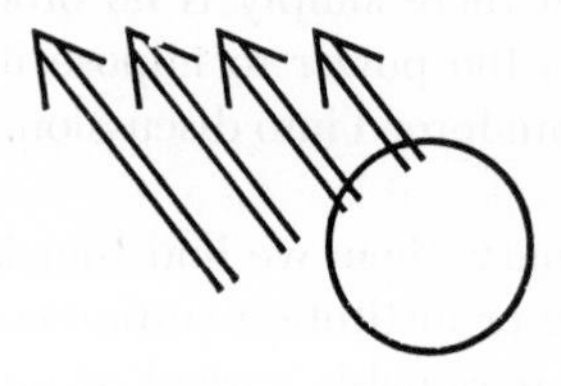

Groups and the Individual

THE DAY OF THE HERMIT IS OVER. Few people in modern times work out their destinies in a social vacuum. As one observer aptly put it, "We lead hyphenated lives." That well-known "man in the street" is a member of a union local, a faithful supporter of the PTA, a trustee of his church, and a block leader for the United Fund. He leads a "hyphenated life" in the sense that he is nearly always a part of one group or another. His role in each of these groups brings out a somewhat different aspect of his personality; as a member of the school board he behaves differently than as a coach in the Little League.

Even when we are physically alone in the privacy of our room, we carry many of our groups about with us in our imagination. How we react to a particular request is determined partly by the social context in which we see ourselves at the moment. Our view of ourselves — what the psychologist would call our ego-image — changes as we think of ourselves as a "party cut-up," a "good neighbor," a "liberal democrat," or a "devoted husband." This has led psychologists to recognize that there are not liars *per se* so much as there are lying situations; not juvenile delinquents so much as social settings which elicit delinquent behavior. Public opinion pollsters have learned, sometimes to their dismay, that the replies given to their questions are very different when asked of the same person in the lobby of his church and in the locker room of his club. To understand human beings and human behavior we must see people, not as isolated individuals, but as they interact and affect one another in the groups to which they belong.

The Multiplicity of Groups

The number of groups that make up the fabric of human society is incalculable. Chester Barnard writes at one point that "the number of formal organizations in the United States is many millions, and it is possible that the number is greater than that of the total population." [1] When the number of casual and accidental associations is added to this figure there is no doubt but that there are many times more groups than individuals in a given society.

A democratic society should, and does, encourage diversity in groups as well as individuals. Some idea of the broad scope of human associations may be obtained by examining the groups cited by one college student in a profile of his memberships:

St. Paul's Choir
Marching Band
Alumnus of Wilson High School
Family
Swimming Team
Sunday School Teacher
Film Society
Spanish Drill Section
Dormitory Council
Cheering Section, Stadium
Seminar in Sociology
"C" Skow Fleet
Jazz Combo
Representative at Model U.N.
Audience at Auditorium
Young Republicans
Sports Car Club of America
Staff of Summer Camp for Handicapped Children

To be complete, however, this list should also include the endless number of groups of people with whom this person relaxes and socializes. Then we begin to get some idea of the richness of our organizational life. We may understand, at this point, why so much attention is paid by social scientists to the conditions of group life, for it is in them that we assimilate our culture and, paradoxically, express our individuality. For the purposes of this book we will want to cut through this maze of associations and identify those

[1] Chester Barnard, *The Functions of the Executive* (Harvard University Press, 1948), p. 4.

groups which are based upon or use discussion as their principal mode of interaction.

The Nature of Groups

To begin with, what do we mean by a group? This seemingly trivial question will be found, upon inspection, to pose a larger problem than appears at first glance. How, for example, are we to differentiate between people who are physically associated, as on the beach or in an elevator, and the persons we find in a mob, an audience, or a committee meeting?

What transforms a collection of people into a group? It is not enough for individuals simply to be together in the same room at the same time. They must be psychologically, as well as physically, related; there must be some feeling of identification with each other. The moment there is an awareness of a problem, activity, or sentiment which they all share in common an aggregation becomes a group. Businessmen riding in a commuter coach lack this common bond. Should a crisis arise, should the air conditioning fail on a hot day or the train jump the tracks, this new ingredient could be expected to convert a coach full of people into a group with some sense of identification, some feeling of affiliation.

This broad definition still includes a tremendous variety of groups — bridge clubs, families, committees, arbitration boards, athletic teams, and audiences. These can be further classified in many ways. Social psychologists have categorized them according to the length of association as "temporary" or "permanent," on the basis of the needs they satisfy as "psyche" or "socio" groups, or according to the part they play in the development of personality as "primary" or "secondary." Even the size of the group has been used as a basis of classification on the grounds that the number of people in a group has much to do with the sort of relationship that can be maintained.

We can isolate the type of group this book is concerned with most accurately by differentiating between formal groups and informal groups. It is obvious that the members of an audience at a theatre or concert are related in a different way than are the members of a basketball team or a committee. In formal groups the interaction is focused; all members of the group attend and respond to a common source of stimulation which may be an orchestra, a speaker, or a film. Furthermore, those present tend to react in relatively passive and stereotyped ways, at least outwardly. Interaction occurs between the performer(s) or leader(s) and the audience as a whole, rather than taking place among the individual members of the group. There is, in addition, a certain anonymity in formal groups, and members seldom recall afterwards the specific personalities of those who attended.

Quite different conditions prevail in the informal group. For one thing, the group is usually smaller in size. There is a significant difference, too, in the way participants relate to each other. Robert Bales notes that in informal groups "each member receives some impression or perception of each other member distinct enough so that he can, either at that time, or in later questioning, give some reaction to each of the others as individual persons, even though it be only to recall that the other was present." [2] This sort of intimacy is seldom found in the formal group setting. The roles played by members of informal groups are also less stereotyped, less predictable. The person who starts the group may soon drift out of the center of attention and later reappear as he responds to someone else's participation. Behavior in the informal group is likely to be more spontaneous and uninhibited. Communication is unrestricted and may change direction at any moment. The informal group, then, is characterized by its fluid pattern of interaction, the fact that its members are aware of each other as individuals, and its spontaneity. Krech and Crutchfield describe two criteria which help to identify the informal group:

> . . . the criteria for establishing whether or not a given set of individuals constitute a psychological group are mainly two: (1) All the members must exist in the psychological field of each individual, i.e., be perceived and reacted to as a group member; (2) The various members must be in dynamic interaction with each other.[3]

There are, of course, many groups that meet these requirements. The members of a basketball team coming down the floor in a fast break are interacting as dynamically as a group can. Some of our great jazz groups, such as the Dave Brubeck Quartet, or the Benny Goodman Sextet, interact in exceedingly spontaneous, fluid,

[2] Robert Bales, *Interaction Process Analysis* (Addison-Wesley, 1950), p. 33.

[3] D. Krech and R. S. Crutchfield, *Theory and Problems in Social Psychology* (McGraw-Hill, 1948), p. 368.

and we might add, effective ways. In the *discussion* group, however, this interaction is carried on principally through speech. The changes that occur in the group are produced primarily by words, by what people say to one another and how they say it. In summarizing the nature of discussion groups we may say that *they consist of a number of persons who perceive each other as participants in a common activity, who interact dynamically with one another, and who communicate their responses chiefly through words.*

Variety of Discussion Groups

The dynamic verbal interaction that we call discussion takes place in many settings and is used to achieve a variety of purposes. We talk to establish rapport with others, to break silence. We air our petty irritations and deeper anxieties by discussing them with friends and associates. We do business through conferences. We deliberate together when we discover differences in viewpoint that have to be reconciled. Most of the vital matters affecting our families, our communities, and our nation are settled through discussion. If we examine the purposes that motivate discussion we may begin to appreciate the multiplicity of forms it takes. An examination of the goals of discussion will also permit us to say something about the criteria to be used in evaluating the suitability of certain discussion practices.

On the continuum below have been placed five representative types of discussion groups. As a beginning we can note that the groups on the left hand side of the continuum, in general, exist to

TYPES OF DISCUSSION GROUPS

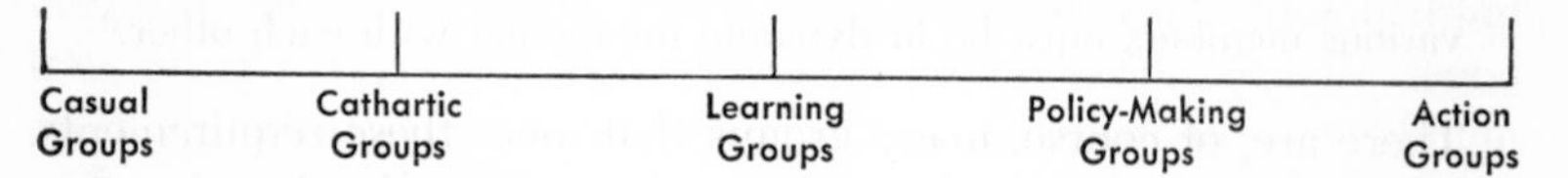

satisfy personal needs. To participate in them is an end in itself. They meet our need to be recognized as unique personalities. Through them we preserve our contact with other persons. They provide security and support for us in times of stress, or they may simply establish communication lines for the sharing of experiences. To say that membership in these groups is an end in itself is to say that these groups need not accomplish anything beyond maintaining satisfying human relationships.

Interaction in the groups on the right side of the continuum usually is a means to an end rather than an end in itself. Environmental, rather than personal, pressures account for the formation of these groups. Citizens, aroused about the facilities for medical care in their community, may form a committee to investigate the problem. Executives meet to confer with each other about company policy. Practical decisions must be forthcoming from groups of this type if they are to fulfill their purpose. It should be kept in mind, however, that these groups are situated on a continuum and each has some of the characteristics of the other. Most groups must create a reasonably satisfying human relationship *and* make some progress toward accomplishing their tasks. It is only the balance between personal and social goals that shifts as one moves from the left to the right across this diagram.

Casual Groups

Let us begin by studying the conditions of discussion in each of these groups. The Casual Group is probably the most familiar type of discussion group known. Within a day most of us are in dozens of spontaneous discussions with friends and acquaintances. Conversational groups form anywhere — on a street corner, over a cup of coffee, among the members of a car pool. On occasions the group is thrown together by social accident, at other times people will go to great lengths to participate in a particular Kaffee Klatsch or bull session. Here phatic communion, as Malinowski termed it, prevails — that is, communication carried on for the purpose of establishing warm human relationships, laying the groundwork for more practical communications at other times, or simply to overcome silence. The topics discussed are often predictable and mundane — the weather, sports, news of the day — though they need not be. Talk is generally directionless, it proceeds by free association. The statements one makes in conversation are normally not subjected to rigorous examination or critical testing; personal experiences need not lead to documented conclusions.

This should not be interpreted to mean that Casual Groups are unimportant. They are the main link between us and our society. Cooley called the attention of sociologists to the vital role they play in forming the personality of the individual. Most of what we know of them, however, is speculation for there has been almost no scientific study of this important, but elusive, group experience. Why do we seek out some of these groups and avoid others? Why are some more satisfying than others? When they are enjoyed is their success related to the subject discussed, the spontaneity of the group, or the sparkling quality of the repartee? Preliminary observation would suggest that tighter control of topics or more carefully prescribed agenda would not improve them. Their attraction for us seems to lie in the intimacy of human contact and the opportunity for self-expression that they provide. The charm of these groups is captured very well in one of William Hazlitt's essays:

> The best kind of conversation is that which may be called *thinking aloud.* I like very well to speak my mind on any subject (or to hear another do so) and to go into the question according to the degree of interest it naturally inspires, but not to have to get up a thesis upon every topic. . . . You thus lose the two great ends of conversation, which are to learn the sentiments of others, and see what they think of yours.[4]

Cathartic Groups

Another reason for discussing matters with other people is to find an outlet for the accumulated tensions and irritations of everyday life. Groups formed for this purpose can be called Cathartic Groups. They will be found in any industrial plant, on any campus, in most human institutions of any size. The student union of a university will be filled with people satisfying their need for catharsis immediately following the semester examination period. Employees will be found in earnest conversation around the water coolers, the coffeepot, or in the corridors, discussing shifts in company policy and, unconsciously, getting rid of some of the anxieties that each decision creates.

Sometimes this need is institutionalized, and men have been amazingly ingenious in forming groups to help each other in periods of personal crisis. Consider, for example, the Tall Girls Society, Divorcees Anonymous, the Wives of Flying Air Force Men, and, perhaps most famous of all, Alcoholics Anonymous. Labor grievance

[4] William Hazlitt, "Characteristics," in Geoffrey Keynes (ed.), *Selected Essays of William Hazlitt* (Random House, 1930), p. 217.

meetings and military gripe sessions recognize the need for discharging the accumulated hostility that lurks in all of us. Even the uncomplaining British found life more bearable during the Battle of Britain in World War II if they were able to talk out the frustrations of wartime.

> Yet the good citizens of Britain organized "grumble clubs" whose sole purpose was to provide a verbal vent for aggressions, irritations, and wartime complaints. After an evening of "beefing" the members felt purged and calmed, and thereafter were ready to attack their tough assignments with greater objectivity and balance.[5]

The line separating the Casual Group and the Cathartic Group is not a sharp one. It is difficult, sometimes, to tell them apart. Discussion in both groups is highly informal and spirited. There is the same need for rapport among the members. To limit or control communication in either substance or direction may only increase the tension and thus defeat the purpose of the group. But there are some subtle differences. A group of angry students or of complaining workmen have a common irritation uppermost in their minds and this will give them a sharper awareness of their problem. While "anything goes" in a Casual Group, the members of Cathartic Groups are more likely to focus their remarks around the irritation which provokes their hostility or depression. As we move down the continuum, then, we find there is a greater awareness of the specific problem that brings people together and a sharper sense of direction.

In some instances the Cathartic Group permits people not only to give vent to their emotions, but also to learn something about themselves. This, in effect, moves us closer to the Learning Group. The doctor and patient during a psychiatric session, for example, through talking about the troubles of the patient, hope to better understand the underlying motives that produce the conflicts and tensions in his life. But learning about ourselves does not have to be a deep psychological experience or confined to the psychoanalytic couch. A meeting sponsored by the Mental Health Association on the problems of parenthood or a workshop on "What should we do about our prejudices?" held under the auspices of a Human Relations Commission may give us a chance to air our frustrations

[5] Gordon Allport, "Catharsis and the Reduction of Prejudice," *Journal of Social Issues* (August, 1945), p. 3.

and also develop insight into ourselves. Membership in Cathartic Groups, then, is likely to contribute to a reduction in interpersonal hostility, to a deeper understanding of one's own motivations, and to more mature social behavior. Those who participate in such groups will be likely to get some insight into their own behavior with, perhaps, added incentive for further improvement.

Learning Groups

We join in groups, also, to learn more about the world around us. Discussion is widely used in our schools — in seminars, quiz sections, laboratories, and in the classroom generally — to help students assimilate information, to teach them to evaluate ideas critically, and to stimulate original thinking. Adult education programs, which have enjoyed such an accelerated growth recently, permit those beyond school age to satisfy their curiosity about world politics, science, or literature. Businessmen, teachers, scientists, and professional men also find it useful to meet regularly at conventions, seminars, or workshops to exchange ideas, compare new methods, and talk over common problems. An informal gathering of a group of neighbors may spring from the desire, not just to chat, but to explore thoughtfully different views of parental discipline. Hobby groups, made up of stamp collectors, or radio hams, or theatregoers, satisfy our seemingly insatiable appetite for coming to appreciate more deeply some aspect of human experience that interests us. When a Casual Group turns to serious talk about the latest best-selling novel or to a discussion of contemporary architecture, the conditions of its talk and the expectations of its members change. If such a discussion does not inform group members or produce new insights it is regarded as a failure or a "waste of time" by those who joined in the conversation.

How do the conditions of interaction in Learning Groups differ from the earlier groups we described? To make any progress at all requires that participants have a clearer definition of the problem under discussion. Group members, whether in the classroom or outside, are expected to have a general knowledge of the subject, or to have made specific preparation for the meeting. With the problem more clearly understood, participants can be expected to watch more carefully so as to keep their remarks relevant, and they may be more disposed to warn others about "getting off on tangents."

The question of how deeply members should become personally involved in a learning type discussion is a controversial issue. Some say that learning groups, particularly in the classroom, should be as objective as possible; that the scientific posture is best for learning. This view — one would be tempted to call it the "cerebral school of thought" — emphasizes the "intellectual" side of learning, and aims primarily at the accumulation and objective testing of facts. This view is strongly urged by Mortimer Adler.

> Emotions should have no place in the classroom or in discussion. We must distinguish between the heart-to-heart talk (such as between lovers) where emotions are the whole of it, and the mind-to-mind talk which is discussion. *Emotions should have no place in mind-to-mind talk.* (*Italics ours*) [6]

Adler does not, however, rule out the *possibility* of emotions forcing their way into the discussion, only that they should be avoided wherever possible for they interfere with the objective consideration of ideas.

> We have feelings about our thoughts and so emotions will enter. The point is not to suppose that you can be emotionless but rather to watch what emotions do, for they can disturb discussion. Anger, all the forms of personal aggression, personal antagonism, impatience, all these things will interfere with discussion.[7]

The "gut school of learning" holds, on the other hand, that learning must be visceral — it must affect the blood stream and the nervous system of the person doing the learning. If the feelings of participants are not affected, then what is assimilated will be only skin-deep and will have little effect upon the subsequent behavior of those in the group. As evidence, the proponents of this school would cite how few of us are changed in any pervasive way by the facts we read in our papers and textbooks compared to the fundamental changes in personality produced by psychiatric sessions where feelings are not excluded.

To extricate ourselves from this dilemma we would hold that both views need to be combined. Attractive as Mr. Adler's metaphor is, his "mind-to-mind" and "heart-to-heart" distinction has no scientific validity. One cannot partition the human personality, and

[6] Mortimer J. Adler, "Teaching by Discussion," mimeographed address (September 9, 1954), p. 11.

[7] *Ibid.*

attempts to do so only lead to distortions which add to the immaturity of the individual. For this reason we have placed the Learning Group in the middle of our continuum, for to us it seems a compromise between the deeply personal experience of the Cathartic Group and the rigorous objectivity to be found in the Action Group. One does not merely *feel* about school desegregation; there are also facts. But the facts do not by themselves settle the issue for us. Learning Groups may function more effectively when they admit that personal attitudes, prejudices, and sets of values are part of the "facts" of discussion, but that they must be tested against the more objective and scientific knowledge available on the problem.

The Learning Group is likely to benefit, also, from having some plan for its meeting. It is difficult to conduct a coherent discussion if people are constantly changing the subject. At the same time, too faithful a commitment to an intricate and inflexible agenda may stifle original ideas.

As we move along this continuum to the right, then, we find that groups have a clearer view of their problems, are able to determine more sharply the relevance of their remarks, and are increasingly objective in their attitude toward the issue discussed and toward themselves.

Policy-Making Groups

Perhaps the most common image to arise in peoples' minds whenever the word "discussion" is mentioned is a committee consisting of a group of people appointed to make decisions about matters of policy. Corporations, universities, religious and fraternal organizations all rely heavily upon them for conducting their affairs. The committee has become such an integral part of our way of life that some observers describe democracy as "government by committee."

Policy-Making Groups usually come into existence because something goes wrong in our environment — schools become overcrowded, labor-management relations deteriorate, foreign powers complain about trade agreements, communities want to rehabilitate slum areas. Groups of this type assume, or are given from a higher administrative unit, authority over a particular problem. They may be asked simply to investigate the conditions leading to the problem, or they may be charged with discovering and evaluating possible courses of action. Most important of all, Policy-Making Groups are expected to develop carefully worked out recommendations that will elicit the support of those vitally affected by the problem.

The complexity of the problems considered by deliberative groups of this type will change the character of their discussion. As problems become more complicated and well defined, members may feel that some organization is necessary. An agenda is one way to insure that all vital aspects of the problem receive appropriate attention and that the group will move systematically from issue to issue.

External restraints also are often placed on Policy-Making Groups: (1) They are normally given a target date by which to complete their investigation — a week, a month, or longer. (2) They are expected to produce decisions that are practical as well as theoretically sound. These restraints tend to give group members a greater sense of responsibility for what they say in their meetings and affect how critically they appraise the ideas that are exchanged. After all, a military strategy or a new fiscal policy has to be lived with for a long time. And the consequences of a wrong decision sometimes may be fatal. We should remember that discussions in Learning Groups, while they may not culminate in any sort of mutual agreement, may also result in individual members making personal decisions about future actions. A discussion of foreign policy in the League of Women Voters, though academic in one sense of the word, may well change the way individuals in the League vote in the next election. In general, discussion in the Policy-Making Group, however, tends to be more objective and more structured, while preserving much of the spontaneity and informality of the previous groups we have described.

Action Groups

The last group on our continuum is the Action Group. The reason for considering the Policy-Making and Action Groups separately lies in the nature of the tasks they are assigned. Policy-Making Groups, for the most part, take up issues that are intricate and require serious and lengthy investigation. The decisions that are reached will commit an organization to a relatively permanent course of action. Action Groups, on the other hand, are created to determine how and when policies will be carried out. The administration of policies, in contrast to the formulation of them, involves making dozens of practical decisions each one of which is relatively insignificant in itself. Consider a university about to change its admissions policy, or a large corporation weighing the merits of diversifying its line of products. Who is to be admitted to the university — that is, what shall be the new criteria of admission — is a matter of policy. So is the question of whether or not to manufacture a new line of products. But once these broad questions have been answered many other committees will be needed to execute the decisions. Admissions officers and members of the faculty will have to decide the fate of hundreds of applicants in the light of the standards they have been given. Within the corporation, heads of departments will have to confer about new materials and changes in production schedules.

No other discussion group works under such pressures. The large number of points to be taken up leaves little opportunity for social conversation. There is usually no time to attend to the personal needs of committee members. Severe limitations are often imposed, either because policies carry with them deadlines or because what happens in one Action Group has to be coordinated with decisions made by committees working on other aspects of the problem. As a result, digressions from the items on the agenda are likely to be frowned upon as interfering with the job of the group. Decisions made by Action Groups tend to be about concrete and tangible matters — the scheduling of workmen or the purchase of equipment — and hence committee members are expected to be objective and impartial in their remarks. On the whole we can expect Action Groups to place greater emphasis on communicating objectively, upon a fairly strict agenda, and upon efficiency in general.

Overlapping Group Purposes

It is important, however, to avoid classifying discussion groups too rigidly and thus stereotype our reaction to them. The five groups that have been described were placed on a continuum to emphasize that although differences among them are significant, the differences are subtle ones. On certain occasions it may be difficult to decide whether a group is forming to pass the time of day or to release tensions, whether catharsis carries with it new insight, or whether a committee is dealing with a matter of policy or action.

Some groups pursue a single objective over a long period of time. A group of neighbors may meet socially for a lifetime without ever engaging in anything more serious than casual conversation. The members of a board of directors may have virtually no social contact with each other and meet only when they have to decide practical questions of management. Some groups become institutionalized, that is to say, they acquire a long term set of goals and a permanent organizational structure to go with these goals. A Great Books Discussion Group or a chapter of Alcoholics Anonymous may become identified in peoples' minds with only one of the purposes described.

The majority of groups, however, change their purposes from meeting to meeting, or even within a single meeting. A group of students chatting together over coffee may find they share very strong feelings about a campus issue and use the group as an outlet for their aggressiveness as well as simply to make friends. A policy-making committee, finding its way blocked by intense prejudices or personal animosities, may have to provide time for "clearing the air" before any constructive analysis of the problem can be started. Sometimes groups run the gamut of the continuum; they start out casually, even accidentally, and then go on to investigate, to formulate policy, and to carry out their decisions.

To describe the operation of every sort of group from a Kaffee Klatsch to a "meeting at the summit" is an unmanageable undertaking in a book of this length. Some lines of demarcation have to be drawn. In this book we have chosen to concentrate mainly on the conduct of those groups in the middle range of the continuum. This should not imply that Casual Groups are not important for, in our opinion, they are. It is only that Casual Groups are so short-lived and move from point to point so unpredictably that it is difficult to describe or assess them. Chit-chat, in some ways, defies analysis. Action Groups, for different reasons, will also be left out of our consideration. Pressures for a multitude of decisions force them to function largely on an assembly-line basis. When there is time or the need for extended discussion of issues, the methods of Policy-Making Groups are applicable.

Each of the groups we have mentioned, however, throws light

on some aspect of the discussion process and each will help to explain some of the problems encountered in discussion. From our experience in Casual Groups we will learn something about the interpersonal relationships that are conducive to effective co-operation. If we want to know more about accomplishing tasks quickly and efficiently, we will get some clues from the way Action Groups operate.

As we move from left to right along our diagram we will find that these groups engage in a series of activities which suggest a natural sequence of communication when people try to work together on common tasks. From the groups we have described we can derive six basic functions carried out by means of discussion. They are: *Ventilation, Clarification, Fact-Finding, Discovery, Evaluation,* and *Decision-Making.* Later we shall find that these are the fundamental processes associated with any complete act of problem-solving.

In this chapter a number of groups have been described to which most of us belong at one time or another. It is apparent that discussion is used to satisfy a variety of personal and social needs. It is obvious, too, that no rules can be laid down which will apply with equal validity to all the groups we have considered. Almost any prescription will be right for some group at some time, and wrong for another group at another time. Rigid control of the conversation in Casual Groups is as inconsistent with its purpose as no control of irrelevant talk is in an Action Group. However, this survey of the uses of discussion will give us a basis for answering many technical questions about procedures. Knowing what kind of a group we are dealing with will allow us to decide more intelligently on what kind of leadership is required, what sort of agenda may prove helpful, and what degree of objectivity will help to fulfill the group's purpose.

In spite of social critics who spout alarms about the dangers of creating "organization men," the question we face in the twentieth century is not *if* we should participate in groups. That has already been answered for us.

> Modern life is group life. The individual of the modern world who has no vital adherence to and expression through a group is an individual who plays a diminishing role; he is insignificant and

> unimportant to the social process in direct proportion to his lack of membership in a functioning group.[8]

The question to ask is what *conditions* should prevail within the groups we belong to so that they will yield the maximum social benefit without sacrificing human individuality. In other chapters of this book we shall explore some of these conditions of group life and try to arrive at ways of accomplishing both these ends.

[8] Eduard C. Lindeman, *Social Discovery* (Republic Publishing House, 1924), p. 111.

RECOMMENDED READINGS

Chase, Stuart. *Roads to Agreement.* Harper and Brothers, 1951.

Coyle, Grace. *Group Experience and Democratic Values.* The Woman's Press, 1947.

Homans, George C. *The Human Group.* Harcourt, Brace & Company, Inc., 1950.

Krech, D., and R. Crutchfield. *Theory and Problems of Social Psychology.* McGraw-Hill Book Company, Inc., 1948.

Thelen, Herbert. *Dynamics of Groups at Work.* University of Chicago Press, 1954.

Chapter Three

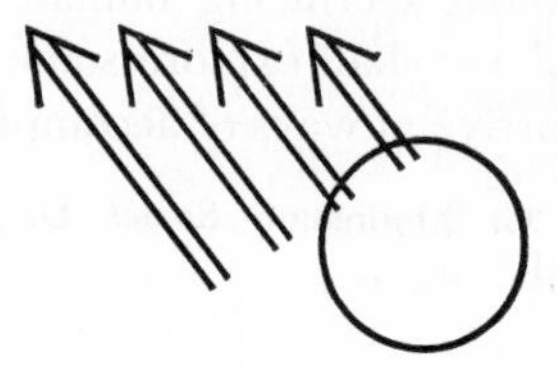

Motives and Conflict

We have spoken of the many purposes for which a group may meet in discussion. In doing so, we have thought of the group as a single unit, as is often done in everyday conversation when people talk about the morale or *esprit de corps* of a particular organization, or about its power and prestige. But these are generalizations which, if not properly understood, can be misleading. A group is not an undifferentiated mass with a monolithic personality or mind of its own. It consists of individuals who may differ in any number of ways, even in their purposes for meeting together.

If we are to understand fully the complexities of group discussion we first must be aware of the multitude of motivations present in a situation. For it is probable that no two people in a group will bring to it exactly the same kinds or intensities of purpose.

The first and most obvious reason for a person to join with others in a discussion is an interest in the publicly stated goals of the group. If he wants to learn something about international affairs, he signs up for an adult education course in World Politics. If he wishes to discourage people from seeing movies he regards as immoral, he may join the Legion of Decency, which is dedicated to such a purpose. Or, if he desires to oppose the censorship of movies, he may become a member of the American Civil Liberties Union. If such adherence to the publicly avowed goals of a group were the sole motivating force behind participation in an organization, students of the discussion process would have a much easier time of it than they do. But their study might also be rather dull. The dynamics of discussion are, in fact, more complex and thus much more interesting.

Although it is likely that most of the members of any organization will share, to some extent at least, the publicly stated purpose of the group, it is just as likely that they will have private goals which are variations upon it. Many are also apt to be motivated by purposes which are additions to, or even substitutions for, the publicly agreed upon objectives. Let us look first at how the variations upon a group's publicly stated goals might operate.

Variations on the Public Purpose

In many neighborhoods in large cities across the country there have come into existence in recent years organizations which are variously known as block clubs, neighborhood improvement associations, or area conservation societies. Their major purpose is to stem the tide of deterioration of homes and properties in the area. To achieve this end residents of the neighborhood come together in meetings to talk over common problems and to work out courses of action. Even granting that all share the same major goal — the prevention of blight — we find in these groups an infinite number of variations upon this central theme. One home owner, for example, is primarily interested in preserving a clean and wholesome environment in which his children may play and grow. Another, who is planning to move in two or three years, is primarily interested in seeing to it that the monetary value of his house does not drop before he sells it. The personnel director of a large business enterprise in the area is concerned only that the neighborhood be safe enough that employees will not hesitate to accept jobs there. An old-time resident feels that the neighborhood can be kept from deteriorating only if Negroes are prevented from moving in, whereas a young college professor who lives there thinks a racially integrated and well-maintained area would serve as a fine example to other communities that integration does not necessarily mean deterioration. One can see immediately that the task of arriving at satisfactory decisions in such a group is going to be much more complicated than if there were greater similarity in the motives that brought the members of the group together.

But even variations do not pose the complications which are introduced when members of a discussion group have, as they usually do, private goals which go beyond the central purpose of the organization or society. Such goals may be classified into two categories — those where the group is seen by the member as a means to some private end, and those where group interaction is an end in itself.

The Group as a Means to Private Ends

Illustrations of the use of groups as means to the private ends of their members abound in any gathering or collection of people. There is the coed who goes to college not only to get an education, but to find a husband; the college student who joins a fraternity or sorority as a means of getting ahead in campus politics; the business or professional man who joins the Lions, Rotary, or Kiwanis club in order to make contacts which will lead to customers or clients; the housewife who participates in charity fund-raising campaigns in order to move up the social ladder; and church members who attend services to see their friends and show off their clothing as well as to worship — these are all instances of the use of groups as means to private ends. There is no reason why such private goals need conflict with the publicly avowed purpose of the group, or why people should feel guilty about them, but these motives will certainly have an effect on the nature of the individual's participation in the group. A woman, for example, who is involved in a drive to raise funds for cancer research because she has lost a child to the disease is more likely to disagree with some questionable campaign idea proposed by the committee's chairman than another woman who, in addition to raising money, is also eager to be invited to join the committee chairman's country club.

Group Interaction as an End in Itself

Group membership may also be an end in itself. An individual may value so highly the friendship of the other members of a group that he participates in their discussions not only for the purpose of solving some common problem but also for the sheer pleasure of being with people whose companionship he needs and enjoys. This person's behavior will be considerably different from that of another member who obtains his primary social satisfactions elsewhere, and whose only motivation with regard to this particular group is to accomplish the task to which they have publicly committed themselves. The latter individual, for example, is more likely to desire an orderly procedure and be less inclined to "waste time" than the former member. Since we know that the human being is a social animal, with strong needs for companionship and an aversion to long stretches of loneliness, it is safe to assume that participation in most groups is, to one degree or another and for most members, an end in itself.

Conflicting Purposes

We have seen now that the participants in a group discussion may possess different degrees of interest in the publicly stated purposes of the group, that they may be committed to many private variations of the public goal, and that they may be motivated by additional goals which lie within or beyond the group. We have also seen that these variations and additions, although increasing the complexity of the group's operations, may be entirely compatible with its common public objectives. There are instances, however, and they are not uncommon, where private goals may be substitutions for or may conflict with the group's avowed purposes. The most extreme example of this would be the FBI agent who, incognito, joins the Communist Party in order to keep tab on its activities, or the foreign agent who works his way into a vital defense agency in order to collect secret data or to sabotage its policies. In such unusual cases as these, the agent's participation in group discussion will be handled with professional skill and is not likely to seem different from that of any other member. There are, in everyday life, however, less extreme and less conscious instances of group subversion, and these do create difficulties for discussion that are rather widespread.

One common illustration is the business official who is assigned by his boss to a committee whose task he regards as unimportant or useless. Such an individual may feel that the hours of time he spends in discussion with the other members of the committee may either result in a policy recommendation which their superior will file in the wastebasket, or may culminate in such a microscopic change as to make his effort seem fruitless. Such an attitude on the part of one or more committee members, whether justified or not, will obviously have an influence, either overt or indirect, on the course of the discussions.

Another example of conflicting purposes is the extent to which grades have become a substitute goal for learning in our school and college classrooms. Whether the fault lies with the students, the teachers, the system, or all three, is beside the point here. The fact remains that when class discussions take place they are frequently not motivated by an undiluted interest in knowledge for its own sake, but are complicated by the needs of students (and teacher!) to impress favorably those who hear the sound of their voices.

One can find illustrations of this problem in government too. The President of the United States is sometimes accused by his opponents of appointing men to public commissions whose personal views are not in accord with the purposes which those commissions were set up to achieve. It was charged, for instance, that a recent President appointed a man to the TVA who did not basically believe in government ownership of public utilities, and that a man named to be Federal Housing Director was not in sympathy with the idea of public housing. If these assertions were true, it does not require much imagination to understand how policy discussions in those agencies would be influenced in ways contrary to the avowed purposes of the organization.

Misunderstandings About Motives

Frequently conflicts between the public goal of a group and the private goals of some of its members are due more to misunderstanding than to deliberate attempts at subversion. Let us look again, for instance, at the teacher-student relationship. There are many teachers who are more impressed by students who, in their eagerness to learn, ask questions that reveal their present ignorance, than by students who, in their eagerness to impress, reveal an unwillingness to learn. These latter students might happily substitute the goal of learning for the competition over grades. Instead, they fail to pick up the cues that this is what the teacher wants too, and go on behaving as though their real goal were the grade.

The authors of this book once knew of a community group which had been organized around the ostensible purpose of meeting informally once a month to read and discuss plays. After attending the first few meetings some of the members came to realize that the publicly avowed goal of the group — play-reading — was not, in actuality, the major goal of the majority. It seemed that for most of the members the group was primarily a source of social satisfaction, and for some a vehicle for social climbing. The majority was apparently quite content with these goals and had somehow understood from the beginning the nature of the group. Since the needs for companionship of the members of the minority were adequately satisfied elsewhere, they dropped out as soon as they came to understand the situation.

This brings us to an important point regarding the motives of individuals in a group. One of the factors which makes our comprehension of the subject so difficult, creates misunderstandings on the part of group members, and builds barriers to communication in discussion, is that so often people cannot or will not openly admit their own motivations.

One of the reasons for this situation is that often these objectives are not socially acceptable, or are not regarded as socially acceptable by the people holding them. Hence, in the play-reading group it was apparently felt necessary to have some public excuse — reading plays — to justify bringing this particular collection of people into social contact. The White Citizens Councils which have sprung up in the South since the Supreme Court's ruling on desegregation in the public schools find it expedient, in the light of national public opinion, to phrase their objectives in less belligerently anti-Negro language than the members would probably use in private. The individual in an organization who volunteers for a committee chairmanship in order to build prestige so that he may run for a higher elective office the following year cannot very well announce to his committee members at their first meeting that this is the main reason he has become their chairman.

On the other hand, people sometimes regard their own motives as socially unacceptable, and hence avoid revealing them, when in actuality there is no good reason for such reticence. The employee who attends a meeting because his boss has asked him to do so, or the student who takes a course because he needs a particular number of credit hours in that field, should not automatically assume that these facts must be kept secret — particularly when there is no necessary conflict between his private motivations and the purposes of the group. The fact that the employee may participate in a discussion under compulsion need not prevent his becoming a useful contributor. Many students become interested and learn a great deal from courses in which they enrolled originally for other reasons. The person who derives pleasure from chatting with his friends on the church steps need not be ashamed to admit that this is *one* of the reasons he attends worship services. Nor is there anything wrong with the Rotary Club member admitting to himself and others that he hopes to make some business contacts through the organization. A boy or girl can find a spouse at college and still get a good education — in fact, there may be fewer distractions from studying as a result of having a less turbulent and uncertain love life. In short, were people franker with themselves and others about the variety of motivations which bring them to a group many of the enigmas of the discussion process would be dissipated.

Unconscious Motivations and Hidden Agenda

There is, however, another reason why these private goals may not be revealed: the individuals themselves can be unconscious of their own motivations. The college freshman, for example, who joins a fraternity or sorority, may not actually be doing so for any of the conscious reasons he could state, but primarily because he feels socially insecure in the strange new university environment in which he finds himself, and desires the aid, comfort, and protection of belonging to some clique or in-group. The apparently civic-minded woman who is an active participant and leader in several community organizations may not be aware that she is using these activities as an escape from an unhappy home life or as a means of satisfying some excessive craving for attention. The businessman who devotes tremendous amounts of energy to his company, and is one of the most forceful and vocal members of its inner councils, may not fully realize how much of his behavior is a compensation for his basic feelings of inferiority. And a teacher, leading a classroom discussion, may be completely oblivious to the way in which he exploits the group to satisfy his own ego-needs.

Indeed, research on small group behavior indicates that a vast amount of the interaction that takes place in a discussion is motivated by unconscious determinants such as these. If we are to understand the process fully we must not be so naïve as to believe that all the remarks of participants can be interpreted solely as attempts to reach the publicly stated common objectives of the group. Rather, it must be assumed that the contributions made to a discussion are motivated by a variety of objectives, some conscious and some unconscious, some relevant to the common goals of the group and some to the private purposes of the individual members. Thus, when Joe disagrees vehemently with Jack's proposal it may be that he really thinks it is a poor idea, or it may be that he is trying to put Jack in his place because he feels Jack has been having things too much his own way lately. It may also be that unconsciously he is competing with Jack for the group's leadership. Or he may fear that if Jack's proposal were adopted the group might finish its work and disband sooner than he would like it to.

Whenever a situation exists where there are a significant number of private motives, either conscious or unconscious, lurking beneath the surface and influencing the course of the discussion in subtle, indirect ways, we refer to the group as having "hidden agenda." In other words, there may be items of "business"—a rebellion against the leader, for example—which some or many members of the group are unaware of or which, for one reason or another, are not talked about openly. Although it is probable that every group, even the most frank and intimate, has some hidden agenda, the problem becomes serious only when the nature of the items on the hidden agenda is such as to interfere with the effective pursuit of the group's avowed purposes. We will have more to say about hidden agenda later in this book.

Task Motives and Interpersonal Relations

A convenient way of summarizing the various kinds of goals or motives which we have been discussing in this chapter is to divide them into two large categories. The first category consists of those motives, either private or public, conscious or unconscious, under the surface or above it, which have to do with the primary purpose, task, or work for which the group has come into existence. If it is a jury in a criminal trial, the task of the group is to render a decision on the guilt or innocence of the defendant, and all the members will be motivated, to one degree or another, to solve that problem. The activity arising from these motives can be described as "task-oriented" or "problem-centered"—that is, designed to get the job done, or to deal with the problem which has brought them together. Similarly, in an adult education course in World Politics, those remarks primarily aimed at an exploration of the subject matter of the course would be considered task-oriented, in contrast to a remark whose primary purpose, for example, is to put an overtalkative member in his place.

This brings us to the second general category of motives—those having to do primarily with the establishment and maintenance of a satisfactory pattern of interpersonal relationships among the members of the group. Every group, no matter what its task, devotes some time and energy to this process of "oiling the machinery," as it were. The degree of concern given to these human relationships will depend, of course, on how smoothly they run without special attention, on the extent to which members have joined the group for social rather than business reasons, and upon the time limits under which the group is working. In an industrial firm where production is presumably the overriding goal, attention to group morale will assume a subsidiary role—although even here recognition of the ultimate impact of morale upon production may cause concern. In a bridge club, on the other hand, attention to playing the game may become subsidiary to the gossip that takes place at the table—although, again, the two categories are usually recognized as interdependent and there is an awareness that if no bridge is played at all the group may fall apart.[1]

In other words, there is in every group an element of production and an element of morale, an element of objectivity and an element of subjectivity, or whatever other similar pair of nouns one wishes to use to describe these phenomena.[2] The distinction has been recognized in this book by the separation between Part II, Group Thinking, and Part III, Interpersonal Relations. George C. Homans, one of the leading writers on small group behavior, speaks

[1] The theories and research of Robert F. Bales, *op. cit.*, would suggest, in fact, that all groups, in order to survive, must maintain an equilibrium between what he calls the task and the social-emotional areas.

[2] The advice contained in the two conflicting aphorisms—"Don't mix business with pleasure" and "All work and no play makes Jack a dull boy"—shows an awareness of the two categories we have been discussing.

of the external system and the internal system of a group.[3] As Homans describes it, the external system of a group is that set of motives and activities aimed at the survival of the group in its environment. The internal system is that set of motives, activities, and interactions — the pattern of interpersonal relationships in other words — which arises out of the external system and then, as he points out, reacts upon it.

Recognition of this interdependence of what Homans calls the external and internal systems is of crucial importance if we are fully to understand what goes on in any discussion group. As a group works together on whatever its task may be, the members build up attitudes and feelings toward one another. These attitudes, whether positive or negative, then affect the way they work together, and the way they work together in turn further affects the attitudes. The tendency for one man to reject another man's ideas because he dislikes the man rather than because he finds anything wrong with the idea is so universal a phenomenon that it cannot be dismissed lightly as something abnormal.[4] The way in which the internal system affects the external can also be seen in the fact that many people will speak more forthrightly when persons of higher status are absent from their group than when they are present.[5] This also cannot be passed off as a neurotic reaction. Man is not a compartmentalized being. Our needs to produce and create and our needs to like and be liked become intertwined in intricate and complex patterns — and what is more, these patterns are constantly changing. Man is motivated by many forces, and the various goals he pursues assume greater or lesser importance as his attention shifts from one to another, or as he grows in understanding and maturity. Although the complexity of the problem should not discourage us from exploring it further, we must always remain skeptical of too simple or too easy an explanation.

[3] George C. Homans, *The Human Group* (Harcourt, Brace, 1950).

[4] Research supporting this point may be found in M. W. Horowitz, J. Lyons, and H. V. Perlmutter, "Induction of Forces in Discussion Groups," *Human Relations* (1951); also K. W. Back, "Influence through Social Communication," *Journal of Abnormal and Social Psychology* (1951).

[5] See Leon Festinger, S. Schachter, and K. Back, *Social Pressures in Informal Groups* (Harper, 1950); also E. Paul Torrance, "Some Consequences of Power Differences on Decision-Making in Permanent and Temporary Three-Man Groups," in A. Paul Hare, Edgar F. Borgatta, and Robert F. Bales, *Small Groups* (Knopf, 1955).

Complementary and Antagonistic Goals

Just because there are a wide variety of individual motives present in any group, affecting and influencing one another, it does not follow that their total impact will necessarily be detrimental. Much depends upon whether or not the various goals sought are complementary or mutually exclusive. There is no reason, for example, why the finance committee of an organization cannot plan and execute a successful fund-raising drive, while at the same time contributing to the personal prestige of the chairman, who may be elected president of the organization the following year. Nor is there any reason why two other members of the committee cannot fall in love and get married, nor why all of the members of the group may not enjoy thoroughly each other's company at the meetings. Under circumstances such as these a spirit of complete cooperation can prevail.

On the other hand, if two members of the committee *both* seek to use the group as a stepping stone to the presidency of the organization for the following year, we have a situation of antagonistic or mutually exclusive motives. If one succeeds the other must fail. Under such conditions, no matter how much commonality of purpose there may be regarding the major activity of the group, there is bound to be some lack of teamwork in the meetings. How destructive this will be depends on the comparative importance to the individuals involved of their conflicting, as opposed to their common, goals. It will also depend on the degree to which they feel they must keep these motives disguised, thus remaining less amenable to the possible working out of mutually satisfactory modifications. It is conceivable that our two presidential aspirants, realizing the overriding importance of their committee's task and the hazards involved in their personal conflict, might sit down together and agree to support each other for the presidency in two successive terms and thus remove from the arena of the committee's deliberations this particular hidden agenda item.

Unfortunately there are many situations where this kind of reconciliation is never achieved. What is even sadder, there are innumerable groups where the major goals of individuals are not really antagonistic but are nevertheless perceived so by the members, who act accordingly. Labor-management conflicts provide us with perhaps the most classic examples of this sort of phenomenon. For here the parties to the dispute have vast areas of common interest — to keep their industry in production, to maintain it as a profitable enterprise, to make it a pleasant place to work, and to contribute to the kind of national economy which, in the long run, will be to the benefit of both management and labor. To be sure, there may be real differences of opinion as to how these goals can best be achieved, and there may be some truly conflicting interests with regard to how large a slice of the pie each party should have. But frequently disputants become so embroiled in conflict that they tend to overemphasize their differences and to overlook their common desires, or to see how these desires might be reconciled. This is not only true of management and labor but, to some extent, of all human relationships. So often when people stop viewing each other as implacable foes and sit down together in calm deliberation, they find their interests are not as divergent or as irreconcilable as they had appeared. One can point to any number of rather bitterly contested labor contracts, for instance, in which mutually satisfactory agreements eventually have been worked out and have stood the test of workability for long periods of time thereafter.

Motives and the Handling of Conflict

We can conclude, then, that the perception which people have of their own motives and the motives of others will have a significant bearing on the ways in which conflict among them is handled. Whether or not agreements can be achieved through discussion will depend not only on the true nature of the interests at stake but also on the perspective from which they are viewed. This would suggest that not all conflict which appears irreconcilable is really so, and that the methods by which conflict is handled are sometimes inappropriate. Let us be more specific.

There are basically three ways in which differences are commonly dealt with in a group, organization, or society where the power to settle these differences is equally distributed among the members.[6] They are majority vote, arbitration, and consensus.

[6] We have already noted in Chapter 1 that where the distribution of power is unequal, conflicts of interests usually are settled arbitrarily by those holding the power.

Majority vote

Majority vote is probably the most widely employed method of handling conflict. Under this system, as is well known, those individuals in a group or society who have interests or views to promote lay their arguments before the rest of the membership. These are discussed back and forth and finally a proposed settlement is submitted to a vote. If a simple majority (or in some special cases two-thirds or three-fourths) of the members approve, the proposition becomes binding upon all, including the minority. Majority rule, therefore, is in a sense a kind of power settlement, although it is a power of numbers in contrast to the physical or economic coercion employed in nondemocratic methods. Presumably every member has an equal opportunity to persuade the majority to his point of view, and presumably if he is not willing to abide by the vote of the majority he can withdraw from the group.

Although a vote is sometimes used simply to formalize or make record of a unanimous or a compromise agreement, it is more frequently employed as a means of actually settling a disagreement. Here the assumption is made either that further talk will not change anyone else's mind, or that the issue is not worth the time it might take for more prolonged discussion. In short, the group has decided that, at least for practical purposes, the conflicting interests are irreconcilable, and that a choice must be made between them. Each member is expected to vote in behalf of his own best interests and, therefore, "the greatest good for the greatest number" will emerge.

We might note several questionable assumptions here. First, are the motives of the members really so much in conflict that, given more time for exploration, they might not be able to come to an agreement? Second, is time really at a premium?[7] Third, will a majority vote truly produce the greatest good for the greatest number, when the members of that majority have not had an opportunity to come to a full appreciation of the minority's feelings? As Socrates is reported to have asked, "How many votes does it take to change a lie into the truth?"

Granted, there are innumerable situations when the answer to

[7] As a result of rushing a matter to a vote, much more time might be wasted in the long run trying to get the minority to cooperate in implementing a decision for which they feel no enthusiasm or loyalty.

these three questions is "Yes." If so, the method of majority vote would certainly be appropriate. However, there are also many circumstances where voting takes place when further discussion might better have served the purpose. Voting tends to encourage an argumentative atmosphere in which members commit themselves too quickly to one faction or another without examining the possibilities of finding a settlement agreeable to all. The knowledge that matters will be settled ultimately by a vote makes it too easy for members of the group (particularly those who think they have a majority on their side) to close their minds on the question and not listen to reason. As Mary Follett put it, "Voting creates nothing. It merely records what has already been created." Finally, the method of majority rule provides no practical solution to such conflicts as labor-management disputes or marital difficulties where there is no immediate larger organization to which the parties can turn for a vote to settle their dispute.

Arbitration

Partly as an answer to some of the shortcomings of majority vote, a second way of handling differences has evolved in many power-sharing societies. This method, known as arbitration, consists of airing the controversy before an impartial third party whose decision the disputants have agreed in advance to accept. This third party may be a single person, such as a judge in our civil courts, or an arbiter in a labor dispute. It may be a panel of three persons, such as the judges in our courts of appeal, or the boards of arbitration in some industrial conflicts or international disputes. It may even be a jury of twelve, as in major criminal court trials.

As in the case of majority rule, arbitration is a kind of power settlement, although, again, this power of decision-making presumably has been voluntarily delegated and voluntarily acceded to by the disputants. Further, the assumption is made here, too, that the conflict is irreconcilable (though sometimes the proceedings are interrupted by a settlement out of court), and that positions will be won or lost. It is hoped that because of the presumed impartiality of the arbiters justice will be done. Obviously this is not always what happens. Nor do individuals, having freely and voluntarily set up a system of courts, always gracefully accept the settlements which are handed down to them. Reactions to the

United States Supreme Court's decision on desegregation of the public schools is ample evidence of this point. Still, most of us would agree that the system is far superior to settlements by force and violence, and in many instances provides a necessary supplement to the method of majority vote.

Consensus

The third means by which a democratic group or society can settle differences among its members is by continuing to discuss the problem until minds are changed or solutions found which make agreement possible. This is sometimes referred to as consensus, sometimes as integration, sometimes as unanimous consent. It is a method by which various groups, like the Quakers, as well as juries, conduct all their business. If agreement cannot be reached, no group action is taken. In the case of the Quakers, discussion may go on for years (as it did in the mid-nineteenth century over the question of harboring fugitive slaves) and in the meanwhile each individual does as his own conscience dictates. In the case of a hung jury, the group is dismissed and another one impaneled to rehear the trial.

Of all the methods for handling conflict this is the most demanding in terms of persistence and creativity. It is also the most likely to produce in group members a willingness to expose and re-examine their own motives and their perceptions of the motives of others in order to find common purposes and to re-adjust conflicting ones. Keen analysis and humane consideration for others are essential if all the variety of interests present are to be satisfactorily incorporated in the final agreement. Hence the decision is likely to be a good one, and once it is reached, the chance of cooperation in its implementation are at their optimum. These, in our opinion, are values highly to be desired; and it is the primary purpose of this book to provide aid to those who are interested in pushing discussion to these frontiers.

The limitations of consensus

Having said all this, we would still remind the reader that consensus is not always attainable and that other methods of handling conflict should not be abandoned. There are, in some circumstances, truly conflicting motives or interests which should not be glossed over with a coating of superficial harmony. The so-called "happy medium" is not always so happy. Although compromising on a goal here and there may often be preferable to a total defeat, there are some compromises which are worse. (The old story of Solomon offering to cut a child in two in order to settle the dispute between conflicting "mothers" amply illustrates this truth.) The easy assumption that "Reasonable, intelligent men with a common objective, in the presence of the facts, do not have too much trouble coming into agreement" (a quotation reportedly on the office wall of a former Secretary of Defense) ignores the possibility that people may even disagree over the validity of so-called facts. Furthermore, whereas a religious group like the Quakers can afford to "agree to disagree," and let each member go his own way, governing bodies like a parliament or board of directors *must* come to decisions, sometimes in a severely limited amount of time. It should be added in this connection, though, that most groups tend to overlook the possibility of adopting broad permissive policies which leave a wide range of alternatives open to individuals within the organization.

Sometimes a minority does not care to explain or argue for its desires beyond a certain point but would rather simply record its dissenting votes and then go along with the majority. Individuals in such a minority may feel that their views are nobody else's business, and that rather than discuss the matter they would prefer to submit to the majority will. Or they may not want to assume the kind of responsibility which would ensue from their having participated fully in the decision-making process. Opposition political parties, for example, have been known to reject a government's offer to them to participate in bipartisan policy-making because the minority party has felt that it could perform a more useful function by criticizing from the outside and thus keeping the government on its toes.

Finally, it should be noted that true consensus, freely and rationally arrived at, is not the same as social conformity. If a group's attempts to reach consensus result in social pressures coming into play which drive minority individuals unwillingly or unwittingly into line, then it is far preferable to reinstitute the protections not only of a vote, but perhaps a secret one at that. We have observed a number of groups where vote-taking has been abandoned for the sake of making meetings more informal, or on the grounds that the members can all trust each other and it can therefore be assumed that "silence means assent." These are dangerous premises — appropriate sometimes, to be sure, but not to be lightly or uncritically accepted. If agreements thus gained are the result of social pressure they will be certainly no more viable than those attained under majority rule. It is more likely that they will suffer from the same defects as settlements imposed from above by power-figures.

Debate and Discussion

Some of our readers may be wondering where debate fits into the picture we have painted of the democratic methods of resolving conflict. Debate is usually thought of as that kind of discourse which takes place, prior to a vote or arbitration, between individuals who have fixed positions on a subject and who are trying to persuade others to accept their point of view. Discussion, on the other hand, is ordinarily considered to be a flexible, cooperative process which precedes settlement by consensus. It should be clear by now that in real life such a sharp distinction cannot be made. Probably no human being is so completely open-minded on all phases of a subject that he can engage in lengthy discussion of it without at some moments engaging in debate. Nor is it likely that there is anyone whose mind is so utterly closed that, given the proper environment, he might not learn and accept something new from his fellow men. Discussion can, and frequently does reach a point where unanimous agreement is unattainable and a settlement, if there is to be one, must be made by a vote. Contrariwise, debaters occasionally discover that they have more in common than they thought, and are able to resolve their argument through consensus.

Often, too, what appears to be a debate is not really so. It may simply be that the rules of the game require the participants to act *as though* they had irreconcilable points of view. Thus school debaters engage in forensic exercises designed to sharpen their wits and cultivate their communicative skills. They do not necessarily believe in the propositions they support, and they usually end a debating season somewhere in the middle of the road on the questions they have argued. Thus, too, opposing lawyers who appear in the courtroom to be deadly foes, may actually be the best of friends, simply fulfilling their professional obligation to attack or defend the litigants with all the resources at their command. And why? Because society has found this to be an effective technique for making certain that all of the relevant information and arguments are brought to light for the judges or jury to *explore and discuss.* This is much like the mock debates in which students of philosophy so often engage, wherein they argue vehemently on opposite sides of a question, but do so only because they are interested in searching for the truth together. In short, what appears on the surface to be debate may, when viewed in its larger context, be part of a discussion process.

This is not to say that there is no such thing as a conflict in which a direct clash of interests is present, and in which serious debate takes place. We are merely pointing out that people do not ordinarily engage even in this kind of an argument unless they hold some hope that influence can be exerted on the opposition and that at least a modicum of change can be brought about. If the parties to the dispute feel they have nothing whatsoever in common they are not likely to continue talking to one another. In other words, we are suggesting that in most human relationships there is a mosaic of interests, some compatible and some not, which make any simple distinctions between debate and discussion unrealistic.

In summary, we have found that the members of most groups possess a wide variety of individual motives, which may be more or less compatible with the publicly stated purposes of the group. Each member will, in all probability, interpret that group purpose somewhat differently. Some may regard group membership as a means to a private end or as an end in itself. The motives which individuals have may be hidden from others or even from themselves. In any case, it is out of the interplay of all these forces, whether concerned with the task or with interpersonal relations, that both conflict and cooperation emerge. Although consensus is an ideal which all discussion might well strive to attain, the constellation of motives operating in a particular situation may make it necessary, after a certain point, to settle for majority rule or arbitration. We have seen that within the total course of the same discussion some points might be voted upon, some submitted to arbitration, and some talked out to unanimity. Finally, we have observed that debate and discussion need not be thought of as distinctly separate processes, but as typically woven together into the total fabric with which the members of a democratic society seek to resolve their differences.

RECOMMENDED READINGS

Bales, Robert F. *Interaction Process Analysis.* Addison-Wesley Publishing Company, Inc., 1949.

Bradford, Leland. "The Case of the Hidden Agenda," *Adult Leadership* (September, 1952).

Cartwright, Dorwin, and Alvin Zander. *Group Dynamics.* Row, Peterson and Company, 1953.

Part Two

GROUP THINKING

Chapter Four

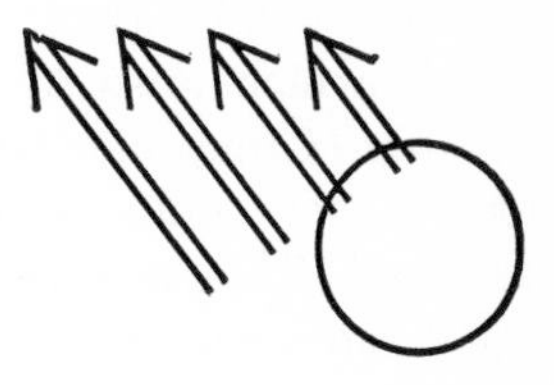

The Origin and Nature of Problems for Discussion

A GROUP OF HARVARD UNDERGRADUATES are huddled over a table studying and discussing a half-played game of chess. Through one-way windows and a set of microphones their conversation is being watched and overheard by observers in the next room. Each comment that is made is categorized and recorded on a tape which rolls through a machine in front of the observers. These are the first stages of a long-term program of research on interaction in small groups under the direction of Dr. Robert F. Bales of the Harvard University Department of Social Relations.

Professor Bales has set up twelve columns into which observers may choose to place the contributions being made in the discussion. Six of these categories provide for comments which are "task-oriented" — that is, which have primarily to do with the problem the group is discussing — such as "asking for information" or "giving opinions." The other six are for "social-emotional" activities, such as "deflating the status of another member" or "telling a joke to relieve tension." These two broad areas of group interaction — the methods by which a group handles its *topic* of discussion, and the personal relationships which develop among participants as they engage in discourse with one another — have come to be recognized generally by researchers in this field as the basic "stuff" of the discussion process. A student or critic may focus his attention on either or both. Part II of this book, Group Thinking, will be addressed to the former of these areas of concern. Part III, Interpersonal Relations, will deal with the latter.

The problems which arise in the area of group thinking are several in number. Group members may have only a vague notion of the nature of their problem and, hence, of the responsibilities they have assumed. They may be unable to organize their thinking so that relevant aspects of the problem are given the consideration they deserve. They may not know when or how to integrate the conflicting viewpoints expressed in the course of their meetings. The first of these obstacles to effective group thinking, clarification of the specific kind of problem before the group, will be analyzed in this chapter. Chapter 5 will deal with the problems of organizing group thinking, Chapter 6 with the handling of the raw materials of discussion, and Chapter 7 with the uses of authority and reason. In Chapter 8 we shall study some of the methods of resolving differences and formulating decisions.

When any of us looks in on a gathering of individuals engaged in discussion, the natural question that first comes to mind is "What are these people talking about?" We are interested in determining the topic of discussion, and we may also find it helpful to know how they happen to be talking about it. These are the same first questions which the critic or student of discussion must answer if he is to understand and improve the process. Why and how does a group become involved with a particular kind of subject? There are a number of possibilities.

Personal Needs of Group Members

Each of us, in the course of pursuing the needs of our daily lives, encounters frustrations of one sort or another. They may range from the minor irritations growing out of our contacts with teachers, bosses, or co-workers to extreme anxiety over such issues as one's job, health, or relationships with the opposite sex. Regardless of the degree of severity of the problem, we often find considerable relief and help from talking the matter over with other persons. These others may be interested in discussing the question with us because they have had experience with it in the past, because they themselves are currently having similar difficulties, or simply because they like us and want to help in whatever way they can. It is out of such mutuality of personal interests that gripe sessions, bull sessions, "man-to-man talks," or therapy groups grow. And the topic, of course, is determined by the nature of the tensions or problems felt by the individuals in the group.

Demands of the Environment

Frequently, however, our choice of discussion topics is not quite so free. Problems from our external environment demand our attention. A community may be inundated by flood waters, struck by a tornado, hit by a serious flu epidemic, or otherwise harassed by the forces of nature, and people will need to come together to talk over what to do about it. Economic difficulties may also plague a group or society — inflation, depression, shortages or surpluses of food, inadequacies of housing, schools, transportation; all of these may call for meetings to explore possible courses of action together. Then, too, there are problems which men, through prejudice, ignorance, or greed create for themselves or for others. Difficulties of intergroup or interracial relations — in employment, in housing, in education, in recreational facilities, and in social contact — consume hundreds of thousands of man-hours of meeting time, as do problems of juvenile delinquency, drug addiction, racketeering, and so on. Sometimes just one incidence of trouble (such as a tragic fire in a school as the result of violations of safety regulations) is sufficient to provoke discussion, but frequently before meetings occur there is an accumulation of related instances which finally become generalized into a broad problem such as "juvenile delinquency in our city," or "the rate of highway accidents."

Many of the situations we have thus far described are ones in which no group existed until problems arose. In other words, it is the presence of a particular problem which evokes the formation of a group. A therapy group for alcoholics gets started when a number of persons, sharing this problem, come together for help. A community emergency housing council is created when a storm destroys a large area of the town. On the other hand, the group may antedate the problem. For instance, a half-dozen friends, neighbors, or colleagues may gather together regularly over coffee or lunch twice a month, each time discussing a different subject about which they are all concerned.

Delegation of Problems

Often discussion occurs as the result of an assignment from an executive to his subordinates or by delegation from a legislative body to one of its sub-groups. An employer may set up a staff meeting or create a committee to consider an issue which he deems to be important and upon which he may wish advice or recommendations. He may even grant the group some decision-making power. Likewise, most sizable organizations — whether it be the Congress of the United States, the local PTA, or a college social fraternity — operate through a committee structure. When problems arise the parent body assigns them to the appropriate committee for study and for either recommendations or decision.

As in the case of problems arising from demands of the environment, committees with delegated responsibilities may exist in advance of the occurrence of particular problems or they may be created especially to deal with a unique circumstance. Congress, for example, has regular *standing* committees in such fields as foreign relations, finance, agriculture, and military affairs to which problems arising in those areas are referred. In addition, temporary or *ad hoc* committees are often appointed to deal with unusual topics, such as the special "select" committee which was assigned the task of studying the possible censure of the late Senator Joseph McCarthy.

Sometimes discussion groups which are set up by higher authorities or by steering and executive boards are given considerable leeway or autonomy in the choice of particular subjects to which they may turn their attention, with only the general area being specified. This would be the case when a professional convention of the "workshop" type is planned, when a Great Books or World Politics course is established, or when a branch of the American Civil Liberties Union is organized to deal with local problems. It is also often true of a legislative assembly such as the Congress, where committees have grown greatly in importance and exercise considerable initiative in the choice of issues which they may explore.

The thought may have occurred to the reader, particularly since we have used Congress for illustrative purposes, that many organizations create a far more elaborate committee structure than is really necessary. Staff meetings are called without much forethought or justification. Certainly our Congress, particularly in the duplication of committees in the House and the Senate, might profitably be streamlined. Often committees are created just to give everyone in an organization a position, even though there is actually little or no work for them to do. We have probably all belonged to a group at one time or another which seemed to have outlived its usefulness — that is, it persisted in surviving and holding meetings even though the problems it was founded to deal with had long since disappeared. Although the question of whether group meetings are really needed in a particular situation is well worth our attention, we will postpone consideration of that issue until Chapter 15 on the uses and abuses of discussion. At this point, having gained some insight into the sources from which topics originate, it is important that we consider the manner in which they are formulated and presented to a group. For the nature of a problem will determine the way it is phrased and how it will be approached.

Questions of Fact or Perception

Probably the least complicated of all the kinds of problems with which a discussion group may be confronted are those we call questions of fact or perception. Indeed, many topics of this type do not require discussion at all. These are the sorts of problems where there is some doubt as to the facts or where the members of a group may have incomplete understanding or different perceptions of the situation and are attempting to come to some agreement on a more complete and satisfactory description. Let us take two illustrations — one in which discussion would be inappropriate, and another where it might prove helpful. Assume that the members of the local Board of Education are uncertain whether or not the majority of parents in their school district would oppose the introduction of sex education in the elementary schools. Although each of the board members may be familiar with a different segment of the population, and there might be some value in their sitting down together at a meeting and pooling their impressions, it would be more sensible for them to devote that time and effort to making a scientific survey of the community — even if on a limited and amateur scale. On the other hand, let us suppose that a committee of the National Conference of Christians and Jews is interested in determining whether the problem of anti-Semitism in the United States is as extensive today as it was fifteen years ago. This is not a question which lends itself so easily to a survey. Indeed, a survey on such a matter could be a tremendously costly undertaking and might only bring results that were rather superficial. However, a group of experienced experts in human relations from various parts of the country, who have worked on this problem over the years, might quite profitably come together, pool and discuss their perceptions of the situation, and piece together an informative portrait of the nation.

There are other circumstances, too, where group discussion on questions of fact or perception may be interesting and useful. A group of people may get together to discuss a difficult book which they have all read, and may spend an entire meeting simply sharing with one another their impressions of what the author was trying to say. A profitable session may be spent by a group discussing, "What is Zen Buddhism?," where the purpose of the meeting is to bring to light as much information as the participants may have been able to gather concerning this particular religious philosophy, in the hope of getting a larger view of the subject. Similarly, students of world affairs might find it worth their while to devote a number of meetings to exploring the question, "Of what does the Communist philosophy consist?"

The classic example of the value of these types of discussion is the fable of the blind men and the elephant. Each had his hand on a different portion of the animal's anatomy, and hence had an entirely different impression of the nature of the beast in question. Only through pooling and organizing their respective bits of knowledge could they secure a more satisfactory understanding of the elephant. Questions of fact or perception, then, involve a group primarily in the sharing of data which the members may possess or may have collected specifically for the purpose of the discussion. The participants engage in little or no interpretation or evaluation of material, for that is not their aim. To be sure, psychologists tell us that even our perceptions are influenced by our needs or *Weltanschauung* (world view); that we do not see simply what is "out there" in the world about us, but that our vision is colored by the workings of our own nervous systems. Nevertheless, we can, if we try, be *relatively* objective — and this is what members of a group discussing a question of fact attempt to do. The process is aided tremendously by their interaction, for each can offset the biases and limitations of the others.

Problems of Diagnosis or Understanding

The second kind of problem a group might discuss goes beyond the sharing and organizing of data to include interpretation as well. These we call problems of diagnosis or understanding. The participants must not only come to some agreement on their perceptions of the situation, but they must also attempt to interpret or make inferences about what they see. Hypotheses as to the causes of the difficulty may be proposed and discussed, or predictions as to possible future trends may be examined and evaluated.

Thus, the medical staff of a psychiatric hospital may meet for an hour each morning to share their observations of a patient's behavior and then to probe the possible explanations of his difficulties or make prognoses regarding the future course of his illness. A class in American history might discuss the different interpretations of the causes of World War I, attempting to determine which of them seems to have the greatest validity. A father and mother might hold a conference to try to figure out why Johnny has been acting so strangely lately. The staff of the National Association for the Advancement of Colored People might discuss the probable consequences of their pressing a court test of school segregation in rural Mississippi. The United States National Security Council might attempt to determine why the Soviet Union is making such rapid strides in missile development and what their rate of progress is likely to be during the next five years.

In all of these examples the purpose is diagnosis or understanding. The problem posed requires not only the collection of facts but raises such questions as, "What do we make of these facts?" "How did this situation come about?" "What course are events likely to take in the future?" These problems are thus more in the realm of the unknown or the disputable than are questions of fact or perception. It is for this reason that the discussion of them, with many minds brought to bear on the matter, can be of such great benefit. As in the case of questions of perception, it may be that there are some circumstances — such as a "bull session" about the relationship between cigarette smoking and lung cancer — where a scientific study might be more useful than a discussion. In general, however, because of the possibility of many interpretations of data, diagnostic group discussions can be extremely enlightening.

It should be noted that problems of diagnosis or understanding can be classified on the basis of the points in time with which they deal. Some, such as an historical discussion about the causes of a particular war, deal entirely with the past. Others, such as "What is bothering Johnny?" are concerned with the present. Still others, such as the question of Soviet missile development during the next five years, have to do with the future. But in all cases it is understanding or insight which is sought.

Problems of Attitude or Feeling

It must be apparent to the reader that much of the discussion that takes place in the course of a normal day's events has to do with problems that are more subjective in nature than those already explained here. We are often concerned not so much that something is so, or why it is so, or what, objectively, is likely to happen, but rather how we ought to feel about it. Presumably, or at least ideally, when such questions arise, we already have some understanding of a situation and are now wondering what attitude we should take toward it.

For instance, we know that there is discrimination against minority groups, both in the North and in the South, regarding the availability to them of certain kinds of housing. We also know a good deal about the reasons for this, the means by which the pattern is perpetuated, and the likelihood of its continuation into the immediate future. But there still remains the question of how we feel about all this. Do we agree that there *ought* to be segregation in housing? That Negroes, or Orientals, or Puerto Ricans, or Mexicans, or Italians, or Jews, ought to live primarily in their own areas? Would we ourselves be opposed to residing in the same neighborhood or apartment building with the members of these minority groups? Do we believe it is wrong for real estate agents to have informal "gentlemen's agreements" that they will not show houses in a certain neighborhood to Jews or that they will not cooperate in the sale of a home to a Negro? Would we ourselves feel justified in selling our own home to a member of a minority group? These are questions of attitude or feeling, and they involve making judgments in which our personal values are the criteria for evaluation. No one can tell us how we ought to feel. They can only expose us to their own attitudes, and to the facts, logic, and values which lie behind those attitudes, and hope that through discussion we may modify our own.

Similarly, let us assume that the fact has been established that there is a greater chance of a man's contracting lung cancer if he smokes heavily than if he does not, and that the cause definitely has been found to lie in the cigarette. There still might be the question for some men whether they would rather take a chance on dying younger and have had the pleasure of smoking, or whether it is more important to them to live to a ripe and healthy old age. This, again, is a problem of feeling or attitude, open to discussion and modification, to be sure, but ultimately to be decided by the individual on the basis of his own needs and values.

There are a host of other classic problems of this type which have no doubt consumed endless hours of discussion time, in this country and others. Is suicide ever justified? Are college fraternities and sororities undesirable? Is euthanasia immoral? Is capitalism better than socialism? Was it wrong for the United States to drop atomic bombs on Hiroshima and Nagasaki? Is homosexuality morally wrong? Is the President of the United States doing a good job? Some of these topics have to do only with the past, some with both present and future. All involve considerations either of goodness or badness, rightness and wrongness, or morality and immorality. In other words, the participants in such a discussion must explore the personal standards of judgment they bring to the topic.

Problems of Policy or Behavior

It may seem but a fine line of distinction between the kinds of problems we have labeled attitude or feeling and those we are about to describe as problems of policy or behavior. However, the difference can be significant. For a question of policy or behavior is one about which the group must decide what to *do.* Frequently how we *feel* about an issue and what we *do* about it are not quite the same. When it comes to action, a new set of criteria may come into play which did not concern us when we were discussing the matter only theoretically. We may think it is perfectly proper, morally and otherwise, to sell a house in an all-white neighborhood to a Negro family, but whether we will actually do so may be quite another story. We may believe that mercy killing is justified, but whether we would vote to legalize it raises a number of *practical* considerations, having to do with the administration of such a law, which might throw the matter into an entirely different light. In other words, answers to questions of policy or behavior involve not only our personal goals and desires with regard to the main issue at hand, but require us to think about the practical effectiveness of a particular course of action in ultimately achieving *all* of the things we may want.

The heavy smoker who becomes convinced that he *ought* to give up cigarettes should ask himself whether he will simply replace this habit with the potentially more deleterious one of overeating. Although the members of a society may come to agree that mercy killing is sometimes a permissible act, it may well be that they will still decide not to legalize it. Admittedly this places doctors in the ambiguous position of not knowing where they stand if they participate in euthanasia, but at least the society has avoided giving legal sanction, and hence possible encouragement, to the act. It may be desirable that doctors carry this weighty burden of responsibility on their own shoulders should they decide to relieve a patient of his suffering through death.

It is important to recognize that for a discussion of policy or behavior to occur, ordinarily there must be some basic agreement in the group on attitudes toward the subject, as well as on a diagnosis of the problem. The discussion of policy must either be preceded by a diagnostic discussion and a discussion of attitudes, or the members of the group must in some other way have determined that they are of one mind on these matters. It would be foolish for a group of college students to sit around discussing possible ways to improve fraternities and sororities if first they had not agreed something was wrong with the system. Likewise, a city council could spend endless hours in fruitless discussion of possible means of raising funds for a new recreation center if the aldermen were not really committed to the idea of building such a center in the first place. For members of a group to argue about the ways and means of gaining some goal which they have not even agreed is desirable is certainly to put the cart before the horse.

It is conceivable, however, that in some instances a discussion of possible courses of action — which forces the participants to come down from the level of theory to a consideration of concrete cases — might actually help a group to decide what its attitude toward a problem should be. For example, through an exploration of possible ways and means of discouraging their daughter from the pursuit of a particular love interest, parents might arrive at the conclusion that they ought not try at all. Or, the members of a city council who are uncertain about the wisdom of constructing a new recreation center might be aided in making up their minds by an exploration of what would be involved in attempting to finance it. Nevertheless, this is not the normal or usual sequence of events. Most groups either would not be in existence or would not be talking about a particular subject unless some feeling of a common purpose had brought the members together. If we do not agree that we dislike the way the president of our organization is leading us we will not be getting together to talk about how to unseat him. Therefore, it is somewhat unrealistic for students who are engaged in practice discussions to talk about a question such as, "How can we overcome racial prejudice?" if all the members of the group do not really feel that it is desirable to eliminate such prejudice. In this instance they ought to be discussing, "Is racial prejudice really a bad thing?" Furthermore, it would be unwise of them to discuss either of these questions without first understanding some of the causes of the problem.

Finally, we would note that the discussion of problems of policy or behavior need not be confined only to those kinds of groups which are actually responsible for making a decision. To be sure, the discussion is likely to be taken more seriously if the group in question, such as the Board of Trustees of a university, possesses the power to act on its decisions. But frequently a committee may have only the right to *recommend* action. As a matter of fact, many civic and professional groups, such as the American Medical Association, American Bar Association, National Education Association, and League of Women Voters, have as one of their central purposes investigating problems and drawing up recommendations which can only be acted upon by appropriate branches of government. This does not change the basic nature of the problems they discuss, although it will have an influence on the climate in which they work. Even a Learning Group may discuss questions of policy. An adult education class in international politics, for instance, might talk about what the United States ought to do in the Middle East. Although the group has not even the power to recommend action, the discussion might very well influence the way in which members of the group will vote in the next election. It is even conceivable that if they all reach an agreement they might write a joint letter to the State Department or their Senator submitting their proposal.

There are also situations which we might call practice policy-making discussions where the members of the group lack any power to act but still derive great benefit from pretending that they do. A bull session revolving around such comments as, "This is what I'd do if I were running the show," might not only be broadly educational for the participants but, if intelligently handled, might provide valuable training in decision-making for people who may some day be in positions of responsible leadership. High school and college students who have taken part in mock Congresses, mock political conventions, mock United Nations sessions, or regular courses in discussion will appreciate the training value of such activities.

Problems Posed by Books, Plays, Films, Lectures

Many group discussions are provoked by the stimulus of new ideas to which all the participants may have been exposed. They may all have read the same controversial book or article, seen the same play or movie, or heard the same lecture, and may as a result have been moved to talk further about this common experience. The kinds of problems which might arise, however, can still be classified in one of the four categories we have already enumerated.

For example, the discussion might center around the questions, "What was this author trying to say?" or "What message was the play attempting to communicate?" Here we would have questions of fact or perception regarding which the participants could share their observations. Or the subject might be posed, "Was the speaker's analysis of the causes of our economic difficulties correct?" In other words, the group would be confronted with the task of evaluating the speaker's interpretation of events and comparing it with their own. This would be a problem of diagnosis or understanding.

A third possibility would be whether or not the group members agree with the attitudes expressed by the writer or speaker. Do they feel as he does, for instance, that there is too much conformity in American society today? Or that most religious groups are too authoritarian? These are problems of attitude or feeling. Finally, they might discuss problems of policy such as whether we should follow the author's suggestions to work for world government or to adopt a plan of socialized medicine.

Regardless of the source from which a topic originally arises, it will ordinarily fall into one of the four areas explained in this chapter. It is important for a discussion group to recognize the type of problem which is before it, because this knowledge will clarify and govern not only what is expected to come out of the discussion as an end product but will also inform the participants as to the character of preparation needed. Further, it will indicate aspects of the topic which are beyond the scope of that particular meeting.

Open-Ended and Specific Questions

Another way in which discussion topics may be classified is whether or not they are posed as open-ended or as specific questions. A problem which presents itself in open-ended form is one that allows for a wide variety of possible answers. The people who are confronted by the problem are unrestricted in their choice of responses. A specific question, on the other hand, is one that places before the group members a limited number of alternative solutions which they may accept or reject but which they are not expected to go beyond. The difference is similar to that between examination questions of the essay type calling upon a student to formulate his own answer and those allowing only a choice between or among alternatives, as in the true-false or multiple choice test.

Each of the four kinds of problems presented above may occur in open-ended or specific form. An open-ended question of fact about juvenile delinquency might be: "What is the nature and extent of juvenile delinquency in our community?" A specific question on the same subject would be: "Is juvenile delinquency on the increase?" It should be noted that the latter question can be answered either "Yes" or "No," whereas the former can elicit a variety of answers. "What are the causes of schizophrenia?" is an open-ended diagnostic type problem, whereas "Is schizophrenia inherited?" sets forth a specific diagnostic proposition which may be accepted or rejected.

In the area of attitudes, a group might discuss the question, "How do we feel about homosexuals?" This is an open-ended problem. If, however, the group is asked, "Do you think that homosexuality should be looked upon with scorn?" the focus of discussion is considerably narrowed. Similarly, in the field of policy, we might approach the topic of immigration by raising the broad and open question, "What changes should be made in our immigration laws?" or we might confine the discussion to the more specific problem, "Should the national origins quota system be abolished?" or "Should the McCarran-Walter Act be repealed?"

The question now arises as to whether it is preferable for a group to phrase its topic in an open-ended or specific way. In many cases this is an academic issue. Group members may have no choice. The problem has presented itself or has been handed to them in one form or the other, and they may not have the power to change it. A congressional sub-committee, for example, may not be authorized by its parent body to explore the entire immigration question but simply to study the relative merits of abolishing the national origins quota system. A fraternity social committee may not be asked to decide "What kind of a party shall we have?" but rather "Shall we have a barn dance or a house party?" Sometimes a group may think it is more limited than it is, and could broaden the scope of its discussions if it really tried to do so. But the question still remains, for this kind of group as well as for one with complete freedom to prescribe its own topic, whether the open-ended phrasing is more desirable.

It is our view that in most circumstances a group would do well, if it has some choice in the matter, to state its problems in open-ended rather than specific fashion. Open-ended topics provide more freedom and flexibility for the group. They are more likely to promote a spirit of inquiry and creativity in the participants than a specific phrasing which, by its either-or nature, may predispose them to taking sides and falling into an argumentative posture.

On the other hand, it should be said in behalf of specific phrasings that they do give more focus and direction to a discussion, and frequently they help a group to get to the core of a matter much more quickly. Furthermore, if the group is a competent and mature one, the participants should be able to maintain an atmosphere of inquiry regardless of how a problem is worded. It is, after all, their attitude which is the important thing. Although a particular phrasing may have the power to *predispose* people toward certain approaches, it cannot *control* them unless they allow themselves to be so dominated.

Having said all this, we would still point out that most groups are not as mature as we might ideally like them to be, and if there are no special reasons for preferring the specific wording of a question it is ordinarily best to avoid the pitfalls involved in that form and to utilize the open-ended phrasing instead. An interesting illustration of the extent to which the phrasing of a topic for discussion can make a meeting less effective than it might otherwise be occurred in an industry with which we are familiar. In an attempt by the employers to open up new channels of communication with their employees, a series of "grievance meetings" was scheduled. The management was dismayed by the argumentative and antagonistic atmosphere which prevailed in these discussions. When it was suggested that this might be due in part to their having advertised the meetings as *grievance* sessions, they experimented with a change of title. They discovered that a much more constructive attitude was being displayed when the meetings were called "weekly conferences," and that "grievances" became "problems" which needed to be solved.

Other Difficulties of Phrasing

Before leaving the matter of the semantics of problem-formulation, there are two or three other points it might be helpful to consider. One has to do with the difficulties created by a problem that is stated so broadly and ambiguously that no one knows quite where to take hold of it. It may encompass an impossibly large area, or it may include several topics which are not vitally related to one another. For example, the problem "What should be done about discrimination against minority groups?" is simply too big for any single discussion group to bite into effectively. What kinds of discrimination are to be discussed? Housing? Employment? Social? Recreational? Educational? And which minority groups? Are not the problems with regard to Negroes sufficiently different from those with respect to Jews, and the problems of Jews sufficiently distinct from those of Catholics or atheists that it would be hopeless to try to lump them all together? Difficulties such as this can be avoided by a more careful refinement of the topic to be discussed.

Another common source of confusion is a topic which confronts a group with a combination attitude-policy type problem. "What, *if anything*, should be done about our immigration laws?" creates this kind of difficulty. Those in the group who are satisfied with the *status quo* will want to argue that nothing should be done, while those who favor a change will be anxious to talk about what kind of changes should be made. The chaos which might ensue should be evident. It would be better either to have the entire group address itself directly to the question, "What is our attitude toward present immigration policy?" or else let those who are agreed that changes are necessary go off by themselves to discuss "What should be done about our immigration laws?" If the group, as a whole, for "the sake of discussion," agrees to *assume* the desirability of a change and then go on to talk about the kinds of change that would be advantageous, it may, by virtue of strong self-discipline on the part of those who really favor the *status quo*, be able to conduct a fairly good discussion. However it is more likely — particularly if the kind of clarification just described is not expressed — that such a discussion would be plagued by conflicts generated as a result of "sabotage" on the part of those who are really not in sympathy with what the others are trying to accomplish.

The last point to be made about the phrasing of discussion topics is the importance of avoiding loaded language. Frequently questions will be laid before a group which are slanted in such a way as to bias the entire discussion or which presume agreement on ideas that are still in dispute. This creates conflict which could easily have been avoided by a more objective approach to the problem. By way of a light illustration, a college student once proposed that his class discuss, "Is it fair for the Women's Christian Temperance Union to further its beliefs and practices in view of the fact that a man's personal habits are his own business and should not be interfered with by society?" Not quite so humorous are proposals to discuss "atheistic Communism," the "monopolistic press," the "excessive powers of Big Labor," the "reactionary policies of the American Medical Association," or "creeping Socialism." None of these phrases is likely to encourage intelligent deliberation.

The subjects which a group of people discuss may arise in a number of ways. They may grow out of personal tensions in the lives of the participants or from the demands of their physical and social environment. Or, problems may be delegated to them by authorities to whom they are subordinate or by larger groups of which they are a part. Sometimes the group antedates the problem, and sometimes it is born in response to a problem.

There are basically four kinds of discussion problems — fact or perception, diagnosis or understanding, attitude or feeling, and policy or behavior. These problems may deal with the past, present, or future. Policy discussions may take place not only in groups with power to act, but also in groups with power to recommend, in Learning Groups, and even in make-believe policy groups. Discussions which arise out of books, plays, films, or lectures are no different in kind from the four categories already enumerated.

Discussion topics may be phrased either as open-ended or specific questions. Ordinarily the former are more conducive to a spirit of inquiry, although the attitudes of the participants are a more important determinant of the atmosphere than the phrasing of the topic. Problems which are phrased too broadly or ambiguously, which attempt to combine attitude and policy questions in one discussion, or which are stated in loaded language, tend to create unnecessary confusion and conflict.

RECOMMENDED READINGS

Dewey, John. *How We Think.* D. C. Heath & Company, Inc., 1933.

Larrabee, Harold A. *Reliable Knowledge.* Houghton Mifflin Company, 1945.

McBurney, James H., and Kenneth G. Hance. *Discussion in Human Affairs.* Harper and Brothers, 1950.

Chapter Five

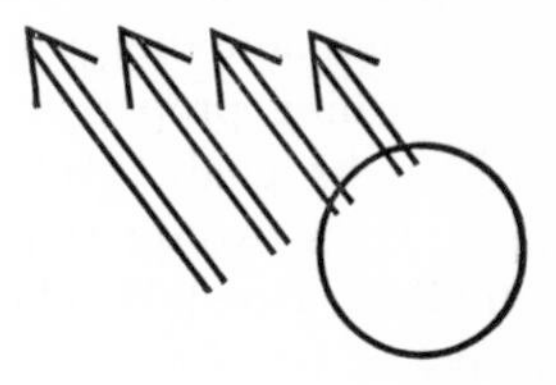

Organizing Group Thinking

A GREAT DEAL OF CRITICISM has been leveled at the operation of the typical committee. Meetings seem to consume endless hours of valuable time only to lead to questionable decisions, or to no decisions at all. The criticism comes from many quarters — from social scientists, from businessmen, even from committee chairmen themselves. Dissatisfaction with the conduct of policy-making bodies has led one wag to satirize a committee as "a group of the incompetent, appointed by the unwilling, to do the unnecessary." A somewhat more serious analysis of the situation is offered by Leland Bradford who describes the problem in these terms:

> Against this background of desperate need for understanding and skill in group productivity is the really tragic picture of the almost universal inability of people to operate effectively in group situations. Anyone familiar with the average committee, with its difficulties in reaching decisions, its incomplete discussions and immature ideas, its personality clashes and emotional stress, and its inability to move from decision into action, should have no difficulty accepting this statement.[1]

Other critics claim we underestimate the magnitude of the problem

[1] Leland Bradford, "Introduction," *Journal of Social Issues* (Spring, 1948), p. 3.

because we do not apply the same rigorous standards of efficiency to group meetings that we use in evaluating performance on the assembly line and in the office. We can expect this flood of criticism to continue until remedies are found that will improve the quality of group thinking.

Much of the time and energy lost in meetings is a result of lack of skill in establishing proper procedures for the group to follow in accomplishing its goals. Any group of persons, according to Ronald Lippitt, faces two questions that must be cleared up before productive thinking can take place. First, group members "must reach some sort of agreement on the problems they are going to tackle" and then they "must reach some kind of understanding and acceptance of the way in which they are going to work together toward the solution of these problems."[2] In the last chapter we treated the first of these questions; we turn now to the latter.

Like so many other problems, this one can be settled consciously or unconsciously. The question of whether or not to follow an agenda can be brought to the attention of group members at the outset of the meeting, or it can be dealt with simply by allowing "nature to take its course." Our preference — as will become apparent in subsequent chapters — is consciously to decide such procedural questions. No matter whether the group chooses to follow what McBurney and Hance call the "hew to the line" or the "skirmish and consolidate" method for exploring its problem, ordinarily it should be a reasoned decision in which all committee members participate. To let matters be decided nonverbally may create confusion and encourage hidden and conflicting goals.

Freedom and Control

The question still remains, should a committee choose to adopt a plan for its sessions or should the members decide simply to "dive into" the matter before them? When we discuss, should we move from point to point in a systematic way, or should we go wherever our feelings take us? Some would answer that people have been talking with each other without the benefit of guide lines for thousands of years and that any interference with this free and uninhibited exchange is likely not only to irritate people but also to hamper them in trying to communicate with each other.

[2] Ronald Lippitt, *Training in Community Relations* (Harper, 1949), p. 79.

Those who oppose this view would reply that only through the adoption of some sort of plan will group members have a clear idea of what they are discussing and hence be able to communicate coherently.

There is some danger in answering this question too glibly without examining the larger issue that lies behind what seems to be a purely technical or practical decision. That issue concerns the balance we want to achieve, or that is healthy to achieve in human affairs, between freedom and control.

Many of us, for example, in preparing for a vacation reject the notion of planning and prefer to leave decisions about our trip to chance. We want to go where the spirit moves us, stay wherever we find an attractive lodge or inn, wander off the beaten track in the hope of finding something unusual and exciting. Often the high point of such a trip, and one that we delight in telling friends about for years afterwards, is a discovery that everyone else missed because they slavishly followed a pre-arranged plan and never deviated from it.

But following this method can also lead to misadventure. After a long day's journey, we sometimes are unable to find a place to stay. We may run out of gas in an isolated part of the country or find, to our disappointment, that the coffee shop we stumble upon is a "discovery" all right but one that would never merit a connoisseur's rating. Then we may remember other trips when we followed a recommended itinerary. We may have been irked, at times, by sticking so closely to a plan, but we travelled the most scenic routes and when we arrived at our destination, tired and hungry, a good meal and pleasant room were waiting for us.

This same theme — of conflict between a disciplined and undisciplined approach to problems — also pervades the arts. Some creative artists work consciously and deliberately, others by intuition. A number of painters, dramatists, and musicians say that they work according to a plan, step by step. They carry in their minds a rather carefully worked out model of what they are trying to do and can tell at any moment how nearly they are coming to realizing their conception in stone or canvas. However, many equally talented artists work according to the inspiration of the moment. One line across a canvas dictates another, a mass of color here requires a balancing mass there, and so on until the painting is finished. If one were to ask a sculptor who worked according to this principle what he is trying to sculpt he might answer with only a shrug of his shoulders, for he, himself, does not know where his hammer and chisel will lead him. The statue he creates is not something formed according to a blueprint prepared in advance, but something he discovers in the stone or the clay as he works it.

Theodor Reik, a well-known psychoanalyst, remarks in one of his books that we can and should be rational and analytical about most of life's decisions but that there are also areas where it is better to solve our problems impulsively and intuitively. We are ambivalent in our attitudes toward freedom and control: we like to discipline our thinking on some occasions, but prefer not to on others. We solve some problems intuitively, by sudden and seemingly unexplainable insight, and approach other problems in an analytical and systematic way. We sometimes enjoy making snap judgments but often weigh alternatives carefully before coming to a decision. These competing orientations, when applied to the process of problem-solving, have sometimes been referred to as synthetic and analytic modes of thinking.

Synthetic Thinking [3]

We think synthetically when, as individuals, we solve problems through free association, letting ideas pop into our minds according to chance. (Or at least we shall have to describe it as "chance" until more is known about the laws of free association.[4]) Sometimes we decide matters in a flash of intuition or insight; that is, we familiarize ourselves with a problem and, without selecting and studying each element in the situation separately, suddenly form a conclusion about it. Both the method of free association and of intuition might be described as "synthetic modes of thinking," for in them the thinker allows his mind to wander over many aspects of the problem indiscriminately, without attempting to bring each facet of it into sharp relief so that it can be analyzed and evaluated. His approach is impressionistic; what "thinking" takes place occurs almost entirely at a subconscious level and it is usually impossible to explain to another person the route he has followed

[3] This has sometimes been referred to as syncretistic thinking. See Jean Piaget, *The Language and Thought of the Child* (Meridian Books, 1955).

[4] A start has been made toward the analysis of the laws of verbal association in a study by Charles Osgood, George Suci, and Percy Tannenbaum, *The Measurement of Meaning* (University of Illinois Press, 1957).

in reaching his conclusion. This sort of thinking seems to play a large part in what we call creative work.

Groups, too, can choose to follow this method of free association. The group simply picks out the most interesting point and begins its attack on the problem there. A suggestion by one member leads to a remark by someone else, but no attempt is made to stay with an issue until it is settled, or to relate contributions to each other. From time to time, someone in the group, perhaps the chairman if there is one, may review the ground that has been covered and try to consolidate it by phrasing a summary statement. This may lead to further talk in an effort to refine the conclusion, or it may be a signal for someone else to open a new issue. Few directives can be given concerning the conduct of such a discussion — except to have as many outspoken advocates of divergent views as possible in the group — for free association largely manages itself. There are ways of stimulating such a discussion and of summarizing the opinions expressed, but suggestions on these matters will be found in a later chapter. It should be remembered, however, that no matter how rigidly the procedure of any group is controlled some free association of ideas will go on. The question is only one of degree.

Analytic Thinking

Although many problems have been solved by sudden insight growing out of the random association of ideas, there have been as many, or more, that have been solved by careful and systematic investigation. The scientist has long been admired as a model for the way in which he uses his intelligence. And rightly so. Few other figures in human history have evidenced so much curiosity about the world we live in, have worked so conscientiously to unravel the mysteries of the universe, or have produced so many sound and usable predictions about the future.

While the scientist makes use of intuition, especially in formulating new theories, his approach, in general, is analytic rather than synthetic. Instead of throwing himself at a problem willy-nilly he tends to approach it methodically. As a result of following a plan he can be reasonably sure that no crucial aspect or important variable will be omitted from consideration, and that each phase of his investigation will be a part of an overall pattern leading logically to a conclusion. The phrase "scientific method" emphasizes the extent to which the scientist relies on disciplined thinking.

The scientific method does not require well-equipped laboratories, complicated instrumentation, or mechanical computers (though they may help). Its most important ingredient is a disciplined mind. As Thomas Huxley once commented, science is nothing but organized common sense. The following newspaper story gives us a glimpse into the scientific mind at work.

> Stevens Point, Wis. — The mystery of the Buena Vista marsh has been solved.
>
> For more than 30 years there have been strange accounts, often hushed up, of the continuous loss of calves from abortion among the cattle grazing on this 55,000 acres of meadow marshland in Portage county.
>
> In 1954, when physicians, bankers and veterinarians decided to find out the truth about the "killer," there were 400 cases of bovine abortion on this giant marsh. . . .
>
> Even more serious, the number of miscarriages among mothers residing on or near these lowlands attracted the attention of the physicians. . . . When expectant mothers stayed away from the area during pregnancy, the birth generally was normal.
>
> Why?
>
> Over the years there have been a lot of ominous accounts and whispers, often exaggerated folk tales, of some unexplained "curse" or plague on this strange marsh land. Men of research knew this was not true. They have now disproved this tale of a black magic "hex" on the marsh.
>
> Until recent years it was generally accepted that the cause of the unusually high number of bovine abortions was from Brucellosis (Bang's disease). Farmers finding dead calves from both their dairy and beef cows kept quiet about it, blaming the deaths on this highly infectious cattle disease.
>
> But when the state, through its costly program of seeking out and eradicating infected cattle, cleaned out the Brucellosis, the abortion of cattle continued just as high on parts of these marshes as before. Something else, mysterious and unknown, was causing so many calves to be born dead or to live but a short time. . . .
>
> These tales of abortion persisted. There must be an explanation.
>
> Two years ago an agronomist trained in soils at the University of Wisconsin, Julian Sund . . . went to work on the Buena Vista and Leola marshes trying to solve this mystery.

Sund went to work much like a detective tracking down an unknown killer — and this trouble was indeed a killer.

He visited most of the farms. He checked accounts of apparently healthy cows suddenly aborting, even cattle which had passed accurate blood tests and been found free of brucellosis.

Then came the first clue. He noticed that the cattle which fed on good, well developed pastures, where the grass land had been limed and properly fertilized, seldom aborted.

But when cattle grazed in the partly wild land, where there was a mixture of weeds and meadow grass, the rate of abortion jumped. That herd had trouble.

The conclusion reached was that the cause was some toxic weed or plant.

So Harold Border of the UW botany staff explored the hundreds of acres of undeveloped swamp meadow. He identified some 90 different weeds. None of them were known to be toxic or even really dangerous to animals or humans.

But examination of the dead calves by the veterinarians showed a strange distortion of tissues. Something was wrong, but what?

The bankers pitched in to help, paying for heifers to be put on the marsh when known to be in calf.

Those feeding on the wild land aborted. Those on the more developed land — where potash, phosphorous and nitrogen, the big three plant foods when in proper balance along with trace elements — thrived and had frisky normal calves.

Then they tried controlled feeding in the farmyards. Sure enough, those given forage from the fertilized pastures had healthy offspring. Those fed the semideveloped or wild mixtures of weeds and meadow grass generally aborted.

Through careful deduction the soil sleuths found out the swamp killers — weeds, chuck full of nitrates and nitrites.

The four worst villains were the stinging nettle, the red berry elder, the common golden-rod and boneset. . . .

These weeds are all nontoxic under normal growing conditions. But this converted marsh is naturally very high in nitrogen and deficient in potash and phosphorus, the two other vital plant foods that must be in reasonable balance for healthy growth.

"Being starved for potash and phosphorus, the weeds were unable to convert the oversupply of nitrogen into plant protein and utilize the surplus nitrogen," explained Sund. "So these weeds were loaded with highly toxic nitrates and nitrites. When eaten by the cattle they caused the abortions. . . ."

There are three steps recommended to solve the trouble on the lowlands plagued by these high nitrate weeds:

Complete renovation of the pastures or grassland, plowing up to reseed and fertilize properly.

Use of the modern chemical weed killers, including 2-4-D, to eradicate these toxic weeds.

Keeping all pregnant animals out of these areas.[5]

The major features of what we call the "scientific method" can easily be extracted from the solving of the "mystery of the marsh killer."

(1) Recognition of the sizable number of cases of cattle abortion.
(2) Those affected by the deaths reject superstition and decide to seek a solution to the problem.
(3) Experts, with some knowledge of cattle diseases, and some experience as scientists, are called in.
(4) The first hypotheses, that the abortions are due to Bang's disease, is tested by eliminating Brucellosis.
(5) Further observation indicates that even healthy cattle abort when fed on the marshland.
(6) A new hypothesis, that the cause of the trouble lies in the plants being eaten by the cattle, is formulated.
(7) A careful study of the marsh weeds is made, but none are found toxic under normal conditions.
(8) An experiment is set up to eliminate other variables in the situation.
(9) It is found that cattle fed the marsh fodder, even in farmyards away from the marsh still abort, while those not fed the marsh weeds do not.
(10) Controlled feeding definitely fixes the cause in the mixture of wild weeds. Laboratory tests are made.
(11) The "villain" is isolated and a solution to the problem is found. An action program, designed to correct the problem, is drawn up.

This, in general, is what is meant by scientific thinking. It is orderly, conscious, systematic. One cannot say that intuition is ruled out, but by and large it is analytic rather than synthetic thinking; the problem-solver isolates one aspect of the problem at a time, considers it carefully and critically, and moves from one

[5] Lewis C. French, "Mystery of Marsh 'Killer' Cracked by UW Sleuths," *The Milwaukee Journal* (July 21, 1957), Part II, p. 1.

step to another according to an over-all pattern, a pattern that is designed to insure that each issue is taken up in a logical order leading to a final conclusion or plan of action.

Factors in Determining the Degree of Organization

Obviously there is no simple, pat answer to the question of the proper balance between freedom and control in planning for discussion. Too strict control of a conversation may discourage some people from participating and may curb original thinking. Yet an unsystematic and chaotic approach to a complicated problem may overlook vital issues and make it difficult to explore arguments carefully and critically. We do not plan to settle this question for the reader (a principle which we shall try to observe throughout this book) but rather would like to call his attention to some of the factors that will need to be considered in whatever decision he makes regarding the degree of organization to be followed in his group.

Factors of time and size

Among the factors which influence whether a group will approach its problem spontaneously or follow a detailed agenda are some that are purely administrative in character. If a committee has little time in which to solve a complicated problem it may wish to adopt a plan of some sort to reduce the time wasted on irrelevant matters. If deadlines are to be taken seriously, then members of the committee will expect and usually accept some restrictions on how they contribute to a meeting. Where there is no deadline, however, some relaxation in, or complete abolition of, procedural limitations might be indicated.

Also, as the group grows in size, as more and more people are added to a committee, greater self-control as well as greater group control may prove desirable in the interest of keeping order, in providing openings for less aggressive committee members, or in the interest of maintaining some coherent connection between remarks. Committees of four or six people can enjoy a freedom from formal procedures that might lead to chaos in a group of twenty or thirty people. The extent to which we accept spontaneity in behavior is somewhat linked to the size of any "society."

The nature of the problem

The nature of the problem being discussed and the attitudes of group members toward it are factors that should also influence the decision about the degree of control. As problems become increasingly difficult to unravel, more systematic investigation may be necessary. It is a relatively simple matter to follow a conversation about homecoming arrangements or about the hiring and firing policies in a small company. But when groups begin to talk about our foreign policy in the Far East, or try to thread their way through the planning of a complicated budget, the same casualness may interfere with intelligent decision-making. On the most involved questions it is difficult to make sense unless each contribution is somehow related to the issue being discussed.

The depth of people's emotional involvement in the problem also deserves consideration. When we discuss matters about which we have strong feelings — when there is likely to be a high level of ego-involvement — it may be difficult to hold members to a plan. To control thinking either tends to make the airing of honest feelings difficult, or it disguises them so that they become more difficult to understand and cope with. The psychiatrist is more aware than most of us of the hazards of directing an emotionally upset person and of trying to make him conform to a logical pattern in his communication with others. As the problem becomes more complex, more careful control of the meeting seems to be indicated. Yet as groups discuss sensitive issues on which committee members have strong, if not violent, feelings, less and less control seems feasible.

The purposes of the group

The different motives that prompt people to hold a meeting also affect the degree of planning the members may find helpful. The members of Cathartic Groups, as we found earlier, are likely to find that adopting an agenda is incompatible with their purpose of establishing close interpersonal relationships with one another as a basis for sharing feelings of anxiety, guilt, or depression. In a seminar in a university, where the principal objective is to provoke new ideas, we would also expect to find a high degree of "free-wheeling" to stimulate original thinking on the part of students. A vigorous and undirected argument may heighten the interest of members of a Great Books Discussion Group or the League of Women Voters, and this increased interest may lead those who attend to subject the ideas that are contributed to more critical examination. Further, this competition in ideas may increase participants' awareness of the principles to be used in forming their own private opinion on the topic. Decision-making groups, on the other hand, often find that in order to complete their investigation of a problem they need some sort of guide so they will be certain to give all vital issues the consideration they deserve. At the same time we must remember that feelings are also expressed in Policy-Making Groups — that company officials are likely to be emotionally involved in carrying out a reorganization of a large company, particularly when it involves their own position in the hierarchy of administration. We must avoid making too sharp a distinction between what Mortimer Adler called "heart-to-heart" and "mind-to-mind" talk.

Personal desire for order

It is clear, both from personal observation and from psychoanalytic writing, that each of us can tolerate different amounts of order and disorder in our lives. This is often evident in the way we respond even to physical objects in our environment. Some persons are made uncomfortable by a misplaced chair or a picture that hangs slightly askew, while others seem perfectly at ease in settings of wild confusion. A recent book, *Nonverbal Communication,* documents some of the ways in which we mirror these needs for order in our lives through the way we arrange furniture, the way we smoke a cigarette, or by the way we care for personal belongings.[6]

This is true of our relations with people as well as objects. Some persons want very badly to "know their place." They are uncomfortable when the exact role they are to play in a group is not defined. These group members experience mild to serious anxiety when thrown into ambiguous situations where they are expected to

[6] Jurgen Ruesch and Weldon Kees, *Nonverbal Communication* (University of California Press, 1956).

relate to others in informal ways. Often they are persons who prefer to be formally introduced, who like to work under an elected chairman and secretary, and who feel that procedural rules will allow everyone "to get along better and accomplish more." To a large extent these reactions reflect a low tolerance for spontaneous human relationships and, according to some, an "escape from freedom." One way of protecting oneself from the need to behave spontaneously is to get the group to operate on the basis of formal rules. These needs for order are particularly pressing in the early moments of a group's association.

> During the initial stages of group development, especially when a group is struggling to solve its first problem, it often tries to seek refuge from the existing chaos and from its own internal tensions by grasping for formal or mechanistic procedures. Finding a lack of structure in the group discussion, a group seeks escape in formalism and "official structure." The reasons for the tendency to escape into formalism are complex, because formalism stems both from factors within our culture which encourage and reward it and from certain needs within individuals which suppress informality and spontaneity.[7]

As we have suggested, the justifications for adopting any sort of organizational plan in a group include more than just an emotional need for order. Some demands for control are quite rational and spring from other needs of the group and from the general setting itself. However, if these external pressures are not present but the group is composed of persons who cannot do without rules to regulate their interpersonal relationships, then their desire for a plan may have to be honored if the discussion is to succeed. The coin, however, has another side. If committee members have grown accustomed to operating spontaneously and informally, it may prove equally difficult to get them to adopt controls when the situation demands some regulation of participation. One type of person can be as much of an obstacle to intelligent problem-solving as the other.

Interpersonal attitudes

Finally we need to consider the sorts of attitudes people in the meeting have toward one another. To disregard the factor of

[7] Thomas Gordon, *Group-Centered Leadership* (Houghton Mifflin, 1955), p. 235.

hostility when labor and management begin negotiating after a long and bitter strike, or the mutual distrust with which two representatives of different racial groups sit down to confer about discrimination in housing, is to be naïve about human behavior. The anger people feel toward those with whom they disagree, either because of the organizations they represent or because of interpersonal frictions growing out of earlier incidents, cannot be overlooked in deciding procedural questions. It is even more difficult to know what to do when the group is made up of persons who hide deep-seated suspicions of one another behind a smoke screen of amiability.

That this is an important factor in deciding on the character of the agenda is apparent from experience in many areas of negotiation. Unfriendly nations almost always insist upon establishing a detailed agenda before beginning high-level talks, while nations enjoying friendly relations generally do not. This same rule holds true for talks between conflicting races, competing corporate entities, between special interest groups of all kinds. It is also illustrated at the level of ordinary social intercourse; people normally are more "cool" or formal with each other when they first meet or after a "falling out." Later, when they get to understand each other better, this formality is usually discarded.

In some cases, groups which start out by following a very flexible plan may find they must resort later to stricter control. This may mean that members have become more aware of the difficulties they face in solving the problem, or it may mean that something has gone sour in their relationships. In either event, whether procedures are set up as a precaution at the outset of a meeting or later as a consequence of interaction between participants, the adopting of elaborate procedural machinery in a group underscores a basic fact—that frank and uninhibited expression usually requires an accepting and permissive atmosphere. When people do not trust each other, or do not respect each other, protection, through rules or regulations, is sometimes necessary.

On the other hand, procedural control may not always be the answer. Perhaps we are too prone to curb and restrain our personal feelings. Trying to constrain a child with a temper tantrum by forcing him to be quiet is not the only, or the best way of dealing with him. Indeed it often increases his anger and aggravates the problem. In groups, too, it might be helpful sometimes if group members had a chance to air their hostile feelings frankly and vigorously. Providing this sort of catharsis may clear the air for more constructive talk. Group members, after finding out how strongly others feel about an issue, may be more inclined to settle down and view their problem more calmly and with greater objectivity.

Patterns of Group Thinking

Let us assume that the members of a group are aware of the factors that might increase or decrease their need for procedural restrictions. Let us also assume that they wish to discuss the pattern of organization and, insofar as possible, make a cooperative decision about it. What are the various ways of organizing thinking so as to improve the quality and efficiency of group meetings?

Perhaps some of the time and energy normally wasted in meetings could be eliminated by following in the footsteps of the scientist. Several patterns, each of which incorporates some of the steps of the scientific method, are available as guides to group thinking and can be easily adapted to fit the specific goals of any group.

Agenda Based on Reflective Thinking

The most carefully worked out set of recommendations for improving human decision-making, and the one which we shall study therefore in the greatest detail, is based on a mode of analytic thinking called the "reflective pattern of thought."

Reflective thinking was first described in a slim volume written by John Dewey which appeared in 1910 and was destined to become something of a classic. It was called, simply, *How We Think.*[8] It was an attempt on the part of this well-known philosopher to distinguish among the various kinds of mental activity in which human beings engage in solving a wide variety of problems. Not only did the author describe how we *do* think — using intuition, reverie, creative imagination — but he also formulated how we *ought* to think. He found, as we have suggested earlier, that scientists in their investigations of physical and social phenomena have followed a method that has been instrumental in producing the great discoveries they have made. As Dewey and many others since him have noted, it is not the *results* of science that can be

[8] John Dewey, *How We Think* (Heath, 1910).

transferred from one field to another, it is the *method* of science. From the records of their achievements he attempted to distill the elements which were a part of scientific thinking and make them applicable to the solving of social problems. Human affairs, in his opinion, would be greatly improved if the methods of science were applied to the solving of social, political, and economic problems.

To think reflectively requires both an *attitude* and a *method.* According to Dewey, reflective thinking begins with the "active, persistent, and careful consideration of any belief or supposed form of knowledge in the light of the grounds that support it and the further conclusions to which it tends." [9] This implies that reflection starts with an inclination on the part of the problem-solver to find better, more dependable beliefs on which to base his actions than those currently popular. Too often, unfortunately, there is a slavish dedication to the *pattern* of reflective thinking while violating the whole *spirit* of reflection. When people do not sincerely want, or urgently need, more valid conclusions, reflective thinking is not going to help them.

As to the method of reflection, Dewey states that it is a unique kind of thinking. "Reflection," he says, "involves not simply a sequence of ideas, but a *con*-sequence — a consecutive ordering in such a way that each determines the next as its proper outcome, while each outcome in turn leans back on, or refers to, its predecessors." [10] At another point he adds that "only when the succession is so controlled that it is an orderly sequence leading up to a conclusion that contains the intellectual force of the preceding ideas, do we have reflective thought." [11] Thus, reflective thinking begins with the desire on the part of the problem solver to form more valid conclusions and leads to an organization of his thinking so that he will move logically from one issue or one part of the problem to the next. It is simply a mechanical scheme based on the scientific method.

Dewey finds there are five major steps in this sequence. He describes them as follows:

1. The occurrence of some difficulty.
2. Location and definition of the problem.
3. The formulation of possible hypotheses or solutions.
4. The elaboration of their consequences.
5. Further testing or experimentation.[12]

[9] *Ibid.*, p. 6. [10] *Ibid.* (1933 edition), p. 4. [11] *Ibid.*, p. 47.
[12] These steps are best described in Chapter VI of the original 1910 edition.

If we consider each of these steps in turn, and modify the terminology, we may see how the pattern of reflective thinking can be easily adapted to fit the needs of discussion groups when attempting to solve complicated problems. First we shall take up the steps in solving a full-fledged or "complete problem"; later we shall consider how to modify the pattern of reflective thinking to deal with abbreviated or "truncated problems."

Ventilation

As Dewey noted, thinking begins when we find ourselves facing a perplexing or confusing situation, when we discover that our present patterns of behavior are not adequate to allow us to reach the goals we desire. A problem, as we found earlier, may arise out of personal needs that are not being satisfied (an unsuccessful disciplinary rule in the home or failure to make constructive use of leisure time), out of environmental pressures (the need to forestall bankruptcy or to accomplish political reforms), or out of many other sorts of interpersonal, intergroup, or international frictions. The problem may take the form of an "ambiguous situation" where we vaguely sense that "something is wrong," or the form of a "forked road situation" where we face a choice between clearly defined but competing courses of action.

Like an athlete about to participate in a contest, group members need some time to "warm up" to a problem. Participants can make profitable use of this interval to try to formulate in their own minds what is troubling them. By talking over the situation briefly in general terms, committee members can learn whether the persons in the group are apathetic, bitter, or belligerent in their attitudes toward the problem, the committee, or both, and can take these feelings into account in beginning their work. A few minutes, or even longer, spent in ventilating feelings can help group members to establish rapport with one another and to obtain a clearer idea of their goals.

Clarification

Before an investigation can get under way, however, the exact problem will have to be phrased precisely. (A well-phrased question, it is said, is half answered.) Dewey would say that the emotional state of participants has to be intellectualized; that is to say, the vague feelings people have about a situation have to be objectified and made conscious. This we do, of course, in groups whenever we verbalize a discussion topic. However several more steps may be necessary in order to clarify a problem sufficiently for effective discussion of it.

Some agreement must be reached on the limits to be placed on the topic and on the meaning of key terms to be used in the discussion. If a group is to take up the question, "What sort of federal aid should be given to education?" committee members will avoid many communication breakdowns and misunderstandings if, at the outset, they agree on what to include and exclude in the discussion. Is the group to consider aid to elementary or secondary schools, to public or private schools, to colleges or adult education centers? Furthermore, it is often desirable, early in the meeting, to define terms, not only those which appear in the phrasing of the question but which will have to be used in investigating the topic. If the problem is "What sort of labor legislation do we need?" participants had better spend some time, before getting too deeply into the discussion, defining terms such as "closed shop," "open shop," "jurisdictional dispute," "lockout," and so on. Some consistency in the use of terms will help members of the group to understand each other better. In the clarification step, in short, group members are trying to answer the question, "What is the specific nature of our problem?" The result of completing this step is for the group to reach a common understanding of the type of problem it faces.

Fact-finding

The third step in thinking reflectively is to gather and assess the information available on the problem. The aim is to find answers to the question, "What are the relevant facts on this problem?" This information may take the form of factual statements or authoritative opinions concerning the history and background of the problem or may have to do with its current symptoms. We get some idea of how to carry out fact-finding from observing the behavior of those who ordinarily use reflective thinking in their jobs — the doctor in examining a patient, the mechanic as he checks an engine, the repairman who clears trouble in a television set. A doctor, for example, does not jump to a conclusion about a patient and begin to operate on him without making an exhaustive study of his condition. He will gather all sorts of information from conversation with the patient, from a careful physical examination of him, from extensive laboratory tests, and only after carrying out these steps will he later attempt to derive the causes of the patient's discomfort. Similarly, in solving a problem in an industrial plant, a school system, or a family, it is essential that people collect all the available data and assess them before trying to determine the causes of the trouble.

Discovery

In the next step, hypotheses or solutions should be discovered and proposed. Group members will try, in this stage of problem-solving, to determine, "What are the possible answers to this question?" Note that the question asks for "possible answers," not for a single answer. This means that more than one hypothesis or solution should be suggested. If this is done, groups will avoid becoming committed too early to a single explanation or course of action when there may be many other — and better — ways of dealing with the problem. The wider the group's range of selection, the wiser the final choice is likely to be.

How does a group go about discovering new and better ways of solving a problem? To begin with, intelligent solutions are partly a product of adequate fact-finding. As group members study and isolate the conditions that underlie the problem they inevitably will be led to thinking about some of the hypotheses or correctives that may be needed.

The discovery stage of reflective thinking requires some talent for imaginative and original thought. Unfortunately, little is known about the factors that stimulate inventiveness. Those who have made studies of creative imagination say only that it requires a full knowledge of the problem combined with a willingness to discard old patterns of thought and action.

> One who prides himself to-day on his conservatism, on the ground that man is naturally an anarchic and disorderly creature who is held in check by the far-seeing Tory, is almost exactly reversing the truth. Mankind is conservative by nature and readily generates restraints on himself and obstacles to change which have served to keep him

> in a state of savagery during almost his entire existence on the earth, and which still perpetuate all sorts of primitive barbarism in modern society. The conservative "on principle" is therefore a most unmistakably primitive person in his attitude. His only advance beyond the savage mood lies in the specious reasons he is able to advance for his remaining of the same mind.[13]

Albert Einstein may have had something like this in mind when, in replying to a question as to how he discovered the principle of relativity he replied, "By refusing to accept an axiom." One of the great barriers to the optimum use of human intelligence lies in our intense desire to cling to traditional theories and familiar institutional practices. To draft new hypotheses requires, perhaps most of all, courage.

> For that reason the hypothesis-maker must add to familiarity with the subject-matter the vital spark of originality; the capacity to explore imaginatively new and un-dreamed of possibilities in search of ideas "not yet wordable" and to fuse old elements in novel combinations. The explanatory hypothesis is sometimes described as a "leap in the dark"; often it takes a kind of rash intellectual courage and freedom from convention. . . . As we should express it, the ideal source of fruitful, relevant hypotheses is a fusion of the two elements, past experience and imagination, in the *disciplined imagination* of the scientist.[14]

In this step ordinarily the group should avoid the temptation to evaluate. To suggest a novel solution is, for many people, an open invitation to rip it apart with devastating criticism. It is essential, of course, to evaluate suggestions that are made, but experience seems to indicate that critical thinking and original thinking often go forward best when each is handled separately.

Evaluation

Finally, a group must examine the consequences of accepting any of its hypotheses or proposals. Some assessment must be made to answer the question, "How adequate is each hypothesis in explaining the problem?" or "How effective is each solution in correcting the difficulty?" This will require that the suggestions be

[13] James H. Robinson, *The Mind in the Making* (Harper, 1921), p. 93.

[14] Harold A. Larrabee, *Reliable Knowledge* (Houghton Mifflin, 1945), p. 172.

taken up in turn and the validity or invalidity of each hypothesis or solution be considered. In a problem of policy, the workability of any proposal, in addition to its theoretical soundness, will have to be estimated. Out of this evaluation will come a group's decision.

Decision-making

The last step in reflective thinking is accomplished when this question has been answered: "Precisely what decisions have we reached on this problem?" It involves nothing more than the formulation, verbally, of the conclusions reached by the discussants. It is important that groups complete this final step, or they run the risk of leaving the meeting in the belief that the problem has been solved when actually each person may have a different impression of what was decided. The decisions may be stated orally, or in written form if that is required. The problems of decision-making and the preparation of reports will be taken up in Chapter 8.

This completes our description of the steps in reflective thinking. However, the reader may have been confused by our use of alternate terms, "hypotheses or solutions," in the Discovery step. The reason for this can be made clear by referring to the types of problems described in Chapter 4. Problems of perception, where a committee is merely concerned with sharing information, involve only the first three steps in reflective thinking — Ventilation, Clarification, Fact-finding. Problems of diagnosis require the use of all six steps — Ventilation, Clarification, Fact-finding, Discovery, Evaluation, and Decision-making — but in steps four and five the group will be concerned only with Discovery of Hypotheses and Evaluation of Hypotheses. When a group discusses a problem of attitude or action, however, it will have to complete steps one through six in order to diagnose the problem and then repeat steps four and five — this time taking up the Discovery of Solutions and the Evaluation of Solutions in order to formulate and weigh alternative courses of action — before going on to Decision-making.

Reflective thinking, then, involves a systematic ordering of the processes of investigation so that each issue may be taken up in the most logical sequence leading to the decision(s) that must be made by the group. Dewey calls attention to one other characteristic of reflective thinking that should be kept in mind — each step in the pattern grows out of preceding steps and also may "reflect" back upon earlier stages. The six steps are not independent of each other: the scope of fact-finding will be determined by the limits that are set up in clarifying the problem; the facts lead, in turn, to the hypotheses regarding the causes of the problem and to possible solutions. In addition, later stages may reveal that there are additional terms that need clarifying or may indicate that the limits originally agreed upon are too restrictive. A group may find itself, therefore, first going ahead and then returning from one stage to another in order to complete its investigation.

Truncated Problems

Groups are often assigned truncated problems, questions that do not involve all the steps in a complete act of problem-solving. In this case the group will have to adapt the procedures described earlier to the specific requirements of their assignment. Some of the common departures from the pattern we described above will now be considered.

Problems of discovery only

Sometimes groups are handed problems of attitude or policy that have already been diagnosed and are asked only to suggest ways of dealing with them. After a club has decided what is wrong with its monthly meetings, it may then appoint a committee to suggest some new types of programs. The senior class of a college or high school may name some of its members to a committee to do nothing but outline ways of raising funds for their class gift. An advertising agency may arrange meetings to formulate new advertising plans for one of its clients. In these instances the group is responsible only for proposing a wide variety of solutions from which a choice may later be made. Their agenda need only include three steps: (1) summary of the diagnosis; (2) suggestions for correcting the situation; (3) editing of the proposals.

A new technique has been developed lately for solving problems of discovery. It is called "brainstorming." It is based on the principle, stated earlier by Dewey, that creative thinking and critical thinking are best separated because they interfere with each other. The rules for brainstorming are simple and few in number:

(1) Anyone may contribute an idea. Talk out whenever you get an idea no matter how naïve it may seem.
(2) No criticism or evaluation is permitted. Questions or comments only distract from the purpose of the meeting.
(3) The more ideas the better. Even a bad idea may provoke a better one from someone else.
(4) Ideas can be edited later. Some suggestions can be combined, others improved on.[15]

"Brainstorming" seems to be a simple and practical way of solving a truncated problem which involves only the discovery of new solutions.

Problems of evaluation only

On occasion, committees and boards are called upon to judge which of alternative policies should be adopted. Problems such as these — Should the company locate its new plant in Rockford, Oshkosh, or Ithaca? Should my children go to Columbia, Dartmouth, or the University of Michigan? Is the country better off under Republican or Democratic administrations? — force groups to choose between different ideas, policies, or actions. The agenda, in this case, consists of only two steps: (1) summary of available courses of action; (2) the discussion of advantages and disadvantages flowing from the proposed solutions.

Sometimes groups both propose new solutions *and* evaluate them. In cases of this type, should groups "brainstorm" first and then evaluate, or engage in both simultaneously? To suggest solutions first has the advantage of keeping creative and critical processes isolated, and might help members who are shy or afraid of being criticized get into the conversation. The competition between participants in "brainstorming" is also stimulating. (We have found the members of a group to formulate dozens of hypotheses under these conditions when, without this stimulation, virtually nothing was being accomplished.) The simplicity of the method leaves

[15] *Report of the Proceedings of the Third Annual Creative Problem-Solving Institute* (University of Buffalo, July, 1957), p. 5.

group members free to devote their whole attention to the business of thinking up new ideas.

On the other hand, Discovery and Evaluation can be intermingled with profit on some problems. When the question is a difficult one and the solutions likely to be complicated, members cannot simply call out a word or phrase and expect the idea to be really assimilated. "Brainstorming" sessions often produce a lot of silly suggestions along with occasional good ones. One also wonders if the technique is necessary when permissive conditions exist in the group and people are creative enough not to require the artificial stimulus of a a game to help them think productively.

Criteria

Some readers may be wondering where criteria — our personal standards of value — come into the process of problem-solving. How can the members of a committee expect to reach agreement in the evaluation of alternative courses of action unless they first agree upon their goals, or on what they want to use as criteria in measuring the merits of a particular solution? To say something is desirable implies some agreement as to what is good and what is bad.

There are conflicting views about the desirability of including the discussion of values as a separate step.[16] One point of view argues that our private standards of judgment so greatly influence our opinions on any problem that these values should not remain unexpressed. In a discussion of socialized medicine, for example, some participants may feel that any interference with private medical practice is automatically undesirable, while others feel that securing medical care for everyone is such a humane end that no one could possibly dispute it. Members of a committee who hold these different views will collect different facts, interpret them differently, and propose quite different solutions to the problem. To try to settle each of these differences, it is argued, is not an efficient way of running a discussion. It would be wiser to bring out the more fundamental of these assumptions so

[16] Even among those who agree on the merit of including such a step there are differences as to when it should occur. Some favor doing it as a part of Clarification, some between Discovery and Evaluation, and others during Evaluation.

that they can be faced and resolved openly. Once the critera are agreed upon, group members can work much more efficiently on suggesting solutions to the problem and evaluating them.

Another "school" holds that the discussion of criteria is a waste of time. In some cases it ends up with group members merely agreeing on a set of extremely abstract statements which they will continue to interpret differently when it comes to applying them to the concrete conditions of the problem. For example, a group may agree in a discussion of socialized medicine, that their target is "to provide the greatest good for the greatest number." Fine. Now that they have agreed on this statement, what does it mean? When solutions are proposed, those in favor of socialization will argue that "this is the greatest good for the greatest number" for it will bring medical care to those who lack it. Those who oppose government-insured medical care will argue just the reverse, that free medicine, even with all its limitations, has provided and will continue to provide better care for all. In other cases it can be claimed that when a committee agrees that a solution should be "workable," "economically sound," and "flexible," they have only verbalized something that is so apparent that it was unnecessary to state it in the first place. In other words, criteria are sometimes phrased in such general terms that they only serve to cover up real differences of opinion that will come to light as soon as the group gets down to specifics. Why not, instead, discuss the assumptions and values of group members as they reveal themselves in the concrete context of the solutions that are proposed?

We can not adjudicate for the reader between these conflicting schools of thought since there is some difference of opinion on the matter between the authors themselves. We would rather suggest that there is merit in both sides of the question, that specific circumstances might make one or the other approach most fruitful, and that one ought to experiment for himself with each method.

Agenda Based on Laboratory Observations

Another way of dealing with the problem of organizing group thinking is suggested by the experimental work of Robert F. Bales. He found the following activities ordinarily to occur in the solving of human relations case studies under controlled laboratory conditions.

> (a) With regard to *orientation,* members of the group have some degree of ignorance and uncertainty about the relevant facts, but individually possess facts relevant to the decision. Their problem of arriving at a common cognitive orientation or definition of the situation must be solved, if at all, through interaction.
>
> (b) With regard to problems of *evaluation,* the members of the group ordinarily possess somewhat different values or interests and the task is such that it involves several different values and interests as criteria by which the facts of the situation and the proposed course of action are to be judged. . . .
>
> (c) With regard to problems of *control,* (that is, attempts of the members to influence directly the action of each other and arrive at a concrete plan) the acceptance of the task sets up in most instances a moderately strong pressure for group decision, with the expectation that the excellence of the decision can and will be evaluated by each of them. . . .[17]

Bales go on to say, "These abstract conditions, with emphasis varying according to circumstances, are met in very much this form and emphasis in a great many group conferences, work groups, committees, and the like."[18] While less detailed than the six-step pattern of reflective thinking, it could easily be translated into an agenda for a group to follow. In this case, the "orientation" would include Ventilation, Clarification, and Fact-finding, so that participants could obtain a clear idea of the difficulty they were attempting to remedy. The group would then consider the values each member wished to have the group observe in assessing the facts and judging alternative solutions. Finally, committee members would apply these criteria to the available solutions and hammer out their decision.

The Experimental Approach

It is to be expected that groups which base their agenda on one of the patterns described in this chapter will encounter some difficulties

[17] Robert F. Bales, "The Equilibrium Problem in Small Groups," in Hare, Borgatta, and Bales, *Small Groups* (Knopf, 1955), pp. 425–426.

[18] *Ibid.,* p. 426.

in following it, especially the first few times. To think well as an individual, much less as a member of a group, has to be learned. It takes a great deal of patience for the members of a committee to master the difficult art of thinking cooperatively and systematically. Discussants, after casually attempting to follow a pattern, may throw it overboard in disgust because it is so restrictive.

> It may be objected that for many purposes this approach is too formal. The plain man, it is true, often resents any orderly conduct of discussion. To talk at random appears to him his God-given right. And sometimes he suspects that any interference with that freedom gives an advantage to someone smarter than he. No one likes to be shown that his thinking is confused or in some other way inadequate for the occasion. Few realize that their own thinking might greatly improve with a little self discipline.[19]

If a group finds that the method is too demanding or discovers that members are giving more attention to maintaining their agenda than to the problem — and in the course of doing so are becoming increasingly irritated with the restrictions it places on them — then the time may have come to jettison the method. On the other hand, this may mean surrendering too easily to the blandishments of the superficial, ill-informed, or irrational members of the group. The "easiest way out" is not often the path to mature decision-making.

There are basically three reasons for desiring some degree of order in discussion: (1) To permit group members to sub-divide a problem into more manageable portions; (2) To allow the participants to think together more efficiently by preventing the intrusion of irrelevant matters; (3) To make communication more coherent so that each member of the group can successfully connect his ideas to the remarks of the previous speakers. The decision to adopt a plan or not should be made consciously and cooperatively whenever possible. The degree to which a loose or strict agenda should be followed can only be determined by weighing the various situational factors and these include: (1) factors of time and group size; (2) the nature of the problem; (3) the purposes of the group; (4) personal desires for order; (5) interpersonal attitudes of group members. If a group is sticking grimly to a pre-

[19] Bruno Lasker, *Democracy Through Discussion* (H. W. Wilson, 1949), p. 294.

arranged agenda in spite of interpersonal conflicts, regardless of the appearance of new and unexpected issues, or despite a change in purpose, they are probably abusing a valid technique. There is little profit in following a detailed agenda if it places so many limitations on members that they devote more energy to procedural matters than to solving the problem itself. As Dewey himself cautioned:

> The disciplined, or logically trained, mind — the aim of the educative process — is the mind able to judge how far each of these steps needs to be carried in any particular situation. No cast-iron rules can be laid down. Each case has to be dealt with as it arises, on the basis of its importance and of the context in which it occurs. To take too much pains in one case is as foolish — as illogical — as to take too little in another. At one extreme, almost any conclusion that insures prompt and unified action may be better than any long delayed conclusion; while at the other, decision may have to be postponed for a long period — perhaps for a lifetime. The trained mind is the one that best grasps the degree of observation, forming of ideas, reasoning, and experimental testing required in any special case, and that profits the most, in future thinking, by mistakes made in the past. What is important is that the mind should be sensitive to problems and skilled in methods of attack and solution.[20]

Group members, therefore, will have to determine for themselves the appropriate amount of control. "Complete" problems require a somewhat more elaborate organization than do "truncated" problems, where some of the steps in reflective thinking have been completed before the meeting gets under way.

Whether control of a discussion is desirable or not in the interest of organizing peoples' thinking, and what degree of control is needed, cannot be answered intelligently by laying down a rule; something as complex and dynamic as human relationships must be met instead with sensitivity and good sense.

RECOMMENDED READINGS

Bryson, L., L. Finkelstein, R. M. MacIver, and R. McKeon (eds.), *Freedom and Authority in Our Time.* Harper and Brothers, 1953.

[20] John Dewey, *op. cit.* (1910), p. 78.

Columbia Associates in Philosophy. *Introduction to Reflective Thinking.* Houghton Mifflin Company, 1923.
Dewey, John. *How We Think.* D.C. Heath & Company, 1910.
Elliott, Harrison. *The Process of Group Thinking.* Association Press, 1928.
Robinson, James H. *The Mind in the Making.* Harper and Brothers, 1921.

Chapter Six

The Raw Materials of Discussion

ADOPTING A PLAN OF ORGANIZATION may help to give direction, order, and coherence to a discussion when it is needed, but it does not guarantee that wise decisions will automatically be forthcoming from a group. A procedure is, after all, nothing more than a vehicle for arranging issues in a logical progression to help participants relate to the topic and to one another. What goes into this machinery, the sort of information and ideas, also determines the validity of any conclusions reached. An automated factory designed to produce engine blocks may appear to be foolproof, and may actually be so, but if inferior metals are used, each engine will turn out to be defective in some way. This idea is expressed less gracefully in the old adage, "You can't make a silk purse out of a sow's ear." That is to say, it is difficult, no matter how skillful we are in technique, to make something attractive and useful out of the wrong materials. It is the same in human affairs — both the way we go about things (process) and the raw materials with which we work (content) determine the quality of the final product.

Fact and Fancy

Man, from antiquity to modern times, has been troubled by the problem of distinguishing in his thinking between fact and fancy.

How can he ascertain the appropriateness and validity of his information so that in everyday affairs he will make judgments that are trustworthy and sensible? This perennial question has been asked, in one form or another, by the writers of nearly every age.

Plato, writing in *The Republic* over two thousand years ago, dramatized this issue through an allegory, the allegory of the men in the cave. Take a group of men when they are very young, he writes, and chain them inside a cave in such a way that they cannot see anything but the wall of the cave before them. Behind them, on a low parapet, place a number of objects so that light coming in through the entrance, and from nearby fires, strikes these objects and casts their shadows on the side of the cave before the men. After leaving them there for many years, with only shadows to look at and to talk about, one day unlock their chains and take them outside the cave so they may see hills, trees, grass, and clouds. Then will not these men assert that the shadows they saw in the cave were real and the physical objects they now observe merely a trick of their imagination? By means of this parable Plato dramatizes one of the eternal questions facing man — how can he learn to distinguish between the things that are real and those that are imaginary?

Many centuries later, the same question was posited in the writings of Francis Bacon. As the foremost of the scientific philosophers he attacked the scholasticism of the academic mind and warned against the dangers of speculating endlessly about problems without tying abstractions to reality through fact.

> The wit and mind of man, if it worketh upon matter . . . worketh according to the stuff . . . but if it work upon itself, as the spider worketh his web, then it is endless, and brings forth indeed cobwebs of learning, admirable for the fineness of thread and work, but of no substance or profit.[1]

Though the warning may be dated, the danger of spinning out elaborate theories without adequate foundation in fact is a tempation that threatens the efforts of thinkers of any time or place. Not long ago a delegate at a student governing board meeting of a midwestern university was heard to advocate support of his resolution

[1] Francis Bacon, "Advancement of Learning," in Robert Hutchins (ed.), *Great Books of the Western World* (Encyclopedia Britannica, 1952), p. 12.

on the ground that "it was a general principle which applied to no specific situation." No one present seemed to find anything specious or objectionable in his argument.

The problem is still with us and, because of the character of the questions we face today, with us in an aggravated form. Walter Lippmann, writing in the 1920's, brought out a popular book called *Public Opinion.*[2] The opening chapter in this volume, entitled "The World Outside and the Pictures in Our Heads," cryptically states the issue, an issue in Lippmann's judgment that is one of the great tests of modern times. How can we, he asks, get inside our minds a picture that corresponds to the complex and rapidly changing environment in which we live? We must if we are to meet the challenges of our age. If we cannot, then modern man, and democracy certainly, are obsolete.

Public and Private Problems

Man stands alone as the most reasonable and intelligent organism to grace our planet. And the average man displays, in some areas of thought and action, a vigor and toughness in his thinking that would honor our leading scientists. The ordinary garage mechanic, serious hobbyist, farmer, and housewife may, on occasion, deal with day-to-day problems in ways that would put experts to shame.

> When we compare the discussion in the United States Senate in regard to the League of Nations with the consideration of a broken-down car in a roadside garage the contrast is shocking. The rural mechanic thinks scientifically; his only aim is to avail himself of his knowledge of the nature and workings of the car, with a view to making it run once more. The Senator, on the other hand, appears too often to have little idea of the nature and workings of nations, and he relies on rhetoric and appeals to vague fears and hopes or mere partisan animosity.[3]

On some kinds of problems people tend to observe carefully, demand to know the facts on which decisions must rest, and critically assess what they know before coming to a decision. Unfortunately, this same caution and respect for facts is all too often cast aside when they move to issues outside their special field of expertness.

[2] Walter Lippmann, *Public Opinion* (Penguin Books, 1922).
[3] James H. Robinson, *op. cit.*, pp. 8–9.

The temptation to substitute wishful thinking for fact seems to increase geometrically as we move from problems that can be solved through the intelligent use of personal observation to those that necessitate the use of information from other sources.

> Yet there is now a gap between the ordinary experience of ordinary people in their daily lives and the events that break in on them from the outside world of government and international affairs. And this gap has become steadily harder to bridge. The ordinary rules and judgments by which we get around successfully in our private lives just don't apply to public events. And when common sense leaves us in the lurch, we find ourselves without intellectual defenses, fusing fantasy with fact, and confusing the impossible with the possible. We fall back on ways of thinking we would effortlessly reject when we are fixing a car or building a house or playing bridge—on animistic styles of thought, on the belief in invisible conspiracies, on a faith in occult forces or in superhuman beings.[4]

Our ability to "see the facts" on many questions seems to hinge partly on how farsighted we really wish to be and partly on how remote the issues are which we must settle; in any case it is safe to say that the horizons of most men of the twentieth century have widened beyond all expectation. More and more problems, which heretofore were private problems, no longer are. Problems have expanded so in size and complexity that it is unusual to find anyone in a position of authority who sincerely believes that he is well enough informed to settle questions of policy all by himself. Imagine leaving the reorganization of a giant corporation or the question of public housing in a large metropolitan center to the necessarily circumscribed vision of one man. It is simply impossible for a single human being, in these days, to see enough, hear enough, experience enough, to get "all way round" the questions we must answer. "The big real environment," in the words of Lippmann, "is altogether too big, too complex, and too fleeting for direct acquaintance. We are not equipped to deal with so much subtlety, so much variety, so many permutations and combinations."[5] Nearly all our problems, in a sense, have become "foreign" problems.

[4] Charles Frankel, "Are We Really Crazy?" *Harper's Magazine* (June, 1955), p. 67.
[5] Lippmann, *op. cit.*, pp. 10–11.

The Exchange of Symbols

One way to meet this unprecedented challenge may be found in exploiting to a larger degree man's capacity for communication. His unique potentialities have led various writers in different disciplines to characterize him as a "culture creator," "symbol user," or "time-binder." No matter which term is preferred, each phrase points to man's unique faculty for representing his experiences in symbolic form — in some sort of language — so they may be transmitted from one member of a society to another, or from one generation to another. We have, in short, a special capacity for making use of the nervous systems of other people, those of the past and the present, and thus utilizing their observations for our own advantage. We use this endowment in both simple and complicated ways. We use symbols on one occasion to warn someone about a dangerous intersection, and on another to report on the level of unemployment in certain sections of the nation.

Forming a group is, in itself, an act of time-binding. Groups come into existence because of the tacit admission that something can be gained from an exchange of personal experiences or points of view. A discussion is simply a way of arranging communications within a family, an industrial organziation, or a nation, so that all of the resources of that particular society can be utilized in accomplishing a given task. Each person brings to a group a unique set of facts and experiences growing out of his familiarity with the problem. Out of the sifting and weighing of these private experiences the group seeks to obtain a larger and more balanced view of the problem to be solved. This has led one theorist to formulate a principle applying to the appointment of people to a discussion group. It is called the "Principle of Least Group Size." [6] It states that whenever a problem is to be investigated, a board or committee should include on it all persons who have knowledge or skills that are relevant to the solution of the problem, but no one whose information or talent duplicates that of another.

This is a beginning. Consultation is a partial answer to the increased size and complexity of contemporary problems. It en-

[6] Herbert Thelen, "Principle of Least Group Size," *The School Review* (March, 1949).

ables isolated individuals to draw upon the combined experience of many persons who have familiarity with different aspects of the situation. But groups, unfortunately, must often tackle issues that extend even beyond the limits of the combined knowledge of all the group members. The gap between private citizens and public problems is an enormous and ever widening one. To bridge this gap we must learn how to use information that comes to us from sources outside the face-to-face groups to which we belong, information that comes from a reporter in China, a diplomat in South America, a scientist working for the Atomic Energy Commission, an engineer at Bell Laboratories, or a psychologist at the Institute for Advanced Study in the Behavioral Sciences. This is no small task.

It was William James who originally made the distinction between "knowledge of acquaintance," which grows out of personal observation, and "knowledge about," which one gets indirectly through the reports of others. Discussions seldom rely on one of these types of knowledge to the exclusion of the other. Management officials, in conferring about the utilization of new equipment, will certainly want to draw upon the experience of skilled workers, supervisors, and engineers within their plant, but will also find it prudent to study technical journals and to read reports prepared by designers of the equipment. Citizens who wish to get rid of racial discrimination in housing or employment would do well both to consult with local officials and to study the experience of comparable communities which have enacted legislation to eliminate these barriers. The members of the League of Women Voters or the students in a classroom may have to depend very heavily upon the library for evidence on political and economic topics, on facts and figures supplied by outside sources.

In the case of "knowledge of acquaintance," where members of the group draw upon their own personal understanding of a situation, people are usually confident of the reliability of their own information. Participants are sometimes, however, so confident that they display unwarranted hostility toward those who criticize or question their knowledge. They insist that, after all, "they were there." Simply because an assertion rests on direct acquaintance with the situation does not, or should not, free committee members from the obligation to test the accuracy and completeness of the facts on which the assertion rests. Another danger, and perhaps a greater one, in relying on private knowledge, may come from overestimating the extensiveness and typicality of one's own experience. However, where several members of a committee are all familiar with some aspects of a problem, the dangers of distortion and error are materially reduced.

When a group must work with second-hand information, meaning data reported in books, magazines, newspapers, or over radio and television, assessment of the facts is much more hazardous. And committees must often make use of evidence that is not second-hand, but third-hand, fourth-hand, or tenth-hand. Few of our senators have personal acquaintanceship with conditions in the Far East, but they will have to learn enough about them to act with intelligence on measures to give financial aid to that area. In changing company policies a board of directors will have to depend heavily upon the reports of company officials thousands of miles away. Not only do committee members have to contend — as they did in the case of "knowledge of acquaintance" — with the possibility of errors in observation, but in addition, they now have to take into account distortions due to the reporter's motives, his habits of thought, including his prejudices, and his ability to state his observations clearly and unambiguously.

The linguistic barrier is one of the most serious of all. Thousands of lines of copy filed by observers must be reduced in volume to a few inches in a newspaper column or magazine and each of the people involved in this process (expert, reporter, rewrite man, editor, copy reader) may alter the final copy. From the original story, which is itself a vast abstraction involving the loss of hundreds of details that might be relevant, lines are deleted, others added, statements are rephrased, local color is emphasized, etc., etc. The semanticists are finally beginning to make us cognizant of the hidden dangers in a naïve acceptance of the reported statements of others.

> To be manageable at all, every bulky reality has to be pulled down into something it isn't — some tight little representation of itself, a symbol or cryptogram, such as converting 10,000 real sheep into a flicker of teletype. New York would be buried in half a day by the physical substance it handles symbolically in the same day. . . .
>
> It follows that, in handling such volumes of physical material by spirit rather than sense, the mind feels a bit guilty. It feels that it ought to know more about the outside world, it ought to make

> some effort to connect up with the reality behind the symbol but, hang it all, there isn't time. You can't go high-tailing it off to Butte to learn about copper, of off to Kansas to learn about wheat. So you come to rely more and more on imagined concepts of what the outside world would be like if you could ever bring it into the field of sensation. These imagined concepts are fortified by no end of information services, respected because of their brevity. They presume to tell us in one paragraph what Iowa is thinking or what California wants. But such summarization carries the mind, not closer to reality, but farther from it. The net effect has been to increase, rather than diminish, reliance on the symbol.[7]

According to Lippmann, the greatest threat to the effective use of human intelligence lies in this inevitable "insertion between man and his environment of a pseudo-environment," the world of words.[8]

Sources of Information

Information about the "world outside" comes to us through many different channels. When the latest information is needed, newspapers are usually the best source. A list of the most reliable papers would certainly include the following: the "good, grey" *New York Times,* the *Christian Science Monitor,* the *London Times,* the *Manchester Guardian,* and other less widely circulated ones such as the *St. Louis Post-Dispatch* and *The Milwaukee Journal.* These newspapers rank high in the estimation of professional journalists not only because they have large and independent staffs of reporters covering a wide field of activities but because, through the years, they have maintained the highest standards both in accuracy and range of coverage.

Newsmen, of course, work under severe limitations in covering the news of the world. The constant pressure on writers for speed — for scoring scoops — often prevents them from giving enough details so that readers can understand the full significance of the events covered. When it comes to reporting on a political or economic crisis, news staffs ordinarily do not have the time — nor are they given the space — to fill in a background so that current

[7] Thomas Ferril, "Western Half-Acre," *Harper's Magazine* (July, 1946), pp. 79–80. Reprinted by special permission of the author.

[8] Lippmann, *op. cit.,* p. 10.

incidents can be placed in context. This other dimension is partially supplied by news magazines. Their less pressing deadlines allow writers to take a longer view of a problem, to learn something about the history and background of the current conflict. A list of the leading news magazines in this country would include *Time, Newsweek, U.S. News and World Report,* and *The Reporter.* Unfortunately, the first three of these are often indistinguishable in their point of view. All except *The Reporter* reflect a predominantly Republican economic and political bias. Nevertheless, the careful reader will find in them a wealth of background information that will help him to establish the significance of an incident in Little Rock, Berlin, or Soviet Russia.

Newspapers and news magazines, however, do not usually take up the more fundamental problems of society unless these tensions happen to erupt in an immediate and pressing crisis. Also, their staffs are seldom expert enough to diagnose or predict the course of events. For an analysis of underlying political, economic, and social trends the members of a discussion group may need to turn to publications such as *Harper's, Fortune, Atlantic Monthly, Commonweal, Commentary, Christian Century, New Republic,* and *The Progressive.* The articles appearing in these journals almost achieve the status of contemporary history. Here the reader is likely to find penetrating observations prepared by experts who are not so much reporters as analysts. Facts about current events will appear here, too, but only as part of an extensive coverage of a problem which is likely to include its history along with a diagnosis of its major causes.

Beyond these sources, of course, are many others. There are almanacs, such as the *World Almanac* and *Statistical Abstracts,* which provide long tables of data on subjects from population growth to imports and exports. Encyclopedias are often helpful in introducing the reader to topics with which he may be unfamiliar. There are also standard reference works in most of the major fields of specialization, along with trade journals, for those interested in technical information. A seldom consulted, but very useful, source of expert opinion is to be found in various professional journals, ranging from those of general interest, such as the *Annals of the American Academy of Political and Social Science,* the *Bulletin of the American Association of University Professors,* and *Foreign Affairs,* to the more specialized, such as the scholarly publications in psychology, sociology, education, economics, law, and political science. In addition, there are digests of books, and abstracts of periodical literature.

When problems are being investigated that have been with us for a long time such as inflation, housing, divorce, race relations, interfaith marriage, free trade, or government regulation, there are many books that will prove useful. Often they are written by persons with a special theory or point of view to propound—thus it is important to consult a number of authors of various persuasions—but they will be written, by and large, by men qualified by training and experience to explain and interpret the facts.

There are many other ways of getting needed information. Whether committee members choose to obtain their evidence through reading or through other methods (interviewing, surveying, experimenting) depends on the kind of knowledge they need. The students in a class about to discuss submarginal housing might read available texts in social pathology, talk with members of the community planning commission, or make a firsthand study of slum conditions themselves. A couple thinking of marrying across religious lines may consult books and articles on this subject or talk to friends who have attempted interfaith marriages. A family planning a vacation trip is likely to ask acquaintances and neighbors for their recommendations. They may supplement this information, however, by subscribing to a film series, writing for travel brochures, or by checking into travel materials in their local library. A group of business executives undertaking to improve communications in their company could consult with psychologists and communication experts, write to the American Management Association for advice, read pertinent articles in *Nation's Business* or the *Harvard Business Review*, and study the large number of research reports on this subject. A group of parents interested in revising public school curricula might not only write to the National Education Association for pamphlets on the subject, but could actually attend classes in their schools and talk with teachers.

Acquiring facts is a slow and painstaking process. But group members, if they genuinely want to solve a problem, must make the effort. A group can rise no higher than its level of knowledge about a subject. Discussion is often criticized for being nothing more than a "pooling of ignorance." Unfortunately this is all too often the case. The blame in these instances should be directed not at discussion itself, but at the inertia of group members who expect to invest nothing in the way of research but hope to take away from the group valid opinions and decisions. In the absence of a reasonable amount of information, groups tend to base their decisions on shared prejudice rather than realities. It might be shocking but helpful to know how many unwise policies and unrealistic decisions rest upon the unwillingness of people to accept the responsibility for being informed.

Kinds of Evidence

The term "evidence" is commonly used by scientists, lawyers, and laymen alike. Despite the widespread usage of the term, there is, unfortunately, little agreement on precisely what it means. Some writers regard evidence as the "real world," the world of reality, no matter what it looks like to human observers. It is simply "what is out there." Others, particularly philosophers and logicians, tend to look upon evidence as anything that serves as a basis for belief or action; whatever is used as ground for an assertion constitutes evidence. Scientists, on the other hand, tend to regard evidence as any observation by one human being that can be confirmed by other qualified observers. Our function here is not to act as a final arbiter among these opinions. Each of the definitions seems to highlight some aspect of what we think of as evidence. We shall use the term evidence very broadly to refer to any kind of information which provides a person or group with knowledge about the world.

A number of questions come to mind almost immediately. Where does evidence originate? Are there different kinds of evidence? If so, what are they, and how do they differ? How can the accuracy of evidence be determined?

To answer these questions, one must begin with the process of perception, the method by which human beings acquire knowledge. A fact, in the opinion of psychologists, begins with a sensation — an impingement upon a human nervous system of some sight, sound, color, touch, and so on — emanating from our environment. Lately experts in perception theory have described a fact as a "transaction" between a human observer and the events that take place inside and outside his skin.

Certain implications flow from this explanation. For one thing, it is obvious that facts will always be personal, they will always involve the nervous system of some human being at some time and place. Further, since nervous systems respond differently depending upon surrounding conditions, upon the sensitivity of our receptors, and upon the mood we are in, we are going to have somewhat different perceptions even when they are observations of the "same" event. Since people are limited in what they see and hear, the facts known to any one person must necessarily be incomplete; it is impossible to know "all" about any happening. Also, what we observe in any case is going to be affected by the past experiences, the assumptions, the desires and needs we bring to that event, for these will profoundly affect what we perceive and the meaning or significance it has for us. Finally, since the real world is dynamic and undergoing constant change, facts (perceptions of it) will also change in time.

Information must be symbolized — put into language of some sort — before it can be communicated and used by others. Most of the evidence used in solving problems comes to group members in one of two linguistic forms: (1) statements of fact or description, and (2) statements of inference. The differences between these two kinds of information will have to be understood before ways can be described for determining the accuracy or validity of each of them.

Statements of fact, to begin with, can only be made *after* an observation of some sort, since they symbolize a sensation or perception. One obviously cannot make a statement of fact without any sensory data on which to base it. Normally, descriptive statements stay very close to the actual observation that was made. Factual statements, like facts themselves are, of course, incomplete, since they derive from sensations which are themselves limited by the sensitivity of the observer and the conditions under which the observation was made. As our ability to observe improves through perfecting our methods and instruments, the number of factual details noted also increases. However, no sophisticated person is arrogant enough to suggest that his factual statements "tell all" about the complexity of any event. Statements of fact are, themselves, static because once they are verbalized they are available for all time; but reality itself and perceptions of it are constantly undergoing change and thus there is no end of new facts to be discovered. The usefulness of a descriptive statement depends to a large extent upon the agreement it elicits from those with similar experiences. Since observations are personally conditioned and incomplete, it is clear that persons have different facts and that it is possible to find conflicting factual statements. However, the likelihood of agreement at the level of descriptive statements is higher than with almost any other kind of statement because discrepancies in our perceptions are easier to check. It is relatively simple to ascertain the accuracy of assertions about the wholesale price of coffee or the wages paid to workers in a particular plant compared to the difficulty in obtaining agreement on an opinion that workers are underpaid or that the economy is sliding into a period of recession.

Inferential statements differ from factual statements considerably, and it is important to understand the difference if intelligent use is to be made of this second type of evidence. Inferential statements consist, not of raw observations, but of conclusions, judgments, predictions, interpretations. Inferences always involve some sort of "leap in the dark," a leap into the unknown and unobserved. As such they usually reflect to a much greater degree than factual statements the habits of thought, the personal prejudices, the training and experience, of the speaker or writer. A medical diagnosis and a political prediction, for example, go beyond mere facts. An inference can be made at any time. It does not have to follow an observation, although it often does; inferences can be made before observing or even without ever observing an event. To ascertain the reliability of such statements requires quite different criteria. While factual statements can often be checked through further observation, inferences are more difficult to assess. Since inferences are less dependent upon perception, and more upon the intelligence, education, and experience of the person drawing the inference, there is far greater opportunity for different opinions and it is far more difficult to resolve divergent views when they do appear. Imagine the difficulties in trying to get a union representative and members of management to agree to the conclusion that profits are excessive, or in attempting to resolve the differences in opinion between an advocate of free trade and a protectionist on the desirability of tariffs.

This should not lead the reader to the conclusion that descriptive statements are better than inferential statements. An inference of an Einstein, a Niebuhr, an Oppenheimer, or a Menninger may be worth far more to the human community than the factual observations of these or other men. Both are important. Both are necessary. A cartoon appeared in the *New Yorker* magazine a number of years ago which captured this point very well. The drawing showed a man sitting all by himself at a crowded cocktail party. Two people nearby were discussing him and one was saying, "Oh, him, he just knows facts!"

Testing Factual Statements

How can people use these different types of evidence to think more effectively in solving problems? How can a group determine the degree of confidence it should place in information brought into the discussion? In the remainder of this chapter some guides will be suggested for evaluating and making intelligent use of factual or descriptive statements; in the following chapter the assessment of inferential evidence will be considered.

Is it clearly stated?

Factual statements can be found in great abundance on matters such as crime, divorce, religious affiliation, profits, immigration, traffic accidents, and national income — about virtually any subject vital to human welfare. Often, though, the statements are deceptively specific in their phrasing. The reader is tempted to believe that he has at last got his hands on a piece of reality. But has he? The Information Service of the National Council of Churches, for example, released figures to show that, in 1954, 60.3 per cent of the total population were members of some church. But what is meant by a "church member?" The figure of 60.3 per cent means nothing without further clarification:

> There is no agreement as to what constitutes a church member. "For example, Jewish (groups) estimate the number of Jews in communities having congregations. The Eastern Orthodox churches include the persons in the cultural or nationality group served. Roman Catholics, and a few Protestant bodies, number all baptized persons, including children, in the membership. Most Protestant bodies include only so-called adults . . . persons usually beyond 13 years of age, as members. Yet in the *Yearbook of American Churches,* 1945,

> it was estimated that about 5,000,000 members of Protestant churches were under 13 years of age."[9]

And, as *Time* magazine points out, "the statistics of the religious bodies often depend for their figures on the unchecked estimates of local pastors."[10] When reports appear that indicate an increased interest in religion, how is this interest determined? Does it represent a growth in the number of persons who have taken religious vows, the number of churchgoers, the number who contribute to religious organizations, the number who attend regularly or once or twice a year?

Statements which report on the number of criminals in the United States, membership in political parties, or the size of profits will have to be carefully scrutinized before conclusions are drawn. Is a criminal, for example, one who commits any kind of antisocial act (in which case we had better all be counted), one who is arrested, one who is convicted, or one who serves out a sentence? Each of these definitions will give a different result and justify different judgments about the current state of crime. Some years ago a statement was issued to the effect that 50 per cent of the coal in this nation was being wasted. But did that mean that half the coal was submarginal and not worth mining, that 50 per cent of it was lost in the process of refining it, or that this represented the wastage due to inefficient utilization? Until we know what the terms represent in a factual statement we do not know very much; in fact we may be deceived into drawing specious conclusions from it. Although it is necessary in drawing inferences to reach beyond the observable, committee members should know at least how secure a base they are using for their "leap in the dark."

Are the statistical units understood?

Among the most necessary (and most neglected) of foreign languages is the language of statistics. Many of the descriptive statements found in newspapers, magazines, technical journals, and books will report observations in numerical form. Statistics constitute a sort of shorthand, a way of summarizing vast numbers of specific instances. But an unsophisticated reading of evidence

[9] "Those Church Statistics," *Time* (October 31, 1955), p. 37.
[10] *Ibid.*

in statistical terminology may confuse or mislead rather than inform.

A delightful exposé of some of the commonest errors resulting from the abuse of statistics was written some years ago by Darrell Huff. The author analyzes in his book, *How To Lie With Statistics*, a number of pitfalls into which people fall with great regularity when it comes to interpreting figures: the misinterpretation of measures of central tendency—mean, median, mode; the misuse of graphed data; the maximizing or minimizing of significant differences; the too ready acceptance of facts gathered by sampling procedures; and so on.

When one reads, for example, that Britain shipped four times as much grain to China one year than the year before, what has been learned? Not very much until the quantity shipped originally is known. If only a hundred pounds were shipped in the base year a fourfold increase would amount to only four hundred pounds. Quadrupling a million tons, on the other hand, would add up to a sizable export business. In one case the significance of the increase is trivial; in the other case it deserves serious consideration. A percentage, a proportion, or a product means little unless it can be related to its base. It is not difficult to gather data that will show that production is up on almost any commodity by simply relating current production to an earlier period. If output is not higher than last month, then you can use last year, or the year before that, or the figures from five years ago as the basis for the comparison.

If the public opinion pollsters report that Candidate A has 48 per cent of the vote and Candidate B only 45 per cent, we cannot conclude that Candidate A is ahead at this point until we know something of the margin of error that is normal in polls of this kind. If the pollsters run true to form their margin is likely to be around a plus or minus 3 per cent. In this case either candidate might actually be in the lead, and some caution should be exercised in placing one's bets.

The mean score obtained from the intelligence tests given to two high school classes may be identical, but this may only hide the great differences between them. The amount of variability (deviation) from these means also has to be known. The I.Q.'s of a few exceptional students combined with the I.Q.'s of the mentally retarded in one class will give the same mean as will be obtained from the scores of a homogeneous group of students with average intelligence. Decisions about instruction in these two classes cannot be made intelligently without some knowledge of what lies behind the over-all statistic.

Major decisions in business, government, and education will often rest at some point on data reported in statistical terminology. Some analysis of the figures needs to be made if a group is not to commit grievous errors in judgment. It was a statistics tenderfoot who died of drowning in a stream that averaged only six inches deep.

Is the evidence consistent?

What should a group do if it finds statements of fact that seem inconsistent with one another? What if the reports conflict? First of all, it is quite possible for reporters to form different impressions about any country, group of people, or even about one person. It may be that descriptions do not square with one another because they were made at different times, under different conditons, or based on a different sample. Mr. X goes to his New York branch office, confers with company officials there and returns home. Later Mr. Y makes a similar trip. When it comes to planning personnel changes in the New York office, Mr. X and Mr. Y find they see the problem quite differently. One is not necessarily right and the other wrong; one does not have the facts and the other falsehoods. Their knowledge, in both cases, may be incomplete.

The ratings assigned by two different media research organizations may give the same program a high and a low rating. Such a discrepancy can probably be ironed out by comparing the sampling techniques of the investigators and deciding which is likely to be more accurate. The facts, where there is "external inconsistency" — that is, where the data given by two different observers or research organizations conflict — should be reconcilable if both reports were carefully prepared.

Sometimes, however, evidence is "internally inconsistent." That is, observations made by Mr. X are inconsistent with other facts he reported from the same visit. As Abraham Lincoln sharply noted in one of his trials, if the moon was not shining, as the witness had testified, then he could not have seen the alleged criminal in a clearing in the woods as he claimed. In instances of this type a careful review should be made of the facts to determine if any errors in reporting have been made; if not, the evidence should remain suspect until the paradox can be satisfactorily explained.

Is the fact placed in context?

Incomplete or partial data are also misleading. "Half truths" which lead to false conclusions may be more dangerous than no information at all, because they encourage one to construct a false picture of reality.

Recorded deaths due to some forms of cancer have shown a steady increase during the last two decades. This fact, even when recorded in a precise statistic, does not give sufficient information to permit people to draw conclusions without scrutinizing the context of this fact. Before an intelligent appraisal of this one piece of evidence is possible a host of surrounding and complicating facts must be taken into account. Does the rising curve of deaths due to cancer merely reflect the rising number of people in our population? Have cancer deaths increased because the proportion of older people in our population has grown? To what extent do current figures merely reflect improvement in our ability to define the disease rather than reflecting any genuine increase in cancer fatalities? Without these and other facts a single statement can give an extremely distorted impression of what is actually happening.

An article appearing in the *American Association of University Professors Bulletin* and bearing the engaging title, "Black Horses Eat More Than White Horses," illustrates how carefully one must analyze the context of factual evidence. A report published in a magazine of national circulation in this country pretended to sum up the unfortunate state of affairs in secondary education in America. The picture was almost uniformly dismal: We, as a nation, were far less well educated in 1950 than in 1900. More than half the schools in the United States offered instruction in neither chemistry nor physics. Where 86 per cent of secondary school students once studied mathematics, only 55 per cent do today. According to the *AAUP Bulletin* critic, Harold C. Hand, these data are grossly misleading. A radically different picture of American education emerges when the facts are put into context. In 1900 only 8 per cent of those of high school age actually attended high school; in 1950 the figure was 64 per cent. It is true that less than half the high schools offer physics and chemistry but over 1800 of our high schools enroll fewer than 50 pupils each and thus altogether educate less than 2 per cent of the total secondary school *population.* The figures on training in mathematics and science also need further explanation. The figure of 55 per cent was probably obtained from U.S. Office of Education figures on enrollments for the year 1948–1949: algebra, 27 per cent; general mathematics, 13 per cent; geometry, 13 per cent; trigonometry, 2 per cent. By adding them one comes out with a total figure of 55 per cent. But this is a report for *just one year* and students normally attend high school for four years. With this factor taken into account it turns out that "98 per cent . . . studied mathematics in their first year of high school, 47 per cent . . . had done so in their sophomore year, 30 per cent of those who were in high school as long as three years had taken mathematics . . . and at least 16 per cent had enrolled in either trignometry or solid geometry . . . during their senior year." [11] The few objective studies of the quality of education then and now, as determined by the College Entrance Board, by college records, and other criteria, all point to the high schools doing as well or better in educating their students. A balanced view, in short, is difficult to obtain from isolated or fragmentary statements about reality.

Is the source reliable?

The dangers of "lifting out of context" may be counteracted in some cases by gathering sufficient additional information so that a context can be constructed which will allow group members to evaluate the isolated scraps of evidence. In other cases, especially where information is of a technical sort or where access to data is limited, committee members may be unable or unqualified to make their own appraisal. They may have to assess the evidence indirectly, by ascertaining the reliability of the source from which the evidence issues. This, of course, is not easy to do and, in many cases, is a highly subjective matter. Some years ago two groups of clergymen traveled behind the iron curtain to determine the ex-

[11] Harold C. Hand, "Black Horses Eat More Than White Horses," *American Association of University Professors Bulletin* (June, 1957), p. 270.

tent of religious freedom. The first group reported "great freedom of worship," but it later turned out that they were sympathizers with the Soviet Union. The second contingent found just the opposite. This group was made up of vehement anti-communists. In this case, both sets of observations should be suspect.

A group needs to determine if there are reasons, first of all, why a witness could not give a reliable report. That is, are there physical or geographic obstacles which prevent him from making accurate observations? We obviously should not place great trust in what an observer claims he saw or heard if he suffers from partial blindness or defective hearing. People also need to view with some skepticism so-called "inside pictures" of the Russian Politburo or reports on the economy of China when prepared by persons who are in no position to have firsthand knowledge of these situations.

In addition there are many psychological barriers to objective reporting. Many publications look for the dramatic, the eye-catching, the unusual, and this may leave the impression that what is described is typical, a regular occurrence. Take, for example, stories about the televising of the U.N. Security Council debates on the Lebanon crisis in 1958. Several leading papers and periodicals conveyed a picture of a nation full of TV viewers angrily objecting to having their favorite soap operas, murder mysteries, and comedy shows replaced by the U.N. proceedings. Robert Lewis Shayon, radio and TV critic for the *Saturday Review* points out, however, that these reports seriously distorted what actually happened: CBS received a total of ten letters on the subject, six of which were critical; NBC's mailbag contained 110 letters with only 17 objecting to the change in programming; ABC received virtually no protests of any kind. By careful selection a few dramatic calls or letters were parlayed into an indictment of the listening habits and general maturity of the average TV viewer.[12] Lincoln Steffens, in his police reporting days, noticed that crime waves were often nothing but journalistic devices; ordinarily crime went unreported but when there was nothing else that was newsworthy reporters created a crime wave simply by playing up these stories.

Much of our information today emanates from the national headquarters of special interest groups with an "axe to grind." A great many corporations and large-scale professional organizations

[12] Robert L. Shayon, "Time, Popeye, and the U.N.," *Saturday Review* (August 30, 1958), p. 25.

maintain private "research" institutes to provide the public with facts favorable to their cause. For example, conflicting statements from labor and management, from the Department of Public Health and the American Medical Association, from Republican and Democratic candidates for office, need to be viewed critically since the data are supplied by sources that stand to gain from the acceptance of their version of the truth. This danger is most obvious in the advertisements of companies who have hired "independent research foundations" to conduct "scientific studies" of their product.

Some of the information coming from the sources described above is, of course, reliable, and some can be checked to determine its reliability. But the reader is often forced, because of lack of information regarding the methods of research or lack of access to original source material, to fall back upon an analysis of the motives that prompted the gathering of the data. Integrity, unfortunately, is a difficult commodity to price.

How was the information obtained?

One of the best, but unfortunately one of the most difficult, of all tests to apply is to determine how the information was gathered. It is a standard requirement in scientific reporting to describe exactly how data were collected. Research papers normally include a statement of "Objectives," "Materials," "Procedures," "Results," and "Conclusions," with a sharp line drawn between the first four steps and the final one. Such statements enable readers not only to use the findings but to ascertain the appropriateness and validity of the method used to gather the facts. It is tragic that with all the improvements in mass communication in modern society, methods of gathering information are so seldom reported.

Consumers, for example, are exposed with some regularity to data concerning the tar and nicotine content of leading cigarettes. Frequently the figures seem in conflict — the same brand is reported to contain 17 or 30 milligrams of tar — depending on which article is read. The discrepancy in studies of this sort is oftentimes, however, a result of following two different research techniques. The "chloroform method" yields lower weights than the "total solids" method.[13] Thus the apparent inconsistency in the facts only results

[13] Lois Miller and James Monahan, "The Cigarette Industry Changed Its Mind," *Reader's Digest* (July, 1958), p. 40.

from a different technique of analysis which, if known to the user of the facts, would be helpful to him in assessing how the data should be interpreted and used.

Some of the consumer motivation studies in the automotive field have led to interesting observations about buying habits. It was found by one automobile company that consumers were interested almost exclusively in the design features of modern cars. Mention was not made of the fact that the company in doing this study made no inquiries of customers in regard to car safety, original price, maintenance costs, ease of handling, or other matters that related to the actual use of the automobile.[14]

A few years ago a leading research organization was asked by a corporation to determine whether a name they had been using on their product had trademark value, that is, if it would be recognized by customers as a name of a specific product manufactured by one company rather than as a generic name for a type of equipment. In the legal fight that ensued over the use of this trademark it was revealed that in the survey of opinion: (1) Only three Eastern cities were sampled out of a universe that included the entire nation. (2) Only religious officials were included in the sample despite the marketing of the product outside as well as within religious institutions. (3) Interviewers who gathered the data were allowed to select the people they would interview out of a list of eligible respondents and therefore tended to interview only those who were easily accessible in downtown districts. (4) The questionnaire was never adequately pre-tested and contained several leading questions as well as a number with double or triple meanings. (5) Two different sets of summary figures could be derived from the data depending on who did the tabulating.[15]

A claim to knowledge, when there is any possibility of doubt about its validity, ought to be supported by a description of the claimant's method for collecting the information he reports. Obviously these techniques vary greatly from field to field. The physical and natural scientist works with variables that are much more discrete and that can be measured with greater objectivity than those observed by the social scientist. Ultimately, however, the

[14] "Economics for Consumer," *Consumer Reports* (April, 1958), pp. 216–218.

[15] Information contained in "Brief on Behalf of Opposer" in the U.S. Patent Office Case number 34,161.

assessment of any descriptive information turns on an investigation of the motives and techniques of the person who reports the facts.

Critical Attitudes

The problem of getting reliable information as a basis for thought is a vital need everywhere but a particularly pressing one in discussion groups since so many important issues are settled in such groups.

The problem of bridging the gap between the world outside and our own private mental processes is no casual and haphazard undertaking. It requires a *desire* to know as well as *techniques* for assessing what is claimed to be known. Some people, unfortunately, display almost no critical capacity whatsoever. They act, but they do not think.

> Many men in nearly all things, and nearly all men in some things, are content and even anxious to be partially deceived. They are satisfied to act without explicit knowledge, or to accept alleged knowledge without testing it, as long as it suits their immediate needs, even though in the long run it may prove to be wholly unreliable.[16]

It is so easy, in the absence of undeniable facts, to follow one's prejudices and not bother about what the world is really like. Such people display a basically uncritical attitude toward evidence. They are satisfied too easily. To them, one opinion is just as good as any other. For a while they may escape the consequences of this posture, but eventually the world will overtake them. Each distortion of reality carried around in our nervous systems at some time, in some place — and often sooner and more frequently than we care to admit — will exact its toll in the form of prejudiced decisions, inappropriate action, wasteful methods, unpleasant human relationships, or in other kinds of breakdowns.

There are others, however, who expect too much. They insist upon having incontrovertible evidence to support every opinion. Their desire for information exceeds the capacity of human beings to know or understand the world. These are the ones who want to know "all the facts" before reaching any decision. Of course, to know "all the facts" is an impossible demand. Reality is constantly changing and as soon as one observation is completed, another could

[16] Larrabee, *op. cit.*, p. 23.

be started. The story, probably apocryphal, is told of the professor who spent a lifetime gathering data about a species of insect. Colleagues urged him to publish his most significant findings, but the world never gained anything from his work for he steadfastly refused, believing that somewhere a gap might exist in his data. The hypercritical person is paralyzed by inaction when decisions must be reached. His caution about accepting evidence becomes a perverted demand for absolute knowledge, for final TRUTH. His failure to move from fact to decision is as unfortunate in its consequences as the unwillingness of the uncritical person to move from opinion back to fact.

Between these two extremes can be found the person of critical judgment. He neither demands too little nor expects too much. He is curious to know, when it is possible to find out. He prefers to act on an informed intelligence, but will act in any case. How rigorously he appraises evidence will depend upon a realistic evaluation of surrounding circumstances — on the pressure for decision, on the time available for investigation, on the accessibility of the evidence. The most important of the situational factors he will consider is the character of the problem itself. He would regard as stupid the person who uses reflective thinking to find a lost cuff link (unless, of course, it happened to be a diamond one). He would think it equally absurd to decentralize a corporation, prepare a federal budget, or plan a military invasion in the casual way one orders lunch.

Speculation is undeniably worthwhile. But when based on ignorance it seems pointless, if not dangerous. Group members should demand that opinions expressed in discussion have some foundation in reality. We need men everywhere, but particularly in discussion groups where the pressures toward conformity may be great, who question assumptions, who have the courage to doubt, and who are not afraid to follow the facts to whatever conclusions they lead.

The problem of making intelligent decisions, as the King of Siam commented, "is a puzzlement." As issues become broader in scope and increase in complexity it becomes more and more difficult to solve them rationally. The forming of a committee is, itself, an attempt to arrange communications to get the maximum benefit from combining the experience of many people. Another way of coping with the widening gap between the public and its problems is to obtain trustworthy information from outside sources. Knowledge about the world beyond our experience can be obtained through a variety of communication media which differ in the accuracy, completeness, and authoritativeness of their coverage. Distinguishing between the reliable and unreliable in this torrent of information can be accomplished by testing each factual statement and seeing to what degree it meets certain conditions: (1) Is it clearly stated? (2) Are the statistical units understood? (3) Is the evidence consistent? (4) Is the fact placed in context? (5) Is the source reliable? (6) How was the information obtained? More important, perhaps, than the method of testing data is the attitude of the problem-solver. Will he accept what John Erskine called "the moral obligation to be intelligent" —will he know when to insist that a factual foundation be placed under "claims to knowledge" and when to act without having complete and absolute truth in his grasp?

RECOMMENDED READINGS

Hayakawa, S. I. *Language in Thought and Action.* Harcourt, Brace & Company, Inc., 1949.

Huff, Darrell. *How To Lie With Statistics.* W. W. Norton & Company, Inc., 1954.

Larrabee, Harold A. *Reliable Knowledge.* Houghton Mifflin Company, 1945.

Lippmann, Walter. *Public Opinion.* Penguin Books, 1922.

Mayer, Milton. "How To Read the Chicago Tribune," *Harper's Magazine* (April, 1949).

Chapter Seven

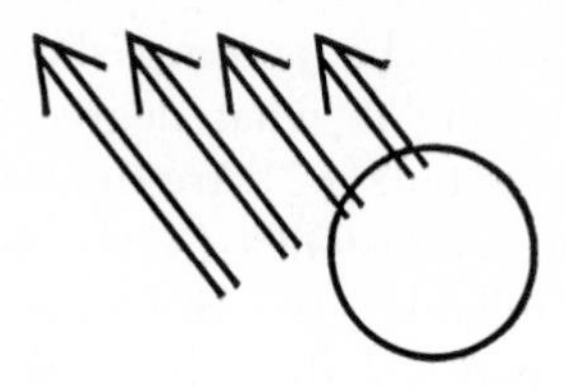

The Uses of Authority and Reason

THE FOLLOWING INTERCHANGE, or one much like it, might have been overheard in any of a hundred discussions across the nation during the past few years:

A: Well, I don't think we ought to pour so much money down this foreign aid rat-hole. It doesn't really win us any friends, and most of it gets wasted anyhow. I know that when I was in the Air Force, stationed in France, I saw how anti-American those people are. A lot of good all our help to them has done us.

B: I don't agree with that. I've had lots of friends who've been stationed overseas or traveled in Europe during the summer, and they tell me that the people they've met were grateful to the United States for not just pulling out right after the war and leaving them to sink or swim. I don't think you can say our aid hasn't done us any good.

C: It seems to me that this foreign aid must be a pretty important thing. After all, every President and Secretary of State, Republican or Democrat, since the end of the war has been for it. In fact they're always trying to get more and more money out of Congress for foreign aid. They must be convinced that it's doing us some good.

D: I think that just because there may be some anti-American feeling in France and other places doesn't prove our aid hasn't done any good. It's only human for people to be kind of resentful about having to be on a dole, even if deep down they really appreciate it. I think that in spite of some of their grievances, if it really came to a show-down they'd be on our side.

This bit of dialogue contains within it the four basic kinds of material with which any discussion group must work. "A" has presented some observations from his personal experience in France. "B" has reported the personal experiences of people other than himself — of friends who have traveled or been stationed overseas. "C" has introduced the opinions of individuals who are presumed to be authorities — Presidents and Secretaries of State. "D" has put forward some ideas which reflect his own thinking on the subject. In the preceding chapter we explored the uses of the first two types of information — statements based on the direct experience of the participants and observations coming to them from secondary sources. We turn now to some of the difficulties arising from the use of the latter two kinds of material — the inferences of others, and our own reasoning processes.

Opinions of Others

If we were to examine the bases upon which our beliefs and actions rest we might be astonished to discover the extent to which we rely upon the opinions of other people. The views of our parents and teachers are profoundly influential, particularly in the early years of life. Later our friends come to play an important part in shaping our thinking, as do the authors of books and articles we read, or speeches by clergymen and public officials. We rely heavily on the opinions of doctors in matters concerning our health, and often upon lawyers in questions of taxation, home purchasing, or even family difficulties. As in the case of individuals, so discussion groups draw upon the inferences of others to guide them in their deliberations. A jury, for example, listens carefully to the testimony of handwriting experts or psychiatrists in order to help determine the guilt or innocence of a defendant.

The courtroom is a good place to begin our study of the problems involved in relying on the opinions of others, for here great care is exercised in this matter. A sharp distinction is made between "expert" and "ordinary" opinion, and only that of experts is admissible as evidence. According to our legal system the average witness is simply to report observations or facts. Inferences which are expressed by an "ordinary" witness may be stricken from the record. He is not expected to make interpretations. That is left to the members of the jury, and it is felt that they should not be prejudiced by the views of others who are presumed to be no better qualified than they. However, on the question of a defendant's sanity at the time of a crime — a judgment which also involves the making of inference — the opinions of a witness, if he be a qualified psychiatrist, are not only admitted but are eagerly explored. Here the typical juror is not sufficiently well-trained to draw his own conclusions from the facts. It is therefore desirable that he hear the advice of authorities. Likewise, in determining whether the handwriting in a particular letter is that of the defendant — another question involving inferences or opinion — men with experience in that line of work are called upon for their judgments.

The average discussion group does not, and need not, make as rigid a distinction between expert and ordinary opinion as is required in our courts of law. The opinions of laymen can be quite helpful on the kinds of problems with which discussion groups are typically confronted — provided those laymen are individuals whose judgment we respect. We assume that the individuals being relied upon have had some kind of experience, and hence have acquired a degree of expertness which has earned them our respect. If young people seriously take into account the opinions of their parents in making some personal decision, it is because they feel that those parents, having lived through similar experiences, may have greater wisdom on the subject. If we listen with respect to the views of a friend on some topic concerned with human relations, it may be because we feel he has "been around" more than we have. If he has not, we would be inclined to figure it out for ourselves.

Thus, whether the opinion-giver be a legally qualified expert, or whether we have informally attributed some degree of expertness to him because of his experience, we are in either case treating him as an authority on the subject being discussed. We will tend to turn to such authorities whenever we are confronted by situations in which we feel incompetent to draw adequate inferences from the facts which we possess. An individual may know that he does not feel well, and be able to describe his *symptoms* quite accurately, but he will still go to the doctor to find out what is wrong. If our car will not start, and we cannot find the difficulty for ourselves, we call an automobile mechanic to analyze the problem. As was suggested earlier, if we were to count the number of times in the course of a day that we rely, to one extent or another, on the judgment of authorities, we would find that their opinions constitute a major influence in our decision-making processes.

An important question, then, needs to be raised here. Does the average group, or individual, rely too much upon authoritative opinion? Or too little? How much of this dependence on the opinions of others is necessary, or healthy, either for a discussion group or an individual decision-maker? In short, what is the proper role of authority in our problem-solving processes?

The Proper Role of Authority

There are some people who maintain that the only legitimate function of an authority is to provide us with factual information from his field of specialization or experience, thus forcing us to make our own interpretations or draw our own conclusions. This school of thought holds that, given the facts, we are overly dependent upon authorities if we ask them to do our inference-making too. Proponents of this approach, in effect, would rule out any reliance on the opinions of others in making our decisions. We would make use of our own observations and the *observations* of others, and from that point on we would reason entirely for ourselves.

A prominent example of this point of view is to be found in the field of counseling, and is known as nondirective or client-centered therapy. It is the belief of Dr. Carl Rogers, the leading spokesman of this school, that, in the area of emotional problems at least, every human being possesses the potential ability to solve his own problems. Any attempt to direct a patient's behavior will only serve to delay him in growing to maturity.

Although, so far as we know, Dr. Rogers has not claimed that this philosophy is appropriate in all other areas of life — such as politics or economics — there are individuals who do take that extreme position, or one close to it. They feel there is no reason why any fairly intelligent person or group, *if* provided with sufficient factual data, cannot adequately interpret the material for themselves. Indeed it is argued that this is a basic premise of a democratic society.

At the other extreme are those who see no danger at all in relying extensively on authoritative opinion, so long as we have confidence in the integrity and ability of the authorities upon whom we depend. According to this school of thought, the citizen in a democracy has done his job when he goes to the polls and casts his ballot. After that it is up to the men whom he elects to do his political thinking for him. If he is not satisfied, he can turn them out of office on his next trip to the voting booth.

There are hundreds of thousands of people who behave in accordance with this philosophy, particularly in such areas as medicine and religion. The patient who places himself unquestioningly in the hands of his doctor, or the individual who looks to his church to prescribe for him what is right and wrong in the field of morals, exemplifies this point of view.

One can take a position somewhere between the two extremes we have described. It should be noted, however, that the pressures in our complicated, modern world seem to be pushing us farther and farther toward the latter pole. The average individual seems not to have enough time to familiarize himself sufficiently with the facts of a problem to be able to interpret them for himself. There is nothing to prevent a person who is planning to discuss the school desegregation issue from going to the library and reading the crucial 1954 Supreme Court decision on this matter rather than relying on some newspaper editorialist's interpretation of that document. Similarly, in a discussion of sexual mores, copies of the Kinsey Report are not difficult to obtain if one wants to study the original document rather than depend on the sometimes grossly distorted interpretations of its contents. But such research does take some time and effort, and so the temptation is great to turn to authorities to digest and interpret the information.

But, even if time were available, there are many subjects on which exposure to the facts might leave us reeling in confusion because we lack the technical training to understand them. Anyone who is doubtful about the legitimacy of a particular income tax deduction he is considering can get a copy of the Internal Revenue Act and read its provisions. But whether he will understand the implications of what he has read is another question. A lawyer or accountant, however, who has been trained in this field, and is accustomed to working with legal documents, might more easily be able to determine what should be done. The same is true of such questions as the dangers of radioactive fall-out from nuclear explosions or the effects of a devaluation of the pound sterling on world markets. Overawed by such technicalities we look to the scientists, economists, and mathematicians to lead us through the jungle of what appear to be meaningless data.

Finally, in many instances it is felt by the authorities themselves that the people with whom they deal are not mature enough — emotionally or intellectually — to be presented with the facts and allowed to make their own decisions. Many physicians feel this way about their patients. And, as we know, there has been controversy in the field of education for many years between the "progressive educators" who believe that students should be given less direction by their teachers and more opportunity to control their own courses of study and the "traditionalists" who feel that young people are not competent to determine such matters. This same issue is now spilling over into the world of business, with the advocates of "participative management" arguing for more self-determination on the part of workers, and the "old school" maintaining that employees are not sufficiently responsible to be given a greater degree of independence.

What can one logically conclude from this clash of viewpoints? To what extent *should* a discussion group rely upon the opinions of authorities? We shall try to state our position on the matter and let the reader decide whether or not he should be influenced by *our* authority!

We would point out that the mere fact of a group's having undertaken to discuss a subject suggests that the members must feel they have some competence to make their own inferences on the matter. If this were not true then they ought not to be holding a discussion at all, but listening to a lecture or reading an authoritative book on the subject. It is our feeling, however, that there are actually not many problems with which people of average intelligence cannot cope, given access to the facts and the *aid* of expert *advice*. We are skeptical of those authorities who claim that the people they deal with are not responsible enough or sufficiently well-informed to make independent judgments. We have observed too many situations where this is a distorted picture of the people being described. When it is true, we frequently find that the immaturity or ignorance that exist are a result of the authorities themselves having withheld information or having prevented opportunities for the development of more responsible behavior. In other words, the "ignorance of the masses" is used as an excuse for perpetuating the same policies which have produced that ignorance. This we regard as a self-defeating philosophy.

We believe, on the contrary, that the average discussion group is or can learn to become competent in the interpretation of evidence in almost any field. This does *not* mean that we advocate the rejection of authoritative opinion. We recognize the complexities and technicalities involved in many areas, the pressures of time, and the limitations people may have in background and training. Therefore we believe that the *aid and advice* which can be provided by experts in analyzing data and helping to find solutions to problems can be invaluable. Authority is abused only when unquestioningly accepted. We have no objection to listening respectfully to the opinions of the doctor, psychotherapist, scientist, clergyman, economist, lawyer, or teacher — in fact, it is foolish to ignore whatever wisdom they may be able to contribute in their special areas of competence. However, we do feel it is a mistake to accept their views as infallible, or to allow ourselves to be so dominated by their opinions that we abdicate the responsibility of thinking for ourselves and of ultimately making our own decisions. In short, we do not believe in the unqualified acceptance of authoritative opinion or in its unqualified rejection. We feel that it should be used whenever helpful and appropriate, but that insofar as we are capable we should subject it to the careful and critical scrutiny of our own judgment. Mary Follett recognized this problem many years ago when she said, "The indispensability of the expert is accepted; what we need is a clearer understanding of his relation to ourselves." [1] And Harold Laski provided what we think to be the answer when he said of the expert, "He is an invaluable servant and an impossible master.[2]

[1] Mary P. Follett, *Creative Experience* (Longmans, 1924), p. 21.
[2] Harold Laski, "The Limitations of the Expert," *Harper's Magazine* (December, 1930), p. 106.

Evaluating Authoritative Opinion

Let us assume that we are now in a situation where authoritative opinions have been introduced into a discussion, and that we wish to use them intelligently. How do we evaluate these opinions? This becomes an especially crucial problem when the authorities are in disagreement with one another and we have to find some basis for choosing among them. But even where only one expert is involved we must still determine the extent to which his views can be trusted. There are a number of tests which can be applied.

What are the expert's personal qualifications in this field?

Whenever we rely upon the opinions of other persons, we must have sufficient grounds for confidence in their judgment on the problem under consideration. We should know something about their intelligence, their experience with matters of this sort, and their educational background. Obviously the more intelligent they are, the more experience they have had, and the more training they have undergone, the greater will be our tendency to trust their opinions.

An interesting question which sometimes confronts us is how much weight we should give to intelligence *versus* experience *versus* formal training. It goes without saying that if a man possesses all three elements to a high degree his views will be given preference over someone in whom all three qualities are absent. But what of the case where two authorities on politics make conflicting predictions about the outcome of an approaching election, one of whom is a leading university professor of political science and the other a noted practical politician with years of experience in campaign work? Which shall we believe? To make the issue even sharper, let us assume that the professor has never had any practical experience in politics and that the politician has only a sixth-grade education.

Our first reaction is likely to be that we ought to find still another authority with *both* academic *and* practical background. For we recognize that purely formal training, with no exposure to real-life situations, may leave even a natively intelligent man somewhat naïve in his judgments. On the other hand, we are also aware that although the school of hard knocks may teach many valuable lessons, its pupils are frequently parochial in outlook and less carefully analytical in their thinking than is the scholar. Therefore, the ideal authority would be a man of intelligence who is both experienced and formally trained in the field. We tend to be justly skeptical of individuals who are one-sided in these respects. But if we cannot have both, and must make a choice, our decision should probably rest upon the nature of the matter in dispute. In a question of the outcome of an election the experienced, though uneducated, politician may provide a sounder judgment than the trained, but inexperienced, political scientist. However, if it is a question of whether a proposed bill is likely to be regarded as unconstitutional by the Supreme Court we would be inclined to give the nod to the political scientist. Fortunately the choice is not usually between such extremes, and it is often quite clear, upon examination, which authority possesses the best combination of talents.

One further caution needs to be noted here. There is a tendency for what is known as a "halo" effect to operate in the evaluation of authoritative opinion. If an individual is a recognized authority in one field, his prestige tends to carry over to other fields. People are prone to give more weight to his opinions about matters outside his true scope of competence than they properly should. For instance, Albert Einstein, in the years just preceding his death, made a number of public statements on the question of world government. Because of Einstein's position as the foremost scientist of our age his opinions were given wide publicity and undoubtedly exerted considerable influence upon many people. But he was not an authority on international affairs. True, he was a genius, and for this reason alone one could justifiably be more interested in his opinions on *any* subject than in those of an average individual, since intelligence is *one* of the personal qualifications of an expert. However, we would be in error to allow his general intelligence and his expertness *as a scientist* to cast such a halo over his opinions as to obliterate the fact that he was neither formally trained nor particularly experienced in international relations. Historically there have been many illustrations of this fallacy —people who gave undue weight, for example, to the *political* opinions of the *industrial* genius, Henry Ford, of the *aeronautical* expert, Charles Lindbergh, or of the *religious* leader, Father Coughlin. There are people today who make this same mistake — who assume that a successful general is automatically qualified to be a good President, or that a clergyman is competent to expound on almost any subject under the sun.

Is the expert in a position to know the facts?

Although we are not concerned here with the evaluation of factual statements, we must recognize that the validity of an *opinion* or inference rests *in part* upon the adequacy of the facts with which one begins. Occasionally, experts who are well qualified, in terms of their intelligence, training, and experience to pass judgment on a subject, are unable to do so because they do not have adequate access to facts. For instance, a man may be a leading authority on China — having grown up there, having studied its history and culture, and having written many books on Chinese affairs. But if, since the Communists came into control, he has not been able to visit the country, we must regard his interpretations of what is happening there with less confidence than we would the judgments of another man whose background was perhaps somewhat less profound but who had just spent the past two years within Red China. This does not mean that we should discount entirely the first man's lifetime of experience and training, for even on the basis of second-hand factual reports he may have more insight than someone of lesser training who has been right on the scene. The latter individual may have visited only a part of the country. He may have been exposed only to its economic or its political life. He may have lacked the training to notice what was significant, or he may have missed the point of certain changes because of his lack of historical understanding. For all of these reasons the first man may be a more trustworthy authority. Yet we cannot ignore the possible limitations imposed upon him by his inability to get directly at the facts.

Is the expert relatively free from bias?

Considerable nonsense has been spoken and written about the need for objectivity on the part of authority figures. It has been suggested that if an expert is at all biased we cannot rely upon his opinion; that in order to be trusted he must be completely free of prejudice, or have no vested interest in the subjects upon which he passes judgment. We call this nonsense because there is no human being who fulfills these criteria. Everyone, of necessity, views the world from his own frame of reference. We have seen how this is true even at the level of sheer perception. How much more then must it be true at the level of inference or judgment? We will find *no* satisfactory authoritative opinions if we pursue such an absolute ideal.

This does not mean, however, that some people do not do better on this score than others. *Relatively* speaking, there are some individuals who seem more able than others to climb outside of their own skins, as it were, and gain a broader perspective of their environment. The high regard we hold for the scientific method is due to the fact that it is an attempt to achieve relative objectivity, or relative freedom from bias. The question which it makes sense to ask of our authorities, then, is not "Are they completely pure?" but rather "How pure are they?" Some so-called experts are notably prejudiced, allowing their own needs and interests to color almost everything they say. They are known as men with axes to grind, and are trusted only by those who happen to share their prejudices. Other authorities are widely respected in their fields because they have a reputation for intellectual honesty. This is to say that they approach problems with as open a mind as possible and make a sincere effort to keep what they think relatively uncontaminated by what they *wish* to think. The contrast between radio commentators such as Fulton Lewis, Jr. and Eric Sevareid, between columnists like Westbrook Pegler and Walter Lippmann, or between newspapers such as the *Chicago Tribune* and the *New York Times* provides dramatic illustration of this principle.

But, even if aware of this test, how do the members of a discussion group ascertain whether or not the authorities whom they have read or heard are relatively free from bias? One clue may be found in the material itself. If opinions tend to be stated in an unqualified manner, full of emotionally loaded language, and phrased in ways which reveal wishful thinking, one might well be suspicious of the objectivity of the author. "There is no doubt in my mind that . . ." or "This is unquestionably . . ." are phrases that typify this approach. Conversely, if the authority presents his views calmly and clearly, gives reasons, and admits possible sources of error, we are inclined to believe him more trustworthy. A phrase like "Other things being equal, it is probable that . . ." conveys such a temperate mood.

Then, too, it is helpful to know for whom the authority works or to whom he is beholden. Not long ago, for example, it was suggested that the responsibility for protecting the public's health from the dangers of radioactive fall-out should be taken away from the Atomic Energy Commission and given to an independent agency. The AEC's statements on this matter could not be trusted, it was argued, because they are primarily interested in weapons development and thus tend to underplay the dangers of their own nuclear testing program. Likewise one can be skeptical of election predictions which are made by the Democratic or Republican national chairmen. This is not to say that a man should *automatically* be discredited if he draws his pay check from a source which has some vested interest in the topic under discussion. However, the question of financing should at least be kept in mind when evaluating any authority, since even the most honorable of us are not entirely immune to pressure.

What is the expert's past record of independence?

Closely related to the question of possible bias due to an authority's source of financial support is the matter of distortions due either to rigidity or flightiness in his thinking processes. Such habits can often be ascertained by examining his past record, or following his present opinions over a period of time. If he is an individual who consistently follows one party line or who analyzes all problems according to the same set of assumptions, we will have reason to doubt his independence, hence reliability, of judgment. "A foolish consistency," said Emerson, "is the hobgoblin of little minds." On the other hand, there is no virtue in inconsistency for its own sake. We have reason to be equally suspicious of the expert who flits lightly from one position to another, revealing a lack of depth or continuity in his thinking. A child, for instance, will have little confidence in the opinions of a parent or teacher who takes one position one minute and another the next. It would seem that what is required in the "ideal" expert is a fine balance between independence and consistency.

Does the selected opinion appear to be consistent with the expert's general point of view?

Every once in a while an authoritative opinion will be introduced into a discussion which, to put it bluntly, sounds "fishy." That is to say, it does not seem like the kind of viewpoint which the particular expert in question would express, because it appears to be inconsistent with his general approach to problems of this sort. In such instances it is well for the group members to check back for the context from which the opinion has been taken — the entire book, article, or speech, as the case may be — to determine whether, by chance, the expert has been misquoted, or whether there is some other explanation for the apparent contradiction.

In recent years, for example, the advocates of continued racial segregation have grown fond of quoting excerpts from some of Abraham Lincoln's speeches in the Lincoln-Douglas debates to the effect that Negroes should not be given "social and political equality." When first confronted with such evidence one is likely to disbelieve that the Great Emancipator could have said any such thing. But if we check the record we will find that, on this point at least, Lincoln has not been misquoted. He did say, more than once in fact, that he did not believe in political or social equality for the Negro. However, in order properly to interpret these statements one must understand Lincoln's *total* thinking on the Negro question at that point in his career. He believed (and said so) that Negroes have "natural rights to life, liberty, and the pursuit of happiness," and he objected to any policy which would deny those rights. However, he did not then see that the granting of political and social *equality* was necessary for the achievement of the Negro's rights to life, liberty, and the pursuit of happiness. To what extent he later changed his mind, or was swept along by the tide of subsequent events, is not entirely clear. What is certain is that it is an oversimplification to assert without qualification that Lincoln, in 1858, was either for or against the rights of Negroes.[3]

[3] See Roy P. Basler, *Abraham Lincoln: His Speeches and Writings* (World Publishing Company, 1946), pp. 403–404; and Edwin E. Sparks, *Collections of the Illinois State Historical Library,* Lincoln Series, Volume I (Illinois State Historical Library, 1908), pp. 100–102, 267–268, 348–349, and 432 ff.

Does the opinion meet the tests of valid reasoning?

We have said that a reliable authority will usually not state his opinion without giving the thinking which lies behind it. When this is the case, a final method of evaluating authoritative opinion is to examine the validity of the reasoning itself. Does the position he has taken seem to be a logical one? Do his arguments appear to be valid? Since this process of evaluation is the same as will apply when we test the reasoning of the other members of a discussion group, we shall now turn to a general consideration of the uses of reason and the possible errors which may occur in its employment.

The Nature of Reasoning

In order to develop our ability to test the validity of reasoning processes — whether of an authority, of other members of a discussion group, or our own — it is first necessary to understand some of the basic characteristics of reasoning. We have already discussed these to some extent in the previous chapter, having pointed out that reasoning, or inference-making as it is sometimes called, is a process in which the individual goes beyond what he perceives, to make a "leap into the dark." He takes hold of the raw material presented to him by his environment and filters it through his own mind. He draws conclusions, makes interpretations, judgments, or predictions. If we examine this process we will see that all reasoning has two basic characteristics: (1) It involves an element of probability, and (2) it involves an attempt to establish relationships.

The concept of probability

What do we mean when we say that all reasoning involves an element of probability? Very simply, we mean that one can never be *certain* of the truth of an inference. There is always a chance that the opinion may be erroneous. To be sure, some inferences are more probable, less "chancy" than others. But, by their very nature, none can be absolute. This principle can best be illustrated by one of the most common forms of reasoning found in group discussions — namely, the process of *generalization,* or as it is sometimes called, reasoning from example. A generalization is a statement about a group or class of people, objects, or events on the basis of observations of a small sample from that group. Thus an individual might generalize, on the basis of four or five foreign restaurants at which he has eaten, that foreigners tend to be better cooks than Americans. A medical research man, having successfully tested a new polio shot on one hundred persons, might conclude that he has discovered a vaccine which will be effective with the public as a whole. A Newton, by studying apples falling from a tree, might develop a law of gravity which applies to all objects on earth. The Gallup poll, by sampling a cross section of 5,000 voters, may assert that Candidate A would defeat Candidate B if a nationwide election were to be held.

It should be clear from these illustrations why some generalizations have a higher degree of probability than others. For one thing it depends upon the size of the sample. Experience with only five foreign restaurants is probably not sufficient proof that foreigners tend to be better cooks than Americans. On the other hand, any of us would be willing to wager that it will become dark tonight and light again tomorrow morning. Yet this is not a fact; it has not yet been observed. It is an inference based upon the daily experience of an entire lifetime. The size of our sample is as large as the number of days we have lived, and with that kind of evidence we are confident of our prediction.

The representativeness of the sample is also a factor in determining a generalization's degree of probability. Mr. Gallup, on the basis of only 5,000 interviews, can make statements about what many millions of people are likely to do because his sample is a carefully selected one, designed to represent, in the proper proportions, every significant segment of the population. In contrast, many false generalizations are made about minority groups because they are so often based upon extreme or nontypical cases.

Some people have the mistaken notion that generalizations should never be spoken or accepted unless they are stated statistically. That is, we should never say of a group of people that "In general, they are hard workers," or that "Most of them are lazy." Rather we must say "52 per cent of them are hard workers and 48 per cent of them are lazy." Actually this is equivalent to demanding that we not use our reasoning powers at all, but confine ourselves to statements of fact. For if we are able to reduce a generalization to precise statistical percentages, it is no longer an inference but a report of observed cases. If we can get such facts, that is highly to be desired. But often it is impossible. To be sure, we take a risk of error when we talk in generalities, but if we did not generalize we could not think at all. Every law of physics, every principle of economics, every theory of human behavior, is a generalization. If it is a highly probable one, we dignify it with the title "law" or "principle." If it is still largely untested we call it an hypothesis or a hunch. But in all instances there is some chance that it might not be true. This does not prevent us from operating on the basis of generalizations. Every time we take medicine we make the assumption, based on past experiences, that it will improve our health. Every time we drive over a new bridge we are trusting that the principles of engineering employed in its design are valid and that the bridge will not fall down. Every time we avoid insulting another person we are assuming that insults *generally* create strained relationships.

Furthermore, it should not be taken for granted that just because a statement contains statistics it is no longer an opinion. Any prediction about future events must of necessity be an inference, regardless of how statistically it may be expressed. If Gallup, on the basis of 5,000 interviews, suggests that when several million people go to the polls 55 per cent of them will vote Democratic, this is reasoning by example. On the basis of 5,000 specific instances he is generalizing about what millions will do. Thus, there is the possibility of error. He can even tell us, statistically, what the chances of error are. When, however, he reports that 55 percent *of his sample* said they would vote Democratic, this is a statement of fact about the 5,000.

In short, we can never be certain about generalizations, for like all forms of reasoning they involve an element of probability. This does not mean we cannot use them, or that statements of fact are necessarily to be preferred. It means only that we should be aware of their fallible nature, and do what we can to ascertain their degree of probability.

Another form of reasoning which commonly occurs in group discussion, and which also illustrates the principle of probability, is *reasoning by analogy*. An analogy can best be described as thinking which employs a comparison to reach a conclusion. We begin with a known fact, for example, that socialized medicine has worked well in Scandinavia, and then infer from this that it will work well in the United States. Or it may be asserted that since it is unwise to change horses in the middle of a stream, therefore a country should not change leaders in the middle of a national crisis. Or that since prohibitive legislation was an ineffective way of dealing with liquor control in the United States, for that reason prohibitive legislation will not be successful in controlling racial discrimination.

We can see the element of probability at work in these three illustrations. Although an effort has been made in each case, as in all reasoning by analogy, to find two situations which are enough alike that what is true of one will hold true of the other, we know that no two situations are ever *exactly* alike. Thus there is always room for error in this kind of thinking. The degree of probability of an analogy will depend upon how like or unlike the two things being compared really are.

Some writers on reasoning argue that figurative analogies, such as the horses-leaders comparison cited above (where a real situation is compared to an imaginary one) prove nothing. They maintain that only comparisons between actual events have any logical validity. Some writers go so far as to assert that *no* analogy proves anything, even though admitting that argument by comparison may be persuasive to listeners. We fail to understand the logic of this position. If what the writers mean is that one cannot be certain of conclusions drawn from comparisons, then their criticism would apply equally to *all* forms of reasoning. If the objection to figurative analogies is (as it usually is) that they involve a dissimilar order of events or objects, we would reply that all comparisons — figurative or literal — involve some dissimilarity, and that the important question to be asked is whether or not the dissimilarities are significant. If the principle involved is the same in both instances being compared, why should we not be able to reason from one to the other? It appears to us that the process of testing an analogy must be the same whether the comparison be between horses and leaders, streams and national crises, Scandinavia and the United States, or liquor consumption and racial discrimination — namely, are the two cases sufficiently alike in significant respects for us to conclude that what holds good for one may hold good for the other?

Induction and deduction.

Reasoning by analogy is closely related to reasoning by generalization. Indeed, it is simply an extension of it. For if we examine carefully the logic of an analogy we will find that essentially two steps are involved. First, a generalization is made — although not explicitly stated. For example, we observe that socialized medicine has worked well in Scandinavia and derive from this the general principle that socialized medicine works well. Second, we apply that principle to another concrete situation, the United States, and conclude that socialized medicine will work well here too. In the first step, we have engaged in what is known as an *inductive* process of thinking — that is, reasoning from the particular to the general. In the second step, we have employed *deductive* reasoning — that is, applying a general principle or premise to a particular case. In everyday discussion, however, one does not usually verbalize this entire chain of logic. When we use analogies we jump directly from one case to the other, implying rather than expressing the general principle that lies between the two. Thus, when one argues against fair employment practices legislation or open occupancy ordinances by comparing them to the prohibition of liquor one is really saying the following: (a) The Eighteenth Amendment did not work and had to be repealed, therefore, (b) prohibitive legislation is ineffective in matters of this sort, therefore, (c) it will not work with regard to racial discrimination.

The deductive process is employed in other forms of reasoning in addition to analogies. Whenever a general principle is used as a major premise, and is applied to specific cases, deduction has taken place. This is sometimes called "formal" logic, and the classic example runs as follows:

All men are mortal.
Socrates is a man.
Therefore Socrates is mortal.

We do not propose to delve here into the technicalities of formal logic, such as the various moods of the syllogism, which are explained at length in textbooks on argumentation and logic. It is our impression that errors of deduction are not common in group discussion, and that when they occur they are rather quickly detected by others, since they violate one's common sense. The most troublesome errors of reasoning appear to lie within the inductive realm, for it is there that new knowledge is being created.[4] Once a theory, law, principle, or hypothesis has been reliably established, it is relatively easy to apply it. Given that all men are mortal, it requires no stroke of genius to deduce that Socrates, a man, is therefore mortal. As one authority has said:

> The value of deduction is grounded in its emptiness. For the very reason that deduction does not add anything to the premises, it may always be applied without a risk of leading to failure. . . . It is the logical function of deduction to transfer truth from given statements to other statements — but that is all it can do.[5]

The concept of relationships

In addition to the element of probability, reasoning processes have a second basic characteristic. All reasoning is an attempt to establish relationships Induction, as we have seen, pulls together a number of isolated events in an effort to discover common threads or principles. Deduction applies these principles to specific instances. In both cases, the demonstration of relationships is involved.

We have also seen that the amount of confidence one can place in an inference is dependent upon its *degree* of probability. Therefore men are usually eager to establish theories or predictions which have a high probability of truth. One way of doing this is to seek and find *causal* relationships, for if we know the cause of something we are in a better position to make valid interpretations of past events and reliable predictions of future events. The study of human psychology, for example, is based upon the assumption that "all human behavior is caused"; and efforts are constantly being made in this field to discover laws or principles which will explain why people behave as they do under various circumstances. Likewise economists try to find out the causes of inflation, and diplomats the causes of war, so that when they express opinions on these subjects they may have some confidence that what they say will prove to be true. If there were no such thing as "cause"

[4] The preceding two assertions are generalizations which the writers regard as hypotheses that need further testing.

[5] Hans Reichenbach, *The Rise of Scientific Philosophy* (University of California Press, 1951), pp. 37–38.

or "causes" — that is to say, if one thing did not predictably lead to another — there could be no process of reasoning or inferring. Reasoning depends upon there being a certain degree of consistency or lawfulness in the universe. If everything were completely chaotic, we could find no stable relationships, make no assumptions — in short, do no reasoning. The fact that we are often able to predict the behavior of people or physical objects (e.g., If I telephone my girl she will be pleased; if I turn the ignition key my car will start) makes it possible for us to act thoughtfully rather than irrationally.

If it can be established, as some claim, that the violence and immorality portrayed in "comic" books and other literature of ill repute is causally related to juvenile delinquency, we would have good reason to attempt to control the distribution and sale of this kind of material. But such a causal relationship has by no means been conclusively demonstrated. In fact, some studies even suggest that the readers of such trash are less likely than others to engage in actual immoral *behavior,* having satisfied their impulses through the act of reading. At best we can only conclude that this is a question which needs further study before valid inferences can be made. The same can be said for the question of the relationship between religion and crime. Although it is often asserted that there is a causal relationship between lack of religious faith and acts of criminality, no actual studies that we know of have demonstrated any such connection. Likewise, many people assume that we dare not abolish capital punishment because it acts as a deterrent to crime. Yet statistics reveal that the crime rate is no higher in nations or states which have abolished the death penalty than in those which have retained it. Apparently a causal relationship has been assumed to exist which, in fact, may not. These three illustrations should serve as warnings to us of one of the possible pitfalls of causal reasoning — that is, falsely assuming the presence of a relationship which in reality may not exist.

There are other considerations, too, which should lead us to some modesty in our attempts to find and assert causal relationships. In the first place, the universe is not as perfectly "lawful" as is sometimes assumed. Modern science has come to accept the validity of Heisenberg's Principle of Uncertainty which holds that nothing in the realm of matter and energy is completely predictable. Some degree of indeterminacy, or chaos, is present in all things of this world. Therefore, although we may make generalizations and predictions which hold true in a high percentage of instances, we can never be absolutely sure that they will hold true of the next case which comes along.

A second reason for caution is that there usually is no single, simple cause for any event. The behavior of any human being, for example, is the result of many forces which play upon him — his heredity, his family, his living conditions, his friends, his schooling, his financial needs, his religious or ethical values, as well as his impulses of the moment and the environment in which he currently finds himself. To attribute his beliefs or actions to any one of these factors to the exclusion of the others is vastly to oversimplify the picture. Most social problems which are dealt with by discussion groups will be found, upon investigation, to have many causes. An inference which suggests only one should be viewed with suspicion. Thus the historian who tries to explain all historical events in terms of economic causation, or in terms of the personalities of great leaders, or in terms of an inevitable rise and fall of civilizations, needs to be evaluated with some skepticism.

Closely related to this notion of multiple causality, if not simply a different way of stating it, is the increasingly prevalent realization that causal relationships can be discussed at various levels, depending upon one's point of view. Thus, one might say that a Chinese peasant feels hungry because there is a general shortage of food in his country, or because what food there is available is going to people of higher social standing, or because the food he is getting is not sufficiently nutritious, or because the nerve endings in his stomach are sending hunger messages to his brain. The first is an economic analysis, the second a sociological interpretation, the third a biological explanation, and the last a physiological reason. Each one may be quite correct, but each tells only part of the story. If we were discussing this matter we would choose those levels in which we happened to be interested, but we should not forget that there are other possibilities.

Causation versus correlation

Finally, one needs to remain constantly aware of the difference between causal connections and another type of relationship, known as a correlation, in which no causal connection has been demonstrated. Often we find that two things commonly "go together"—that is, there seems to be a correlation between them. It may be red hair and quick temper, Communism and atheism, ice cream sales and auto accidents, or cigarette smoking and lung cancer. Of what value is the discovery of such relationships? If in the past we have found these things consistently appearing together, can we then reason that the next redhead we see will be quick tempered, the next atheist a Communist, and that the next heavy smoker we encounter will die of lung cancer? Our reaction to each of these predictions is likely to depend on how much sense the relationship seems to make to us. This is simply another way of saying that if we have some reason to believe that there *might* be a causal connection between the two things in question we are more willing to trust an inference based on the correlation than if we can see no "reason" why they are necessarily related. No matter how many quick-tempered redheads we have known, our knowledge of human behavior makes us skeptical that the color of one's hair can dictate his temperament. On the other hand, it is quite easy to believe that there might be something about a cigarette or cigarette smoke that could cause lung cancer. Furthermore, the correlation between heavy smoking and lung cancer, at least among men, has overwhelming statistical support, whereas the red-hair–quick-temper relationship is based upon random, and probably selective observation. That is, we tend to notice the redheads who are hot tempered and overlook those who are not.

But even with as much statistical data as we have, there is still objection made by some authorities to the logic of the cigarette smoking–lung cancer argument. It is pointed out that just because two things go together and the correlation *seems* to make sense does not mean that they necessarily have any direct causal relationship. It has been suggested, for example, that there may be a certain type of personality, or a certain kind of psychological tension, which creates susceptibility or proneness to both heavy smoking and lung cancer. There is no attempt made by these authorities to deny the consistency of the correlation between smoking and cancer, but rather to propose that both factors are a result of some third cause, and that the first two do not necessarily lead to one another. Similarly, the parallel rise in ice cream sales and automobile accidents can be attributed to the onset of warm weather, and thus these phenomena have nothing *directly* to do with each other.

Likewise, since we know that there are many atheists who are not Communists, we would guess that the relationship between them is not a directly causal one, even though we may not be able to explain it.

Does this mean, then, that correlations in which no causal connection can be found are useless as a basis for inference-making? Not necessarily. If, for instance, one were in the ice cream manufacturing business and knew that the sale of his product were consistently related, over the years, to the number of automobile accidents, but did not know the causative factor — namely, the weather — would it not be better for him to guide his production schedule by the National Safety Council's predictions on automobile accidents rather than to rely on pure guesswork? To be sure, if he knew that the weather were the causative agent, and could follow the Weather Bureau's predictions, this would be a more direct and reliable method. But frequently we do not know causal relationships. We do not understand completely how or why certain medical cures work. All we know is that they do work, and surely this knowledge is better than none. Even granting that it may ultimately be found that cigarette smoking is not the cause of lung cancer, the consistency of correlation is so impressive that it cannot be brushed off lightly. Until we do know more, a reasonable man who values his life will think twice before opening his second pack of cigarettes. To those who maintain that we may make mistakes if we operate on the basis of simple correlations we would answer that *no* reasoning, even where causality has been shown, is infallible. It is always a question of "how probable is this?" Naturally, the degree of probability is greater if we know, or have reason to believe that a direct causal connection is present. But lacking this knowledge, we accept the next best thing. Otherwise we must abandon reason altogether and fall back on intuition or authority.

Common Errors in Reasoning

In the course of examining the nature of reasoning processes we have alluded to a number of ways in which flaws in thinking can occur. It might be well at this point to review the most common of these fallacies, as they arise in group discussions, so that we may be on our guard against them.

Confusion of fact and inference

The most basic error in reasoning that one can commit is not to recognize that one is engaged in an inference-making process, but rather to regard opinions, judgments, and predictions as though they were statements of fact. Trouble arises here because the statement is endowed with a greater degree of certainty than it deserves. The element of probability is overlooked. Hence, if the President of the United States assures us that our defenses are adequate to meet any military threat from abroad, and if we fail to recognize that such an assertion, by its very nature, is an opinion rather than a fact, we may be led to place more confidence in it than we should. It is quite possible that his opinion may be correct. But we can never be certain.

Faulty generalizations

We have seen that there are several reasons why a generalization may be invalid. First, it may be based on too few examples. We cannot very well conclude, from sampling the opinions of a handful of Europeans, that the majority of them do not appreciate the economic aid we have sent them. Second, a generalization may be based on an unrepresentative or atypical sample. The science of psychology, for instance, has been criticized for deriving its general principles either from experimentation with college sophomores or from clinical observations of emotionally disturbed patients. Third, there may be a failure to see or to take into account specific instances which contradict the generalization, hence leading to what we call stereotyping. For example, it cannot be assumed that most labor unions are corrupt. There are too many cases to the contrary. Finally, one might forget that the world is in a constant state of change, and that a generalization which holds true today may no longer apply tomorrow. It can hardly be disputed that, as of today, most Americans look with disfavor upon intermarriage between members of the white and Negro races. We cannot assume, however, that this will always be so.

Faulty analogies

A comparison may be fallacious if there are significant differences between the phenomena being compared. Inasmuch as no two situations are exactly alike, analogies are tricky, and there is always a chance that the difference may be one that "makes a difference." The best we can do is examine the argument in order to satisfy ourselves that the people, objects, events, or phenomena being compared are sufficiently comparable that what is true of one is likely to be true of the other. Because prohibition failed it does not necessarily follow that antidiscrimination legislation will not work. The first was an attempt to control a behavior which many people were not convinced was undesirable. The second is an attempt to control behavior which most people, even though they practice it, will admit is rationally indefensible.

Non sequiturs

Non sequitur is the Latin expression for "it does not follow." As we have seen, it does not necessarily follow that if one is religious he will not commit antisocial acts; that if a child reads obscene literature this will contribute to his becoming a sexual pervert; or that capital punishment is a deterrent to criminals. Each of these arguments is an illustration of an alleged causal relationship which, in actuality, has not been proven to exist.

Oversimplification

Another common error in causal reasoning is to attribute to one source what in reality has sprung from many roots, or may be interpreted at many different levels. It is too easy to blame all the world's problems on the subversive influence of Communism, or to explain the rising tide of juvenile delinquency with the simple assertion that there is a lack of discipline in the home.

Confusing causation and correlation

The popular label for this kind of fallacy is "guilt by association." Just because a relationship has been observed between two phenomena, or because two people "go around together," does not mean that there is any necessary connection between them. There may be, but we should be most cautious in making any assumptions without sufficient investigation of the meaning of the relationship. An even more subtle form of this error might be termed "credit by association." Some newspapers seem to feel they are doing minority groups a service by playing up the good deeds of individual members of those groups and emphasizing the fact that these fine citizens are Negroes or Puerto Ricans or Nisei. Logically there is no more reason to conclude from such stories that the majority of individuals in those groups are upstanding citizens than there is to conclude that the majority are criminals because of the crimes of a few.

Other Logical Errors

There are a number of other errors of thinking which commonly occur in discussion that are not so much fallacies within the reasoning itself as they are perversions of the total process. We would like to remind the reader of a few of these.

Extending an argument

Occasionally one finds an otherwise entirely reasonable argument misused because it is pushed too far. For example, it is quite logical to assume that ever-increasing opportunities for contact between racial groups will lead to a narrowing of the cultural gap between them and perhaps eventually to a certain amount of intermarriage. But to use this as a basis for opposing school desegregation, on the grounds that integration will somehow force a sudden upsurge of undesirable and unwanted intermarriage upon us, is to carry the chain of logic to a ridiculous extreme. This is sometimes called *reductio ad absurdum* (reduction to the absurd).

Another illustration of this perversion of good reasoning is found in the concept of "creeping socialism." Here it is argued that if we socialize medicine, or public utilities, or any other single facet of our economy, we will open the door to a flood of further socialistic measures. Some textbooks call this the "slim entering wedge" type of argument. "Give a person a finger and he will take a whole hand." The fallacy in this type of thinking is evident when we note that the United States has for years had a "socialized" postal system, a "socialized" public school system, innumerable "socialized" local transportation, water, and electric companies, and has still retained a free economy.

This is not to say that it is *always* invalid to extend an argument.

There are circumstances in which a person who is given a finger *may* take a whole hand. There might be some merit to the notion that if we legalize euthanasia for certain kinds of incurable diseases pressure may build up to extend this policy to other areas of life—such as physically defective children or imbeciles and idiots. Once the principle that medicine should devote itself exclusively to the prolongation of life is breached, other invasions may be easier to make. This does not excuse us, however, from examining the proposal in question on its own merits. The possible extensions of it, while they may be matters we ought to consider, should not be overplayed.

Arguing ad hominem

Frequently members of a discussion group will approach a particular opinion or argument by attacking the motives of the speaker rather than by examining the logic of his position. Although a questioning of the personal qualifications of the author of an opinion is one of the legitimate ways of determining his competence as an authority, there is no need to resort to this kind of test if we have the necessary information to study and evaluate his *reasoning* processes. Often, questioning a man's motives is simply a convenient way of avoiding the task of dealing with his logic. If we can label the advocates of a particular social reform as "radicals" or "do-gooders" or its opponents as "reactionaries" or "selfish interests" we can discount what they have to say without facing up to the merit or lack of it inherent in their arguments. This kind of fallacy has been recognized for centuries, and the Latin phrase *ad hominem* (against the man) has been used to describe it.

As in the case of extending an argument, the questioning of personal motives is not *always* entirely irrelevant. Knowing the personal reasons for a man's viewpoints, or the psychological causes for his interest in a topic, may give us clues to possible biases in his thinking. But again, this does not exempt us from evaluating the merit of his views. There has been considerable discussion recently regarding the legitimacy of taking into account a man's membership in the Catholic church in evaluating him for the presidency of the United States. Is doing so committing the fallacy of *ad hominem?* This depends on why and how it is done. There are certain public questions, such as the dissemination of birth control information, movie censorship, and public aid to parochial schools, on which it is possible that being a Catholic might influence one's thinking. To inquire as to a Catholic presidential nominee's views on these subjects is no more erroneous than to ask a Christian Scientist how he would feel about public health matters, a Southerner for his opinions on the race problem, or a millionaire about his attitude toward the graduated income tax. The only mistake would be to assume that just because a man belongs to one of these groups, his logic will necessarily be unduly affected. Such a fallacy is not only arguing *ad hominem*, but is also an example of guilt by association.

Wishful thinking

Occasionally one encounters a chain of reasoning in discussion which, from a logical point of view, appears to be impeccable. The only trouble is that the proponent of the view has carefully developed this airtight logical scheme *after* having already made up his mind about the conclusion. In other words, the conclusion did not arise out of the reasoning, but the reasoning was engineered to fit a preconceived conclusion. This is sometimes called rationalization, and is called into play when an individual has a strong emotional need to believe something but also feels some obligation to give it logical support. It is amazing, for example, to observe the great lengths to which some theologians will go to prove rationally that there is a God. More often than not this belief is one they actually accept on faith, and the logic has come after the fact. We do not mean to ridicule people who make an honest effort to think through their beliefs in order to test their logical validity. We would simply caution people to be skeptical of those whose aim is persuasion rather than inquiry.

Avoiding an issue

There are two rather common methods by which members of a discussion group may avoid an issue altogether. The first we call the "irrelevant counterattack" or the "you're another" approach. The Southerner who, instead of answering the logical arguments presented against racial segregation, retorts by reminding the Northerner that he too practices discrimination is employing this technique. It may be quite true that the North, in its own way, has as many problems and shortcomings as the South, but this is no answer to the question of discrimination *in the South.*

The second method of avoiding an issue is the "appeal to irrelevant emotions." Promoting an idea because "everyone is doing it" (the band-wagon technique) or attacking it by pinning an unfavorable label on it ("the Commies are behind this") are just a few illustrations of this means of argument. They have nothing to do with the validity of the idea itself.

There may be other fallacies in thinking which we have not discussed here. We have attempted to point out only some which strike us as particularly troublesome and which discussion groups need to guard against.

In summary, an astonishing amount of what we believe is based upon the opinions of others. Whether these others be recognized authorities or friends, we tend to rely upon them if we have confidence in their judgment on the matter under consideration. There are some people who feel that we should practically never rely upon the opinions of others, but should figure most things out for ourselves. There are others who are quite uncritical about the degree to which they accept the authority of alleged experts. The pressures of time and lack of training push many of us into this latter position. So do many experts themselves who feel that the "masses" are too immature to make their own judgments. It is our belief that there are not many problems with which people of average intelligence, given access to the facts, cannot cope if they have the aid and advice of experts. In other words, we do not believe either in the unqualified acceptance or rejection of authoritative opinion, but rather in its intelligent and critical usage.

When we are doubtful about the merits of an authority's opinion, or when the experts are in conflict, there are a number of ways in which we can evaluate them. What are the expert's personal qualifications in his field? Is he intelligent, experienced, well-trained? Is he in a position to know the facts upon which to base an opinion? Is he relatively free from bias? Does the particular opinion given appear to be consistent with his general views?

Whether dealing with expert opinion, or with the opinions of those about us, we can also examine the validity of the reasoning process itself. We have found that all reasoning has two basic characteristics. First, it is only probable, never certain. Second, it attempts to establish relationships. We must always remain aware of its fallible nature and seek to ascertain whether the phenomena assertedly related actually have any connection with one another. Some of the most common fallacies found in reasoning are the confusion of fact and inference; faulty generalizations which are based on insufficient or atypical examples; faulty analogies in which the matters being compared have significant differences; *non sequiturs;* oversimplification of causes; and the confusion of causation and correlation.

Perversions of the reasoning process may take place in the form of extending an argument, arguing *ad hominem,* rationalization, and avoiding an issue altogether. The members of any discussion group would do well to remain aware of this comment by Herbert Muller:

> I assume that for interpreting the past and choosing a future we must begin with a full acknowledgment of the claims of reason: a humble reason that makes no claim to finality or metaphysical certitude, because such claims cannot be rationally substantiated, and that recognizes its finiteness and fallibility; a proud reason that nevertheless maintains its authority as the final judge of all claims to truth, insisting that its tested knowledge is no less real and reliable because it is not a knowledge of ultimate reality, and that only by a further exercise of reason can its limitations and its fallacies be clearly discerned. . . . The only possible virtue in being a civilized man instead of a barbarian, an ignoramus, or a moron is in being a free, responsible individual with a mind of one's own.[6]

[6] Herbert J. Muller, *The Uses of the Past* (Oxford, 1953), pp. 70–71.

RECOMMENDED READINGS

Chase, Stuart. *Guides to Straight Thinking.* Harper and Brothers, 1956.

Larrabee, Harold A. *Reliable Knowledge.* Houghton Mifflin Company, 1945.

Laski, Harold. "The Limitations of the Expert," *Harper's Magazine* (December, 1930).

Chapter Eight

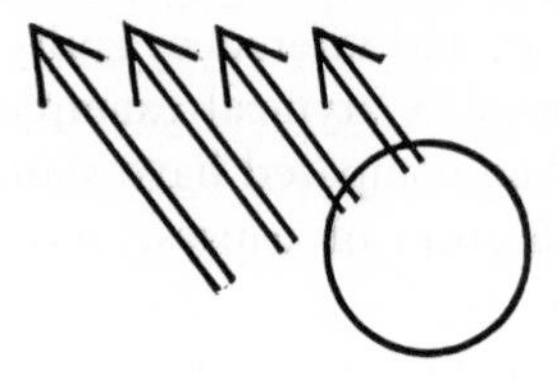

Resolving Differences

The long history of the human race is a study of conflict in ideas. Whether one turns to the subject of politics, religion, economics, or the arts, the record of the past is marked by disagreement, controversy, schism, and revolution. Our books of history are filled very largely with accounts of what men have disputed about, how their disputes arose, and how they were finally settled. The occurrence of disagreement has led one civilization after another to experiement with a variety of methods for coping with controversy.

Suppression of Conflict

In the main, those who have held positions of power have used their influence to suppress divergent points of view. Often the resort has been to physical coercion. The critic has been threatened with death or expulsion from society. "The world," according to Ivor Brown, "has been continually tormented by the people who thought they had the one secret, the one God, the one political party that gives salvation. So they determined to force everybody inside their tabernacle, burning, racking, imprisoning, killing all objectors, closing the mind, denying the use of body and brain." [1]

[1] Ivor Brown, "The Ethics of the Golden Mean," *The Listener* (July 24, 1947).

The innovator, as Ibsen suggests, has been regarded as "an enemy of the people." In psychological brain washing, the twentieth century may have invented a new technique for silencing the skeptic, but the aim and over-all effect is the same as in physical coercion — to stifle those who question the norms of any social system.

Some have found it easier to deal with conflict by circumventing it altogether. So individuals, and at times whole peoples, have fled to some sanctuary where they would be safe from the questions or objections of those of different persuasions. "Members of the faith" have then been able to develop and protect their monolithic systems of political or religious thought safely sealed off from the scrutiny and criticism of others.

The status quo has sometimes been preserved, and conflict suppressed, by manipulating social pressures and using them against the members of a society who do not conform in thought or action. In this way the ends of coercion are accomplished without the bloodshed or destruction that usually accompanies the use of force. Uncongenial points of view are not espoused simply because the goals of every member of the society — whether it be family, fraternity, or large-scale corporation — have been brought into perfect alignment. This involves, of course, the wearing away of the individuality of the members of that society, but it is an extremely effective way of throttling controversy before it gets started. The *Brave New World* of Aldous Huxley is not a piece of science fiction so much as it is a biting commentary on trends in our own society leading toward the elimination of human individuality. If uniformly conditioned, as were Huxley's test tube babies, humans would not be motivated to want dissimilar things or to express discordant opinions.

In short, "the overwhelming mass of mankind in time and space," in the words of Adlai Stevenson, "have believed in a fixed social order, guided by those in authority which individual men and women are expected not to criticize but to accept." [2]

Sources of Conflict

Those who regard controversy as an unnecessary irritant in what could be an entirely tranquil and serene existence make a false

[2] Adlai Stevenson, "Party of the Second Part," *Harper's Magazine* (February, 1956), p. 32.

assumption about its role in the growth of an individual or a society. One is impressed in reading history with the fact that our periods of greatest social upheaval have often turned out to be our periods of greatest social progress. The crisis in Little Rock over school desegregation seems terrible in some of its repercussions but, as Harry Belafonte pointed out, "There's something wonderful about it, too. You can't view Little Rock as anything but a sign of progress." Discord seems to signal the approach of change, and struggle always accompanies social, as well as personal, growth. Despite all efforts to suppress it, controversy may prove to be not only an ineradicable condition of human existence, but an exceedingly desirable and enriching one as well.

Differences of opinion, as Madison argued in *The Federalist,* spring from human diversity, and this cannot be eliminated except by destroying the freedom which makes individuality possible. Persons differ in temperament, in religious affiliation, in social experience, in modes of perception, in intelligence, in educational background, in the assumptions they live by, in their choices of humane or material values, and these differences manifest themselves in their approach to anything from love-making to national defense. What we call "conditioning" — our experiences as a member of a particular family circle, our successes and failures in school or business, our habits of reading and thought — shapes the personality we form and the values to which we become committed. True, within a given group or society, there tends to be some agreement on common values, but there is often a substantial difference in the intensity and depth of these convictions. It is not very difficult to imagine how dissimilar backgrounds will lead a steel worker and an executive in the same company to bring conflicting motives and perceptions to the bargaining table. In *Man's Emerging Mind,* N. J. Berrill points out that "Individualism is a greater attribute of the human species than of any other kind of living organism and much of the hate so rampant in human relations stems from this essential diversity and our failure to accept and understand it." [3]

Furthermore, we question whether most of us would want to be rid of conflict. Some might be willing to trade places with the ants and the bees, but that is a high price to pay for peace and

[3] N. J. Berrill, *Man's Emerging Mind* (Fawcett World Library, 1957), p. 194.

harmony. Without variety and contrast life would lose most of its color and spice. Each person with whom we associate confronts us with an opportunity to deepen and enlarge our own awareness of life. To live in a world where everyone is a carbon copy of everyone else is a discouraging fate. Difference, however, is not only of direct personal advantage. Its benefits spread throughout society and contribute to what we call human advancement. As long as disagreement does not culminate in violence, it can be used to improve society.

> It is wretched advice that the healthy system is one in which the individual feels no conflict. Every great advance has come about, and always will, because someone was frustrated by the status quo, because someone exercised skepticism, the questioning, and the kind of curiosity which, to borrow a phrase, blows the lid off everything.[4]

On some occasions we may be satisfied to write off our differences, after exchanging points of view, by "agreeing to disagree." It may be enjoyable and enlightening for a Protestant and Jew to discuss their religious differences, but neither feels forced to sacrifice his own theology in order to reach a common conclusion. A devotee of jazz and a student of classical music can learn much in the course of discussing their private musical passions, but neither feels a need to start a movement to exterminate the other. However, even the right to disagree can be abused by people when they use it as a defense against new courses of action. Mortimer Adler was thinking of its abuse in the classroom when he wrote:

> But the trouble is that many people regard disagreement as unrelated to either teaching or being taught. They think that everything is just a matter of opinion. I have mine. You have yours. Our right to our opinion is as inviolable as our right to private property. On such a view communication cannot be profitable if the profit to be gained is an increase in knowledge. Conversation is hardly better than a ping-pong game of opposed opinions, a game in which no one keeps score, no one wins, and everyone is satisfied because he ends up holding the same opinions he started with.[5]

"Agreeing to disagree" is not always possible. Where we must act as a society — whether in factory, home, or United Nations —

[4] William H. Whyte, Jr., "The New Illiteracy," *Saturday Review* (November 21, 1953), p. 35.

[5] Mortimer Adler, *How To Read a Book* (Simon & Schuster, 1940), p. 248.

we *must* find ways of ameliorating the differences so that we can combine our efforts in accomplishing common purposes. Too often people use their right to have an opinion as a protective shield to ward off criticism from others and to escape from the responsibility of coming to decisions.

Fortunate or not, each of us cannot do as he pleases about national defense. Labor and management cannot go their separate ways. And while we may differ about theology, we cannot "agree to disagree" when it comes to passing laws about censorship, divorce, capital punishment, or the distribution of information on birth control. Those who hold different points of view are often forced by social circumstances to explore, to negotiate, to resolve their conflicting demands so that society is not stalled on dead center.

Alternatives to Coercion

The extent and seriousness of conflict in our time has, if anything, increased. Partly this is the result of the breaking down of external restraints imposed by authoritarian systems of political domination, and partly it has come about because of the gradual freeing of men's minds from the internal barriers of ignorance, suspicion, and belief in magic. In autocratic systems, as we saw earlier, conflict is simply outlawed: to differ is to die. While coercion, through physical or psychological forms of torture, is still used, modern societies have discovered a number of alternatives to banishment or incarceration. The emergence of popular governments has led to the formation of legislative assemblies, courts of justice, international tribunals, regulatory boards and commissions. Each of these provides a forum for the peaceful settlement of disputes through arbitrator, judge, jury, or ballot box. There is little question but that these constitute a vast improvement over earlier methods and have done much to protect our right to hold different opinions.

The substitution of the ballot box for the firing squad has brought with it many advantages. Advocates of different policies now defend their causes in public, thus informing those who must ultimately decide the fate of society. Competition between persons of different convictions is stimulating and likely to bring about a more penetrating analysis of a problem. Public forums also furnish an outlet for the airing of grievances which if bottled up might become violent and destructive in character. Most important of all, legislative and judicial processes make it possible for societies to revamp their institutions peaceably and thus keep pace with changing environmental conditions.

As was found earlier, however, these methods have their limitations. Disputes conducted under the rules of courts, legislative bodies, and arbitration boards limit participation in policy making to the official representatives of the conflicting groups. Not all persons who have an interest in the issue or who have relevant knowledge contribute to the final solution. The conditions of debate, following parliamentary rules, force controversy into a partisan mold where people must commit themselves to either attack or defend the proposal under consideration. Thus, differences in point of view are exaggerated and it becomes difficult to change positions. The ballot box forces a choice between two mutually exclusive solutions — either a motion passes or it fails — and this weakens the position of moderates. Because battle lines are so sharply defined more energy may be spent in defending foregone conclusions than in creating new solutions.

Finally, and most important of all, the decision rests on a quantitative rather than a qualitative basis — the number of votes that can be marshaled by either side. A decision means that a powerful majority has brought a minority to its knees, or that a compromise between competing factions has been arranged. Settling disputes through voting does permit a group to act (and this is often important), but it does not really resolve the differences nor change people's minds about the nature of the problem. A vote seldom produces greater unity of thought or feeling within a group. Often the defeated members of an organization work, thereafter, not to execute the policy, but to bring about a realignment in the balance of power so that the matter can be brought up again and the decision changed. A compromise may be nothing more than an uneasy truce with the losing side working, consciously or unconsciously, to sabotage the decision and vindicate itself.

Discussion and Conflict

Discussion represents a relatively new method for dealing with controversy. "Discussion at its best," according to Emory Bogardus, "is the highest form of conflict." Insofar as it is conducted successfully, it has many advantages.

For one thing, discussion draws upon and uses the total resources of a group or organization. Anyone with vital information or a worthwhile idea may bring it before the group for consideration. Participation is not restricted to "recognized delegates," "counsel for the prosecution or defense," or "official representatives"; contributions are invited from anyone who is vitally affected by the problem or seriously concerned about the outcome.

The permissiveness that characterizes a healthy discussion encourages independent thought. People need not hold back their opinions, as they might under the competitive atmosphere of debate, because what they are going to say reverses a position taken earlier. Nor need they be afraid to express views because they happen to be unpopular or incompletely worked out. There is no need to carefully calculate the phrasing of ideas so as to manipulate others in order to win a point in a verbal boxing match.

Also the conditions of discussion encourage flexibility rather than rigidity in viewpoint. Participants are free to change their minds as ideas are suggested, scrutinized, and found worthy or wanting. The aim is to create a common solution to a problem rather than to conquer an opponent.

> I do not go to a committee meeting merely to give my own ideas. If that were all, I might write my fellow-members a letter. But neither do I go to learn other people's ideas. If that were all, I might ask each to write me a letter. I go to a committee meeting in order that all together we may create a group idea, an idea which will be better than any one of our ideas alone, moreover which will be better than all our ideas added together. For this group idea will not be produced by any process of addition, but by the interpenetration of us all.[6]

Integration — the combining of each person's ideas in a group idea — is the aim of discussion. The final decision should reflect, insofar as it is possible to do so, the facts, insights, and attitudes of all members of the group. This, according to Mary Follett, is the essence of democracy.

> The aim of democracy should be integrating-desires. I have said that truth emerges from difference. In the ballot-box there is no confronting of difference, hence no possibility of integrating, hence no creating; self government is a creative process and nothing else. Thus the suggestion box of the modern factory is not a democratic device al-

[6] Mary Follett, *The New State* (Longmans, 1926), p. 24.

> though often so-called. Nor is a factory democratically organized when questions are put formally to a committee of workmen and a Yes or No vote taken. Democracy does not register various opinions; it is an attempt to create unity.[7]

If integration can be achieved, the decision will be wiser because it embodies the combined intelligence of the whole group, and will be more lasting because it will not be sabotaged by disappointed or defeated members of an organization.

This is not to imply that discussion is a panacea or cure-all. It is a different method of dealing with conflict, and it has unique characteristics that offset some of the limitations of other methods of decision-making. But it also has drawbacks. There is the problem of maintaining a permissive atmosphere for the exchange of opinions. More serious still is the danger of giving only superficial consideration to issues because of the lack of stimulation, or in order to preserve pleasant interpersonal relationships. Sometimes the desires of persons who disagree will turn out to be actually antagonistic and competing ones which cannot be integrated. Finally, great skill in analysis and communication are required to attain consensus. Ultimately, of course, the processes of discussion may have to yield to the method of voting, of compromise, or of arbitration. But even these may be more effectively employed to resolve differences when the points at issue have first been explored in a free and unrestricted way.

Attitudes Toward Conflict

While discussion *may* provide a more constructive setting for the voicing of differences, while it *may* create a situation in which people need not be so defensive about their ideas, and while it *may* lead to decisions incorporating different views of the problem, whether discussion actually does these things or not depends, in large part, upon the attitudes that members of a group hold toward the idea of disagreeing itself. Some so-called discussions differ from debates or trials only in the fact that the chairs are arranged in a circle.

To use conflict constructively — that is for mutual rather than private advantage — requires skill, to be sure. But most important is a healthy respect for the right of people to disagree. Nothing is

[7] Follett, *Creative Experience*, p. 209.

gained from placing conflicts in the context of discussion if group members continue to regard disagreement as something unpleasant, unfortunate, embarrassing — or an opportunity for winning dialectical battles. To quote Follett again: "Unity, not uniformity, must be our aim. We attain unity only through variety. Differences must be integrated, not annihilated, nor absorbed. . . . As long as we think of difference as that which divides us, we shall dislike it; when we think of it as that which unites us we shall cherish it."[8] This is very close to the sentiment expressed by Antoine de Saint-Exupéry, the French aviator and writer, when he said of his reconnaisance group in World War II, "When we of Group 2–33 argue of an evening, our arguments do not strain our fraternity, they re-enforce it. For no man seeks to hear his own echo, or to find his reflection in the glass."[9]

Committee members who are unaware of the value of disagreement, or who have no idea of how to deal with conflict, may become upset at the prospect of an argument. In their distress over not knowing what to do, they may act (without being fully aware of their motive) to stifle or choke off controversy before it can be studied by the group. The attempt to suppress arguments in discussion is expressed in many ways — in verbal appeals for unanimity; in pleas for speedy, even if superficial, decisions; in premature requests to submit the matter to a vote.

Or discussants may side-step issues about which people feel strongly or try to postpone consideration of "difficult" questions. The desire to maintain an atmosphere of "sweetness and light" reminds one of the saying that the only sin some people can never forgive in others is a difference of opinion. Indeed one of the most frightening developments of recent years is the practice in social conversation of avoiding talk about religion, politics, or any other really vital human topic because it might lead to argument. When the tie that holds people together in the human community is as fragile as this, no knowledge of techniques for resolving conflict will compensate for it.

A group is also "sick" when its members exert pressures on everyone to conform to a single view of the problem. Differences that are suppressed, glossed over, or ignored not only debase our relations

[8] Follett, *The New State*, p. 40.

[9] Antoine de Saint-Exupéry, *Airman's Odyssey* (Reynal & Hitchcock, 1942), p. 420.

with each other but threaten the foundation of survival in a free society. In a nation committed to freedom of inquiry and freedom of communication we would hold, along with Adlai Stevenson, that "it is better to discuss a question without settling it than to settle a question without discussing it."

Improvement in our techniques for handling controversy must begin with a mutual respect for the diverse experiences, points of view, and personal criteria which committee members bring to any meeting. Conflict is the essence, the heart, of any problem-solving method, and participants in discussion will find it much easier to develop constructive ways of dealing with it once they accept disagreement as a normal and desirable feature of group life. Differences can become a springboard to more enlightened decisions — both personal and organizational.

> And throughout our participation in the group process we must be ever on our guard that we do not confuse differences and antagonisms, that diversity does not arouse hostility. Suppose a friend says something with which I do not agree. It may be that instantly I feel antagonistic, feel as if we were on opposite sides, and my emotions are at once tinged with some of the enmity which being on opposite sides usually brings. Our relations become slightly strained, we change the subject as soon as possible, etc. But suppose we were really civilized beings, then we should think: "How interesting this is, this idea has evidently a much larger content than I realized; if my friend and I can unify this material we shall separate with a larger idea than either of us had before." If my friend and I are always trying to find the things upon which we agree, what is the use of our meeting? Because the consciousness of agreement makes us happy? It is a shallow happiness, only felt by people too superficial or too shut-up or too vain to feel that richer joy which comes from having taken part in an act of creation — created a new idea by the uniting of differences.[10]

As committee members begin to sense that conflicting beliefs are a source of strength — that differences can contribute to individual growth and social progress — then the group is likely to create an atmosphere more congenial to a frank and vigorous exchange of opinions. Participants will begin to feel secure in expressing objections, in offering criticism, in arguing their convictions. No one will feel threatened any longer because his views happen to be unusual or unpopular. Coercive behavior, whether expressed overtly in

[10] Follett, *The New State*, pp. 40–41.

hostile acts or indirectly through the manipulation of social pressures, will disappear. Members of the group will know that any opinion they offer will receive calm and thoughtful consideration.

The Creative Use of Conflict

What we seek, in short, is a way of "taming social conflict," of "resolving difference without destroying it." Since the purpose of most committees is to make decisions, group members are obligated to find a way of working out or combining their conflicting views. In order to discover ways of using conflict creatively, we need to examine the different levels at which it arises, the risk of allowing it to persist at these levels, and what participants can do to exploit it for their mutual advantage. Arguments seldom resolve themselves. As one writer noted, "Unless there is a contrary influence, conflict tends to take a line from bad to worse."

Level of assertion

Controversy usually begins with the assertion of conflicting statements of personal preference or belief. "Agricultural price supports are a waste of money." "This is the worst political administration in twenty years." "The schools should return to a classical curriculum." "Capital punishment should be abolished." "Union labor is too powerful." Opinions such as these, when germane to the problem under discussion, deserve to be analyzed and explored.

Why do arguments so frequently start with statements of this type? The answer is quite apparent. They are the easiest and least demanding remarks for people to make. To state a fact one must know and recall something specific about a subject — the percentage of unionized labor, the current level of parity prices, the rate of capital crimes. To justify or explain a belief requires reflection. One has to review his assumptions and examine them critically to state the premises on which his judgment rests. But simply to express what one likes or dislikes requires nothing more than a facile tongue.

Also, it should be noted how often the statements that open a dispute (or an issue within a larger topic) are phrased in abstract language. The global generalizations given above cover such a vast territory that agreement at this level of talk is most unlikely. Certainly there must be something that can be said in behalf of labor unions, capital punishment, or price supports. Someone, therefore, denies the original assertion and the battle lines are drawn.

Upon examination, the difference of opinion may turn out to be nothing more than a semantic problem. If so, then once the opposing members clear up what they mean by their statements the disagreement will dissolve. For example, what one person means by "socialized medicine" may turn out to be a government-supported private insurance program, which is what the opposition favors too. The members of a group who disagree over farm price supports may find that their difference of opinion turns on whether the program is a flexible or fixed one. If this is the case, committee members need only limit their statements, or define their terms, to resolve the difference.

The conflict, however, may be more than simply a verbal one. If so — and the disagreement is genuine — group members are likely to continue at the same level of assertion, repeating their remarks over and over again in the hope of discouraging the opposition. The person who argued for a return to a classical curriculum will state that "The schools must cut out the frills added to the curriculum in the last three decades," or "The schools must get back to subjects that discipline the mind, rather than entertain the student." These statements add virtually nothing but emphasis to the original assertion. And, after several restatements of the same opinion on both sides of the question, members of the group will find themselves in a stalemate. The argument, then, may degenerate into a conflict of personalities. Those who disagree, after running out of ways of repeating their views, may question the integrity or intelligence of those who oppose them. Through insinuation they may imply that other group members know very little about the subject or have not thought about it sufficiently. Someone may suggest, "You ought to visit the schools and see what's *really* going on!" or "Do you *honestly* believe that labor unions control our economy?" or "Where did you *ever* get that idea?" What began as a legitimate and valuable conflict in ideas is now in danger of becoming nothing more than an unnecessary and fruitless clash between people. At this point the group faces not one, but two, problems — how to settle the issue itself and how to re-establish healthy relations among the committee members.

It is particularly disastrous to the progress of a discussion to carry on in the abstract the consideration of agreements or disagreements.

To no two persons in the group will these principles, stated in the abstract, mean the same. Such abstract discussion causes heat when there is disagreement, but throws little light on the issue; and an agreement on general principles often causes confusion because it may prove to be in fact a disagreement. To argue in general whether brotherhood, race equality, respect for personality, democratic participation, industrial democracy are practical and desirable often means that no party to the discussion knows what the other person is talking about. All sorts of fears and defense reactions are aroused because of that which each person reads into the terms.[11]

If, on the other hand, a new dimension can be added before the conflict deteriorates into a clash of personalities it may be possible to explore the disagreement further.

Level of reasoning

One way of moving into such a deadlocked situation is to take the argument to another level of talk. Sydney Smith once commented in observing two housewives screaming at each other over their back fences that they could not agree because they were arguing from different premises! Someone in the group needs to ask those locked in argument to state the *reasons* for believing as they do. In answering this request discussants will be forced, of course, to expose the logic of their position and thus enable other members of the group to understand their position better. Group members who believe in capital punishment may argue, for example, that it is necessary "in order to protect society" or "to set an example for others who may be contemplating the same crime." Those who object to farm subsidies may defend their opinion by showing how federal funds lead to undesirable farm practices.

Several beneficial effects follow from forcing the conflict to this new level. First, it minimizes the chances of the argument becoming personal. When people begin to criticize each other it is usually because they have run out of ammunition on the original issue. Also, by asking the disputing parties to be more precise about the bases for their opinions the original generalizations will be given more specific meaning. As we move from abstract to more concrete levels of talk, agreement becomes more likely. If committee mem-

[11] Harrison Elliott, *The Process of Group Thinking* (Association Press, 1928), p. 57.

bers, in defending their views, resort to quoting authorities, or to explaining the line of reasoning they followed, then the experts cited and the modes of reasoning may be evaluated by applying the tests described in the previous chapter. Group members may, in reviewing the bases of their beliefs, begin to see some merit in each other's arguments. Committee members may find themselves clinging less solidly to the dogmatic statements they made earlier. They may even find that it is possible to combine their various arguments and, thus, integrate them. Forcing the argument to the level of explanation, then, may ward off personal attacks, clarify the locus of the disagreement, encourage the testing of arguments, and lead to a settling of the initial dispute.

If this happens — and it sometimes does — all well and good. The conflict has served its purpose. But it may turn out that consensus is still not achieved and the group finds it has exhausted the usefulness of further talk at this level. Again, without being fully aware of why, group members may begin to berate each other, rather than deal with the issue. They may imply that no really valid objections or arguments have been given, or that the explanations were trivial and inconsequential. Before long, members of the group are hastening toward a premature vote on the issue, or are charging each other with being ill-informed or incompetent. This happens, we might add, not so much because people are irrational but because, in their exasperation with themselves, they cannot find a more constructive way of handling their argument.

Level of evidence

If the dispute has not been settled at the second level and the lines of reasoning of the participants have been fully explored, then the conflict should be moved to still another level, the level of evidence. When people disagree over whether or not capital punishment works as a deterrent to crime, figures should be studied on the comparative crime rates in states which have and do not have the death sentence to ascertain which conclusion is supported by the evidence. Arguments over the abuse of labor power or the extent of science training in the schools can be settled, in many instances, by a little fact-finding.

At this level we again increase our chances of coming to an

agreement. For one thing, it is difficult to find facts which absolutely contradict each other. Where inconsistent sets of figures are reported, the committee can make use of the tests described in Chapter 6 to determine which of the pieces of evidence seems the more trustworthy. Also, the facts available to the group may invalidate some of the conflicting opinions and help in this way to reduce the scope of the controversy still further. Finally, the closer we get to reality, through evidence, the more likely we are to form similar conclusions about it. If the group can agree on the facts and carefully follow through on the interpretation of them, some, if not all, of the opinions may be integrated.

If the facts do not decide the entire matter, however, the group again faces the prospect of the dispute turning into a stalemate, forcing recourse to other methods of settlement.

The level of values

Our conflicting beliefs about labor unions, capital punishment, or race relations are not always a product of having been exposed to different facts. Nor do they always reflect a difference in our ability to draw logical inferences from the facts. If this were the case, all controversies, even the most serious, could be resolved in time. But our convictions often turn, instead, on the assumptions we make about what is "good," "desirable," "proper," "just," and "virtuous." These, we say, are questions of value.

A conflict which rests on a difference in values is the most difficult of all to resolve. Disputes over the cost of government subsidies, the effectiveness of birth control in limiting population, the deterrent effects of capital punishment, usually can be settled by referring to the facts or to the testimony of experts. But what sort of investigation will reveal whether or not farm subsidies are "democratic," contraceptives "moral," or capital punishment "inhuman?"

Some persons believe such questions to be unresolvable. They see no possibility of settling differences between Communist and non-Communist nations as long as their underlying political beliefs are so contradictory. They say it is useless to seek agreement between Protestants and Catholics, Republicans and Democrats, or labor and management because their systems of values are so different.

Committee members, when they discover that their dispute is rooted deeply in an ideological difference, may be tempted to conclude that nothing further can be done about it. After all, isn't everyone entitled to his opinion when it comes to matters of morality and taste? This notion exists in most cultures and is expressed in idioms such as the French "chacun à son gout" (each to his own taste) and the Latin "de gustibus non est disputandum" (there is no disputing tastes). The temptation to give up may be great. However, before group members take the position that their own systems of values are "nobody's business but their own" they would do well to consider carefully the consequences of this move.

Take, for example, the question of racial integration. The argument here may turn finally on whether or not it is "right and proper" for members of different races to mix socially. One person argues for bringing the races together because "my religion teaches it" while another opposes racial assimilation on the grounds that "it is not the way I've been brought up to think." If personal standards of judgment are asserted dogmatically, and other members of a group are not permitted to examine their validity, all further attempts to solve the conflict will be stymied. To claim that one's values are sacred and above criticism by one's contemporaries is tantamount to renouncing rational methods of solving social problems altogether. James Harvey Robinson was concerned with this problem when he wrote:

> The person who justifies himself by saying that he holds certain beliefs, or acts in a certain manner "on principle" and yet refuses to examine the basis and expediency of his principle, introduces into his thinking and conduct an irrational, mystical element similar to that which characterized savage prohibitions. Principles unintelligently urged make a great deal of trouble in the free consideration of social readjustment, for they are frequently as recalcitrant and obscurantist as the primitive taboo, and are really scarcely more than an excuse for refusing to reconsider one's convictions and conduct. The psychological conditions lying back of both taboo and this sort of principle are essentially the same.[12]

When a member of a group takes the position that his values are intuitively given, beyond criticism, and incapable of rational justification, there are several alternatives available — he may personally withdraw from the group, the entire issue can be shelved, a vote can be taken, or a group solution reached through undemocratic processes.

[12] Robinson, *op. cit.*, p. 91.

Another position, and one which we endorse, is that preferences and values — like any other form of thought or talk — can be subjected to critical analysis. As the authors of one of the most provocative of the early writings on reflective thinking point out:

> When two men conflict upon these preferences, there can be but one way of reaching agreement. These preferences must themselves be subjected to elaboration and clarification, until it is made plain that the acceptance of one or the other will bring with it still further good upon which the two disputants can agree.[13]

The "elaboration and clarification" of which these authors speak may be carried out in one of two ways: (1) By ferreting out and testing the theoretical assumptions on which the asserted value rests. (2) By examining the consequences of any belief empirically, through experimentation or experience.

Many of our disagreements about what is good or bad, right or wrong, may be tested, first of all, by investigating the premises on which they rest. What are the assumptions, for instance, that lead one to disapprove of racial integration or support a classical system of education? Are the arguments that support certain value judgments superior or inferior to those that lead to the opposite conclusion?

For example, a great many Americans are firmly convinced of the desirability of freedom of thought and speech. But one does not get far in defending this preference simply by arguing that it is an "inalienable right" protected by the Constitution. While the First Amendment prohibits infringements on freedom of communication, it does not explain *why* this is a necessary or desirable provision in human societies. To test this value judgment (which might be expressed in a discussion involving censorship) one must examine the theoretical basis of the principle. In the writings of John Stuart Mill we will find such a defense. Any limits placed on the exchange of opinions is fundamentally unsound, according to Mill, because it robs the human race of new ideas. Four distinct arguments are given in support of the value of free speech.

> First, if any opinion is compelled to silence, that opinion may, for aught we can certainly know, be true. To deny this is to assume our own infallibility.

[13] Columbia Associates in Philosophy, *Introduction to Reflective Thinking* (Houghton Mifflin, 1923), p. 218.

> Secondly, though the silenced opinion be an error, it may, and very commonly does, contain a portion of truth; and since the general or prevailing opinion on any subject is rarely or never the whole truth, it is only by the collision of adverse opinions that the remainder of the truth has any chance of being supplied.
>
> Thirdly, even if the received opinion be not only true, but the whole truth; unless it is suffered to be, and actually is, vigorously and earnestly contested, it will, by most of those who receive it, be held in the manner of a prejudice, with little comprehension or feeling of its rational grounds. And not only this, but, fourthly, the meaning of the doctrine itself will be in danger of being lost, or enfeebled, and deprived of its vital effect on the character and conduct: the dogma becoming a mere formal profession . . . preventing the growth of any real and heartfelt conviction, from reason or personal experience.[14]

Now that free speech has been given a rationale, the members of a group can evaluate whether or not this value judgment deserves support. In a similar way it is possible to explore critically the value structures of a liberal and conservative in an argument over social welfare measures, of labor and management over right-to-work legislation, of teacher and student in a dispute over course requirements.[15]

In the last analysis, the supreme test of the validity of our values is to be found in experience. Freedom must not only be verbally, or theoretically, defensible, it must prove desirable in the day-to-day lives of men. Another way, therefore, of arbitrating conflicts in values is to apply the criterion of experience. An opinion in favor of American literature is hardly to be taken seriously when based upon complete ignorance of Russian or French literature. A preference for realistic or abstract art assumes much greater weight when it is based on a careful study of both forms of painting.

> It may well happen that men disagree upon the appeal of various goods for lack of experience with them. No one who had never heard a single symphony of Beethoven performed would be accepted as a

[14] John Stuart Mill, *On Liberty* (Henry Regnery Company, n.d.), pp. 65–66.

[15] We would remind the reader that Learning Groups have a great advantage in dealing with conflicts in values because they are not so pressed for time and do not have to reach the sort of negotiable decisions that must be made in Policy-Making or Action Groups.

> competent judge of the respective merits of Beethoven and Irving Berlin. . . . And yet not a day passes when we do not make ourselves some judgment of value upon an equally meagre experience.[16]

This test holds not only for matters of taste, but for practical situations as well. Suppose the members of a PTA, in advising their school board, find themselves divided over the relative merits of traditional and progressive methods of teaching. It turns out that the disagreement rests on the relative weight they assign to the importance of order and discipline in teaching. If an examination of the arguments in favor of the two philosophies does not settle the question, committee members might wisely decide to visit classrooms and see for themselves what it is actually like to learn under each of these conditions. Company officials, in deliberating over a change in methods of decision-making, may find that some board members are more interested in increasing productivity while others regard improvement in morale as equally vital. In this case, those who disagree over whether morale or efficiency is the primary value might visit other plants and observe the consequences of different modes of decision-making. Or better still, they might test their assumptions by experimenting within the departments of their own plant. Data will soon be available which will help to confirm or deny the claims made for various decision-making arrangements. Thus, where a conflict in values cannot be settled by argument, it may be dissolved through resort to experience.

By elaborating and critically examining the values which lie behind our judgments we may be able to reduce the area of disagreement beyond what has been accomplished at other levels. But it is not easy. It takes a great deal of time to isolate the assumptions on which our attitudes are based. And often the motivation is lacking. The careful examination of one's private prejudices also can be very threatening to our egos. Most people do not mind adding to or subtracting from their stock of information on a problem; even a slight shift of opinion here or there does not frighten them. But to undertake to change our values is to modify, in some cases, our whole personality. This requires considerable moral courage as well as an alert and critical mind.

[16] Columbia Associates, *op. cit.*, pp. 240–241.

Group goal

If fundamental differences in reasoning, evidence, or values still exist within a group and consensus has not been achieved, the group faces the serious possibility that its members may now withdraw and give up altogether in trying to resolve their conflict through discussion. A married couple may separate or start divorce proceedings against each other. Two nations may stop negotiating, seek alliances, and begin to increase their military forces. A community may be tempted to use violence to coerce intransigent racial or religious minorities. Labor and management may take their dispute to the courts, or begin a long drawn-out strike.

Before all the constructive potential in conflict is destroyed, and people begin to lose their respect for one another, one final course remains. There is one value — beyond all others — which is usually shared in common by the members of a group. That is the goal that brought them together in the first place. A school administration and faculty confer with each other about their differences because they both stand to gain from improvements in the school system. All elements in a community benefit, in some way, from alleviating sources of friction. In fact, in the absence of some common goal, it is difficult to see why consultation should ever take place. "'Pour se discuter il faut être d'accord.' Only among people of equal intention is reasonable deliberation possible."[17] If, by accident, discussion does occur between people with completely antagonistic goals, it is unlikely that agreement will be reached on any of the outstanding points of difference. Simpson makes this point in distinguishing between what he calls "communal" and "non-communal" conflict.

> In non-communal conflict, there is no sense of common ends between the parties to the conflict, each of whom considers itself as a complete community, and its opponents as contradictors and subverters of its final ends and values. Non-communal conflict results when there is no community of ends between the parties to the conflict, or when these parties believe that no common ends can be discovered so that a compromise may be reached.[18]

[17] Joost A. M. Meerloo, *Conversation and Communication* (International Universities Press, 1952), p. 127.

[18] George Simpson, *Conflict and Community* (T. S. Simpson, 1937), p. 41.

The goal that group members share in common must be deeper or more significant than the points of difference if discussion is to be of any value whatsoever.

Perhaps this is best illustrated in the labor-management field. When the representatives of labor and the members of management sit down to negotiate a new contract both stand to benefit from the meeting or there would be no conference. But in emphasizing their private aims each may forget the one purpose they share in common — that they will both benefit from the continued successful performance of the company and the economy as a whole. Some years ago, in a large automobile company, labor and management found it impossible to settle their differences. The representatives of labor demanded a large increase in pay and insisted that the company books, if they were opened, would demonstrate the justice of their demands. Management, facing the prospect of imminent bankruptcy, refused to open their books or meet the demands of the union. The dispute reached such proportions that both parties issued final ultimatums and broke off negotiations. After a few days, however, recognizing that neither would gain from liquidation of the company, both sides agreed to reopen deliberations and a settlement was quickly reached on all outstanding issues.

The same sort of crisis was evident in the armistice talks between the United Nations and Communist forces in Korea. At the outset of the war there was no possibility of talks even being started because each side felt that victory on the battlefield was easily within its grasp. Once both sides concluded that it was to their advantage (despite a world of ideological differences) to conclude this costly affair, agreements were quickly concluded on a wide variety of particulars.

This higher or larger goal which group members share in common can be used in two ways to increase the probability of settling disagreements in discussion. Emphasizing, from time to time, the mutual benefit that will result from ironing out specific differences may make group members less suspicious of one another, may cause them to work harder at discovering ways of integrating their separate aims, and may lead them to be less inclined to take dogmatic and rigid positions on issues. Furthermore, the existence of this common purpose makes it possible to tie controversies over lesser objectives to the attainment of the larger purpose the group is trying to realize. Each short-range, or mediate goal, can be resolved in terms of how it advances or retards the accomplishment of the common, or end, goal. Lest we become too discouraged over the possibilities of integrating deeply felt and opposing values, we should bear in mind this counsel:

> When all has been said in favor of skepticism, it remains clear that men must act, that some acts are better than others, and that some basis of discrimination must be used. The skeptic is right in maintaining that at some point all our knowledge, of sense-fact, of mathematical truth, of inference, of values, rests upon unproved assumptions. Yet it is obviously the better part of reason to make these assumptions as fundamental as possible, to choose those that appear the least uncertain, and to introduce them only when reflection has reached its limits. . . . Nor is it by any means certain that disagreements are as absolute as the moral skeptic affirms. When men have actually experienced several different goods, there is generally fairly unanimous agreement about them.[19]

The Prospects for Integration

The suggestions we have made concerning the creative exploration of conflict in discussion can be summarized in the diagram below.

Cone of Consensus

Assertion...Assertion
Reasons...Reasons
Evidence..Evidence
Values..............................Values
Group Goal

Conflict, as we pointed out, can begin at any level of talk. No matter at what level the controversy begins it must usually be taken to other levels to be understood and/or resolved. When an argument persists at any one level for a long period of time it is likely to go from bad to worse. Sooner or later, participants will begin to attack each other personally, fall back on verbal stratagems and semantic devices to confuse or mislead, or even manipulate social pressures to force agreement. When this happens, the conflict has been compounded.

[19] Columbia Associates, *op. cit.*, pp. 246–247.

The advantages of exploring a disagreement at these various levels of communication are manifold. Each time we examine a point of view at another level we are likely to understand better our opponent's motives and the logical validity of his position. As we admit the facts and arguments that can be marshaled for a position, we may become less dogmatic and less absolute about our own. Zones of agreement and disagreement can be marked off and clarified.

As each person begins to reflect on his own position and that taken by others, several important things can happen to him. First, he may begin to see the problem in a different light than he did originally. Second, participants may find that some of their convictions are not supported by the facts — that assumptions that seemed sound at the time turned out to be questionable or without any foundation later. Third, in listening to the arguments of others, each person will be exposed to some ideas he had not considered seriously before but which turn out, now, to have considerable merit. Fourthly, participants may, and often do, come into a deeper appreciation of their own *real* desires as a result of explaining themselves to others.[20]

We must not underestimate, however, the obstacles in the way of achieving integration. People change their minds slowly.

> For every individual, a group integration involving a transformation of his interests and values is only possible within the limits prescribed by his established pattern of personality. The complete integration of a confirmed open shop manufacturer and a stanch upholder of trade unionism could only be secured by melting them both down in the crucible of experience and running them into new molds. Such conversion, it is true, is not unknown and is a cause of rejoicing. Most of our social relations, however, must rest on the presumption that the personalities of those we deal with are changing slowly under the impact of experience and contain certain relatively stable aspects. As a result the integration of in-

[20] Josephine Klein in her book *The Study of Groups* (Routledge, 1956), p. 141, summarizes the research in decision-making and makes several observations that seem consistent with the theoretical framework we have advanced: (1) "Decision making involves making proposals and securing agreement." (2) "If all members share a set of norms decisions are held up only by lack of information." (3) "If all members share in decision making but differ in norms, decision making is prolonged and group pressure is exerted to secure uniformity of norms."

> dividuals in a group is possible only to the extent that the limits of flexibility of adjustment coincide. When a well considered and rational conviction falls outside those limits the individual cannot, without a loss of his integrity as a person, submerge his differences or allow it to be changed in accordance with the demands of the occasion. He must remain a dissenter. He can "do no other."[21]

If a careful exploration of the conflicting points of view under discussion does not produce agreement, then, in the interests of action, the members of a group must settle upon an alternative method for handling their dispute; they must put the matter to a vote, delegate authority to outside persons, or resort to other methods.

Formulating Decisions

Once having verbally explored their differences, the next step is to translate this talk into clearly stated decisions.[22] As many committee chairmen well know, it is one thing to get people to make up their minds, but quite another to get them to formulate their decisions in so many words, or accept responsibility for implementing their decisions. Members of a group may lack what Dewey called "intellectual responsibility."

> To be intellectually responsible is to consider the consequences of a projected step; it means to be willing to adopt those consequences when they follow reasonably from any position already taken. In-

[21] Grace Coyle, *Social Process in Organized Groups* (Richard Smith, 1930), p. 214.

[22] We would remind the reader that groups sometimes go through a process of "pseudo problem-solving" in which members rationalize, obscure, or subvert their conflicts in order to achieve a questionable integration. Some of the more familiar of these gambits are:

(1) Prove that the problem is widespread and that experts cannot agree on its cure. (Hence it must be unsolvable.)

(2) Agree upon a set of general principles that are so vague that everyone can interpret them as he wishes. (Yet everyone can carry away the impression of "consensus.")

(3) Pick a scapegoat; find someone to blame. (Criticizing others will divert attention away from deep-seated differences that exist within the group.)

(4) Rationalize the status quo as the safest compromise between extremists on both sides. (Coming to grips with the actual division of opinion is hard and dirty work.)

(5) Decide to appoint a new committee, or better yet, several new committees which will study the problem in detail. (Which is what this committee was set up to do in the first place.)

tellectual responsibility secures integrity; that is to say, consistency and harmony in belief. It is not uncommon to see persons continue to accept beliefs whose logical consequences they refuse to acknowledge. They profess certain beliefs but are unwilling to commit themselves to consequences that flow from them. The result is mental confusion.[23]

There are a number of reasons why people are so reluctant to conclude their discussion with a clearly formulated set of recommendations. The members of a group, for one thing, may not have a clear understanding of their assignment. Uncertainty about the specific authority of the committee may cause them to hold back, in fear of offending someone, from verbalizing their decisions.

Some persons have difficulty, also, in moving from thought into action. An individual may make up his mind, but his nervous system remains unaffected. Psychologists say that decisions have to be "internalized" before people are ready to accept their consequences in actual behavior.

At the moment of final decision-making, some participants may realize, more deeply than before, the seriousness of the action they are proposing. Although convinced of the logical necessity of their conclusion, a group may not be prepared to make the personal sacrifices in time, energy, or money, that the decision entails.

Finally, the members of a committee may be individually reluctant to phrase the decision because it is still vague in their own minds, or because it is difficult to summarize the points covered over a period of weeks or months in words that would be acceptable to everyone. Anyone with experience in discussion should be ready to acknowledge that phrasing decisions requires considerable skill, especially when they involve complicated or delicate issues.

Failure to translate talk into decisions is a familiar point of breakdown in group discussion. But an understanding of the forces that lead to this blockage may help group members to deal with these sources of resistance.

Keeping Records

Groups normally must prepare written reports of their activities. This involves two questions of method to which we shall now turn: (1) Should a group keep a running record of its deliberations?

[23] Dewey, *op. cit.* (1933), p. 32.

(2) Who should be responsible for keeping records and preparing the final recommendations of the committee?

Some argue that there is no reason for keeping records in discussion. If all members are present for the meetings and are reasonably alert, everyone should know what has been covered. Furthermore, record-keeping tends to stifle the informality of the meeting and inhibits participation. While these arguments are convincing in groups of small size who work for short periods of time, and are especially convincing in the case of Casual, Cathartic, and Learning Groups, we feel that there is much more to be said for keeping somewhat careful records in Policy-Making and Action Groups.

A major objection to decision-making through discussion comes from the fact that there is so little to show for hours spent in committee meetings. People feel that discussion is not productive. One reason is that no records are kept which might reveal how much ground has been covered and how many important agreements have actually been hammered out. Members of a committee are inclined to remember only the decision of the moment and to forget all the spade work that led to it. By summarizing the discussion periodically (through reference to the minutes) a member can give the group a psychological lift and keep the participants informed on the issues already settled.

Records also serve as a valuable storehouse of information. When facts introduced early in the discussion are forgotten and needed again, they may be recovered with a minimum of lost time. (We might add, in this connection, that a common mistake is for a group to formulate a solution to a different problem than the one they originally diagnosed simply because they have forgotten the conclusions they formed earlier.)

The importance of record-keeping can be emphasized by noting that many states have laws that require decision-making bodies within legally established corporate organizations to keep accurate records of all decisions. It is vital not only to know what has been decided but to be able to fix responsibility for decisions. In short, the arguments for maintaining records in decision-making groups seem compelling.

Should the group take care of the matter by appointing a secretary or should everyone keep notes on the discussion? This may seem an unnecessarily narrow question to take up in a book of this sort but it should be given more thought than it ordinarily is. We would point out that the naming of a secretary — officially or accidentally — raises some issues that must be faced in assigning any permanent roles in a discussion group.

Naming a single person to take notes on the topics discussed and conclusions reached seems the simplest way of insuring that records are kept. Giving this duty to a specific member will fix responsibility for the job. Everyone else will then be able to concentrate more exclusively on the issues before the group. This is a particularly attractive solution when there is someone in the group with talent for digesting and summarizing the meeting concisely.

On the other hand, to give the secretarial duty to one person is an effective way of sterilizing that person altogether. Anyone who takes the job seriously will not be inclined to contribute information or ideas to the group. An even more serious objection is that in placing this responsibility in the hands of one person, a group may give him more authority than they realize. The person who controls the records in a group has considerable power. There has been many a slip twixt the pen and the lip — both unintentional and deliberate.

The group will be less dependent on the secretary if everyone acts as a participant and recorder. If the group members are in the know, at all times, they can take up the slack immediately when the secretary is absent and they can counteract the influence of anyone who abuses the privilege of keeping minutes. One also wonders if it is expecting too much of committee members to ask that they know what has been covered in their earlier deliberations. True, it may be somewhat distracting. But could this be a healthy distraction? They may do a better job of thinking together if they are forced to keep up to date on past decisions. At the same time, there is no denying that spreading this responsibility may result in no one taking the job very seriously.

Whatever arrangement is made for keeping track of the progress of the group, records seem desirable. And many groups would be amazed at the improvement in their efficiency from merely making this one change in their normal procedure.

The Group Report

The question of who should prepare the final report of Policy-Making and Action Groups raises again some of the issues we have just finished exploring. Usually the parent organization, or the person in authority who appoints a committee, expects to have some sort of detailed recommendations supplied by the group that investigated the problem. This is true not only of national and international boards of experts; it is true of committees in industrial plants, schools, and community organizations.

The demands of efficiency again would indicate that a single member of the group should prepare the final statement — either as a draft which could be edited by other members of the committee, or as a final report to the agency that created the group. This view is particularly valid when nothing but a factual record of the committee's action is needed or when everyone fully trusts the member who is given this responsibility. If the person so appointed has a good grasp of the feeling and thinking of the group and has some talent in phrasing ideas, this course recommends itself.

Yet there are times when the gain in efficiency is offset by other considerations. Then the entire committee should help draft its report. One of these circumstances is when the report has a rhetorical, as well as reportorial, purpose to serve. That is, if the committee recommendations are designed to influence readers, thus making the proper choice of words a critical matter, the report might be more effective if everyone contributes in drafting the final statement. The committee appointed by President Truman to investigate civil liberties is a case in point. Their report, *To Secure These Rights,* had a double purpose — to inform and to convince. In cases of this kind, each member may be able to offer useful suggestions on how his public will react to certain words and phrases. Sometimes it is desirable for each person to write that section of the final report on which he is best informed or in which he is most interested. The benefits from preparing a committee report jointly, however, must be weighed against the time available, the talents, and the interests of group members.

A recent advertising slogan reads, "Friction has some uses but mostly it is freedom from friction this world needs." It is the uses of friction, in the form of intellectual disagreement, that we have considered in this chapter.

Down through history people have attempted, in one way or another, to suppress, destroy, and dispel conflict. Despite all attempts, it appears to be an inescapable ingredient of human experience. Conflict arises out of the fact of human individuality which, in turn, has its source in political and intellectual freedom.

Controversy seems desirable both from a personal and a social point of view. But its desirability depends on whether or not it serves constructive or destructive ends. In discussion we find a promising technique for exploiting differences in attitude, conviction, and values. Improvement in our techniques for resolving conflict, however, hinges upon the question of attitude. Until people stop regarding their disagreements as something embarrassing or immoral and begin to see them as invigorating and enriching, there is little point in studying methods of resolving controversy. Once this change in attitude occurs, however, the question of approach becomes critical.

Disagreement among the members of a discussion group can be profitably explored — and often resolved — by examining the conflict, in turn, at the level of assertion, reasoning, evidence, and value. The "Cone of Consensus" diagrams a method whereby a group may study its conflicts at various levels so the members may better understand the roots of their disagreement and seek ways of integrating their various aims. The final, and essential, step in carrying out the group task is to formulate specific decisions and to draw up a statement of recommendations.

RECOMMENDED READINGS

Biddle, William. "The Problem of Conflict," in *The Cultivation of Community Leaders.* Harper and Brothers, 1953.

Dewey, John. *The Public and Its Problems.* Henry Holt & Company, Inc., 1927.

Follett, Mary. *Creative Experience.* Longmans, Green & Company, 1930.

Mill, John Stuart. *On Liberty.* Henry Regnery Company, n.d.

Simpson, George. *Conflict and Community.* T. S. Simpson, 1937.

Stevenson, Adlai. "Party of the Second Part," *Harper's Magazine* (February, 1956).

Part Three

INTERPERSONAL RELATIONS

Chapter Nine

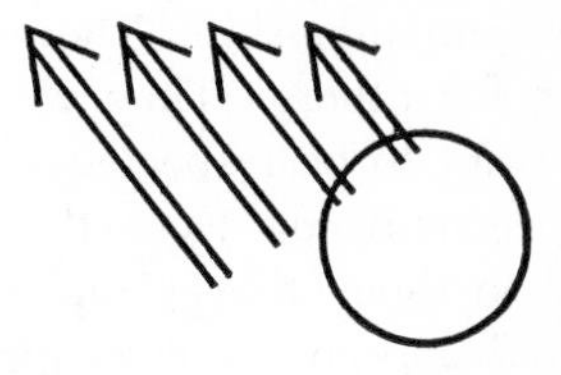

Group Norms and Social Pressure

Modern science has accomplished wondrous things. It has probed the mysteries of the atom and has hurled satellites into outer space. It has even created machines which can think — in some respects more efficiently than the human brain. What it has not done and, we suspect, cannot do is to convert human beings into thinking machines. We feel quite confident that neither individuals nor groups of individuals are soon likely to function devoid of feeling. In Part II of this book we have dealt with discussion groups largely as if they were group thinking machines. It is now time that we correct the balance and turn our attention to the "human" element. In analyzing and attempting to understand any process one is forced to break it down into its elements, thus artificially and verbally separating what in real life is inseparable. To do this is not a mistake and we do not apologize for it. Error occurs only if we omit crucial elements, or if in the end we fail, as with Humpty Dumpty, to put all the pieces back together again.

The Origin of Interpersonal Attitudes

As we saw earlier, the members of any discussion group have a variety of motives which are satisfied by their participation in group activities. Some of these needs are related to the "public" purposes or task of the group — that is, the individual members are interested in solving problems confronting them. The thinking processes we have described in Part II are designed to implement that purpose. But we also found that there are other non-task-oriented motives which operate in any situation. People have desires for human companionship. They want to be liked and to express their liking for others. They want to feel accepted and secure. They also want to be respected as individuals, to feel worthwhile, and to be recognized. Even though engaged in a task of great importance to them, they would prefer to work with people who are congenial and to avoid those toward whom they feel hostile. It is true that if the job to be done is sufficiently urgent, we may be less "choosy" about who helps us than otherwise. An episode in the classic wartime movie, *Lifeboat,* comes to mind here — where the intensely disliked enemy prisoner is the only one aboard with the medical training to amputate a dangerously infected leg of another member of the group. His cooperation is therefore readily accepted. Ordinarily, however, we resist working with those we dislike, and, if forced to do so by circumstances, often find that our productivity suffers. The reason is obvious. Energy which might otherwise be used in working on the problem is channeled off into stresses and strains among the participants.

One of the safest generalizations we can make is to assert that no group has ever existed or will exist in which interpersonal feelings, either positive or negative, are totally absent. The members of even the most task-oriented groups develop personal attitudes toward one another. It is inevitable that when people engage in discussion they will respond not only to each other's *ideas,* but also to each other as *people.* They will go away from the meeting with some evaluation of those with whom they have interacted, and indeed of the process of interaction itself. They may have been antagonized by the manner in which one of the members put forth his ideas, or attracted by the beauty of a girl across the table. They will have liked or disliked, to some degree, the way the meeting was run. Thus are interpersonal relationships developed.

In fact, interpersonal attitudes often start to form before words are exchanged, or even before the members are assembled for the first time. This occurs whenever individuals bring expectations or stereotypes along with them, which is usually the case. For example, if one goes to a meeting expecting to be in a minority he may have a chip on his shoulder before the discussion gets under way. Or, if one is the youngest or least experienced member of the group he may feel and exhibit a sense of deference towards the others. This in turn will elicit positive or negative reactions from them depending upon whether or not they enjoy the deference with which they are treated. When students attend a class meeting for the first time, they have certain notions of how students should act with teachers, just as a couple going out to a dinner party knows that there are certain things which you do not say or do on such an occasion. Their expectations may prove to be wrong, but until that time their behavior will be guided accordingly. As Ruesch and Bateson explain in their provocative book, *Communication: The Social Matrix of Psychiatry*,[1] the way one defines and labels a situation will determine how one communicates within it. In some cultures, such as that of the Japanese, interpersonal relationships are built into the language itself. For instance in Japan one uses a different word for greeting someone of superior status than one uses with an equal.

The Importance of Interpersonal Attitudes

The kinds of interpersonal relationships which exist or develop in a group have a tremendous impact, then, on the way in which the business of the organization is handled. They will determine the extent to which people speak freely or guardedly; whether one can come right to the point or must be indirect; and even what sort of language is appropriate. If we are fully to understand the discussion process and learn to improve it, we must know as much about interpersonal relations and how they develop as about the thinking processes examined in Part II. This is a difficult goal to achieve. In the first place, research in this area is a relatively recent development and we simply do not yet know as much as we should like to about the psychology of group behavior. Furthermore, as we saw in Chapter 3, many of the feelings which members of a group have toward one another are not consciously recognized by them or, if they are, cannot be brought into the open. They remain beneath the surface, on the hidden agenda. By virtue of their less accessible nature they are more difficult to deal with.

For instance, a discussion may be deadly dull, and a casual ob-

[1] Jurgen Ruesch and Gregory Bateson, *Communication: The Social Matrix of Psychiatry* (Norton, 1951).

server might infer that it is because the topic is uninteresting to the members of the group. The real reason may be that the participants are afraid to express an opinion on the subject because they do not want to get into the kind of wrangle they know is likely to be precipitated by some forthright individuals if the argument once gets underway. Or, two factions within the group may be locked in heated conflict over some proposal that is under discussion. If the truth were known, it might reveal that these participants do not really disagree on the proposal itself but, for personal reasons, are each attempting to thwart the other faction.

When we talk about interpersonal relations, then, we are dealing with an elusive matter. We are also dealing with an endlessly complex area if we take into account all the possible cross currents of feeling and combinations of relationships that can exist even in as small a group as six or eight people. In order to make the subject manageable, we will confine ourselves to an examination of those feelings which come to characterize a group as a whole, and will trust that the reader can make his own application of these general principles to relationships within sub-groups and between pairs of individuals. We will also confine ourselves to "continuing groups" — that is, groups which meet more than once and have time to develop somewhat stable patterns. This is not to say that participants in a so-called "one-shot affair" do not develop feelings about each other, or that their interpersonal attitudes are not important to the outcome of the discussion. On the contrary, the same kinds of things that happen in a continuing group are likely to develop, in embryonic form at least, in the most transient of settings. They are simply more difficult to identify there, and the opportunities to do anything constructive about the problems which they may pose are more severely limited. For example, the steamrollering of dissenting opinions can occur in either a continuing or a one-shot discussion group; but the prognosis for understanding and resolving such a difficulty is considerably more promising in the group which meets with some regularity.

The Causes of Group Norms

Just as in the case of an individual, it is possible to speak of the "personality" of a group. By individual personality we usually mean certain traits, attitudes, or patterns of behavior which are a relatively stable or permanent part of a person — those things which *characteristically* occur in him, which we come to expect of him, and which set him off as different from other people. In this same way, a group can be characterized by its typical modes of behavior — the attitudes which prevail within it, its emotional atmosphere, the way in which it functions. Thus we may say of a group that it is a liberal crowd, it is a formal gathering, it is an efficient organization, the members are very status conscious, they are honest with each other, or they are unfriendly to outsiders. Each of these phrases describes one aspect of group behavior, and we assume that the group behaves this way rather characteristically.

Do such descriptions involve us in the "group mind" fallacy of thinking? Not if we are careful and remain aware (as indeed we should when describing individuals, too) that our adjectives are only suggestive — that they are intended to convey an over-all impression of how *most* of the members behave *most* of the time. Taken in this spirit, such labels can be useful to us. They indicate general patterns which have come to be relatively permanent and predictable parts of the group's activities and attitudes. These patterns are sometimes called customs, mores, group standards, and most commonly, group norms.

Why and how do group norms come into existence? In other words, what causes a group to develop stable and predictable patterns of interpersonal relationships? Patterns or customs serve essentially the same basic purpose for a group that they do for an individual. They make it possible for us to function quickly and efficiently without having to stop to figure out every move we are about to make. When an individual awakens in the morning there are certain habitual acts in which he engages without reflection. He washes his face, brushes his teeth, and ties his shoelaces without particularly thinking about what he is doing. These customs, patterns, or habits relieve him of the necessity of expending undue time and energy on ordinary, everyday matters and make it possible for him to devote his attention to the novel situations and problems which he will encounter during the day.

Similarly a *group* of people establish certain working habits, or role relationships, which enable them to function automatically and efficiently in a smooth team operation. Their respective responsibilities are defined — such as the positions on a football team — and they count upon each member to carry his particular share of the load. A group of friends who have bull sessions with some regularity will usually develop a customary gathering place so that time and energy are not expended trying to find one another. If a student can carry into a class certain established ways of relating himself to a teacher, or a couple can make some automatic assumptions about how they should behave at a dinner party, this will save them the trouble of working out an entirely new arrangement every time they enter such situations. To be sure, no two teachers or dinner parties will be exactly alike, and some adaptations will have to be made, but at least the traditional patterns will have provided a base from which to work.

To the extent that a group has not established clearly defined role relationships and customary procedures, there will be considerable clanking and grinding of gears as they go about their work. They will have to expend a larger share of their energy figuring out and establishing a satisfactory pattern of interpersonal relationships. We sometimes wonder if, at the first meeting of any discussion group, anything more is accomplished than getting to know each other — the so-called discussion of the topic being simply a thin veil over the feeling-out of the situation going on at a deeper interpersonal level.

In addition to the need to conserve time and energy, there seems also to be a psychological cause for the development of norms. People have a need to "know their place," to know "where they stand," to know "what is expected of them." Without any guideposts they become anxious, insecure, and sometimes even paralyzed. It is like going into a restaurant and being given a menu which is so long and has so many choices that one does know where to begin the process of elimination. Complete freedom can sometimes be as immobilizing as rigid restriction. And so we search for some kind of pattern which will help to orient us. We develop rules, roles, customs, rituals, habits, norms, or what have you — all designed to bring "order out of chaos" and to give us the sense of security we need in order to function productively.

The Dangers of Group Norms

As we have explored the reasons for the development of group norms we hope the reader has been somewhat frightened as well as enlightened. For at the same time that we come to appreciate the need for customs and the values they serve, we must also recognize the dangers inherent in them. It is, in fact, their potential for great good or ill that has caused traditions to be such a basic bone of contention between liberals and conservatives in any group or society.

Certainly man cannot function without habit. He would go crazy if he had to think anew about every move he was going to make. On the other hand, customs can become so ingrained, so automatic, so unconscious, that they are regarded as unalterable. When the conditions which they were designed to meet change, people may not be sufficiently flexible to change their customs too. Then the individual or group is encumbered with rituals and relationships which are not only meaningless but are downright dangerous. Patterns are useful up to a point, but they can also lull individuals and groups into a false sense of security which is entirely inappropriate in a dynamic and complicated world.

To make this danger clear let us examine a few illustrations. Most groups, meeting for the first time, assume that it is desirable for members to introduce themselves to one another — not only giving their names but perhaps also providing other labels of identification (such as groups, institutions, departments, or geographical areas they may represent, and their jobs or professions). We now have some understanding of the purpose behind this. By identifying one another they are aided in the process of establishing patterns of relationship. They are provided with clues as to what might be expected from each member, and how one ought to behave toward him. They know better with whom they are dealing and where they themselves stand. If they discover that one of the participants is a clergyman they may be more cautious about the use of profanity. If they find that one of their number has had twenty years of professional experience with the problem to be discussed they may be more careful in expressing their own opinions. All of this can be to the good in enabling them to function smoothly and efficiently. But there are also rather obvious negative results. Too much may be assumed on the basis of labels of identification. Because a man is a clergyman does not necessarily mean that he cannot tolerate profanity; because a member comes from the South does not mean he is prejudiced against Negroes. False stereotypes such as these may cause the participants to avoid statements which do not need to be avoided and the expression of which would make everyone feel more comfortable. The awareness that there are people of greater experience or higher status in the group may lead members to inhibit their own worth-while contributions. An experimental study of problem-solving in three-man Air Force discussion groups, consisting of a pilot, a navigator, and a gunner (the first two being officers and the last an enlisted man) revealed that rarely did the groups fail to solve a problem when it was the pilot who had the right answer, but that frequently the group decided on a wrong answer when the gunner knew the right one.[2]

Stabilized patterns of relationship can deprive a group not only of knowledge possessed by low-status members, but also of available skills. Just as a baseball team might waste a good substitute pitcher by confining him to right field, so a discussion group might lose the services of an effective summarizer by expecting that function to be performed exclusively by the leader. Although specialization and division of labor is ordinarily thought of as a means of attaining greater efficiency in an organization, it can, if carried too far, lead to stultification. Everyone keeps his "place," no one learns how to do anyone else's work, and in the event of a death, an emergency, a change in the nature of the task, or the inability of one member to do his job properly, the group is unable to continue functioning. The old truism that a chain is only as strong as its weakest link takes on added significance if there are no substitute links available.

Finally, let us assume that a discussion group has developed as one of its operating norms that members are not supposed to interrupt each other, but are to be patient and courteous at all times. (A norm, incidentally, can be implicitly understood without ever being verbally expressed.) Such a standard might ordinarily be quite helpful in maintaining a maximum of mutual respect and a minimum of frustration within the group. On the other hand, there may be a time when one of the members is quite stirred up about a particular issue and feels that the rest of the group is dangerously complacent. This one individual may also feel, with considerable justification, that action has to be taken rapidly and that there is not sufficient time to sit around and hear everyone expound at length on the matter. So he may become a bit aggressive, interrupting others, and pressing urgent pleas for action upon them.

[2] Torrance, *op. cit.*, pp. 482–492.

If the group is so committed to its norm of courtesy and non-interruption that it resents this member's behavior and freezes him out without listening to what he has to say, the members may later discover to their dismay, if not their downfall, that they should have tossed their precious norm overboard and listened to this deviant.

In sum, a group or society cannot operate without traditions. But when these patterns become so binding that they are not open to re-evaluation, that group or society is on the road to extinction.

Types of Group Norms

In order to understand more fully the processes by which group norms are conceived, developed, and changed, let us select a particular kind of norm to talk about. So far we have alluded to a wide variety of interpersonal relationships which can become stabilized in the form of norms or customs. We have referred to characteristic "tones" with which members interact — formally or informally, honestly or deceitfully, with warmth or unfriendliness, with a high or low degree of status consciousness. We have discussed modes of procedure and organization — specialized or fluid, efficient or inefficient, spontaneous or restrained. There are many other ways in which characteristic aspects of group behavior might be described. What kind of leader-follower relationship does the group have? Is it one of dependency or equality? What sort of personal behavior does the group admire and approve of? Must one be a sharp dresser? Casual? Assertive? Modest? Intellectual? Anti-intellectual? A good drinker? What kinds of opinions does the group frown upon? A belief in racial integration? Sympathy toward labor unions? Leanings toward the Republican Party? We could go on indefinitely exploring many kinds of group norms. However, we choose to select for our purposes a type which is rather comprehensive in nature and is sometimes referred to as the "emotional climate" of a group.

Every group — be it a family, a business staff, a school class, a board, or a committee — has an emotional climate of some sort. Like any group norm, an emotional climate develops as the group works together, and becomes somewhat stabilized, so that after a while one can say that it is characteristic. Emotional climates have been described with different sets of adjectives by various authors. A British psychoanalyst, W. R. Bion, who has worked extensively with therapy groups, has proposed a threefold classification: (1) pairing, (2) dependency, and (3) fight-flight.[3] According to Bion, one of these three climates pervades every group at a given time in its life history. In a "pairing" group, the climate is one of interdependency — that is, the members relate to one another in a spirit of equality and mutual aid. A "dependency" group is one in which the predominant emotional problem being worked on is the relationship between the leader (or father figure) and the group members. In "fight-flight" the members are primarily in a state of mutual antagonism, which is expressed either by direct verbal warfare or by patterns of evasion and withdrawal.

Another popular set of categories are those which were used by Lewin, Lippitt, and White in their experimentation with various styles of leadership in small groups.[4] Although designed primarily to describe different modes of leadership — autocratic, democratic, and laissez-faire — these adjectives are also widely used as labels for the emotional climate which results under the three styles of leadership referred to. An autocratic atmosphere is characterized among other things by competition among group members, scapegoating, buck-passing, and hostility (usually repressed) toward the leader. A democratic atmosphere is similar to what Bion has described as pairing. A laissez-faire situation is one in which there is an absence of impelling group goals, low motivation, and considerable withdrawal.

David Riesman, in his well-known book, *The Lonely Crowd,* characterizes societies as being predominantly tradition-directed, inner-directed, or other-directed. Although he is talking about societies at large, we might apply these categories to discussion groups as well. The tradition-directed group would be one in which the behavior of members is guided heavily by rituals and customs which have been handed down from previous generations or previous meetings. Relationships are highly formalized — virtually prescribed by formula. The Japanese culture referred to earlier, where interpersonal relationships are built into the language, exemplifies this kind of climate. The inner-directed group would be

[3] W. R. Bion, "Experiences in Groups," *Human Relations* (1948, 1949, 1950, 1951).

[4] Ralph White and Ronald Lippitt, "Leader Behavior and Member Reaction in Three 'Social Climates,'" in Dorwin Cartwright and Alvin Zander (eds.), *Group Dynamics* (Row, Peterson, 1953).

rather fiercely competitive — for each member is guided, in Riesman's figure of speech, by a gyroscope which has been set going within him by his parents. He has rather rigidly defined individual goals and notions of right and wrong, and thus finds it difficult to work adaptably with others. A constantly scanning radar set is used by Riesman as the symbol of other-directedness, which is to say that group members are constantly on the lookout for cues from others to guide their beliefs and actions. The urge to conform to the views of other people is their primary goal. Such a group would be compulsively cooperative, and highly uncritical.

Although each of the above sets of classifications is interesting and helpful, we prefer to set up our own list of adjectives, specifically designed to describe the emotional climates commonly found in the kinds of groups with which we are concerned in this book. We make no claims to originality or completeness. Our categories will include some of the concepts described above. They will, like all attempts at classification, overlap each other somewhat. There may be other categories we have omitted. Finally it should be noted that a group need not fit simply into one of these classifications. Its norms may change from time to time, or with shifting circumstances. Nevertheless, we feel it may be useful to identify five types of emotional climate which we have encountered in our observations of group behavior.

The overly cooperative group

The prevailing norm in the overly cooperative group is one of suppression of conflict and of negative feeling. An artificial atmosphere of "sweetness and light" predominates. The positive emotion in evidence is of the "simpy" or "sugary" variety, which is usually the case among people who have repressed or inhibited their feelings of antagonism toward one another. "Togetherness" is the keynote of the relationship. The members are probably Riesman's other-directed individuals, and are engaged in Bion's flight. The leader is probably "super-democratic" — a wolf in sheep's clothing.

The overly cooperative emotional climate is sometimes found in teachers' groups, religious conferences, or at the first meeting of strangers — all of these being situations where the background of the participants and the immediate environmental pressures tend to be against conflict and in favor of the suppression of negative emotion.

The overly competitive group

This is the opposite end of the pole from the overly cooperative situation. Here positive emotion is suppressed, and the emphasis is entirely on conflict. A "dog eat dog" atmosphere prevails. Such groups often operate on the principle of "all business and no pleasure." In fact, the overly competitive atmosphere is most frequently found in business and labor groups, or among young boys who have not yet learned to "civilize" their hostilities. But let us not exonerate the ladies. Many women's clubs, though operating under a thin veneer of "sweetness and light," are, if one scratches the surface lightly, exceedingly competitive. Their modes of expressing hostility are simply more indirect. The overly competitive group is comparable to Bion's fight situation, and the members are likely to be Riesman's inner-directeds. This kind of norm can develop under either autocratic or laissez-faire leadership. It typified much of nineteenth-century American culture, and still persists in many segments of our society.

The anarchic group

The anarchic group can best be characterized as rugged individualism run amuck. The participants are not enough in actual communication with each other to be regarded as competing. Each member is intent on his own ideas and goals, and there is little or no effort to work together on a commonly understood and accepted group objective. The discussions are characterized by aimless wandering and lack of accomplishment. This kind of climate generally develops under laissez-faire leadership and, like the overly cooperative group, represents another mode of flight from genuine interpersonal relationships. Meetings of artists and others of so-called "artistic" temperament frequently fall into this pattern, as often do those of college professors. Each participant is up on his own cloud, and the skies are spacious enough for them all to move around without ever coming into real contact. Our stereotyped — and, to some extent, true — picture of French culture provides the classic illustration of highly anarchic relationships.

The ritualistic group

The prevailing norm in the ritualistic group is strict adherence to traditions and rules. Meetings are conducted very formally—completely dominated by procedural restrictions. Any departure from Robert's Rules of Order, the Dewey pattern of reflective thinking, or whatever other bible the group may happen to believe in, is rigorously discouraged. The expression of emotion, either positive or negative, is made difficult if not impossible by virtue of the fact that behavior is so carefully directed into prescribed forms. This is the small-group counterpart of Riesman's tradition-directed society. It is also a form of Bion's dependency, since such a group is likely to have a dominant leader who is the keeper and enforcer of the rule book. Many of the Oriental cultures are or have been characterized by this type of emotional climate.

The interdependent group

We would regard interdependency as the most mature of the five kinds of emotional climate we are describing. Discussions in a group of this type tend to be direct and free. Differences are frankly expressed and vigorously argued. At the same time, common goals and sympathies are recognized, and verbal indications of support and friendship are common. Tension builds as the group works hard on some problem, and is then released in friendly banter and relaxation. This is Bion's pairing group and Lewin's democratic atmosphere. It is what a group would be like if it consisted of Riesman's "autonomous" individuals—people who are dominated neither by tradition, parental influence, nor the opinions of peers, but who are for the most part able to express their own individuality. There appears to be no particular profession where this kind of emotional climate is more frequently found than in others. However, there are certain national organizations such as the League of Women Voters and the American Civil Liberties Union, in whose local chapters one is more likely than not to discover such an atmosphere.

Norm Development and Change

The fact that all groups have a need for a certain amount of stability and predictability in their patterns of interpersonal relationships explains *why* group norms are developed and maintained. It does not, however, tell us *what kind* of norms a particular group will establish or *how* they are brought about. Why does one committee develop an overly competitive emotional climate and another an anarchic one? It is not enough to assert that it is simply a result of the kind of people who are participating, since each of them is likely to have a somewhat different set of personality traits, and the same people on different occasions may create a different sort of emotional climate. How, then, do some characteristics come to prevail over others? How are these patterns maintained? And how, if at all, can they be changed?

These are questions to which social science has only begun to discover answers. Much more research in the field of group dynamics is necessary before we can say that we truly understand the process. There are a few important insights which have been uncovered, however, and they may help us to see somewhat more clearly what makes a group "tick" at the interpersonal level. One thing we know is that norm development has its inception the moment group members begin to interact with one another. If the meeting has been called together by a leader or some other person of authority, that individual's attitudes, mannerisms, and emotional make-up will have a greater impact than anyone else's upon the shaping of the *initial* norms. If he is a relaxed, warm, direct person a climate of interdependecy will be encouraged. If he is tense and dogmatic, the seeds may be sown for a highly competitive situation.

It is clear, however, that the leader (if there is one) cannot by himself establish a climate which is seriously out of tune with the predispositions of other group members. Anyone who has ever taught a class can testify that in spite of all that a teacher may do to create the kind of atmosphere he or she believes most conducive to learning, a few strong-willed students with different attitudes can make their tone prevail. This same thing is true in every social situation. There are probably none among us who have not had the experience of being "sucked into" a pattern of interpersonal relationships which runs strongly against our grain, no matter how assiduously we have tried to turn it in a different direction. Although it takes two to make a fight it also takes two to make a friendship, and though one may want to be frank and cooperative it is difficult to be so if those to whom one is talking are either hostile or oversolicitous.

Some psychiatrists have speculated that the most seriously neurotic members of a group have a greater influence on the social climate than the more "normal" members. Thus, if one participant has a strong persecution complex, or an overpowering need for attention, he may seduce a group of otherwise relaxed people into a high state of competitive emotional tension. A compulsively formal and orderly person, if he is assertive enough, may impose a more ritualistic pattern on the group than the other members really want. An individual who has serious problems of repression of hostile feelings may make other members so uncomfortable about expressing *their* differences that they too "clam up."

Dr. Fritz Redl, a psychiatrist with wide experience in working with children's groups, suggests that the predominant emotional tone of a group is set by what he calls the "central person." Redl identifies ten different types of such people and describes the kind of emotional effect they have upon others.[5] For example, Type 9: "The Bad Influence":

> In him ["the Bad Influence"] there is no conflict. His drives . . . do not set loose . . . problems for him. He faces them and does not care. Alertness, on the part of the others to this . . . seems sufficient encouragement for the expression of what they had . . . been trying to suppress. This really means . . . that the "unconflicted" personality constellation has an infectious influence on the conflicted wherever they meet. . . . The central person renders a service to the ego of the potential group members. . . . he saves them the expense of guilt feelings, anxieties and conflicts.[6]

Dr. Redl makes another interesting observation in discussing Type 7: "The Seducer," when he calls attention to the importance of the "first act" and reminds us of an experience we have probably all had — that is, seeing a group go in a certain direction merely because of who happened to speak first. The initial comments in any group, whether they come from the official leader or somebody else, and whether they have little or great merit, seem to have an advantage in the determination of norms merely by virtue of their priority in time.

We may conclude then, at least on the basis of present knowledge, that those members of a group who have more authority than the

[5] Fritz Redl, "Group Emotion and Leadership," in Hare, Borgatta, and Bales, *op. cit.*

[6] *Ibid.*, p. 85.

others (the leader, senior members, etc.), those who have disturbed personalities, and those who happen to get attention first are likely to be more influential in shaping group norms than the "average" member. We also know, however, that it requires some social support from others, either via open verbal assent, reinforcing behavior, or passive acceptance, before the leader or central person can see his norms become the established ones. In other words, there must be some who share, at least in part, his needs.

The maintenance of norms

This brings us directly to the next question — how do norms, once introduced and accepted, maintain their force? Or, in George Homans' words, "What makes custom customary?" Homans provides the first answer to this question when he explains that each act of a group member which is in keeping with the norm serves to reinforce that habit and intensify its power.[7] Let us suppose, for example, that the first individual to speak in a discussion carefully avoids revealing any strong feelings toward the topic being considered. If the next two or three contributors follow suit, a climate has already begun to develop in which strong feelings are considered inappropriate. The fourth participant, beginning to sense this atmosphere, therefore avoids committing himself intensely, even though he might have had such an impulse. By refraining from so doing he is not only conforming to the norm that has already been tentatively established, but is actually adding his weight to its further development. For the fifth contributor will be even more likely than the fourth to respect this rapidly developing mood. Like the proverbial snowball rolling downhill, the norm gains momentum as each new individual behaves in conformity with it.

> The routine of a group therefore implies a control: once it is established, you depart from it at your social peril. Conversely, and this is perhaps a more difficult point to grasp, even a hint of peril helps establish the routine. If, fearing the consequences of departure from the group's routine, you act so as to abide by it, you have by that action helped to establish the routine. Custom and control grow up together.[8]

[7] Homans, *op. cit.*, p. 178.
[8] *Ibid.*

We should not assume, however, that a particular norm remains potent simply as a result of the natural tendency of group members to fortify it with their own further actions. For there will always be those who come along with divergent attitudes or behavior patterns. Why do their actions not upset the norms? As we shall see shortly, they sometimes do; but ordinarily the group reacts to deviant behavior in such a way as to preserve the established norms and discourage further violations. The mechanism employed is what we know as "social pressure."

The power of social pressure

A considerable amount of interesting research has been done which demonstrates the power and functioning of social pressure. One of the best known studies is that of Professor S. E. Asch,[9] who conducted experiments in which unsuspecting subjects were individually placed in groups where all the other members were secretly cooperating with the experimenter. The participants were asked to judge the relative length of a number of pairs of lines which were shown to them, the unsuspecting subject being asked for his judgment after all the "fixed" contributors had stated theirs. Sometimes the fixed participants all gave the correct answer, sometimes they all gave the wrong answer, and sometimes they were instructed to be divided in their judgments. It was then possible to determine the extent to which these judgments influenced the naïve subject to contradict what his eyes told him and give wrong answers. It was found that approximately one-third of these subjects yielded to group pressure and distorted their answers in the direction of majority opinion. Of further significance was the finding that majority pressure was more effective when it was unanimous than when the majority was divided. Even when the unsuspecting subject was given just one "true partner" (a participant who gave a right answer when all the other contributors gave the wrong one) he was able to withstand social pressure to a far greater extent than when he stood alone. As Asch puts it:

> It is clear that the presence in the field of *one other* individual who responded correctly was sufficient to deplete the power of the

[9] S. E. Asch, "Effects of Group Pressure upon the Modification and Distortion of Judgments," in Harold Guetzkow (ed.), *Groups, Leadership and Men* (Carnegie Press, 1951).

> majority, and in some cases to destroy it. This finding is all the more striking in the light of other variations which demonstrate the effect of even small majorities, provided they are unanimous. Indeed, we have been able to show that a majority of three is, under given conditions, far more effective than a majority of eight containing one dissenter. That critical subjects will under these conditions free themselves of a majority of seven and join forces with one other person in the minority . . . points to a fundamental psychological difference between the condition of being alone and having a minimum of human support.[10]

The Asch study rather clearly demonstrates the potency of social pressure, for if so many people will succumb to group norms when it is a simple question of visual perception, how much more likely are they to do so when they are confronted with problems where they have had no direct sensory experience which contradicts the prevailing opinion in the group?

The mechanisms of social pressure

Stanley Schachter, in another revealing study of group pressures,[11] provides us with still further insight into the mechanisms of social influence. He found, for one thing, that the more cohesive a group is (that is, the greater the attraction it holds for its members) the more likely it is to bring pressure to bear upon a deviant to conform to the norms, or to reject him if he fails to conform. Also, the exent to which social pressure occurs and rejection takes place is directly proportional to the relevance to the group of the particular norm being challenged. Thus, taking a drink at a gathering of ladies of the Women's Christian Temperance Union would bring greater pressure than wearing an out-of-style dress. Finally, Schachter found that when a participant deviates from group opinion, communication will tend to flow in his direction in an effort on the part of the majority to change his attitude. This concentration of attention on the dissenter will continue either until he has modified his view or until the majority becomes convinced that he is "impossible" (according to the majority's standards) and cuts him off completely from group interaction.

[10] *Ibid.*, p. 186.

[11] Stanley Schachter, "Deviation, Rejection, and Communication," in Cartwright and Zander, *op. cit.*

Changes in norms

One other possibility, of course, which the Schachter study does not deal with, is that the deviant may succeed in modifying the attitudes of the majority. This brings us to the matter of change in group norms. For in spite of the needs which they fulfill, and their general resistance to alteration, traditions are overturned or become transformed. The process by which this occurs is now apparent. Some individual or minority within the group that does not believe a particular standard to be valid either speaks out against it or violates it in action. If there is sufficient latent sympathy within the group for this new point of view, or if a majority can be persuaded to accept the new mode, the old routine is overthrown and a new one established.

Actually this sounds easier than it is. In the first place it requires that individuals who formerly accepted the norm must suddenly become assertive enough to challenge it. This means not only contesting the norm itself but often displacing from their positions of leadership those persons who formerly dominated the scene. They are not likely to withdraw easily. Another common difficulty is that, although under-the-surface dissatisfaction with present norms may be widespread throughout the group, the entrenched leaders may have done such an effective job of dividing and conquering that the other members are either not aware that their desire for change is shared by many others or are unable to unite their forces sufficiently to overcome firmly established patterns. After all, theirs is the uphill battle.

There are, on the other hand, a number of forces which may serve to aid the proponents of change and make it possible for them to overcome the obstacles they confront. Sometimes an alteration in the personnel of the group — through old members leaving or new ones being added —may shift the balance of power sufficiently to make change possible. Sometimes the original norm-makers overextend themselves and alienate so many people that they begin to lose their influence. There is some reason to believe that this is beginning to happen to the extreme racist leaders in the South as the result of their school and synagogue bombings and other forms of mob violence. Sometimes the mere opening up of new channels of communication among the average members of the group — so that they discover that there is social support for a change — may be enough to turn the tide. For instance, frequently when cliques start having coffee together after meetings and begin sharing their grievances about the emotional climate which prevails in the group a kind of revolutionary momentum begins to build up. Finally, there is perhaps no greater help to the advocates of change than the persuasive power of external reality. That is to say, when old group customs no longer fit the demands of a changing world, or are detrimental to the group's continued survival in its environment, they are much more easily abandoned or altered. Thus a group with a highly competitive emotional climate may discover that while its members sit around and bicker with one another, the organization as a whole is rapidly going out of business. The recognition by the group of this threat to its existence may shake up the members sufficiently to bring about a change in their interpersonal relationships.

Group self-evaluation

All of these methods of change may simply just happen without any highly conscious effort on anyone's part. That is, a shift in personnel may automatically bring about modifications. Old leaders may gradually and imperceptibly lose their influence until they are no more. Dissatisfied members, discovering they have support, may simply begin to behave differently and change the norms without talking about it with the entire group. Or, the group may slowly adapt itself to changing environmental conditions without the stresses and strains of a major upheaval. These might all be thought of as natural and unconscious processes. But if these changes do not occur naturally there is still one other way to bring them about. This is through a process of conscious and deliberate "feedback." Feedback is a term which has been borrowed by social scientists from the physical sciences and refers to that process which is illustrated in the operation of a thermostat. Very simply, the thermometer in the dining room records the temperature of the house and feeds it back to the furnace controls, "telling the furnace" whether it is giving off enough heat or needs to change its "behavior" in order to adapt to the changing climatic conditions.

Similarly, the members of a discussion group can occasionally interrupt their regular business and ask, "How are we doing?" Is our pattern of interpersonal relationships satisfactory? What are our norms, in regard to emotional climate for example, and do they serve our purpose? In other words, the group engages in a conscious, critical examination of its own interpersonal patterns with a view to determining what, if any, changes are desirable. In this way the hidden agenda, if there is one, may be brought to the surface and a clearing of the air can take place. Often, merely facing these questions openly will improve the climate. Just as in individual psychoanalysis, the process of making the unconscious conscious, or analyzing the taken-for-granted, can bring about considerable change. It might be that overtalkative participants were not aware of how much they were dominating the conversation, or of the effects of their monopoly on other individuals. Having this brought to their attention might alleviate the situation.

As in psychoanalysis, however, simply bringing a problem into the open and talking about it may not be enough. New habits have to be formed to replace the old ones, and this can be accomplished only through action and experience, not merely by talk. So too a group, once aware of its own unsatisfactory patterns and motivated to do something about them, still must find and establish new norms. It is our hope that a book of this sort may be helpful in providing guidance along these lines.

Finally, there is a point at which our analogy between group feedback and individual psychoanalysis breaks down. Unlike individual therapy, there are certain kinds of norms or hidden agenda in a group which do not lend themselves to open discussion, or (and here the analogy once again becomes valid) are not worth the time and effort to probe. It might be that discussion of such matters would create new problems for the group that are worse than the old ones. Some organizations, particularly social clubs in high schools and colleges, regularly hold what they call "truth sessions" (or some similar title). The purpose of these meetings is for each member to tell the others exactly what he thinks of them. Although presumably such an affair should serve the values we have been discussing above, it is obvious why it might not. Unless skillfully handled, such a meeting might do no more than create hard feelings and compound the tensions that up to that time had been fairly manageable. For someone to accuse another member, in front of the whole group, of overdominating the meetings because of his neurotic need for attention, would not usually serve any constructive purpose.

On the other hand, we do not wish to create the impression that a group should avoid discussing touchy interpersonal matters. If a feeling is widely shared that meetings are a waste of time because the leader is not interested in the group's goals, but is simply using the group as a means for building his prestige on the outside, it might well be that an open facing up to this issue could be the best thing that might happen to that group. If handled with reasonable maturity, such a discussion might reveal to the members that they had to some extent misinterpreted the leader's motives. He, on the other hand, might find it enlightening to know how the members have been reacting to him and the intensity of their feeling. As a result he might, if he can or is so inclined, modify his behavior. Or if not, he might decide to turn his duties over to somebody else. In any case, it is unlikely that after such an airing of feelings the previous patterns of interpersonal relationships will remain unchanged. Whether the change is for the better will depend on how well the process of feedback and evaluation has been handled.

In the past few years, social scientists have developed an impressive body of experience which indicates that group norms can be and are effectively changed by open discussion. In fact, studies like that of Coch and French[12] suggest that discussion and group decision-making (in this case in a manufacturing corporation) are the surest way of overcoming a group's resistance to change and of gaining acceptance of new norms. This is not surprising when we remember that it was only through group acceptance and social support that the original norms became effective. It follows logically that through group acceptance and social support they can most assuredly be changed.

Whenever people meet together, whether for discussion or any other purpose, it is inevitable that they will develop relationships which go beyond the immediate task of the group. As Homans says: "Social life is never wholly utilitarian: it elaborates itself, complicates itself, beyond the demands of the original situation."[13] Not only do interpersonal relationships develop; they tend to stabilize themselves in relatively fixed patterns. Just as an individual develops personality characteristics which set him apart from others, so a group evolves relatively stable patterns or customs. Such pat-

[12] Lester Coch and John R. P. French, Jr., "Overcoming Resistance to Change," in Cartwright and Zander, *op. cit.*

[13] Homans, *op cit.*, p. 109.

terns conserve time and energy for the participants and satisfy their needs for psychological security. If they become inflexible, however, they can also lead to the group's disintegration.

One can talk about many different kinds of group customs or norms. Emotional climate is one of these. Emotional climates can be classified in a number of ways, and we have chosen to identify five rather common types — the overly cooperative group, the overly competitive group, the anarchic group, the ritualistic group, and the interdependent group. The emotional climate of a group, or any other norm, has its inception the moment members first begin to interact with one another. Initially it is greatly influenced by the leader, by certain kinds of emotionally disturbed members, and by those individuals who, for whatever reason, happen to speak first. However, without support, either active or passive, from other members of the group, a particular norm cannot survive. With social support, it becomes extremely difficult to violate or to change. Deviants are subjected to strong group pressure and, if they do not conform, are rejected by the other members.

Nevertheless norms are sometimes changed. The process of alteration is a difficult one, and those who wish to bring it about usually need extra support in the form of some turnover in group personnel, excesses by the entrenched leaders, more adequate communication and organization among the "rank and file," or external pressures for change. Finally, norms may be modified through a deliberate process of group feedback and self-evaluation. This is not always feasible or desirable, but can be extremely effective. The ancient advice to "know thyself" is as applicable to a group as to an individual human being.

RECOMMENDED READINGS

Beukenkamp, Cornelius, Jr., *Fortunate Strangers.* Grove Press, 1958.

Cartwright, Dorwin and Alvin Zander. *Group Dynamics.* Row, Peterson & Company, 1953.

Hare, Paul, Edgar Borgatta, and Robert F. Bales. *Small Groups.* Alfred A. Knopf, Inc., 1955.

Homans, George C. *The Human Group.* Harcourt, Brace & Company, 1950.

Stock, Dorothy, and Herbert A. Thelen. *Emotional Dynamics and Group Culture.* National Training Laboratories, 1958.

Chapter Ten

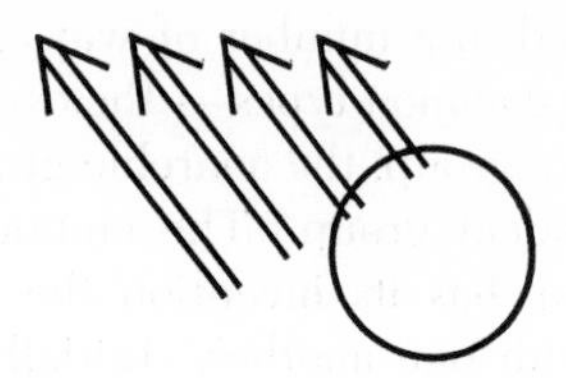

Apathy and the Problem of Involvement

ONE OF THE MOST PERSISTENT and difficult of all problems that beset groups is that of apathy. To be sure, discussions often suffer from lack of organization, inadequate information, improper leadership, and interpersonal friction, but few of these seem as difficult to diagnose or remedy as that of disinterest on the part of group members. A committee plagued with apathy is about as efficient in discharging its responsibilities as an automobile engine without spark plugs.

Here again it is clear that the small, face-to-face group is society in microcosm, that the motives found in groups duplicate those we find in society at large. The apathetic committee member is the counterpart of the apathetic citizen. The recently disclosed abuses of power in labor unions could not develop were it not for an indifferent union membership. McCarthyism would never have gained a foothold in a nation of alert and responsible citizens. The "silent generation" earned its nickname because of the passivity it displayed toward public issues. Students are currently characterized by their teachers as "armed neutrals" because they seem impervious to all challenges involving a personal commitment of any sort. Our political vigor can be questioned when just over 15 per cent of an electorate can name a state's representative to Congress. Erich Fromm, in exploring the case of pre-war Germany, reminds us that apathy has national significance.

> We have been compelled to recognize that millions in Germany were as eager to surrender their freedom as their fathers were to fight for it; that instead of wanting freedom, they sought for ways to escape from it; that other millions were indifferent and did not believe the defense of freedom to be worth fighting and dying for.[1]

Perhaps by studying the phenomenon of apathy in the small, face-to-face group we can learn something of its sources within the individual and how it serves as a means of adjustment to his environment.

There are a number of theories we could borrow and use as a basis for studying this aspect of interpersonal behavior. One of these, presented in the last chapter, that of W.R. Bion, seems particularly helpful. Bion found that interpersonal attitudes in groups led to relationships of interdependency ("pairing"), dependency, or fight-flight. The last of these, the fight-flight pattern, is one in which participants express their motives through personal attack on each other or through withdrawal from participation in the group.

In general, people seem to regard the attitude of fight as the more serious. Teachers label as "problem children" those who are disobedient, demanding, talkative, who do not conform to classroom rules. Few parents look upon a quiet son or daughter with anything but fondness. They worry instead over the child who demands attention, who fights back, or who is difficult to live with. Are these, however, really the "problem children?" Or are they more likely to be the docile and submissive children who make no attempt at all at *self*-expression?

The psychiatrist, for example, finds that treating violent or hostile patients is extremely trying. But he will readily admit that there is no more serious case than the catatonic — the person who has withdrawn so completely from participation in life and relations with other human beings that he cannot even communicate to others about his problem. Violence can be redirected into healthier and socially more acceptable channels, but therapy cannot reach the mentally withdrawn patient. While we do not mean to suggest

[1] Erich Fromm, *Escape From Freedom* (Rinehart, 1941), p. 5.

that the nonparticipating member of a group is a "psychological case," some light is thrown on his motives and patterns of behavior through study of more serious sorts of withdrawal.

Our experience with small groups — in classrooms, industrial plants, churches, civic organizations — forces us to join the psychiatrist in regarding apathy as a more serious problem than hostility. A "sick" group is more likely to suffer from too little rather than too much involvement. Overly aggressive, dominating members of a group undoubtedly cause trouble and discomfort for other members, but they are at least striving, even if unsuccessfully, for some sort of self-realization. The cynical, the passive, the uncommunicative, on the other hand, may be trying to avoid becoming anything at all. In stifling their impulses toward self-expression they can become a burden on the group. We do not mean to underestimate the "fight" side of this question, but shall reserve for the next chapter our analysis of its sources. Here we wish to take up the problem of "flight."

The Sources of Apathy

What explanation can be given for the pattern of flight? Why do people who are physically members of a group withdraw from it psychologically? Why do committee members prefer to remain silent in a meeting when their help is needed? What has paralyzed their creativity? There is probably an infinite list of causes which have their source in the person himself, his family, his group, and his culture. All are part of the pattern that leads to his inertia.

Sources outside the group

The way in which one acquires membership in a group can have a great deal to do with the enthusiasm one feels for participating. Membership on committees is often forced upon people. They are pressured into attending meetings on one pretext or another. Perhaps they are members of a department or organization that needs to be represented in negotiations, or they are accidently present when the committee is being set up, or it is simply their turn to shoulder some of the responsibility for decision-making. Either their stake in the outcome of the meeting has never been made clear to them or, as frequently happens, it does not exist.

It is amazing to find the number of irrelevant criteria used to select the members of deliberative bodies. And it is not surprising that persons appointed on the basis of artificial reasons see little point in investing much energy in the work of the group. Students who are forced to attend college by overzealous and ambitious parents can hardly be expected to attract notice by their enthusiasm in the classroom. Members of a department who are mechanically assigned to committees, regardless of interest, qualification, or personal experience, cannot be expected to enter eagerly into their deliberations.

Apathy is a condition under which many discussion groups begin their investigation of a problem. The "chosen" few feel little or no concern over the issue, they are indifferent to its solution, and they will be unaffected by the decisions that are made. Like the proverbial horse, people may be forced to join a committee, but you cannot make them talk.

Sources within the group

Apathy is sometimes generated by the group itself. Members of the committee are eager to get started and are full of optimism at the outset. But their ardor soon cools. Perhaps the leadership is repressive, the norms of the group restrictive, or the interpersonal relationships strained. Disillusionment is followed by indifference.

To begin with, there simply may not be an opportunity for everyone to participate. A committee of thirty people, for purely physical reasons, may make it difficult to get into the conversation. The presence of a few monopolizers — those who talk too frequently and too long — may leave little chance for others who are less aggressive and unwilling to interrupt. Often the temperamentally excitable, or the exceedingly well-informed, or the effusively enthusiastic, take over a discussion. The more they talk, the less time remains for others. The effect is to "short out" all the less aggressive members. As one wag put it, "Those who hold a conversation ought to let go of it once in awhile." When the overly-talkative do "let go" of an issue, it is usually after it has been thoroughly exhausted and nothing more remains to be said.

Perhaps the most important of the internal conditions that lead to withdrawal is found in the climate of the group. Norms may be established that are inconsistent with the goals of the group. The meetings may be too highly organized (so that spontaneous contributions are stifled) or too disorganized (so that people have no idea where they are on the topic and hence of what to say). The group atmosphere may be too formal or too informal for productive work. The discussion may move forward too rapidly, giving the slower and sometimes the more thoughtful members no chance to enter, or too slowly, discouraging the more alert. The "personality of the group," as it was called in the last chapter, may be too competitive, making it difficult for the less vigorous to obtain a hearing for their ideas. When a member offers an opinion he may be exposed at once to criticism or ostracism, and social pressure is hardly conducive to prolonged participation. An experimental study by Deutsch, for example, shows that members of competing groups tend to withhold information from one another while the members of cooperative groups communicate more freely and learn from one another to a much greater extent.[2] It may appear to some to be childish to withdraw psychologically from a group, for it is strikingly parallel to the behavior of the little girl who, in not getting her way, decides to "take her dolls and dishes and go home." But it is *psycho*-logically sound for one to stop participating if his contributions are systematically ridiculed or he is cut to ribbons by the overcritical. It is safer to remain silent.

Also, failure to participate in the opening moments of a discussion, or in the first of several meetings of a committee, can make it doubly difficult for people to take an active part later on. Having remained silent for a time, a norm is created in the group in which the person begins to see himself as a "nonparticipant" and other members of the group expect him to continue in that role. Getting into the conversation then takes an extra effort to break through the previously established tradition and create a new, and more active, role for one's self. Unless the group is relatively flexible, this may be difficult to do.

Withdrawal is also brought about through the actions of dominant members or cliques. Whereas the monopolist makes it difficult for people to get into the conversation because of his insatiable desire to talk, the dominator discourages people from expressing themselves because he creates a psychologically threatening atmosphere. With the monopolist there just is not time; in the case of the dominant member, it is too dangerous. In these days when

[2] M. Deutsch, "The Effects of Co-operation and Competition upon Group Processes," *Human Relations* (1949).

we hear so much about the need for "rugged individualists" as an answer to excessive emphasis on "togetherness" and group conformity, we should be careful that we do not confuse individualism with stepping all over everyone else. The trouble with *rugged* individualism is that is makes impossible any other kind of individualism. The "dog-eat-dog" or the "show me" climate is one that many people would rather not get mixed up in, so they stop talking and sit back to watch the show.

The attitudes of high-status members of a group also have something to do with participants' eagerness to enter the discussion. Teachers who punish students, via grades, for original or heretical opinions are hardly in a position to complain about student apathy. Yet they sometimes do. Businessmen who create boards of "Yes men" or who monopolize their own meetings are themselves accountable for the irresponsibility they condemn. A survey of communicative practices in factory and office units by Thomas Nilsen supports this analysis. Nilsen found that members of management were disillusioned by the fact that after inviting employees and supervisors to consult with them, they encountered almost total indifference toward the affairs of the company.

> Long-standing habits of communication are difficult to overcome. This would seem at first to be too obvious to mention, but the surveys revealed that management personnel . . . were at a loss to understand why supervisory personnel would not talk when given the opportunity although they had not had such an opportunity before. . . . There were many factors entering into this lack of discussion, but it seems clear that one important factor was that . . . supervisors had never talked frankly to or discussed problems with management in the long history of the company, and habits of non-discussion were firmly established.[3]

Involvement is not brought about, after months or years of abuse, by a few well-chosen words. Enthusiasm cannot be turned on and off like a hot water faucet.

Sources within the individual

Much of what we call apathy, then, is a result of the psychological climate that prevails in a group. But, in addition, each person

[3] Thomas Nilsen, "The Communication Survey: A Study of Communication Problems in Three Office and Factory Units," Unpublished Ph.D. dissertation (August, 1953), Northwestern University, pp. 398–399.

brings to his group a specific personality whose architecture is very largely completed. This personality, with unique needs and patterns of expression, is created out of earlier contacts with parents, friends, and associates. Every human relationship leaves its trace. While one group may bring out a different facet of an individual's personality, or will permit greater or lesser flexibility in roles, there is a strong tendency for personal habits of expression to change very slowly. Freud used the term "transference" to refer to our inclination to behave toward other persons, and to communicate with them, as if they were our parents. People who tended as children to be submissive or dominant in their relations with their parents may repeat these same reactions in a wide variety of human situations. Broadening the meaning of the term somewhat we might say that in any group there is a tendency for people to act out patterns of behavior they have tried and found successful in other groups to which they have belonged. As we experiment with various roles we rely more and more upon those which produce maximum personal satisfaction. The nonparticipant, therefore, may withdraw simply because he has learned from past experience that it is the safest thing for him to do, safest because it makes the least demands upon him and provides maximum protection for his own ego.

Among the personal reasons for voter apathy in democracy, and for nonparticipation in discussion groups, is the fact that many people have never been deprived of the chance to participate and hence, take it for granted and regard it lightly. The immigrant, who highly prizes his new privileges, often puts the native-born citizen to shame. Those who have to fight hardest to gain a voice in decision-making are usually most zealous in exercising their privilege. It seems paradoxical, at first, that so many democratic people are products of authoritarian home environments. But this is less curious when we consider that those who have had to struggle for the right of self-expression are usually most deeply aware of the meaning of participation. The passive committee member may take his prerogatives so much for granted that he feels no need to stir himself to contribute. "Let George do it."

On the other hand, people may be passive because they have never felt the personal satisfaction that comes from contributing to decision-making. The failure to practice democracy in our schools, factories, and homes is hardly calculated to prepare people for effective participation when the opportunity occurs. One is not born with talent for democratic action any more than one is born with the ability to play a Beethoven Sonata. Each failure to submit a problem to discussion deprives people of the chance to develop the confidence and skills which make participation attractive. During World War II, for example, an experiment was conducted at Fort Eustis, Virginia, to test various methods of re-educating German prisoners of war. Former German soldiers were given this training, on a voluntary basis, just before being repatriated. The program consisted of a series of twelve lectures followed by one or two hours of discussion, with further opportunities for attending lectures and films on American institutions. While the POW's showed considerable interest in the programs, they had great difficulty in discussion. Questionnaires completed by nearly all the 20,000 soldiers who took part reveals that they were most dissatisfied with their own inability to think together, to express themselves, to argue rationally, and to conduct orderly meetings.[4] To participate in a group, then, requires more than a favorable climate of opinion; it requires certain technical skills as well. The nonparticipant in discussion may not be really disinterested; he may simply be unsure of how to make use of his intelligence in this sort of social situation.

Then there is the apathetic group member whose withdrawal from discussion springs from cynicism. Having been a member of a number of unsuccessful committees — where decisions were never reached, or were never put into operation — he has become thoroughly disillusioned with democratic processes. He is convinced that nothing will come of it all and by remaining silent does everything in his power to make his prediction come true. Failure to work effectively in group settings in the past is projected into the new situation and provides him with a motive for withdrawal. Often this kind of verbal nonparticipant demoralizes a group because he communicates nonverbally — through posture, facial expression, and gesture — how hopelessly he regards the whole situation.

When one studies the reasons cited by nonparticipants themselves as their reasons for withdrawing from discussion, two other factors can be isolated that deserve comment. First, many peo-

[4] *A Reorientation Program Seen Through the Eyes of German Prisoners of War* (Mimeographed), Special Projects Center, Fort Eustis, Virginia.

ple do not enter discussion because of the risk of exposing their ideas to criticism. Taking a position in a committee meeting carries with it some obligation to explain and defend the position. The threat here is most obvious in the case of a person who has strong feelings that are without logical foundation. To express a prejudice is to take a chance of revealing one's own narrowness or ignorance. It is also to run the risk of having to change a comfortable and familiar belief. Even when the opinion has a solid basis in fact, a group member may not believe he is up to the job of defending his judgment. Persons who are mature in many ways may withdraw from a conversation when they are the only liberal in a group of conservatives, the only believer in racial equality among segregationists, the only independent among fraternity members. Fear of ideas can also take another form. A committee member in a group of well-prepared and well-informed people may doubt that he could have any ideas worthy of their consideration. A mental paralysis, growing out of a feeling of intellectual inferiority, may keep him from contributing. Silence seems the best defense against having our intellectual inferiority — whether real or imagined — displayed publicly.

> Talking can be dangerous. An expressed opinion may produce ridicule, rejection, or retaliation. A person whose opinion is unusual or unpopular may prefer to remain silent rather than risk getting hurt. A person with a bright idea may fear its (and his) fate after it has been gone over by the group. People with little power in an organization know that what they say in the presence of those with greater power may seriously endanger their future in the organization. In the face of such dangers, it is often realistic to be quiet or to say only the right things.[5]

Thus, lack of confidence in our ideas, a fear of becoming involved in a discussion that is over our heads, or of having critical personal beliefs changed, may account for silence on the part of group members.

Another reason for the members of a group withdrawing springs from lack of confidence in their ability to interact successfully with others on an equal basis. Members of a discussion group may not be threatened intellectually, but socially, by the demand for spontaneous and informal human relationships. The possibility of

[5] Dorwin Cartwright, "The Questions People Ask," *Adult Leadership* (December, 1953), p. 11.

getting into arguments, of risking interpersonal frictions and perhaps alienating people, may prompt some members to remain silent. Those who are normally indirect in their relations with others may balk at having to express themselves so frankly and directly, and on such an intimate basis.

The discussion group is one of the most ambiguous of social settings. There are no assigned roles to play. A person facing the first meeting of a newly formed committee may be uncertain about the goals of the group, or how these goals relate to his private purposes. He cannot know in advance whether his associates will be cold and formal, or warm and friendly, in their relations with each other. He seldom knows in advance what sort of hierarchy, or "pecking order" may prevail. There may be certain approved ways of doing things that he, in his ignorance, might violate by acting prematurely. All of this, of course, can make him feel intensely insecure. Finding himself in such an ill-defined social situation, he may withdraw from the group psychologically (particularly when resigning from the committee is impossible) rather than risk social disapproval. Our conversations with some of the more serious of these cases of withdrawal strongly suggest that to be one's own self, in a spontaneous and natural way, is one of the more serious challenges to which the human personality is exposed. Some people prefer to retreat into silence before the challenge.

The Group and the Individual

In explaining the causes of psychological withdrawal we have implied that it is undesirable. But is this really so? Do not the privileges of citizenship include the right to stay away from the polls altogether? Does freedom of speech mean that everyone must publicly announce his private thoughts? One has the right, doesn't he, *not* to contribute to a group? Is it not legitimate for a member to use his membership as he pleases, including the right to remain silent? The issue is far too complicated to permit an easy "Yes" or "No" answer to these questions. Before we proceed to a discussion of how to overcome nonparticipation, we had first better clarify our goals. What is the responsibility of the individual member to the group? And, in turn, what responsibility must the group assume toward its individual members?

If we are going to place individual values above all others then we must say that a person has the right to develop whatever means of personal expression — even of nonexpression — he chooses. Privacy, in some respects, is the greatest of all democratic privileges. But, at some point, a group member or a citizen who fails to accept *some* responsibility for maintaining democratic processes becomes a parasite. The examples of such exploitation are legion: the non-union worker who profits from all the gains scored by dues-paying members of the local; the student who learns from his classmates but refuses to contribute his own ideas; the apathetic member of a committee who gets as much credit as anyone else for formulating wise plans. The member of a crew who does not pull his own oar gets there just as certainly as the others, but at their expense. Any collaborative effort involves us in the sticky question of where the line should be drawn between the obligations of group to member and of member to group.

Individual responsibility

We turn first to the individual. Under what circumstances does he have a responsibility to contribute to a group's deliberations? We would suggest the following:

(1) He should contribute whenever he has *information* that is needed by the group. This does not mean bringing in unnecessary or irrelevant factual material. Nor does it mean "snowing" others with his findings just to impress them.

(2) He should present his *point of view* on the problem whenever that view has not been presented by someone else. He should contribute a promising hypothesis or solution even if he, personally, does not support it.

(3) He should participate, even when he has nothing new to add, in *evaluating* the opinions and information presented by other group members. It is up to each person to examine, criticize, and explore the views of others.

(4) When all the previous items have been taken care of, an individual has some responsibility for assisting in the *process* of discussion. He may be useful to the group in bringing in other members, in clarifying misunderstandings, in resolving conflicts, in formulating decisions, or in keeping records.

(5) Finally — even if the group is functioning intelligently and efficiently — the individual member is obligated to contribute occasionally to show that he *understands and approves* of the action being taken. Even when this requires no more than a nod of the head, a smile of agreement, or the saying of "Aye" or "Nay."

If an individual member can be reasonably sure that these needs are being met by other members of the group, then he is justified generally in remaining silent. Perhaps at a later time, or at subsequent meetings, his skills or knowledge will be required. If not, then he has failed to prepare adequately or his appointment to the committee is without purpose for he duplicates the qualifications of other members of the group.

Group responsibilities

Since many of the causes of apathy have their source in the group, rather than the individual, some of the responsibility for nonparticipation must be shared by the group as a whole. In order to avoid blame for forcing withdrawal of some of its members from a discussion, a group must, in our opinion, maintain two conditions.

First, there must be an equal opportunity for all members to enter the discussion. To attach the stigma of "nonparticipant" to someone who has tried repeatedly to obtain a hearing is totally unwarranted. Free competition in the market place of ideas is as important as in the market place of goods and services. And just as antitrust laws are necessary to protect the relations between corporate entities, so a discussion group must limit those who might abuse the privilege of talking and so prevent others from entering the conversation. This is not to say that everyone must participate equally in the mathematical sense, but that everyone, regardless of status, must have equal access to the floor. There is a great difference between "equality of opportunity" and "equality of participation." Discussion — or for that matter, democracy itself — would not last long if everyone, fool and genius alike, exercised the same influence in public decisions. But all must be given a chance to contribute their ideas so that we can discover which are the wise and which the foolish.

Second, equality of opportunity is not very meaningful unless the group establishes a climate favorable to participation. The right to speak is an empty privilege if social pressures are brought to bear against those who use their time to express unpopular views. A group needs, therefore, to create a permissive psychological climate as well. This means that regardless of who is expressing an opinion, or what the opinion may be, the remark will be discussed openly, honestly, and without prejudice.

It may, on occasion, be necessary to go one step beyond these minimum provisions to secure participation from all members of a group. Some colleges, for example, follow a policy of giving priorities in admission to foreign students. They believe the foreign student deserves extra consideration because of his less fortunate circumstances. So, in a discussion group, the shy, reticent person may temporarily need encouragement before he feels accepted enough to voice his opinions. Everyone is not equally aggressive, equally articulate, equally confident of his convictions. The group should take into account that its members may differ in reaction time, in general spontaneity, and in willingness to engage in an intellectually vigorous argument. A special effort to aid the underprivileged may sometimes be necessary.

This sharp delineation of responsibility between individual and group, however, is not as clear as our treatment suggests. Just how often should a group depart from its assigned task in order to increase the interest and skill of an individual member who is bored or inactive? When should a group give "aid and comfort" to its ineffective members? Some of the critics of discussion may be justified in complaining about groups in which therapy and training are continually given precedence over productivity and efficiency.[6] It takes time away from the group's real business to help people to express themselves. An atmosphere conducive to personal growth may be bought at the expense of speed in making decisions.

Also the individual who justifies his failure to contribute because of his lack of skill in group work sometimes stampedes other members into catering to his deficiencies. A novice card player does this, for example, when he throws himself on the mercy of others and forces them to teach him how to play rather than letting them play the game themselves. On the other hand, a group which disregards the personal needs of its members may fail to cultivate persons who might contribute valuable information, original ideas, or interpersonal talents that may be needed at other times.

The specific point at which training should be given priority over task performance is one to be decided in a particular social context. Participants should bear in mind this principle: the group

[6] See William Foote Whyte, *Leadership and Group Participation* (New York State School of Industrial and Labor Relations, Bulletin No. 24, 1953).

must perform well not only in the short run, which might excuse the group's neglect of some member's needs, but in the long run as well, where the survival value of the group will reflect its ability to marshal the combined capacities of the members.

Handling the Problem of Nonparticipation

A number of techniques for dealing with the problem of apathy recommend themselves and, as has been our habit throughout this book, we shall describe them as objectively as possible, leaving to the reader the issue of selecting the preferred approach.

No matter what methods of handling the nonparticipant are adopted after the meetings are under way, it should be evident that appointment to a committee in the first place should be made, as far as possible, on a voluntary basis. Trying to coerce people into behaving democratically and spontaneously is to engender not only apathy but a host of other motivational problems as well. People can hardly be blamed for indifference, or for dodging their share of the work, when a problem does not touch their lives in any recognizable way. Whenever possible, persons should be named to a committee who already have some experience with the problem or who are deeply affected by current policies concerning it. Committee members will often work surprisingly hard when given a chance to correct problems which they themselves have had to live with.

There are a number of ways of ascertaining interest in a problem, and they range all the way from surveying the members of an organization to simply asking for volunteers. Much of the dead weight found on committees would be reduced if chairmen, presidents, and supervisors stopped appointing people to committees arbitrarily. It is true that everyone cannot always be named to serve on committees of his own choice. Education, training, and expertness, as well as the interests of potential group members, must be taken into account. As in the Army, a military draft may be a temporary and necessary expedient to insure that undesirable or unpleasant duties will be carried out. But organizations should re-examine their committee structure periodically to find out if better use can be made of the natural interests as well as the skills of their members.

The directive approach

Two quite different schools of thought exist concerning the proper way to deal with noncontributing members. The first and most familiar of these can be broadly characterized as directive in method. It is based on the belief that inarticulate people need to be pushed to express themselves more freely and more fully. Through a little prodding here, a few well-placed suggestions there, or some persuasion at another point, nonparticipants will be temporarily pressured into joining the discussion. Before long these artificial techniques of motivation will be unnecessary, for participation will become its own reward; group members who were formerly withdrawn will begin to feel some of the satisfaction that comes from exchanging ideas in a spirited discussion. The directive method is used by a parent when he guides his son or daughter into taking music lessons or attending a day camp from which he believes the child will benefit. The teacher, through provocative lectures, hopes to stimulate and arouse curiosity so that his students, in the future, will motivate themselves to go on learning. The preacher, through inspiring sermons, believes he can raise the moral standards of his parishioners. The psychiatrist who advises his patient how to solve one of his problems hopes that this temporary lift will make his client better able to shoulder other crises in his life by himself. Involvement in discussion, too, can be brought about in a number of directive ways.

Perhaps the committee never gets off the ground because few of the participants are deeply concerned about the topic. In this case, some members might take it upon themselves to deepen the level of emotional involvement. Through the showing of a controversial film on the subject, or from participating in a dramatic re-enactment of some aspect of the problem, the group might obtain a fresh perspective on its topic.[7] A field trip may translate a seemingly abstract issue into more tangible form. There are many students who have taken a fresh interest in mental illness, juvenile delinquency, or the narcotics problem after visiting a mental hospital, accompanying a social worker on her rounds in the slums, or after spending a day in court. A bored discussant may become much more excited about a topic after reading provocative or controversial articles on the subject.

[7] This is one of the many uses of role-playing. See Appendices A and C for instructions on setting up exercises of this type.

The chairman, or any member of the group, may use stronger medicine. For instance, a personal attack on the most popular point of view may draw fire from members who are normally content to let others carry the ball for them. Once a person enters a discussion — takes a stand publicly — he is more inclined to feel a personal stake in the outcome of the meeting.

The "devil's advocate" is a special case of the technique described above. Some member of the group assumes, for the sake of argument, a point of view that is unpopular or that is being disregarded by the group. This tactic is not only effective in producing a higher level of interest, but it can serve as a healthy antidote in groups where unanimity is too often or too readily achieved. The spokesman for the devil may improve decisions by forcing groups that are too homogeneous in their outlook to give consideration to ideas that are unusual, unfamiliar, or original. Maier, for example, in one of his studies of reasoning, found that people are often blocked in trying to solve problems because of habitual "sets" which tend to blind them to other solutions.[8] In another study, this same psychologist in collaboration with a colleague set up an experiment in which college students solved simple math problems, first by themselves, later as a discussion group. In some of the groups, leaders were instructed to encourage participation, to urge group members to explore a wide variety of solutions, and to protect the rights of minorities to disagree. In other groups, the leaders were asked only to record the decisions reached by the members. Maier and Solem found that groups which considered a large number of solutions were more likely to solve problems correctly than those in which this element was missing. In fact, the right answers were often discovered even when none of the individuals originally solved the problem correctly when working alone.[9] Advocacy of seemingly unattractive points of view may stimulate nonparticipating members to contribute and may lead, as well, to a higher level of performance in problem-solving.

Another suggestion is to give inactive members a specific assignment within the group and make them responsible for carrying it out. Students who are shy and withdrawn are often brought out of their "shells" by being given a position of authority in

[8] N. R. F. Maier, "Reasoning in Humans. I: On Direction," *Journal of Comparative Psychology* (April, 1930).

[9] N. R. F. Maier and A. R. Solem, "The Contribution of a Discussion Leader to the Quality of Group Thinking: The Effective Use of Minority Opinions," *Human Relations* (August, 1952).

school activities. Why not do the same for adult members of discussion groups? One person might be made responsible for reporting on this phase of the subject, another on that phase. Or perhaps nonparticipants could be put in charge of summarizing the discussion, keeping records of the meeting, or even leading the group from time to time. This may put some pressure on them to become better informed so they will be prepared to take part. Giving them responsibility for the conduct of meetings may supply the motive for developing the skills they now lack.

In some cases the suggestion is made that active members of a group call on nonparticipants by name and ask them for their opinion. While this may be justified if the nonparticipant is simply shirking his share of the work, it is not always effective in bringing him out. The occasions on which it works must be balanced against the times when it does not work, and when it drives the insecure person still further into seclusion. To be put on the spot for an opinion may be exceedingly embarrassing — as students well know — if one does not happen to have anything worth while to say at that moment.

Sometimes, as we noted earlier, the failure to participate grows more serious from meeting to meeting. Roles become fixed and the nonparticipant is cast permanently and inflexibly in a role from which he cannot depart. The pattern is simply too difficult to upset. By subdividing the group into smaller groups, a large committee occasionally can bring about greater opportunities for participation. Not only does the splitting up of the original committee provide more time for everyone to speak, but it may break down old patterns of communication and allow new ones to develop.

The nondirective approach

The nondirective approach to problems of personal and social adjustment is usually associated with the name of Carl Rogers.[10] The fundamental premise underlying the non-directive approach is that human beings have within themselves constructive impulses which can lead to creative and mature behavior. Much as the

[10] Readers who are interested in studying in detail the applications of nondirective methods in the field of teaching, counseling, and leadership should read Carl Rogers, *Client-Centered Therapy* (Houghton Mifflin, 1951).

body restores itself to health, so the psyche, if permitted, can shrug off its inhibitions. What causes withdrawal from satisfying human relationships is that natural impulses have been subverted through past failure to relate successfully to one's family and culture. As a result a person loses the desire for risking interdependent relationships with other people. Directive and manipulative techniques, according to Thomas Gordon, one of Rogers' students, only intensify reactive and defensive behavior.

> We have seen, too, how authority produces reactive rather than constructive and creative behavior. We have evidence of the reluctance of people to "show their ignorance" in the presence of the expert, or the well-informed person. People apparently must feel secure and free from threat in order to be themselves, in order to participate freely, in order to expose their ideas or feelings to others. Traditional leadership, it seems, rarely gives people such security and freedom.[11]

The job of the nondirective psychotherapist, according to Rogers, is not to manipulate the client — by stimulating him, diagnosing him, or prescribing for him — but to create an accepting situation in which the client may cure himself by re-assessing his patterns of evaluation. The ideal is to make him more autonomous, more self-energizing, not less, and therefore the therapist avoids responding to his appeals for help.

At the level of the small, face-to-face group this means that any member, or its leaders, will simply try to elicit the cooperation of others by maintaining an accepting atmosphere in which to conduct business. It will mean the avoidance of all attempts to stimulate people artificially, to threaten or cajole them into saying something, or to dramatize issues and tease them into the conversation. The hope is that upon reflection and introspection group members will find within themselves reasons for participating more productively in the work of the group.

In a group of apathetic committee members what, specifically, would this mean? Simply that the group would discuss its own processes and through feedback and self-evaluation determine what action, if any, needs to be taken. Someone would call the attention of the group to the prevailing mood of apathy. But

[11] Thomas Gordon, "Group-Centered Leadership and Administration," *ibid.*, p. 334.

there would be no overt gestures on his part to salvage the meeting or the committee members from their predicament. Probably, at this point, it would involve sitting quietly until someone takes the initiative or, if necessary, until the group adjourns. This is tantamount to saying: "I believe we have a problem here. It is not my problem any more than it is yours. We may wish to do something about it but, on the other hand, we may not. I am prepared to listen to whatever anyone has to say."

This is a difficult kind of solution to apply for it puts a strain on the person doing it, and on the rest of the group as well, especially if they are not accustomed to facing up to their interpersonal problems in this way. Unless the initiator of this action is reasonably secure he may be tempted, in the silence that follows his remark, to propose solutions for the problem himself. It is also a strain, however, on the other members of the group who must finally face up to their own inner impulses and motives. It is quite true that this method may lead in many directions — and one who adopts it had better be prepared to accept any outcome. The group may disintegrate, either because the members finally see that there is no real reason for its continued existence, or because they are not up to the self-analysis that such an approach opens up. Or the group may reassess its old goals and formulate new ones that are more realistic. But the group that does survive this kind of self-analysis, or group-analysis, is likely to emerge from it with stronger and more genuine reasons for acting.

Briefly, the result of the directive approach is to revitalize a group through temporary expedients that will keep it going. By stimulating a group artificially it can be kept functioning in the same way that a doctor can force down the temperature of a man with a fever by administering drugs. Simple palliatives may do the job. But apathy or fever may be a symptom of a deeper malady within the organism. If it is, then a different cure may be in order. The group may be pursuing the wrong goals, they may have already achieved their goals, or the members may need to face squarely the motives for withdrawal within their own personalities. If so, less directive methods may be of value.

Apathy is one of the more persistent and serious illnesses from which discussion groups suffer. Committee members who are physically present may not actually take part for a variety of reasons. For one thing, they may have been appointed to the group but have no interest in the problems being investigated. Many persons regard committee work as something inescapable but not to be looked forward to with anticipation. Yet sometimes committees are composed of deeply concerned people whose original interest was snuffed out after a brief time. Withdrawal, in these cases, has its source within the group itself. The overly talkative and dominant members may discourage some people. Others may find the pace too fast, or too slow, too formal, or too anarchic. Social pressure is sometimes manipulated so as to threaten anyone who does not conform in thought, dress, or manner. But nonparticipation may also reflect motives and fears within the individual laid down through past experience. To engage in discussion may be seen as dangerous or difficult — dangerous in the sense that earlier family and group relationships have been personally painful; difficult in the sense that a person may feel incompetent to articulate his ideas successfully. Cynicism, too, can play a part when people have participated in one group after another without feeling any sense of accomplishment.

The group and the individual member share in the responsibility for failure to make maximum use of the talents of group members. The individual is obligated to contribute whenever he has information or ideas to offer, when the opinions of others are not being adequately tested, or when the group needs help in some area of its own process. The group, as a whole, should be held responsible for forcing people out of discussion when it fails to provide equal opportunities for all to participate or when it does not maintain a constructive climate for thought and communication.

The nonparticipating member may be brought into the conversation through directive or nondirective methods. A greater degree of involvement may be produced through reading provocative materials, through field trips, or role-playing scenes. Some members, in taking controversial stands, or by playing the devil's advocate, may "smoke out" some of the less aggressive members. Nonparticipants may be assigned specific duties, or the group may be divided temporarily to allow people to re-establish new roles and new channels of communication. If the non-directive approach is adopted members will simply bring the problem of apathy to the attention of the group, encourage members to analyze their own goals and motives, and be prepared to accept changes in either the aims of the group or the attitudes of committee members.

RECOMMENDED READINGS

Cantor, Nathaniel. *The Dynamics of Learning.* Foster and Stewart, 1946.

Cartwright, Dorwin. "The Questions People Ask," *Adult Leadership* (December, 1953).

Fromm, Erich. *Escape from Freedom.* Rinehart & Company, Inc., 1941.

Gordon, Thomas. *Group-Centered Leadership.* Houghton Mifflin Company, 1955.

Rogers, Carl. *Client-Centered Therapy.* Houghton Mifflin Company, 1951.

Whyte, William F. *Leadership and Group Participation.* New York State School of Industrial and Labor Relations, 1953.

Chapter Eleven

Interpersonal Conflict

There comes a time in the life of most groups when a little apathy on the part of some members, rather than being regarded as a problem, might instead be welcomed with a collective sigh of relief. Although constant and widespread withdrawal may indicate serious interpersonal difficulties, such a state of affairs could look rather attractive to people who are suffering from the discussion equivalent of battle fatigue. It would be difficult to convince them that lack of involvement is a worse ailment than overaggressiveness. "Fighters" seem so much more omnipresent than those who take flight and they cannot so easily be ignored. In fact, one of the most frequent questions asked of experts in the field of discussion is, "What can be done about an overaggressive member?" Of the various problems confronted by discussion groups this is one of which a great many people seem acutely aware.

The problem of fight is closely related to that of apathy. We have seen how overaggressiveness in some members of a group can lead to withdrawal by others. By the same token, apathy in some can lead to overaggressiveness by others who feel that they must assert themselves if anything is to get done. The relationship between lack of involvement and interpersonal conflict is of the chicken and egg variety — that is, it is impossible to say which is more responsible for the other. We would do better to regard them both as elements in a vicious circle, and work at breaking the cycle at whatever point we can. Whether we begin with those who are non-involved or with those who are involved in unproductive ways, the chances are that we will eventually be dealing with both aspects of the problem. Having already explored some of the possible causes of and cures for nonparticipation, we now turn our attention to interpersonal conflict.

Overt Expressions of Hostility

Interpersonal hostility is expressed in group discussion in many ways. Sometimes it flows forth quite openly and directly; at other times it is masked and subtle. Before attempting to analyze the sources from which it springs, or to propose possible remedies, we must make sure that we recognize "fight" behavior when we see it.

One of the most common and easily recognized manifestations of overaggressiveness is that of monopolizing the discussion. One or a few people talk so much that no one else can get into the conversation, or, if they try, they must make a fight for it. In such a group the discussion proceeds at machine-gun-fire rapidity. There is no time for reflection or relaxation. The slow or hesitant members are snowed under. The others either battle for the floor or give up and let control pass to the monopolizers.

But excessive talk is not the only weapon which a fighter can use to dominate a discussion. He may also pull rank if he has any. Military officers are not the only ones who use rank in order to manipulate other individuals. It is done in civilian life every day — by bosses with their employees, by supervisors with their workers, by parents with their children, by senior Congressmen with their juniors, by teachers with their students, by upperclassmen with freshmen. Nor does one need to have rank himself in order to engage in this behavior. He may invoke the authority of somebody else. "The boss won't approve of that idea," or "I'll tell your father," or "Just don't let Sam hear about this," are all attempts to intimidate others through the threat of disapproval by stronger powers.

Persistent negativism is still another way in which interpersonal hostility manifests itself. Every idea that is put before the group is immediately ripped apart. Only the faults and errors of contributions are pointed out — never their merit. Insofar as the fighter listens to other participants at all, he does so not in order to understand them but to refute what they have said. Often he does not confine himself to tearing into what others say, but also goes after them as individuals — questioning their motives, suggesting they are insincere, using ridicule to make them appear stupid, and possibly engaging in outright name-calling. "You don't really believe that, do you?" "How could anyone in his right mind think that?" "You know better than that!" "I've never heard anything quite so foolish." "You really are naïve, aren't you?" "That sounds like a lot of Communist propaganda to me."

Instead of going so much on the offense the belligerent group member may express his hostility in more defensive ways. He may make dogmatic and prejudiced statements and then stick by them stubbornly, refusing to allow the other participants to influence him in any way. He may defend his own ideas with the possessiveness of a miser — inflexible and close-minded to the last, constantly repeating the same point of view over and over again in different words. We must be cautious, however, not to confuse this kind of behavior with the legitimate defense of an honest conviction which happens to be unpopular in a particular group. Often we can tell from the feeling-tone with which the dissenter expresses himself whether he is sincerely defending an honest difference of opinion or just being sticky and "impossible."

Indirect Manifestations of Hostility

Since so much of the education and training in our culture teaches us that it is "not nice" to be openly hostile, nasty, stubborn, or overaggressive, we find a good deal of the fight phenomenon in group discussions expressed in veiled and indirect ways. This is particularly true of the more "educated," "cultured," or "refined" segments of the population. But nevertheless, fight they do — albeit on a hidden agenda basis. Let us look at some of the more "sophisticated" weapons of interpersonal hostility.

The biting joke or "funny" comment which is designed to cut someone down to size or "prick his balloon" is one of the more common modes of hostile expression among sophisticates. An effective jokester can control the atmosphere of an entire group by making it impossible for anyone else to function in constructive and serious ways. He can drive both the timid and the not so timid out of the discussion in fear of the sharpness of his tongue.

So, too, can the moralizer suppress the individuality of other members of the group. By greeting ideas that are original or different with pious remarks suggesting that no "good American" or "good Christian" or "loyal member of the team" could subscribe to such views, the moralizer (sometimes unconscious of his own motives) effectively stifles free discussion and sees to it that his own set of values remains dominant. Such behavior is closely akin to that of the non-verbal "keepers of the norms" who, by their raised eyebrows, shaking heads, knowing glances, smirks, shuffling of papers or of chairs, murmurs of disapproval, and whisperings to their neighbors, let it be known that they do not like what someone is saying or doing.

Finally there is what we might call "blocking" behavior, which is simply negativism cloaked in the outer garments of rationality. The blocker, under the pretense of examining each contribution carefully and critically, actually succeeds in destroying all constructive contributions. His exterior manner of calm, objective, ice-cold reasoning is but a mask for the prejudices and personal goals he is seeking to implement or the goals of others he is seeking to obstruct. Again, he may not even be aware of the hostility he is expressing, but may instead fancy himself to be the only reasonable member of the group, sorely beset by a crowd of irrational associates. The difference between the blocker and the participant who has honest doubts about what other members propose is sometimes difficult to detect, and again one must rely on the feeling-tone of the particular situation to make such a determination.

There are some other, less subjective, clues which can help us to decide whether a group is or is not involved in an under-the-surface interpersonal struggle. If we find that the group is going round and round on the same issue, making no progress or forward movement toward agreement or understanding, we have reason to suspect that personal conflict may be at the root of it. Or if, during the course of the discussion, there are many side conversations which do not appear to be about the topic of discussion, they may indicate that tensions are spilling over into hostile whisperings. If an analysis of the discussion itself reveals that some members of the group are consistently supporting the ideas of certain individuals or opposing those of others, regardless of what is being talked about at the moment, this would suggest the existence of factions engaged in a struggle for power. And if, as the meeting breaks up, small groups go off together involved in animated conversation, they may be releasing antagonisms which have welled up within them during the discussion. (On the other hand they might also be carrying over enthusiasm generated on the topic.)

The Sources of Interpersonal Conflict

What gives rise to the kinds of antagonisms we have been describing? Why are some group members overaggressive, defensive, stubborn, hostile? At the risk of seeming to oversimplify a complex matter, we would propose two general categories of causation — frustration and insecurity. Modern psychological theory would appear to support the notion that these two factors are at the basis of most pugnacious behavior, whether it occurs in a group discussion or in any other social relationship.

Frustration

None of us is immune to frustration. As a matter of fact life would be rather dull if we got everything we wanted and never found ourselves confronted with any obstacles to our desires. But we need not worry about such a state of affairs. Even if it were not for the problems constantly posed by our physical environment or our own lack of talent, there would always be other people with conflicting needs to serve as agents of our frustration. There are a number of different reactions we may have to frustrating conditions. We may be impelled to work at overcoming the obstacles. We may withdraw and give up. Or we may become angry at ourselves or at other people. It is this latter kind of response which leads to interpersonal conflict.

There are all sorts of elements present in a discussion situation which may frustrate a member sufficiently to arouse overaggressiveness in him. We have already noted that the apathy or indifference of other members may make him angry, particularly if he feels that the group has important work to do. Or if problems he wishes to see solved are not being met to his satisfaction — perhaps not quickly enough to suit him or perhaps not in ways he thinks are proper — he may become frustrated and hostile. His ideas may not be receiving the acceptance and support which he feels are due them, or he as a person may not be given the amount of attention or respect he wants and needs. Any of these frustrations may put him in a fighting mood. And the moment he becomes belligerent in the discussion other members are provoked to respond in kind. At this point human physiology enters to complicate the picture. Adrenalin begins to flow faster, blood pressures start to rise, sweat glands function more vigorously, ears and necks redden. This in turn heightens the tension that is felt, and the molehill soon becomes a mountain.

Conflicts which spring from sources such as these are to be expected occasionally in most intimate human relationships and are not necessarily something to be concerned about. So long as these flare-ups are but momentary episodes in a generally positive atmosphere they can be regarded as the normal and healthy draining off of tensions resulting from life's daily frustrations. It is when pugnaciousness becomes chronic — when an individual or group is almost always fighting — that remedies are needed. Although some of the kinds of frustration enumerated above may give rise to chronic interpersonal conflict, it is more likely that we will find the source of serious difficulties rooted in insecurity.

Insecurity

Fifty years ago the notion that a bully or otherwise overaggressive person was basically unsure of himself would have seemed to most of us like a strange and paradoxical idea. But the impact of psychology on popular attitudes has, in the intervening years, been so pervasive that we now have no difficulty in understanding how it is that an insecure person attempts to pretend to himself and others how strong he really is. As Erich Fromm explains it:

> . . . the lust for power is not rooted in strength but in weakness. It is the expression of the inability of the individual self to stand alone and live. It is the desperate attempt to gain secondary strength where genuine strength is lacking.
>
> The word "power" has a twofold meaning. One is the possession of power over somebody, the ability to dominate him; the other mean-

> ing is the possession of power to do something, to be able, to be potent. . . . Far from being identical, these two qualities are mutually exclusive. . . . to the extent to which an individual is potent, that is, able to realize his potentialities on the basis of freedom and integrity of his self, he does not need to dominate and is lacking in the lust for power.[1]

The chronic fighter, then, is often one who feels basically insecure. Ridden by self-doubt, he lashes out at others or becomes defensive with them. Since his experiences with people — his parents in particular — have left him feeling rejected, he now finds it difficult or impossible to relate to group situations in a warm and open way. He keeps people at arm's length, mistrusting them because he mistrusts mankind in general (including himself). If he does not withdraw entirely, he participates in competitive or defensive ways.

It should not be assumed that the pattern of behavior we have here described is manifested only by people who are emotionally ill. There are various degrees of insecurity, and resultant hostility, and all of it need not be traceable to being "dropped on one's head as a baby." Members of minority or underprivileged groups, for example, (whether racial, religious, or economic) often exhibit some of these tendencies in discussion groups. Lacking confidence in their status in society, feeling unaccepted and discriminated against, they frequently develop a chip-on-the-shoulder attitude — defensive, distrustful, argumentative, and brittle. Communication becomes difficult because it is so hard to get through to them. Their unsatisfied needs for status and attention may lead them to talk too much or to talk with a know-it-all air — making desperate (and, ironically, self-defeating) attempts to win the acceptance they so urgently crave.

This behavior is not only harmful to others but serves no good purpose for the fighter himself. Its effect upon the group is to create a tense and competitive atmosphere from which warmth and honesty tend to be excluded. The less aggressive members are, in effect, denied an equal opportunity to participate, and individuals who might otherwise be friendly and cooperative have their worst impulses aroused. The fighter himself gains nothing from the arrangement. No matter how many triumphs he scores his appetite remains insatiable. Although he may gain temporary

[1] Fromm, *op. cit.*, p. 162.

pleasure from a particularly effective cutting remark, or a long-winded speech to the group, his victories are essentially hollow, since what he really wants is not to conquer but to be accepted. Domination over others will never successfully fill the void he feels within himself. Only if he can find some increased sense of inner strength and security will he no longer need to be hostile and defensive with others.

Approaches to Interpersonal Conflict

Having described the sources of interpersonal conflict in such psychiatric terms, we may have led the reader to wonder if anything short of psychotherapy will solve the perennial problem of "what do we do about the overaggressive members of our group?" Although we do not wish to be defeatist, we must admit that with the most severe cases of hostility, referral to a psychiatrist or exclusion from the group may be the only answers. However, there are many degrees of interpersonal hostility — and, though the causes may be psychological, many discussion groups do contain the resources for alleviating such problems, at least to some extent. Even the most task-oriented group has within it some therapeutic capacities — that is, the ability to help an overaggressive member modify his behavior. The less pressing the group's task, of course, the more time and effort it can devote to providing therapy for its problem members.

Simply having the experience of participation in a successfully functioning discussion group may itself be therapeutic for some types of hostile personalities. They may discover, in the frank and free interchange of ideas and feelings, that people are not all as bad as they thought; that it is not necessary forever to be on guard. They may find in this group the sense of worth and belongingness they need to turn their attitudes in more positive directions. The other members of the group may themselves feel sufficiently secure to absorb the attacks of the aggressor with emotional generosity. That is to say, instead of responding in kind, they may show an understanding and acceptance (not necessarily agreement) which takes the steam out of the aggressive thrusts and demonstrates that they are both futile and unnecessary.

Furthermore, a fighter may be helped to achieve more socialized behavior merely by virtue of being confronted, in discussion, with other people who have different needs and who are strong enough to place limits upon him. Chances are that one reason he has developed the aggressive patterns he has is that up until now he has gotten away with them. His parents and others in his life must in some way have submitted to them or the patterns would not have been perpetuated. By interacting with a new set of people who are not so amenable, the aggressor may find himself faced with sturdy realities to which *he* must readjust. An interesting example of this kind of "therapy" is reported by Grant and Grant, who have experimented with group interaction as a means of rehabilitating delinquent servicemen.[2] These investigators have found that with subjects who possessed a minimal degree of "interpersonal maturity," being forced to live and interact intimately with a group of other men succeeded in bringing about substantial improvements in attitude and behavior.

These, then, are some of the automatic or built-in mechanisms which may function in a group to modify hostile actions. There are, in addition, deliberate steps that can be tried when a group is plagued with serious problems of interpersonal conflict. We may, for convenience, classify them into three categories: therapeutic, diversionary, and restrictive.

Therapeutic measures

The most ordinary and probably soundest advice that can be given to avoid or reduce the level of interpersonal conflict in discussion is to provide opportunities for the members of the group to engage in activities together which will enable them to get to know each other as human beings and help build feelings of friendship and rapport. Common sense alone would tell us that if people have dinner or refreshments together before plunging into the business at hand, they are likely to find one another easier to get along with. This is because they will have had an opportunity to discover common ground with one another, be it baseball or children, and to develop some confidence in their relationship. Major Charles Estes, a former staff member of the

[2] J. Douglas Grant and Marguerite Q. Grant, "A Group Dynamics Approach to the Treatment of Non-Conformists in the Navy," *Annals of the American Academy of Political and Social Science* (March, 1959).

Federal Mediation and Conciliation Service, used to tell of a technique he employed in labor-management negotiations which is based on this same principle of building common ground. He would start each meeting by asking the participants to list on the blackboard all of the outstanding issues between them. He would then have them divide the list into two categories: More Controversial and Less Controversial (it was relatively easy to get agreement on this categorization). The next step was to take up the less controversial issues — for here agreement would be most readily achieved. Thus by the time the most controversial issues were reached, a foundation of harmony had been constructed which would tend to lessen the interpersonal tensions that might come into play over the more difficult problems.

A second, and more direct, approach to interpersonal conflict — after it has already begun — is to employ the mechanism of feedback and group self-evaluation discussed previously in this book. Thus if one individual habitually monopolizes the conversation, a discussion in which he is made aware of what he is doing and how others feel about it might serve to effect some change in his pattern. Or if he can be convinced that his sarcasm is getting him nowhere, and is disrupting the group as well, he may be persuaded to soften his remarks. If the antagonisms are too explosive to handle in this way by the group as a whole, private talks might be arranged, separately or jointly, with the parties to the conflict, in the hope of achieving sufficient self-insight to temper their actions in the group.

A third and somewhat debatable mechanism for alleviating interpersonal conflict is for someone in the group to provide a face-saving escape hatch through which a defensive personality can gracefully crawl. So frequently issues remain stalemated in a discussion simply because everyone has taken a firm position and no one wants to give others the personal satisfaction of feeling that a point has been won. If some way of phrasing an agreement can be found which makes it appear that the loser has not given any ground (even though everyone knows that he has), this may be enough to bring the recalcitrant party around. In fact, if he has gotten himself into a sufficiently untenable position he may greatly appreciate the chance to get out of the hole with so little loss of "face." We call this a debatable technique because it may have harmful as well as helpful effects upon both the individual directly concerned and the group as a whole. It is, in essence, a form of coddling the overaggressive one, of treating him as the child he is acting. If this sort of thing is done for him consistently his juvenile behavior is reinforced, and the group may find itself in the position of always having to appease him whenever his support is sought. On the other hand, it can be argued that the end justifies the means. Why make a person lose face if you can achieve a reasonable agreement without wounding his pride? If his problem is basically one of insecurity, why make it worse by cutting the ground from under him? If you try to force him to face reality you may lose him altogether. We leave it to the reader to decide if and when face-saving devices are justified.

Another possible method of reducing overaggressiveness is to place additional power and responsibility in the hands of the fighter. He may be asked to serve as recorder (a job which might also succeed in quieting him down), or summarizer, or even discussion leader. His help might be solicited, outside of the meeting, in drawing out nonparticipating members. This is a risky course of action, one which might just as easily make matters worse rather than better. It can be extremely successful if the aggressor in question has felt only mildly insecure and now finds sufficient self-confidence through his new responsibilities to become a constructive member of the group. The energies which formerly flowed into hostile expression may be redirected to useful purposes. The danger, however, is that if the fighter's feelings of insecurity are deep-seated, additional responsibility and acceptance in the group will not satisfy him. His new powers will merely be added to the arsenal of weapons he already has, and make him a greater menace to the group than he was at the outset.

Finally, the technique of role-playing can sometimes be fruitful in alleviating interpersonal conflict. By asking the parties to the dispute to "act out" a discussion in which each plays the part of the other, new insight may be gained not only into how the other fellow feels but into one's own behavior as well. Malcolm Knowles, in an interesting article called "Role Playing at Home,"[3] has described the successful use of this method in ameliorating a bit of conflict between himself and his young son. By his little boy

[3] Malcolm Knowles, "Role Playing at Home," *Adult Leadership* (November, 1953).

playing the father and himself taking the son's part an improvement in communication between them was achieved.

Diversionary tactics

Sometimes the best that can be done about interpersonal conflict is temporarily to divert the group away from it. This may be accomplished by shifting the discussion to another issue less fraught with personal overtones; by getting the conversation away from the parties to the dispute and into the hands of other people; or, if necessary, by calling for a recess or adjournment. These tactics are based on the premise that the causes of the conflict are largely transitory ones, such as relatively minor frustrations which have been aggravated by the physiological cycle of adrenalin and blood pressure. It is assumed that when the group returns to the same issue at a later date these tensions will have disappeared and rational discussion will be possible. If, however, the conflict is but another manifestation of a chronic pattern of personal hostility within the group, diversion will serve no useful purpose in the long run. Sooner or later the group will have to deal with the problem in more fundamental ways.

Restrictive methods

When all of the more positive methods of redirecting the energies of overaggressive group members have failed, and continued expressions of hostility pose a serious threat to the successful functioning of the group, it may be time to resort to restrictive measures. One of the most effective of these is social quarantine: the other members of the group unite to isolate the fighter, ignoring him and his contributions, and taking or keeping the conversation away from him as much as they possibly can. Assuming that there are only one or two hostile personalities in the group, and that all the others cooperate in the quarantine action, this method can work well.

The difficulty lies in achieving the united action which is required. For one thing, there is sometimes insufficient communication among the members of the group about interpersonal matters for them to have discovered that others are as fed up with the fighters as they and are willing to join in an effort to do something about them. Often the aggressor is shrewd enough to have played a divide-and-conquer game, or the other participants are insensitive to the ways in which they are making things easier for him. We have witnessed countless discussion groups which were troubled by conversation-monopolizers, where other participants, when they did manage to get the ball away from the dominator, would toss it right back to him again by asking him a question or engaging him in an argument. There seems to be something magnetic about the overaggressive person which causes others unwittingly to cooperate in keeping him at the center of attention.

Sometimes it is difficult to achieve unified action because the group members have grown so battle weary that a "what's the use?" attitude has overcome them. They feel that the patterns of hostility are so firmly established that nothing will change them. As we noted in the previous chapter, apathy and withdrawal are frequently the result of an atmosphere of conflict. And this apathy is something which the aggressor, consciously or unconsciously, counts on to aid his cause. For if he can drive everyone else into a state of noninvolvement he then has the entire field to himself.

Finally, the group may fear that social quarantine would so antagonize a pugnacious person that it would be the same as throwing him out of the group. Particularly if the dominator holds a position of official leadership, to attempt to quarantine him would be tantamount to revolution. And, as the signers of the Declaration of Independence proclaimed, "all experience hath shown, that mankind are more disposed to suffer, while evils are sufferable, than to right themselves by abolishing the forms to which they are accustomed."

In spite of these obstacles, effective quarantines can be and often are achieved. They may be facilitated by techniques of communication such as the Kaffee Klatsch, where members get together outside of meetings to share their grievances, or by Post-Meeting Reaction Sheets (sometimes referred to as PMR's) which are filled out anonymously by the participants at the end of each discussion and tabulated and reported at the next meeting. Simply making the members aware of the points we have been discussing here — such as their unconscious tendency to play into the aggressor's hands, or their failure to support those who do attempt to set in motion a more positive atmosphere — may cause the group to swing into united action.

The second category of restrictive methods we would like to discuss has a long and honorable history. We refer to formal controls of a meeting, such as the rules of parliamentary procedure. When one studies parliamentary law it becomes clear that one of the major motivations for its establishment must have been the desire to regulate interpersonal conflict. There are a number of rules that can be cited which have this effect. First is the requirement that before a member can speak he must seek and gain recognition from the chair. This places in the hands of the discussion leader the power to restrict the contributions of anyone he chooses not to notice. Then there is the provision which makes it possible for the assembly to place time limits on the length of speeches, and another that advises the chairman to alternate speaking opportunities among the proponents of opposite sides of the question. Finally we would point to the custom of addressing all remarks to the chair, and of referring to one's enemies in the debate as "my honorable colleague," or "my worthy opponent," or "the distinguished Senator from Illinois" — all of which tend to depersonalize the argument. Although this sort of rhetoric sometimes seems hollow and insincere — and provides but a thin veil over the hostilities that are present — it at least serves to curb the more violent expressions of personal antagonisms. Much as we may hesitate to recommend that a group invoke formal procedures of this sort, there may be situations of interpersonal conflict where such a course of action would be helpful.

When all else has failed, and the fighters continue to obstruct and demoralize discussion, force, if the group has it, may be the only answer. That is, the other members, either directly or through a leader, may discipline the trouble maker. The fraternity president may fine him, the employer may demote him, the military court-martial him, the teacher send him to the principal, his friends give him a tongue lashing, or the members of his gang beat him up. Such methods are hardly the most enlightened way of dealing with a human relations problem — but then again, perhaps enlightenment has its limitations!

Overaggressiveness in group discussion is a problem of which many people are acutely aware. Although certainly no more serious than apathy, its manifestations are more immediately irksome. Hostility may be expressed overtly, through monopolizing a conversation, pulling rank, negativism, and defensiveness, or it may emerge in more indirect and subtle ways — through sarcasm, moralizing, and blocking. Personal aggressiveness appears to spring from two sources — frustration and insecurity. Interpersonal conflict which is due to temporary frustration is much easier to deal with than that which arises from feelings of basic insecurity in the participants.

We have seen that a discussion group has within it a certain "natural" potential for offsetting interpersonal conflict. The sense of freedom and belongingness which it can provide to the aggressor, as well as the limits it places upon him, may in themselves be therapeutic. In addition, there are deliberate and conscious steps which the members of a group may take to alleviate problems of personal hostility. Among the more constructive or therapeutic of these are providing opportunities for discussants to establish common ground with one another, group self-evaluation, face-saving, and placing increased responsibility in the hands of pugnacious individuals. Role-playing may sometimes be useful. At times, diversionary tactics may be called for, and at other times restrictive measures may be all that are feasible. Among the latter possibilities are social quarantine and formal controls such as parliamentary procedure. As our final resort we may revert to primitive impulse and fight fire with fire.

RECOMMENDED READINGS

Chase, Stuart. *Roads to Agreement.* Harper and Brothers, 1951.

Elliott, Harrison. "What to do with Emotional Prejudice and Bias," *The Process of Group Thinking.* Association Press, 1928.

Fromm, Erich. *Escape from Freedom.* Rinehart & Company, Inc., 1941.

Lindgren, Henry Clay. *The Art of Human Relations.* Hermitage Press, 1953.

Chapter Twelve

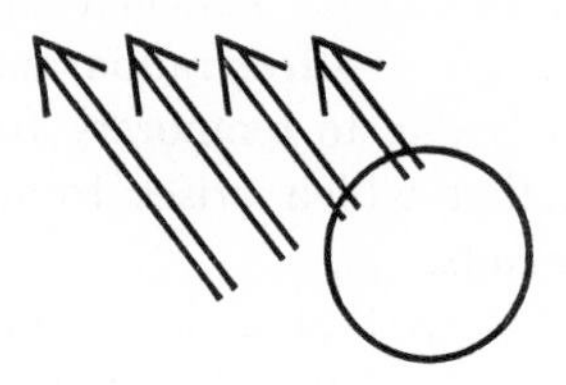

Obstacles to Communication

SOME YEARS AGO Elmer Rice, the American playwright, penned the following dialogue for a scene in a successful play, "The Adding Machine."

Six. Business conditions are sure bad.
Five. Never been worse.
Four. I don't know what we're comin' to.
Three. I look for a big smash-up in about three months.
Two. Wouldn't surprise me a bit.
One. We're sure headin' for trouble.
Mrs. Six. My aunt has gall stones.
Mrs. Five. My husband has bunions.
Mrs. Four. My sister expects next month.
Mrs. Three. My cousin's husband has erysipelas.
Mrs. Two. My niece has St. Vitus's dance.
Mrs. One. My boy has fits.
Mrs. Zero. I never felt better in my life. Knock Wood!
Six. Too damn much agitation, that's at the bottom of it.
Five. That's it! Too damn many strikes.
Four. Foreign agitators, that's what it is.
Three. They ought to be run outa the country.
Two. What the hell do they want, anyhow?
One. They don't know what they want, if you ask me.
Six. America for the Americans is what I say!

All. (in unison) That's it! Damn foreigners! Damn dagoes! Damn Catholics! Damn sheenies! Damn niggers! Jail 'em! shoot 'em! hang 'em! (They all rise) (Sing in unison)

My country 'tis of thee
Sweet land of liberty! [1]

This conversation, bizarre and extravagant as it is, satirizes some of the real difficulties people have in trying to communicate with one another. The breakdowns revealed in this passage — talking past each other, speaking without foundation, engaging in name-calling and vituperation — are just a few of the obstacles that prevent people from understanding each other and dealing successfully with human problems.

Thus far we have looked at interpersonal relations in a group largely as a psychological problem. We quote the above passage in order to suggest that another way of looking at the discussion group is to view it as a communication system and observe the character of the talk that flows through its channels. When this is done one is impressed with the fact that some habits of talk lead to irritation, anxiety, and unnecessary conflict, while others seem to promote understanding and harmony. Some talk divides people; other kinds of talk unite them. The potential for fusion or fission is present not only in nuclear fields, but in human affairs as well, and the quality of our communication may contribute to either result.

An Overview

Before attempting to evaluate communication in discussion groups we will have to form some idea of what we mean by the term. "To communicate," according to Ralph Hefferline, "is, literally, to make common. To say that the parts of a system are in effective communication is to say that activity, excitement, information in one part of the system comes to be shared by, participated in, or, in short, communicated to, the other parts." [2] Thus, in discussion, when we talk of communication we are re-

[1] Copyright by Elmer Rice and published by Samuel French, Inc. Reprinted by permission of author and publisher.

[2] Ralph Hefferline, "Communication Theory I: Integrator of the Arts and Sciences," *Quarterly Journal of Speech* (October, 1955), p. 226.

ferring to how thoroughly, and by what means, "activity, excitement, information" are distributed in a group. As we noted earlier, many groups of people interact dynamically, from jazz bands to basketball teams, but there is only one type, the discussion group, in which this interaction is carried on exclusively through speech. By speech, in this case, we refer to the total communicative behavior of group members, including their use of physical movement, voice, and language, although our primary concern will be with the way ideas are symbolized and expressed in words.

George Homans suggests that the symbol of the social sciences should be a snake biting its own tail, for whenever we analyze human behavior we risk becoming involved in a vicious circle. We decide, let us say, to study racial discrimination. To understand it we must isolate its cause. This we trace to the existence of prejudice in people's minds toward certain races. But where did the prejudice come from? In many instances it results from having been raised in a family or community in which discrimination is regularly practiced. Thus discrimination is a consequence of prejudice, which is a consequence of discrimination. We have come full circle. In a similar manner we find that the way people begin to talk to each other, what they talk about, and the character of their statements establishes certain expectations, or norms, in a group. When this happens we say the group has "structure." Once communication norms are crystallized and recognized they, in turn, will influence the way in which all future ideas will be communicated. Whether or not certain opinions will be expressed, or silenced, and how they circulate in a group will contribute significantly in all probability, to the quality of decisions reached and the degree of enthusiasm with which they will be supported.

In a sense this whole section of the book (Part III) is about communication, since all facets of interpersonal relations — personal motives, apathy, and overaggressiveness — affect, in one way or another, how the members of a group will communicate. And these patterns of communication, once established as norms, will themselves have a subsequent effect upon the personal motives of members, apathy, overaggressiveness, and so on. Patterns of communication, therefore, may be viewed as either the symptoms or the causes of other aspects of interpersonal relations with which we have already dealt. But since they are so influential it is important that we examine the communication process *per se*. Therefore we shall describe in this chapter some of the channels of communication that are likely to develop when people discuss, why they develop, and how they are related to the morale and productivity of a group. Second, we want to examine how language influences the communication of ideas. In other words, we are interested not only in the circuitry in discussion but the kinds of signals that flow through these circuits as people attempt to share their experiences. Finally, we want to offer some suggestions about the attitudes and habits of communication that make it easier for people to understand each other.

Communication Networks

As people begin to talk together they not only develop specialized roles for themselves but they may, as does a river, form well-defined channels for sharing their feelings with one another. A group member who opens one meeting will find that other people, at later meetings, will wait for him to get them started. A person who makes several highly original suggestions will be expected to take the lead whenever the group is engaged in formulating new policies. A person who monopolizes the conversation will find others expecting him to comment frequently on all matters before the group. The infrequent contributor and the nonparticipant will be likely, as time goes on, to play a smaller and smaller part in the group's deliberations. Often the expectations of committee members become so solidified that talk rarely departs from the channels laid down in earlier interactions.

Some of these networks are desirable and effective. They are desirable when they enable the group to make maximum use of the talents of its members, and they are effective when they contribute to speedy decision-making. Valid decisions may not be made, on the other hand, because information in one part of the group fails to reach other parts. In some cases a network may exclude certain members or cliques and thus contribute to division, disruption, or disintegration. Vital facts concerning the group's own processes, as in the case of the hidden agenda, may be suppressed, and their neglect may sabotage the group's efforts. Frequently groups fail, not for lack of ideas, but for lack of channels through which ideas can flow freely and without distortion.

We shall describe four of the more common patterns, why they evolve, and how some of them may be changed if they seriously impair a group's effectiveness.

Recitative pattern

The first communication network is called the "recitative pattern" because it is reminiscent of the sort of interaction one finds in so many classrooms. The teacher initiates all the questions to which, in turn, the pupils are expected to give the right answers. Approval is given for the correct reply, disapproval for any other. In a discussion this means that most of the communication originates from, or is directed toward, one member of the group. The interaction diagram below illustrates this pattern.[3]

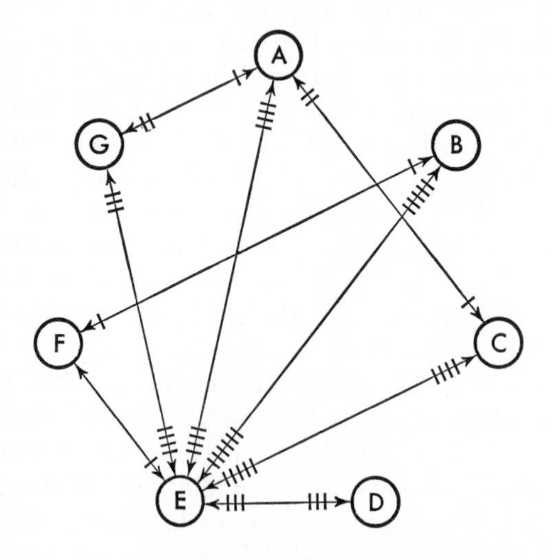

In spite of the absence of formal restrictions upon communication in discussion there is a tendency for talk to center on certain individuals. Participants will almost inevitably direct their remarks toward high-status figures, because they have a greater influence on decisions. A person who happens to be unusually aggressive or dominant will also tend to be at the hub of communications be-

[3] In these diagrams the lines connecting people indicate an interaction between two members of the group. The short intersecting bars represent the number of times this channel was used.

cause he is likely to seize control of the group. Someone with extensive knowledge of the problem normally will find himself in a focal position. The locus of leadership in a group will almost certainly influence who talks to whom. If the leader sees himself as personally responsible for directing and controlling participation, then most of the talk will be aimed in his direction, since his permission must be obtained in order to "get the floor." If, on the other hand, there is no leader, or he plays a nondirective role, there is not as likely to be a consistent or inflexible pattern of communication. The focusing of communication on E in the diagram could indicate the presence of an undemocratic leader who has assumed the responsibility for herding the group along, or it may have resulted from someone monopolizing the conversation and thereby forcing others to speak to him.

Before taking any corrective action it would be wise to make sure that the recitative pattern is not a result of legitimate, temporary factors. The presence of conflict in a group, for example, will often cause a momentary focusing of communication upon a single member. Disagreement is immediately reflected in both the substance and direction of interaction. Leon Festinger, who has directed some of the most successful studies of social influence, notes that "The existence of a discrepancy in the group with respect to opinions and abilities will lead to action on the part of members of that group to reduce the discrepancy."[4] In both laboratory and field studies, Festinger and his colleagues have found that the pressures to communicate are greater the more cohesive the group is and the wider the difference of opinion among the members. This is to say that whenever someone takes a position opposite to that of the group, communication will increase between the group and the deviant to reduce the margin of disagreement and facilitate unified action.

As we saw earlier, however, communication with deviants is likely to decrease after a time. Parties to the dispute may change their minds, or conflicting points of view, as a result of discussion, may be integrated. In some cases the group discovers that the deviant is unalterably and absolutely committed to his position.

[4] Leon Festinger, "A Theory of Social Comparison Processes" in Hare, Borgatta, and Bales, *op. cit.*, p. 171. The interested reader will find further data on social influence in Leon Festinger and J. Thibaut, "Interpersonal Communication in Small Groups," *Journal of Abnormal and Social Psychology* (January, 1951) and in Festinger, Schacter, and Back, *op. cit.*

People may then stop talking to him, not because he disagrees, but because he is unpersuadable and will not yield to any argument. This raises an ethical problem. If the individual has not changed because the members of the group have employed unfair tactics to convince him (social pressure, verbal stratagems), or because the issue has not been thoroughly explored, then the group will only be harming itself by cutting off communication with him. The deviant may turn out to be right. If, on the other hand, the members of the group have explored the controversy intelligently we see no alternative but for the group to go on in spite of his opposition. Otherwise the entire deliberative process will break down.

Any decision to break out of the recitative pattern, therefore, requires some analysis of its causes. If it results from temporary, or healthy, disturbances nothing should be done to change the pattern. But if it reflects the presence of a dominating personality, a monopolizer, or someone who needs to be in the center of attention, some corrective action is indicated.

The first and most democratic way of handling the recitative pattern is to call it to the attention of the group and discuss how to bring about greater freedom and spontaneity. If this fails, or if the narrowing of communication channels is a result of certain members' needs to dominate, then action along the lines described in the last chapter may have to be adopted: the group may have to resort to therapy or quarantine; it may have to shift to new issues where a different combination of people will be brought into the conversation; if none of these succeed, the group may have to preserve its freedom to communicate by adopting rules of procedure for regulating participation and by giving the power to enforce them to someone other than the member now dominating the discussion.

Sub-grouping

In sub-grouping we find private conversations taking place within the framework of the larger discussion. These conversations have the effect of taking certain members out of the discussion and of splitting off attention from the main job of the group. Sub-grouping is illustrated on the next page.

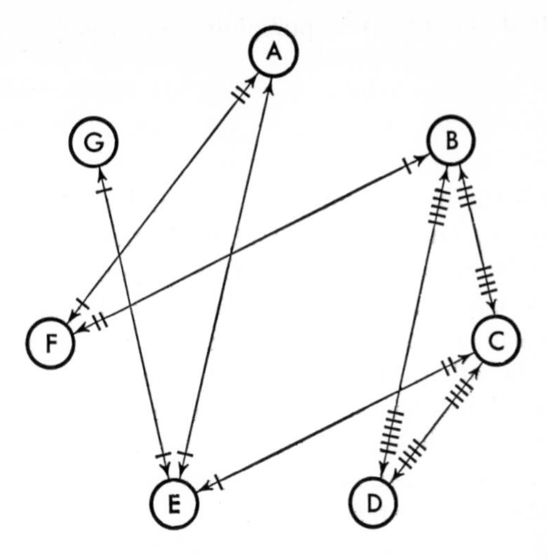

Curiously enough, sub-grouping can occur either because of too much or too little interest in the topic. Participants can become so emotionally upset over an issue that they must express themselves to someone, with the result that they split up into smaller groups to increase the number of available communication pathways. Whispering between neighbors is sometimes interpreted as a sign of apathy. Actually it often means that those engaged in side conversations are so interested that their enthusiasm spills over into private comments for which they do not wish to take the time of the group. Sometimes, however, if the discussion becomes tiresome, members seated beside each other will start a conversation about other matters. Their conversation may deal with more exciting aspects of the topic or with entirely irrelevant matters of personal interest (family problems, dating, vacation plans).

There is no reason to prohibit such occasional conversations, but when they become common and persistent they may indicate that something is seriously wrong. If sub-grouping occurs because it is impossible to break into the larger discussion, then new openings must be made for those forced into private conversations. Again the problem may be brought before the group and talked about openly to determine the cause and agree upon a solution. If the discussion in the sub-groups is on irrelevant topics this may be a clue that the group is pursuing the wrong, or unaccepted, goals.

Dialogue

A special case of sub-grouping is found in the dialogue. A few people carry on their conversation, in this case not privately, but in front of the entire group. One person offers an opinion. Someone else objects. As the two disputants begin to argue they set up a private communication circuit in which each is forced to reply to the other. The remaining group members are driven into the role of helpless spectators, for the two people engaging in argument are oblivious to anyone else who tries to enter the conversation. The diagram below illustrates a group in which two such dialogues have taken place.

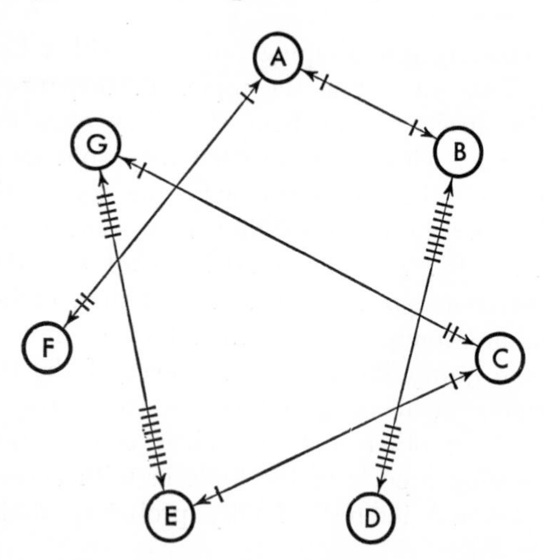

This sort of public dialogue is usually a product of a healthy dispute between members of a committee. If this is the case nothing needs to be done about it immediately. But if the dialogue continues very long it may lead to apathy or interpersonal friction in the group. It can be overcome if other members will be more aggressive in entering such an exclusive conversation, by shifting to another issue, or if necessary, by appointing someone to control participation. Often, however, nothing more is needed than to point out the problem to the parties involved.

Multilateral pattern

What most discussion groups are striving for in the way of a communication pattern is diagrammed below.

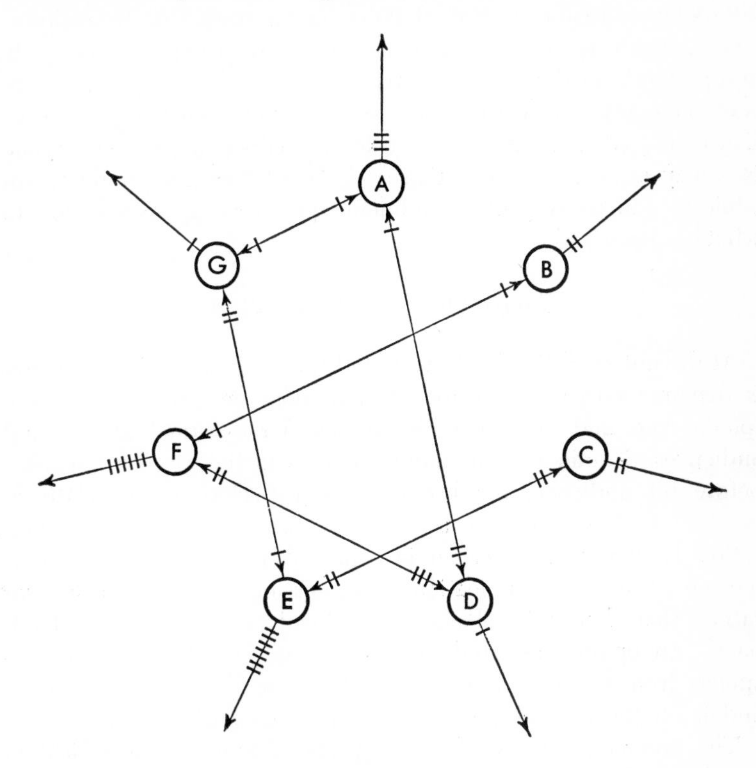

In this instance communication flows freely from person to person according to whoever is moved to speak or whoever has relevant information to contribute. Attention shifts randomly around the group, and departures from this pattern are a result of special issues that arouse conflict, or some other kind of temporary crisis.

On this diagram the reader will notice the addition of a number of lines which, instead of connecting people inside the circle, point away from the group itself. These lines are used to indicate what we shall call "group-centered" remarks, comments that are directed at the group as a whole rather than at a single committee member. One of the characteristics of a mature group seems to be the predominance of group-directed over person-directed contributions. They profoundly improve communications because they tend to open up the communication channels, encourage everyone to offer information and opinions, provide maximum feedback for the correcting of error, and facilitate better interpersonal relations. Robert Bales, in his studies of group interaction, for example, found that those exercising leadership in groups tend, on the whole, to make a larger proportion of group-centered contributions than those who are not regarded as leaders.[5] Expressing ideas in a way that invites comment from everyone is a way of "drawing out" those who may have something worth while to add by way of amendment, qualification, or objection to what has been said.

Two-way Communication

At the outset of this book we noted that interaction in discussion is dynamic rather than static. Communication tends to be more spontaneous and unpredictable than in large formal groups and audiences. In one-way communication, as in the case of a speaker before his audience, the listeners are expected to be relatively passive. In the committee meeting, on the other hand, communication is two-way: everyone is expected to transmit as well as receive ideas. Communication in discussion, in short, is circular rather than linear in character; it involves instantaneous feedback. An opinion asserted by one person provokes a verbal response from another, a further qualification is added by a third, and finally the original speaker completes the circuit.

The greater efficiency of two-way over one-way communication has been demonstrated by Heise and Miller. They found, in asking groups to solve different types of problems using a variety of communication networks, that:

> A closed chain in which only one-way communication was possible between any two persons was by far the least efficient; an open chain which allowed two-way communication between any two adjacent individuals, was intermediate; a closed chain where all members talked and listened to all other members was most efficient.[6]

[5] Robert F. Bales, "The Equilibrium Problem in Small Groups," in Hare, Borgatta, and Bales, *op. cit.*, p. 438.

[6] George Heise and George Miller, "Problem Solving by Small Groups Using Various Communication Nets," in Hare, Borgatta, and Bales, *op. cit.*, p. 366.

The level of performance in small groups, they noted, was definitely related to the communication channels available for solving their problems.

The specific effects of different patterns of feedback were tested in a study by Leavitt and Mueller. In this experiment, instructors were asked to tell groups of students how to construct a series of geometric designs. Four conditions were employed: (1) Zero feedback in which no questions or responses were permitted. (2) A visible audience condition in which speakers and listeners could see each other but where no actual oral exchange was permitted. (3) A yes-no condition in which listeners were able to reply in the affirmative or negative to any instruction. (4) A free feedback condition which permitted questions, interruptions, requests for clarification, and so on. Leavitt and Mueller found that "free feedback" produced greater accuracy in communication, led to better rapport among the communicators, and resulted in greater confidence in the decisions that were made.[7] Maximum feedback seems to help people to understand one another better by reducing the inherent ambiguity in messages. The explanation of the superiority of group decision-making over other modes may lie in the absence of restrictions on communication in the small, face-to-face group.

Morale and Productivity

How are the communication networks in small groups related, if at all, to the productivity and morale of a group? One of the most ingeniously designed studies of group performance under various communication networks has been carried out by H. J. Leavitt.[8] Groups of five subjects each were seated at tables in such a way that they could only communicate with each other by passing slips of paper through partitions which were manipulated to produce a variety of communicative patterns. The four basic networks used in this study are reproduced on the next page.

In the Wheel, members had no choice but to communicate their information to C, who was in a position to communicate with

[7] Harold Leavitt and Ronald Mueller, "Some Effects of Feedback on Communication," in Hare, Borgatta, and Bales, *op. cit.*

[8] H. J. Leavitt, "Some Effects of Certain Communication Patterns on Group Performance," *Journal of Abnormal and Social Psychology* (January, 1951).

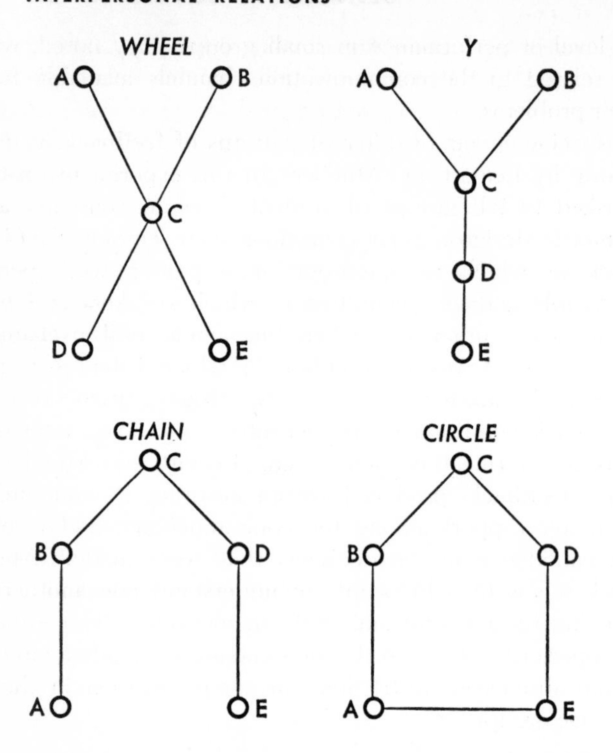

everyone. In the Y, each subject, with the exception of E, could communicate with C, but E was virtually isolated except through D. In the Chain, two members (A and E) found themselves cut off from the group except through B and D, but the remaining members could pass messages to persons on either side of them. In the Circle, every subject was free to communicate either to right or left.

Each of the subjects was given a different set of symbols (information) and the problem was to discover which symbol was held in common by all the group members. Records were kept of the time it took to complete the task, the number of messages communicated, the errors resulting from communication, the morale of the group, an so on. The results raise some interesting points about interaction in small groups: The Circle — the one most closely resembling, but not identical to, the normal discussion situation — proved to be the most active (most messages exchanged) and was characterized by having the least centralization of leadership. More errors were committed, but they were also more readily corrected. Morale in this condition was the highest. In the Wheel, Y, and Chain less errors were made, subjects required fewer messages to complete the task, and found it necessary to organize their work around a central person or leader. But these last three arrangements were less satisfying ones in which to work. The groups did not differ significantly in the time required to solve the problem. Equal efficiency, higher morale, and less dependence upon particular members, therefore, seem to be associated with greater freedom of communication.

The Content of Communication

Next we need to analyze the content of the messages flowing through the channels that become established, for there are other impediments to successful communication beyond the mere circuits themselves. As one listens to committee meetings in which people are trying to talk sense, one is struck by certain recurring habits of personal expression that lead, time after time, to confusion or misunderstanding. Almost everyone agrees that man's greatest faculty is his ability to symbolize and share his experiences with his fellow man, but it is not always clear whether we control our symbols or they control us.

What are the unconscious assumptions we make when we talk together? Whenever human beings begin to wag their tongues at one another they are saying implicitly that they expect to gain from an exchange of information or from sharing their experiences. When this communication is effective it can have both a therapeutic and educational value. Talking together is therapeutic when it gives one insight into his own personality or when it leads to a deeper understanding of other people and their problems. It is educational when it increases our factual knowledge and grasp of social problems. Communication, in short, is the means by which we achieve some sort of agreement as to what is "out there," what it means to us, and how we should act in view of that knowledge.

Yet many of our habits of talk take us precisely in the opposite direction. This is true in part because we are not fully aware of the nature of language and the assumptions carried in its structure. Partly, also, because we seldom appreciate how our personal habits of using words can make it hard for other people to respond intelligently or sympathetically to us. One could prepare a lengthy catalogue of "communication stoppers"—habits of talking that make communication impossible or irritatingly difficult. Sometimes our habitual ways of expressing ourselves halt communication dead in its tracks so that people stop trying to communicate altogether; in other cases our language distorts reality so that it becomes difficult to think straight in spite of our desire to be logical. All too often our words produce a great many sparks but little heat. As symbol users we occasionally reveal an abysmal ignorance of the tool—language—that distinguishes us from other living things.

Norman Kemp Smith remarked at one time that "The history of human thought is the record, not of a progressive discovery of truth, but of gradual emancipation from error." This statement seems to apply in some respects to communication as well. Transcripts of committee meetings reveal that discussion often proceeds by negation. That is, one member introduces a topic by making a statement about it. Someone else objects to a portion of the opening remark and qualifies it. Others then proceed to revise and correct his statement. After many objections have been argued there occurs a brief period of integration and agreement. Soon another issue is raised and the process of negation starts again until the new point is acceptable to all. But many interruptions, detours, blockades, and breakdowns mar this flow. Some of the more prominent will be described in the following pages.

Dismissal Reactions

The dismissal reaction takes many forms (both verbal and nonverbal), but running through all of them is a desire—usually unconscious but no less obstructive for that reason—to cut off communication on the idea under discussion. It may be expressed in a complete rejection of the original suggestion—"That just isn't so!" or "It simply won't work!" Or some member of the committee may declare, "That's the most stupid thing I've ever heard!" To call a suggestion "ridiculous," "naïve," or "absurd," is usually enough to foreclose further talk on it. The effect of such remarks is to fasten a period to any dispute, to put an end to further efforts to talk constructively about it. According to Irving Lee, one of the leading sources of trouble when people talk together is

> *The mood of dismissal,* in which a man makes it clear that he wishes to go no farther, to talk no more about something which is to him impossible, unthinkable, wrong, unnecessary, or just plain out of the question. He has spoken and there is little use in trying to make him see otherwise. If he has his way there will be no further discussion on the matter.[9]

This posture, of course, reveals something about the speaker's personality as well as his understanding of the process of communication itself. Communication, as we suggested earlier, arises out of and is sustained by our need to enlarge our grasp of reality. We do this by exchanging words. None of us is capable of perceiving or reporting more than a fraction of reality. Those who stop talk about any idea display an arrogance that is usually without foundation. The effect of their remarks is to put an end to further efforts to discuss a matter. Denunciation replaces argument. This posture of infallibility and omniscience seems without logical justification.

Evasive Reactions

A second pattern of talk that leads to trouble can be described as evasive communication. Ideas are disposed of, not by meeting them head on, but by detouring around them. One way of accomplishing this is to label a remark, "That's a generalization" or "That's just a personal opinion." The speaker then rests content that he has really dealt with the statement. He of course misses the point. The important question is whether the generalization is valid or the inference justified by the facts. Unfortunately, group members sometimes believe that by categorizing an expression they understand it or have disposed of it.

There are those, too, who somewhat smugly tidy up problems by moralizing about them. Slogans and clichés become substitutes for thought. Platitudes are offered in place of penetrating criticism. "The truth will always prevail," "Idle hands are the devil's workshop," or "You can't change human nature" seem so undeniably true — because they are so familiar — that their specific applicabil-

[9] Irving Lee, *How to Talk with People* (Harper, 1952), p. 46.

ity in a particular instance is never considered. It should be apparent to any reasonably sophisticated person that there is a pat verbalization to cover nearly every problem. If one bromide, "You can't teach an old dog new tricks," does not apply, one can always substitute the opposite saying, "You are never too old to learn."

Another way of avoiding the trouble of grappling with a complex idea is to throw a verbal smoke screen around it. Diplomatic doubletalk is not limited to conferences of foreign ministers; it complicates communication in many perfectly ordinary discussion meetings. While articulateness — the sensitive expressing of ideas in language — is an art to be admired, its cultivation sometimes leads to erecting a curtain of words between one's self and strange or unfamiliar ideas.

> After using a word I have often been chagrined to realize that I relied on its beautiful sound to conceal my actual inability to express myself. Many discussions are aggressive fights with empty phrases; more effort is expended to win the fight than to lay bare the truth. We must realize that our words tend to conceal rather than express meaning.[10]

Talk, in short, is often used to impress, to defend one's ego, to spread confusion, to hide one's ignorance. The emphasis in modern life on our ability to manipulate words encourages us to delude ourselves and others through verbal rationalizations. Clever or witty repartee may displace meaningful talk.

Evasive communication seems to border on what psychiatrists have called "tangential responses." Jurgen Ruesch points out that one can respond to any communication positively, negatively, tangentially, or not at all.[11] In the first two cases both the motive of the speaker and the content of his message are acknowledged. The receiver may say "I agree" or "I disagree," but in either case his reply indicates that the communication circuit has been completed. Positive or negative replies are almost equally satisfying because both indicate a willingness on the part of the listener to continue to reach an understanding with the speaker. When responses are tangential or totally missing, however, the receiver

[10] Joost Meerloo, *Conversation and Communication* (International Universities Press, 1952), p. 121.

[11] Jurgen Ruesch, "Synopsis of the Theory of Human Communication," *Psychiatry* (August, 1953).

rejects not only the substance of the message but the very fact of communication itself. Perhaps none of us has passed through childhood without having experienced this at one time or another. Johnny rushes in to announce a thrilling bit of news only to find his parents so absorbed in something else that he might as well not exist. To have one's contributions ignored, passed over, or disregarded can be a shattering experience. Repeated often enough it may produce intense frustration and psychological withdrawal.

Signal Reactions

The brakes are often applied to a constructive conversation, also, because of people's propensity to react signally. Language is made up of words which we can treat as signs or symbols. Words are used symbolically as long as human beings respond to them critically and conditionally; that is, as long as people are aware of the multiplicity of meanings they may have, and of their limited accuracy in describing a particular event. But words can also be treated as signs. When this is the case people react to them as animals do, uncritically and automatically, without qualification. An animal can be taught to react consistently to a phrase, even when it leads to its own slaughter. A dog can be trained to salivate, bark, or attack a person by building up automatic, or signal, responses in him. To be fully human, of course, is to behave symbolically most of the time. When we act automatically, or blindly, we surrender our birthright.

Unfortunately, participants in discussion often react signally rather than symbolically to words. Suggest that an idea is "radical" and they are against it. Call a proposal "socialistic" and minds snap shut without any examination of particulars. Think of the stigma words that can be associated with an idea that will catapult people into immediate acceptance or rejection of it: "reactionary," "atheistic," "monopolistic," "Christian," "Communist-inspired," "materialistic," "dictatorial," "democratic," and "authoritarian." These are words that divide, that oversimplify, that touch off explosions, words that lead to stereotyped reactions. As Alfred Korzybski once remarked, *dog*matic and *cat*egorical people behave animalistically. Instead of pushing words around, they are pushed around by words. The predilection to react signally cements prevailing attitudes and suspends intelligent talk.

Language and Thought

Breakdowns also occur in discussion as a result of our ignorance of the limitations language imposes on our thought processes. As the linguists Edward Sapir and Benjamin Lee Whorf have pointed out, we are not free to talk about things as we please, but are forced to abide by the categories and relationships available in our language. Words are not sterile tools with which to handle ideas but shape and control the ideas themselves. Every language contains a vast number of silent assumptions about the character of reality and every time we speak we express our thoughts in the logic of that language. Sometimes we expect too much from words and are not sufficiently aware of how our native tongue imposes certain ways of thinking on us.

A speaker frequently fails to realize that his manner of symbolizing an idea generates unnecessary conflicts, misrepresents reality, or obscures a real difference of opinion. The English language with its emphasis on nouns over verbs, its tendency to divide the indivisible, its polarity, its stress on the permanent and unchanging, its mutually exclusive categories, inevitably affects the character of most of our arguments. There is not space here to provide a complete catalogue of these semantic pitfalls; it will have to suffice for us to deal with two that most frequently corrupt communication in discussion.

Polarity

We tend, first of all, to talk in terms of opposites. That is, we regard things in life as belonging to two mutually exclusive categories. Something is either this or that. We choose between peace or war, inflation or deflation, capitalism or Communism, progressive or traditional education. We are for unions or against them; in favor of, or opposed to, the New Deal; a believer in cooperation or competition; a segregationist or integrationist. In our social conversations we describe people as brilliant or stupid, beautiful or homely, informed or ignorant, virtuous or sinful, mature or immature. One must be for modern art or against it. There is no middle ground. As Eduard Lindeman once wrote:

> One of the sicknesses of our time is revealed in the tendency to fall into the trap of false antitheses.

> We are driven to accept one of only two alternatives; communism or fascism, science or the humanities, free enterprise or collectivism, laissez-faire or planning. These are all false antitheses and do not belong to the order of nature. These "Either-ors" are the result of dialectical trickery and those who follow their dictates soon lose the sense of reality. . . . Whoever engages in this type of reflection finally builds a rationalized fantasy world.[12]

That our arguments should so often take on this complexion is no accident. A thesaurus or dictionary will reveal the answer. Our language is basically two-valued; it is organized into synonyms and antonyms.

All of this means that as people discuss they will often be impaled on the horns of their own false dilemmas. To choose between polar opposites is to assume that truth lies on one side and error on the other. Dichotomies of this sort, of course, distort reality in most instances, for much of life takes place on the ground between the opposing categories of language. There are not only blacks and whites, but many shades of grey. People differ in the degree to which they are wise or foolish, honest or corrupt. Not only do "either-or" statements distort reality but they sometimes convert disputes into trivial verbal battles which prevent people from coming to grips with the specific details which words so inadequately represent. In the words of Heywood Broun, "Once a man takes sides he begins to see a little less of the world."

In addition, our polar way of thinking and talking frequently gives discussion a partisan character. We talk as if we were on a battlefield. People feel they must take positions. And this implies that they must be constantly attacking someone else or defending themselves. There is little room left over for speculation, for an open-minded examination of the problem, for careful and dispassionate thought. According to William Hazlitt,

> Nothing was ever learnt by either side in a dispute. You contradict one another, will not allow a grain of sense in what your adversary advances, are blind to whatever makes against yourself, dare not look the question fairly in the face, so that you cannot avail yourself even of your real advantages, insist most on what you feel to be the weakest points of your argument, and get more and more absurd, dogmatical, and violent every moment.[13]

[12] T. V. Smith and Eduard C. Lindeman, *The Democratic Way of Life* (Mentor, 1951), pp. 133–134.

[13] Hazlitt, *op. cit.*, p. 99.

As we become identified with a position we begin to interpret criticism as not only an attack on our side but as an attack on ourselves personally. To admit error or to change position under such partisan conditions, even when secretly convinced, is virtually unthinkable. It involves too much "loss of face." The tendency to talk in terms of "either-ors" thus complicates the process of communication and introduces an element of unreality in our thinking.

Abstracting

Failure to understand the different levels of talk in which people engage can also contribute to confusion and errors in judgment. Consider, for example, the following remarks:

(1) The world is undergoing an economic revolution.
(2) Capitalism is still strong in democratic nations.
(3) The NATO countries have emerged from an economic recession.
(4) France has stabilized her currency.
(5) The Consumer Price Index in the U.S. shows that prices were stable in 1959.
(6) The price of meat declined in Chicago during the last six months of 1959.
(7) I paid twenty-five cents for a box of aspirin at Walgreens.

These statements represent different levels of abstractness. The generalization about the "world economic revolution" is an extremely high-level inference and value judgment. It involves collecting, weighting, and evaluating thousands of specific facts. Furthermore this statement cannot be made intelligently unless its author has had considerable training and wide experience. The statement about the box of aspirin, on the other hand, is a description of a simple, daily occurrence. It should be apparent in comparing these sentences that, all other things being equal (which they rarely are), a high-level abstraction is far more risky than a low-level one simply because of the multitude of factors involved.

The danger, in discussion, comes from what Wendell Johnson calls "dead-stick" abstracting. This means simply that conversation gets stuck at one of these levels; people talk exclusively in terms of high- or low-level abstractions. Low-level statements, of course, are likely to be very accurate or at least highly testable. As we move toward level seven we get closer and closer to reality.

But we also run the risk of becoming mired in trivialities. Obtaining greater accuracy in our talk is sometimes bought at the expense of the significance of the idea. We may learn many particulars but fail to understand what they mean. As one moves to higher level abstractions, to theory, interpretation, diagnosis, generalization, one gains significance but runs the risk of inaccuracy. As the Frenchman is reported to have said, "All generalizations are false, including this one." We gamble on building what Bacon called "faith ladders," complicated systems of belief and theory that lose all touch with reality. Participants in discussion need to be on their guard against talking constantly at any of these levels. The concrete has to be interpreted before it has any meaning; the abstract has to be checked against the facts before its truth can be ascertained. The need for accuracy and significance has to be kept in balance.

In addition, there is the danger that, in the search for agreement, committee members will unwittingly push their way to higher and higher verbalizations. Eventually a generalization is formulated that is so broad that everyone is comfortable under its tent. But ambiguity also increases with abstractness. (Note the vagueness in the first three statements above compared to the last three.) And there is a real danger that the final conclusion will be virtually meaningless. Or that it will only mask genuine differences of opinion that would be revealed if the problem were discussed at more concrete levels.

In short, sophisticated participants in discussion need to become flexible in dealing with the different levels of language; able to abstract from concretes, able to particularize abstractions. They need, also, to be suspicious of overly abstract agreements that may only hide important differences at the level of practical action.

Constructive Communication

Study of the communication process reveals that there are certain attitudes and practices that contribute to constructive talk. Speech can be the medium through which we fulfill ourselves, establish warm and intimate relations with our associates, and penetrate to the heart of provoking problems. We are, above all, symbolizers. "In the beginning was the word." Certainly there must be ways of enriching and improving human communication.

Listening

It takes two to communicate — one to listen, another to talk. To discuss effectively requires ability to function with some skill in both roles. Since listening is the more difficult, and the least developed of the two, we turn first to it.

What are we trying to do when we listen to someone? Few seem to have given serious thought to this question. Perhaps that is why the world is filled with so many bad listeners. Our answer would be that we should be trying to get inside the nervous system of another human being to find out how the world looks to him. Or as Clifton Fadiman has said, "Communication begins when you become interested in exploring the other fellow's mind."

Some idea of what is needed to be a good listener can be gained from a brief look at what most of us do when we are *not* being good listeners. Let us imagine that we were suddenly to interrupt a discussion and were able to look at what was going on in the minds of the participants. First, we would find that many people are not listening at all. They are monitoring the conversation, not listening to it. Like a telegraph operator who is expecting a message, they are vaguely aware of signals passing through the ether but are unconscious of what they mean. One sometimes gets the impression, in discussion, of a number of trains all moving in the same direction but on different tracks. Sydney Harris, newspaper columnist, comments that a good conversation "used to be like tennis, where you returned the other fellow's shot, but now it is like golf, where each man goes on hitting his own ball."

Then there are those, in this imaginary experiment, who would be only partly listening to the conversation. They listen selectively, filtering out an occasional word or phrase that allows them to identify the position of the speaker without going to the trouble of understanding what he is saying. A casual reference, an emotionally charged word, a pattern of phrases, touches off a string of associations in the mind of the "listener." He hears just enough to confirm his guess that the speaker is a Republican, Fraternity Man, Pro-Laborite, or an Intellectual, and then retires to his own private speculations about this fact. His filter lets only certain messages through, and these messages are often emasculated by being lifted out of context.

A sizeable number of participants would be listening to refute. Such persons wait impatiently for a chance to demolish the speaker's arguments and, in the course of rehearsing their own cases, pay slight attention to the logic of their imagined opponents. As someone explains an idea they are busily engaged in finding things wrong with it. These "debaters" — and we use the term here only in the worst sense — are animated by the thrill of disputation. They listen defensively, either so they may protect themselves from the threat of change, or so they may impress others with their dialectical prowess.

Our imaginary group, however, would most likely contain a few persons who knew how to listen. Or we might happen upon the group at one of those rare moments when someone drops his defenses, becomes excited about another member's way of looking at things, and begins to listen to him intently. Silence, then, no longer means withdrawal but active participation in the interaction of the group.

Effective listening is not passive. It means abandoning one's own premises temporarily in order to step inside the assumptive world of another human being. The good listener is able to enter the "frame of reference" of his associates. He shares their perceptions primarily to understand, rather than disprove, them. In this sense, good listening is based on a deep respect for the integrity of the speaker. This sort of communication also involves bringing one's whole attention to bear on understanding the speaker as well as his argument. To really grasp another point of view is virtually impossible without first coming to know the person behind the idea — his hopes, fears, doubts, desires. A man is often the living embodiment of his opinions, and one cannot separate the two without losing a vital ingredient.

Good listening, however, is not exclusively an intellectual matter; it has an emotional dimension as well.

> I wonder if we can't say that the aim of real communication is a kind of communion with the other person, a sharing of one's self and an appreciation for the other which affirms the integrity of each. Real understanding comes, we might say, when there's an unspoken agreement that each recognizes the right to self-hood of the other, a self-hood which is unique and accepted and rejoiced in as such — and further, which eagerly desires to know the other more fully and more deeply than he does before the process of communication begins.[14]

[14] Richard Henry, "The Integrity of the Listener," *Today's Speech* (September, 1957), p. 27.

This kind of listening requires the establishment of genuine rapport between the speaker and listener. To be *en rapport* means that people are in tune with each other, that they have established an interpersonal relationship that conduces to good communication.

Carl Rogers suggests that effective listening has still another facet to it.

> I should like to propose, as a hypothesis for consideration, that the major barrier to mutual interpersonal communication is our very natural tendency to judge, to evaluate, to approve (or disapprove) the statement of the other person or the other group. . . . Suppose I say with some feeling, "I think the Republicans are behaving in ways that show a lot of good sense these days." What is the response in your mind as you listen? The overwhelming likelihood is that it will be evaluative. You will find yourself agreeing, or disagreeing, or making some judgment about me such as "He must be conservative," or "He seems solid in his thinking." [15]

To be a good listener, then, requires the ability to avoid making premature judgments about the speaker or his message. A good listener must be able, in short, to avoid reacting signally. This capacity is most drastically needed, and in shortest supply of course, when critical problems are discussed or when people become deeply involved emotionally.

The avoidance of an evaluative reaction can have an important therapeutic effect on the speaker in return.

> If I can listen to what he can tell me, if I can understand how it seems to him, if I can see its personal meaning for him, if I can sense the emotional flavor which it has for him, then I will be releasing potent forces of change in him. If I can really understand how he hates his father, or hates the university, or hates communists — if I can catch the flavor of his fear of insanity, or his fear of atom bombs, or of Russia — it will be of the greatest help to him in altering those very hatreds and fears, and in establishing realistic and harmonious relationships with the very people and situations toward which he has felt hatred and fear.[16]

Of course this takes some courage. There are few things in life that are harder to do than to leave the security of one's own mental

[15] Carl Rogers, "Communication: Its Blocking and Facilitation," *Northwestern University Information Bulletin,* Vol. XX (April, 1952), p. 11.

[16] *Ibid.*

world and enter the private thoughts of another. As Thomas Gordon writes, "There seems to be something in human nature—whether learned and acquired or rooted in the organic make-up of all organisms—something that predisposes man to defend his world of reality against the threat of change from without." To listen open-mindedly is to run the risk of being changed ourselves, of finding that other ways of looking at events may be more valid or more satisfying. Therapists have found many patients who are willing to undergo treatment only if the psychiatrist will assure them that it will not destroy their beliefs in this or that idea.

Dropping one's defenses, empathizing with others, and delaying evaluation will go a long way toward improving communication. It will remove the irritants that produce the antitoxins of dogmatism, exaggeration, name-calling, and verbal dodging which people now use to defend areas of insecurity within their own egos. But rapport is not an end in itself. It is a means to an end—the attainment of wise decisions on matters of human concern. Once a message and speaker are understood, the information contained in his statement must be extracted and acted upon. This involves testing the assumptions on which it rests, checking it against the experience of other group members, and discovering how much of it can be incorporated into the final decision. The following questions may help as a specific guide to the task of listening critically, as well as empathically, to the ideas of others.

(1) What is the speaker saying? What is he trying to tell us? About the problem? About himself? Do I really feel I understand him? Or should I check my interpretation by asking some questions?
(2) What sort of reaction is he generating in me? Does his idea threaten me, my status, my assumptions? Why? Is my hostility or enthusiasm a reflection of my own insecurity or is it an objective response to the inherent strength of his idea?
(3) What is the basis for his remarks? Are his premises stated or implied? How does he know what he claims to know? Does my experience cover his point?
(4) What can be done with his opinion? Does his view invalidate mine or others? Can the different opinions or information be integrated? How? Where does his idea lead us?

Advice on good listening might be reduced still further to a simple paraphrase of a widely held moral principle: Treat other sides of the question with the same respect that you would have others handle your own point of view. "The true spirit of conversation," as Bulwer-Lytton said, "consists in building on another man's observation, not overturning it."

Speaking

The listener is at one end of the communication circuit. The speaker is at the other. The responsibility for success or failure of communication must be shared by both. We not only want to understand others; we want them to understand us as well.

Let the speaker who urgently wishes to communicate his ideas begin by expressing himself as frankly and sincerely as he dares. Few things so corrupt the relations between teacher and pupil, worker and boss, or parent and child, as deceptive communication. In some circles a premium is placed on hiding one's feelings and covering up one's sentiments. Forthrightness is frowned upon. Discussion is a travesty on communication when people sit and smile pleasantly, verbally stroke each other's egos, and utter sweet inanities at one another while large and vital differences of opinion smolder underneath the surface. Nothing, on the other hand, cuts through this sort of pseudo-communication quite as devastatingly as a person who really says what he thinks. On more than one occasion we have seen a group of "grey flannel mouths" shocked into talking sense by one refreshingly blunt remark.

The effective discussion participant is also aware of the need for succinctness. The "orator" is out of place on a committee. It is difficult for people to deal with lengthy contributions covering an entire series of points. This does not rule out talking about complicated subjects in a discussion but merely means that the speaker should try to limit himself to one issue at a time.

The effective speaker contributes not only his final judgment but the background of assumptions, experiences, and facts that led to his opinion. He lacks what some people have called "idea-possessiveness." An attack by someone on an idea he suggests is not interpreted as a personal criticism. On the contrary, he invites others to scrutinize the logic behind his current conclusions, for an error committed by him and compounded by the group is no less serious a mistake just because he happened to be its author.

No other quality so distinguishes the successful communicator as recognition of his own fallibility. To him, as to the scientist, conclusions are tentative, not absolute. His views are qualified as to time and place, always subject to revision. He is so deeply convinced of the limitations of his own intelligence, of the way his desires may distort his logic, of the incompleteness of his knowledge, that he is suspicious of all unexamined judgments — including his own. John Fischer, writing on the problems of the Cold War, displays this sense of humility in its finest form when he concludes with these words:

> Or so it seems to me. I am well aware that I may be overlooking some vital piece on this complex chessboard, and that these tentative conclusions may therefore be mistaken. If so, I hope that wiser and better informed men will point out where the mistake lies.[17]

It is most important to remember in communicating with each other, as Thomas Gordon has so perceptively written, "that each individual constructs *within himself* the really effective barriers to free communication."

To understand discussion as a communicative process one needs to analyze the network of channels through which information flows, the character of the signals in these channels, and the habits of communicating which may affect the operation of the system.

Discussion, since it provides for two-way communication, for maximum feedback and correction, and for unrestricted interaction should lead to better decisions and improved morale. Conditions in a committee, however, may lead to the formation of informal networks which interfere with intelligent decision-making. The recitative pattern, the dialogue, and sub-grouping are cases of this sort and may weaken the communication system of the group. The multilateral pattern, in which there is spontaneous communication and a preponderance of group-centered over individual-centered remarks, is likely to characterize the more mature group.

Communication is sometimes cut off because of the attitudes of the communicators. A dismissal, evasive, or signal reaction can prematurely terminate a productive conversation. The uncritical use of language, as in the case of false polarities or failure to abstract flexibly, can corrupt communication.

To talk constructively requires positive attitudes on the part of

[17] John Fischer, "The Editor's Easy Chair," *Harper's Magazine* (March, 1959), p. 25.

the listener and speaker. The person who listens to understand, rather than monitor, who enters into the frame of reference of his associates instead of listening only to refute them, helps others to express themselves and enriches his own life in the process. The person who speaks frankly, who speaks to the issue, and who is deeply aware of the limits on his own knowledge will make it easier for himself to learn from others and easier for others to learn from him.

RECOMMENDED READINGS

Hayakawa, S. I. *Language in Thought and Action.* Harcourt, Brace & Company, Inc., 1949.

Johnson, Wendell. *People in Quandries.* Harper and Brothers, 1946.

Lee, Irving J. *Language Habits in Human Affairs.* Harper and Brothers, 1941.

———. *How to Talk with People.* Harper and Brothers, 1952.

Roethlisberger, F. J. "Barriers to Communication Between Men," *Northwestern University Information Bulletin,* April, 1952.

Rogers, Carl. "Communication: Its Blocking and Facilitation," *Northwestern University Information Bulletin,* April, 1952.

Part Four

LEADERSHIP

Chapter Thirteen

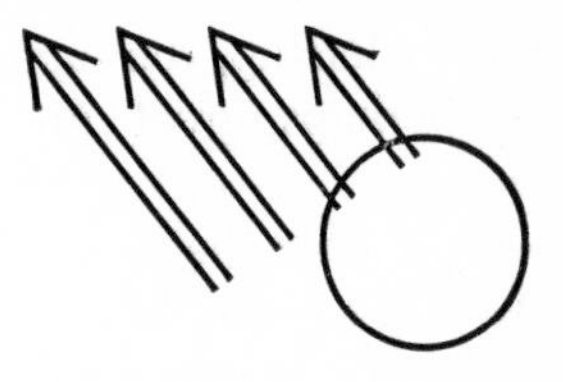

Functions of Leadership

IT IS LIKELY that every reader of this book has been, or in the future will be, charged with some kind of leadership responsibility. Some may be eager for the opportunity — seeing it not only as a chance to help steer their groups toward the accomplishment of desirable goals, but also as an opportunity to fulfill their creative potentialities. Others may assume leadership more reluctantly — having it thrust upon them because their talents, experience, or education are needed by the groups to which they belong. In either case, to perform effectively it is helpful to understand precisely what leadership is, and the relative merits of the forms it may take. As we explore this subject we will discover that everything presented so far in this book has a bearing on the problem of leadership. In a sense, therefore, this section will serve to review and perhaps bring into sharper focus many ideas which have already been touched upon.

The Meanings of Leadership

Most of us, when confronted with the term "leadership" tend to think immediately of a single individual — a committee chairman, a supervisor, a club president, a parent, a teacher, or a military officer — who holds a position of authority in a group. When the members come together for discussion, this leader sits at the head of the table, or stands at the front of the room, and presides over the meeting. Our concept of leadership is thus an image of a person who has been elected or appointed to the task of assuming major responsibility for the group's activities. When we speak of good or poor leadership, the names and personalities of particular individuals — perhaps great presidents or evil tyrants — usually come to mind.

It is understandable that most of us view leadership in this way. Ever since we have been old enough to be aware of group relationships we have been accustomed to the idea of someone's being in charge — be it father, mother, or grandparent in the home; ringleader in the neighborhood gang; teacher in the classroom; president of student government; minister in the pulpit; foreman; boss; or chairman of the committee. Hence, when we go to a meeting where discussion is to take place the assumption is made that some one individual will be in charge, and that he will call the group to order, start and guide the proceedings, verbalize any decisions that are agreed upon, and bring the discussion to a close. This we ordinarily take to be discussion leadership.

There is, however, another possible way of viewing leadership. We can think of it as *any action* which exerts an influence on a group, regardless of its source. With this definition in mind, one sees the "powers behind the throne" to be as much a part of the leadership of the group as the man who happens to hold the gavel. The jokester who breaks up the seriousness of a meeting by provoking outbursts of laughter, or the deviant who delays action on a matter by his disagreement, is also seen as exerting leadership. Even the silent member, by the uncertainty or anxiety he may create in others, or by his contribution to an atmosphere of indifference, has an influence. In short, since every member of the group, if by no other means than his mere presence, has some effect on the discussion, every member is regarded as exerting some degree of leadership.

To view leadership in this way, as the influential *behavior* of all members of a group rather than the authoritative *position* of one, is to see leadership as a more complex and subtle phenomenon than it is often taken to be. Yet, sophisticated and modern as this kind of analysis is thought to be, there have been those whose thinking revealed it many years ago. The writings of the philosophical anarchists, for instance, contained a clear awareness that without "leaders" there could still be "leadership."

> We are not afraid to renounce both judge and priest. . . . We renounce . . . all types of sanction. . . . We are not afraid to say: "Do what you wish, do as you wish" — because we are convinced that the vast majority of men, to the extent that they will be more and more enlightened and rid of actual trammels, will do and act always in a certain direction useful to society. . . .[1]

And the Pilgrim fathers who landed at Provincetown, Massachusetts, wrote this notion into their compact:

> This body politic established and maintained on the bleak and barren edge of a vast wilderness a state without a king or a noble, a church without a bishop or a priest, a democratic commonwealth the members of which were "straightly tied to all care of each other's good and of the whole by everyone." [2]

Astute students of human behavior have probably always been aware of the many sources of power in a society. Surely only a relatively naïve observer could believe that the only leading done in a discussion group is done by the leader. To see leadership simply in terms of the behavior of the person who happens to hold the title of "Chairman" or "President" is vastly to oversimplify the matter. Furthermore, such a view provides no framework of analysis for those many informal groups — bull sessions, Kaffee-Klatsches, and the like — where there is no formal or official leader at all. Yet certainly leadership is present.

The point of view which regards leadership as "functional" — that is, as specific actions which influence a group, regardless of their source — enables us to study and describe the leadership in a discussion more accurately than if our observations are clouded by preoccupations with the individual who happens to be the official leader.

This functional approach — so aptly clarified by Irving Knicker-

[1] Pierre Kropotkine, *La Morale Anarchiste* (Librairie Sociale, n.d.), p. 20. From an unpublished translation by Franklyn S. Haiman.

[2] Inscription on the memorial to the Pilgrims at Provincetown, Massachusetts.

bocker in 1948 [3] —has been found to be both useful and realistic by research workers in the fields of group leadership and group dynamics.[4] It has therefore gained widespread acceptance, and we propose to follow it here. It does pose one dilemma, however. To regard every influence that every member exerts upon a group as leadership (although logically quite plausible) is to broaden the subject to such an extent as to make it virtually unmanageable. For practical reasons it becomes necessary to isolate certain events as being acts of *leadership* and to relegate other actions to the category of *membership* contributions. We have chosen, accordingly, to regard as leadership only that member behavior which exerts *significant* influence upon the group—that is to say, those actions which affect the group as a whole and which have some important bearing on the group's movement (or lack of it) toward its goals. The dividing line between what is regarded as significant or important influence and what is not must be an arbitrary one, governed by our own value judgments. The participant who stirs up an argument may in one group be regarded as having significantly influenced the course of the discussion by this act, whereas in another situation we might consider the same behavior as inconsequential. We would point out, in defense of our rubbery definition of leadership, that any analysis of this subject is bound to be arbitrary. Those who regard leadership as emanating only from the nominal leader arbitrarily exclude from consideration all other significant influences upon the group. Those who regard every contribution alike as leadership arbitrarily fail to discriminate between greater and lesser degrees of influence.

Sources of Influence

When we examine leadership in discussion from the point of view of *significant* influences upon a group we find that there are roughly two ways in which a particular comment or action assumes importance. First, a comment may have an important bearing upon the group as a result of the power, authority, or high status of its author. Second, a contribution may have significance because

[3] Irving Knickerbocker, "Leadership: A Conception and Some Implications," *Journal of Social Issues* (Summer, 1948).

[4] See, for example, Dean C. Barnlund, "Experiments in Leadership Training for Decision-Making Discussion Groups," *Speech Monographs* (March, 1955).

it performs a vital function which is needed at the moment. Let us look at each of these sources of influence in more detail.

Leadership through status

Although it sometimes happens that the nominal or official leader of a group may be something of a nonentity who leaves the actual leading (or functional leadership) to other individuals, he cannot be entirely ignored. Merely by his possession of the office and title, "Leader," "Chairman," "Moderator," or "President," he exerts an influence regardless of what he may or may not do. The best test of the influence of his status *per se* is to imagine what this group would be like if the particular leader in question were just another member. The group would go about its business, paying him no heed. But so long as he occupies "the chair" it is necessary for the real leaders to work with, through, or around him in order to move the group forward. To be sure, if an official leader combines with his position and title the peformance of vital group functions he will be immeasurably more influential. But it is important to recognize that even without providing particular leadership services he still holds control of the focal point in the group and of whatever power and authority that position may command.

Thus, when an administrator who has the power to hire and fire his subordinates conducts a conference with the members of his staff, his mere presence is likely to have a marked effect on the course of the discussions. What members of the group say or do may be carefully calculated to win his approval or avoid his displeasure. The leader, without saying a word, will influence both the general climate of the meeting and the content of the remarks that are made. Similarly, when a teacher in a classroom or a clergyman at a church meeting sits down to participate with his students or his church members in a discussion, his contributions will most likely be listened to more attentively and given more weight than those of anyone else, whether they merit it or not.

To be sure, the degree to which the members of a group are influenced by status alone will depend upon their own personalities as well as upon the attitudes and actions of the leader. If the participants are people who are easily cowed by authority, who uncritically accept the dominance of experts, or who are impressed by the symbols of high office, the position of the leader will have more significance than in a group whose members are of a more independent spirit. If the individual who holds the office of leader is the kind who uses his power to dominate others (such as a former president of a nationally famous mail order company who was noted for firing vice-presidents who disagreed with him), he will naturally have more impact on the group's climate and activities than one who attempts to play down his own authority and to encourage ideas from others. There are many sensitive people in positions of power who are so aware of their potentially dominating effects upon the discussions in which they participate that they will go out of their way to offset these influences. For instance, they may encourage the use of first names, may avoid sitting at the head of the table, or may even ask someone of lesser status to serve as chairman of the meeting. They may emphasize that their opinions are only *opinions,* and that others may see things differently. Of course all of these might be interpreted as empty gestures if not followed up with actions that give them substance.

It is interesting, in this connection, that the laws of parliamentary procedure (as set forth in *Robert's Rules of Order,* for example) require that if the chairman of a meeting wishes to express an opinion on the subject under discussion he must step down from the chair and hand the gavel over to someone else while he makes his remarks. This is an attempt to divest his comments of the aura of authority surrounding his office. Knowing what we do from psychological research about the "halo" phenomenon (i.e., the tendency for a man's prestige in one field to be carried over into others) we are skeptical about the effectiveness of this rule. Nevertheless it does serve to remind us that to be influenced by a man's position rather than the value of his actual contributions to the group is basically incompatible with the ideals of discussion. The democratic process is based upon the premise that contributions should be examined and conflicts resolved on the basis of the merit of the ideas themselves rather than the personality, power, or prestige of their originator. When this is not the case, discussion is likely to be less profitable than it would otherwise be.[5] The ideal discussion, therefore, is one in which all leadership is functional — that is, the

[5] The reader may recall, for example, the Torrance study reported in Chapter 9, where groups consisting of air force pilots, navigators, and gunners sometimes solved problems incorrectly because they allowed themselves to be more influenced by the pilot, who was wrong, than the gunner, who knew the right answer.

group is influenced only by what people do and say, not by who they are.[6]

We would hasten to add that in its pure form this is probably an unattainable goal. To some extent, at least, the influence of position or status is likely to be present in all real-life human relationships. If, however, group leaders and members are aware of it, actions can be taken, as suggested above, to counteract its power. By the same token a leader who is hostile to democratic processes can exploit his status in such a way as to subvert all discussions in which he participates.

Leadership through function

The second way in which a participant may have significant influence on the course of a discussion is through the performance of certain functions which are vital to the progress of the group (or obstruction of the group in the case of negative leadership). Those individuals who are sensitive enough to realize what contributions the group needs, and skillful enough to provide them, will thus be the real leaders.

What are these vital functions? The answer to this question depends in part upon the kind of group one is talking about. In a Cathartic Group, for instance, the most important single need may be for someone who can help establish an atmosphere of acceptance in which other members feel free to bare their innermost thoughts. In a decision-making committee which has a two-hour deadline to meet, the person who can help resolve a conflict and verbalize a satisfactory agreement may be the most important member of the group. In a college seminar the most significant function would probably be the ability to stimulate critical evaluation, whereas in a staff meeting of an advertising agency the man who is most adept at extracting new ideas from others might be considered the most valuable.

The need for certain leadership functions is also dependent on the other people in the group. If, for instance, they are full of ideas and enthusiasm, they will need no further stimulating. Such a situation may even require a calming influence. On the other

[6] A legitimate exception, discussed at length in Chapter 7, would be the use of personal qualifications as a means of adjudicating a dispute between conflicting experts.

hand, a group of apathetic or indifferent individuals may be in dire need of someone who can light a bonfire under them. Similarly the nature of the problem being discussed will affect the kinds of leadership functions that are called for. A complicated subject may require, above all, a member who can help clarify matters, whereas a less complex task may call for leadership in moving the group along rapidly so they do not waste too much time on simple questions.

It is thus impossible to predict in advance what kinds of functions one would have to perform in a particular group in order to provide its members with effective leadership. The best we can do is to make an inventory of all the kinds of functions that are commonly needed by many groups at one time or another, leaving it to the reader to determine which of these is called for in any particular situation. For convenience, we will classify these leadership functions into three broad areas. Category I we shall call Influence, or Leadership, in the area of Creative and Critical Thinking. This might also be thought of as intellectual leadership. The so-called "idea man" is a prototype. Category II we label Influence, or Leadership, in Procedural Matters. Here we have in mind those actions which organize and move the group toward the achievement of its tasks. This might also be thought of as the administrative or managerial set of functions. The "organizer" fits into this classification. Category III is Influence, or Leadership, in the area of Interpersonal Relations. Some writers have called this the "group building," "group maintenance," or "social-emotional" set of functions. The "harmonizer" or the "supporter" might be cited as examples.

Let us turn now to a more detailed exploration of the specific functions that may need to be fulfilled in each of these three general areas — assuming all the while that the other members of the particular group in question are not automatically taking care of these matters, and that the task they are engaged in requires their performance by someone.

As we list and describe each of these leadership functions, we hope it will become apparent to the reader that the present chapter is actually a summary of the entire book to this point. For leadership in discussion is nothing more than helping a group with whatever it needs to make its meetings more effective. To understand the various facets of discussion which have been described in previous chapters, and to learn ways and means of handling them, is to increase one's leadership potential. Specifically, in Chapter 5 we spoke about the problems involved in organizing a discussion; and here, under Leadership in Procedural Matters we will review the leadership functions which were implied in that chapter. In Chapters 6 and 7 we discussed the raw materials of discussion and the uses of authority and reason. Here, under Leadership in Creative and Critical Thinking, will be listed the activities in which one who understood the principles presented in those two chapters would be inclined to engage. In Chapters 9 through 12 we explored several aspects of interpersonal relations in discussion groups. Here, under Leadership in Interpersonal Relations, we will remind the reader of the services needed to solve some of the problems posed in those chapters.

Leadership in Creative and Critical Thinking

Contributing fresh ideas

Every group needs new ideas. A Congressional committee looking for a solution to labor racketeering, a staff of scientists seeking a defense against intercontinental ballistics missiles, a police department attempting to piece together clues that will lead to the explanation of a crime, economists attempting to unravel the problems of agricultural surpluses — all look for leadership to those of their number who can provide fresh and promising suggestions. The psychologist's contributions to a therapy group may be mainly in the form of providing the patients with fresh insights into human emotions. The English teacher's role in class discussion may be to expose the students to new ways of looking at a piece of literature. If group discussion is to be a productive enterprise there must always be those present who can and will open new avenues for exploration.

Provoking original thought in others

Quite as important as the "idea man" who himself keeps pumping fresh leads into a discussion is the individual who can provoke others to do likewise. It is a sad fact that so few people in our society utilize their full creative potential, and that so many need to be stimulated by others before they can become truly productive. When provided with the proper encouragement they sometimes surprise themselves with the new thoughts they can produce. Therefore, we must not be too easily discouraged when we find ourselves in groups that seem lethargic and uncreative. It may be that through such methods as dramatizing the topic for discussion (perhaps by a vivid description of a concrete case) or through provocative and searching questions, the members of that group can be brought to operate on all their cylinders. Surely one of the secrets of great teaching is the ability to stimulate original thought in students.

Critically evaluating the ideas of others

In these days of great emphasis on resolving conflict, harmonious living, and togetherness it is important to remember that unless the ideas which are contributed to a discussion are subjected to critical scrutiny, the group may find itself accepting theories and programs which are full of hidden flaws. One of the dangers of the present "brainstorming" craze among some self-styled experts is that we may be led to believe that all we need in discussion is new ideas, regardless of how inane they may be. What the too-agreeable group needs is individuals who can exercise leadership in the posting of danger signals — who can ask such questions as: How do you know that? On what do you base that opinion? Would that really happen? Are you sure those statistics aren't outdated?

Encouraging critical thought in others

No one individual can or should be expected to discover all the fallacies that can be committed in the course of a group discussion. We need the help of everyone. Yet, as in the case of creative thinking, many discussion participants are not sufficiently accustomed to thinking critically. They fall prey too easily to the glib salesman or the group member with a "good line." Hence they require someone to goad them into making discriminating responses. This can sometimes be achieved by playing the devil's advocate — that is, by arguing quite convincingly for a point of view which is unpopular in the group, thus forcing otherwise complacent listeners to come to the defense of their now-threatened prejudices or opinions. Also, by setting an example of friendly but firm criticism one can demonstrate to others that such behavior is both permissible and valued.

Making the abstract concrete, or the concrete abstract

One of the common causes of fuzzy thinking in group discussion is the carrying on of conversation at levels that are either too abstract or too concrete. In the former instance participants tend to talk in big words and vague generalities, passing each other by without really communicating. In the latter case the group becomes so involved in petty details and individual cases that it loses sight of general goals and principles. In both instances leadership is needed either in lowering or raising the level of generality. If the discussion is too abstract one can pull it down from the clouds by asking for examples and illustrations, or by injecting figurative analogies. If, on the other hand, the conversation is embroiled in minutiae, one can simply ask: What is the point of all this? or, Can we find some general principle at work here?

Leadership in Procedural Matters

Initiating discussion

The obvious first step in getting a discussion group organized is to start the meeting. Whoever does this exerts considerable influence, since the opening remarks may set the tone and direction of the entire conversation. Usually the initiator not only starts the discussion but, directly or indirectly, provides some indication of the purposes for which the meeting is being held. In other words, opening remarks tend to carry with them goal-setting implications, just as the driver of a bus who starts out eastbound from Chicago on U.S. 20 raises a presumption that the riders are heading for South Bend.

Making agenda suggestions

Our analogy of the bus ride can also be used to illustrate the inadequacy of opening remarks in determining the entire course of a discussion. There are many places besides South Bend that one can get to by starting eastward on Route 20 from Chicago. In short, further procedural decisions will have to be made by the members of the group en route as to where they want to go and how they want to get there. In order for these decisions to be made, leadership in the form of either asking for or offering procedural suggestions will have to be provided. Here are a few examples.

Where shall we start?

I suggest that we first discuss movie censorship, then move on to magazines, and take up television last.

Shall we just begin with the first item in the report, and then take up the others in chronological order?

I have a feeling we're getting a little off the track. I'd like to go back to what Bob was saying when. . . .

You know, we've only got fifteen minutes left. Don't you think we had better drop this now and get on to the question of. . . .

Clarifying

Thinking is a difficult enough process when we do it in solitude. How much more complicated it becomes when several people try to make it a joint enterprise! Confusion and misunderstanding are almost certain to arise at some points and the leadership services of a "clarifier" may be extremely helpful. As in the case of the agenda, either questions or suggestions can be useful. By someone asking, "I'm lost. What are we talking about now?" the attention of the group may be called to the fact that obstructions need to be removed from the channels of communication. Clarification can be achieved, also, by contributions which point up the relationship between what group members are saying (e.g., "It seems to me that John's plan is similar to the one Bill was describing at our last meeting") or which otherwise provide helpful links (e.g., "Would that be set up the same way as Division X is now?"). Merely requesting others to explain more fully what they mean, or rephrasing their comments in your own words and asking them if this is what they intended, may also help clarify matters for the entire group.

Summarizing

Another "administrative" problem that arises when groups of people attempt to think together is that as the discussion roves over wide areas of thought, participants tend to forget many ideas that have been proposed or important points that have been made or agreed upon. It therefore becomes necessary occasionally for someone to remind the group of what has been accomplished so that the discussion can be brought back into focus.

> We've had three proposals put before us now — Sam's, Jean's, and Tom's. Are there any others?
>
> We agreed at our last meeting that we've got to do something about the congested conditions at the school, and that whatever we do we can't exceed the present budget. Where do we go from here?

Verbalizing consensus or agreements

An easy way to get rich would be to collect a dollar for every discussion which fails in its purpose because each participant goes away from the meeting with a different idea of what has been decided or agreed upon. Frequently the meeting adjourns with a vague feeling about what has been determined which proves inadequate when it comes to translating that mystical achievement into action. This is such a common ailment among discussion groups because so few people are highly skilled in drawing together the strands of a conversation and making statements which adequately capture the total thinking of the group. To perform this function to the satisfaction of all the diverse elements present requires considerable sensitivity to others as well as a more-than-average talent at verbal expression.

Leadership in Interpersonal Relations

Regulating participation

The fondest hope of a discussant might well be to participate in a group which is so self-disciplined that actions to regulate participation are unnecessary. Unfortunately this is rarely the case. It is the unusual group, indeed, where there is no need whatsoever to draw in nonparticipants, to take or keep the conversation away from overtalkative members, or to restore unity when the discussion splinters into sub-groups. We will have more to say in the next chapter about the different methods of handling this function, and only mention it here as one of the vital elements in the maintenance of effective interpersonal relationships.

Climate making

The establishment and maintenance of an emotional atmosphere that is conducive to the best discussion involves several kinds of leadership services. We would cite first those contributions and actions which help to create a climate of *informality* in the group. This could include everything from the proper arrangement of chairs to suggesting the use of first names or taking off one's coat. But more important than any of these relatively superficial things would be the attitude and manner with which one presents his ideas when he speaks to the group. A cold, impersonal approach, particularly on the part of a member who holds a position of high status, can place a group in a deep freeze, whereas a warm and friendly contribution can set an example of ease and informality for others to follow.

Closely related to inducing informality is stimulating *frankness.* Again, this can perhaps best be accomplished by being frank oneself — for such behavior has a way of becoming contagious unless there happen to be rather potent counterforces present in the situation. Frankness can also be increased sometimes by suggesting to the group directly that "we seem to be beating around the bush" and proposing that "we take off the kid gloves and get down to business."

Providing *emotional support* to other members who are in need of such aid can be another important leadership contribution within the broader category of climate making. Coming to their defense when they are unfairly attacked, helping them to "save face," joining them in opposition to attempted steam-roller tactics — all of these moves would add to the maintenance of a permissive atmosphere in which participants would not fear to become involved.

Instigating group self-analysis

We have found, at a number of points throughout this book, that the most effective answer a group can find to some of its problems may come through a process of self-analysis — a "discussion of the discussion." When this is needed, somebody in the group must become aware of it and instigate the processes. To do so, either by proposing self-analysis to the group or simply by plunging in and starting to analyze without first asking the group's consent, is to exert an extremely important influence.

Helping to Resolve Conflict

We have omitted from our three general categories of leadership functions, and left to the last, a kind of contribution which is no respecter of the boundaries of classification we have set up—namely, helping to resolve conflict. This should serve to remind the reader once again that classifications and categories, though often helpful in setting forth descriptions, are always artificial. For resolving conflict involves elements of all three categories. An effective mediator may be an idea man in that he proposes new solutions which neither of the parties to the dispute had thought of. He is surely a leader in procedural matters—clarifying, summarizing, and separating out what is agreed upon from that which remains in dispute. Finally, he must be a diplomat *par excellence*—remaining on good terms with all parties to the conflict and helping to span the emotional gaps between them.

The Relationship of Status and Function

While we are in the process of erasing boundary lines which, for expository purposes, we have previously drawn, there is one final point that needs to be made. It has to do with the distinction set forth earlier between influence based upon "who a person is" and leadership resulting from "what one does." It is important to recognize that these two phenomena are not entirely unrelated.

In the first place, an individual's position or degree of authority in a group may make it easier or harder for him to perform certain leadership functions successfully. For example, it is extremely difficult for a person such as a boss or teacher, who possesses considerable power over other members of the group, to draw nonparticipants into the discussion without making them feel coerced into speaking. A peer can perform the same function much more gracefully. On the other hand, there are some leadership functions, such as initiating discussion or verbalizing a consensus, for which possession of relatively high status in the group is almost a prerequisite. We have observed a number of meetings where attempts by low-status members to initiate a new phase of the problem or to articulate a group conclusion have been ignored, whereas high-status people, saying virtually the same thing a few minutes later, have met with acceptance. This would suggest that there is a quality about starting a discussion and drawing it to a close which tends to be regarded by most groups as the prerogative of only "duly constituted authorities."

Indeed, there is evidence that one's status in a group affects to some extent his ability to exert any kind of influence. An experimental study of thirty-two groups by Riecken, for instance, tested whether or not a participant who had established himself as the "biggest talker" in a problem-solving group would gain more acceptance for a so-called "elegant" solution (secretly given to him by the experimenter) than a "small talker" similarly provided with this answer. Riecken found that:

> When the top man has the insight needed to solve the problem elegantly, the group accepts this solution more than two-thirds of the time; when the bottom man has the same information, the elegant solution is rejected in more than two-thirds of the groups.[7]

Not only does status determine the ease with which particular functions of leadership may be performed, it may also affect the motivation which an individual will feel to take the initiative about assuming leadership responsibilities. For a group member to come to the support of another individual whom the group is about to drive over with a steam-roller ordinarily requires that the first person be sufficiently secure in his own status that he can afford to stick out his neck in this way. Similarly, a participant who is unsure of himself and of his acceptability to the group is less likely to provoke creative thinking through the injection of radical ideas than one who knows that he cannot or will not be ostracized for his originality. Some of the research that has been done by Bales and his colleagues suggests that discussants who provide a group with leadership functions in our Categories 1 (Creative and Critical Thinking) and 2 (Procedural Matters) are likely to arouse some hostility from other group members who may regard them as taskmasters.[8] If this be true, and if group members sense it, the performance of those functions is likely to be avoided by individuals whose status in the group is already shaky or who cannot tolerate being disliked.

[7] Henry W. Riecken, "The Effect of Talkativeness on Ability to Influence Group Solutions to Problems," *Sociometry* (December, 1958), p. 313.

[8] Bales, "The Equilibrium Problem in Small Groups," in Hare, Borgatta, and Bales, *op. cit.*, pp. 452–456.

Who one is, then, can and does have a bearing on what one does. Not only one's status in the group but also one's own personality characteristics play a part. To exert effective influence in the area of interpersonal relations, for example, calls for a certain amount of empathy in one's responses to other people. To provide stimulation of thinking requires at least a reasonable degree of intelligence. Franz Alexander, the psychoanalyst, even goes so far as to assert that

> The emergence of leaders can be understood only from individual differences between the members of the group. Those who have least emotional dependence and are ready or eager to take responsibility naturally become the leaders of the insecure majority which needs them. . . . The surplus energy accompanying maturity which animates parental care is also the driving power of leadership.[9]

We would not want to leave the impression, nor do we understand Alexander to mean, that the old wives' tale that "leaders are born, not made" is valid. One can wholeheartedly believe in the view that leadership is functional, and that skill in the performance of these functions can be improved,[10] and still recognize that a person's native abilities, environmental background, and current status in the group will influence his motivation to lead, his talent at leading, and the degree to which his attempted leadership will be followed by the other members of his group.

Leadership may be viewed as residing only in the one individual who happens to hold the title of group leader, or it may be seen as any action by a group member which exerts a significant influence on the course of a discussion. The latter approach, referred to as functional leadership, seems to hold the greater promise as a tool for understanding the dynamics of discussion. This is not to deny that groups are influenced by status *per se*, but only to suggest

[9] Franz Alexander, *Our Age of Unreason* (Lippincott, 1951), p. 213.

[10] There is, indeed, considerable experimental evidence that skill in performing leadership functions can be improved by training. See, for example, Dean C. Barnlund, "Experiments in Leadership Training for Decision-Making Discussion Groups, *Speech Monographs* (March, 1955); Alex Bavelas and Kurt Lewin, "Training in Democratic Leadership," *Journal of Abnormal and Social Psychology* (January, 1942); and John R. P. French, Jr., "Retraining an Autocratic Leader," *Journal of Abnormal and Social Psychology* (April, 1944).

that, given the desire by both members and authority figures, it is possible to minimize these effects. This, indeed, is one of the goals of a democratic group.

Leadership functions may be classified roughly into three broad areas: influence in creative and critical thinking, influence in procedural matters, and influence in interpersonal relations. The first category includes such specific actions as contributing fresh ideas, provoking original thought in others, critically evaluating the ideas of others, encouraging critical thought in others, and making the abstract concrete or the concrete abstract. Leadership in procedural matters has to do with initiating discussion, making agenda suggestions, clarifying, summarizing, and verbalizing consensus or agreements. Influence in interpersonal relations refers to such matters as regulating participation, climate-making, and instigating group self-analysis. Helping to resolve conflict cuts across all three general categories and serves to remind us of their interrelatedness.

Finally, we have noted the mutual dependence of status and function in the exerting of effective leadership, and the role played by personality as well.

RECOMMENDED READINGS

Barnard, Chester. *The Functions of the Executive.* Harvard University Press, 1948.

Benne, Kenneth, and Paul Sheats. "Functional Roles of Group Members," *Journal of Social Issues* (Spring, 1948).

Haiman, Franklyn S. *Group Leadership and Democratic Action.* Houghton Mifflin Company, 1951.

Knickerbocker, Irving. "Leadership: A Conception and Some Implications," *Journal of Social Issues* (Summer, 1948).

Ross, Murray G., and Charles E. Hendry. *New Understandings of Leadership.* Association Press, 1957.

Chapter Fourteen

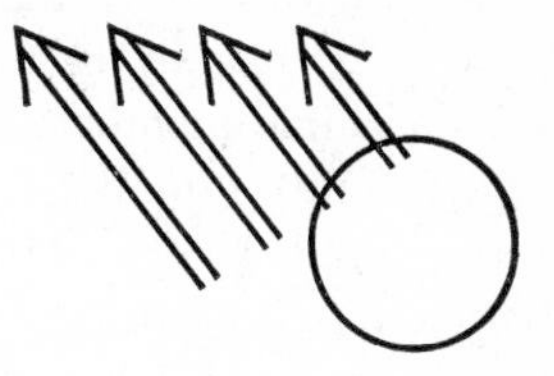

Styles of Leadership

THE CRITICAL IMPORTANCE OF LEADERSHIP in any group or culture is pointed up in these words of Kurt Lewin:

> Any real change in the culture of a group is, therefore, interwoven with the changes of power constellation within the group. From this point it will be easily understood why a change in the methods of leadership is probably the quickest way to bring about a change in the cultural atmosphere of a group.[1]

So far we have defined leadership as a set of functions which must be carried out in order for a group to maintain satisfying human relationships, coordinate its energies, and perform its assigned tasks. Lewin's reference to the "constellation" and "methods" of leadership reveals that there are two further questions that must be faced in this area: (1) *Who* is to provide the group with leadership, i.e., on whom should the responsibility for these functions rest? (2) *How* should these functional needs be met, i.e., should they be imposed upon the group or simply offered? The way any group answers these questions will certainly affect the morale of the members, the character of communication, the quality of thinking, and, indeed, every facet of the discussion process.

[1] Kurt Lewin, *Resolving Social Conflicts* (Harper, 1948), p. 49.

The Locus of Leadership

When leadership is seen as a set of functions or actions, rather than a combination of personality traits or a matter of status, it becomes possible to distribute it in a variety of ways. Authority might be given, as it usually is, to an appointed leader, or placed in the hands of a single member of the group. Or everyone might share the responsibility equally. There is room, also, between the extremes of the single leader and completely diffused leadership, for other patterns of authority. Co-leaders might be named to guide the group. Or a trio of leaders, one functioning in the area of Creative and Critical Thinking, one in the area of Procedural Matters, and one in the area of Interpersonal Relations might divide up the leadership in the group. Committee members with special skills in resolving conflict or formulating decisions might be asked to provide direction only when help was needed on these specific problems.

The fact that so many different patterns are possible has led a number of social scientists to give serious thought to the feasibility of the "leaderless" group. This is a group in which no one is the nominal leader, but in which everyone shares in the coordinating of group action. Some people oppose this concept vigorously and contend that a leaderless group leads only to confusion. Furthermore, this confusion may contribute to disillusionment with the whole idea of democratic decision-making. Still others argue that the leaderless group can work, although admitting that it is not something to be arbitrarily invoked upon first forming a discussion group. One cannot choose intelligently between these alternatives without a more careful examination of the issue.

Most of us are so familiar with the way a group operates under an elected chairman or appointed moderator that we assume it to be the only conceivable and practical way of conducting meetings. The official leader achieves his position either by being elected by the members of the group or from being appointed to the chair by someone in authority. The type of control he exerts over the meeting is based upon his own past experience as a leader, the limits imposed by the situation — passivity of members, complexity of the problem, pressure of time — and by his own needs to dominate others. He is expected to open the meeting, suggest an agenda, arbitrate conflicts, keep peace among the members, and speed their deliberations. He is also expected, normally, to refrain from participating very heavily on the grounds that his services as a leader will be impaired if he gets too involved. By virtue of his position he exerts a greater influence than any other member over the communicative, interpersonal, and intellectual processes of the group. Or, in theory, he should. After all he was presumably chosen because of his superior skill in these areas.

The Leaderless Group

The leaderless group is not so familiar. Or is it? Many of us may not have recognized the countless times we have participated in leaderless groups without knowing it. A dormitory bull session, a serious discussion at the office, a group of workers solving a mechanical breakdown in a piece of machinery, a class subdivided into project committees, may all be operating unconsciously without formal leaders. The direction taken by the group comes spontaneously from whoever sees a better way of running the meeting. His proposal is discussed. Others may modify the original suggestion. Soon a consensus emerges and the group moves forward again. There is no distinction between participant and leader, for each member plays both roles at various times. A person may be in the center of an argument at one moment and an arbitrator at another. On one occasion he suggests a solution to the problem and later he helps to integrate the proposals of others. One person opens the meeting, another may close it. The participant who helps to clarify a semantic misunderstanding early in the meeting finds others, a few minutes later, removing the verbal nettles from his own argument. The person who talks too much, who goes off on tangents, may reappear at another time to open the channels of communication to the less aggressive or may bring the discussion back to the next point on the agenda. This description of a leaderless meeting may make the concept more concrete:

> The members straggle into the meeting room in groups of one to four. Casual conversations fill the air until apparently all who are coming have arrived. Social talk may continue for a short while, perhaps longer than it would if a single leader were present to call the group to order; but soon one of the members who has business

> to present will speak up and state his problem. Others will respond. If two or more begin to talk at once, the ones with the least motivation will stop and perhaps even say, "Go ahead," to the one who seems most eager. Conversation will continue until the issue is resolved by someone who can verbalize a summary to which the rest of the group give their assent. If a conflict arises over a point which the majority are interested in pursuing, but which they do not have time to explore fully, someone who is not too deeply engrossed in the issue will interject the suggestion that time is getting short and that the group had better settle the matter by a vote or else postpone it to another time. . . . When the customary closing time approaches, someone will say, "Let's go home." If he voices the sentiments of the majority, people will begin to get up and leave. If he has interrupted something in which the majority are interested, he will be ignored.[2]

In the leaderless group people simply talk together as effectively, as cooperatively, as intelligently, as they can, utilizing the total leadership capacities of the members. No one person occupies the center of attention. Later, if someone were to ask, "Who was the leader?" it would be difficult to answer because no one was officially recognized as such.

The argument over the proper locus of leadership is complicated by the fact that many people confuse the "leaderless" group with the "leader*ship*less" group. And this distinction is one on which many critics stumble. No group activity, as we see it, from playing sand-lot baseball to negotiating a labor contract, can go on successfully without leadership. To coordinate any mutual undertaking requires somebody to do the coordinating. But in the leaderless group the behavior we call leading is so widely shared, so diffused throughout the membership, that to designate a single leader is inaccurate. The group follows whatever person *at that moment* is sensitive enough and skillful enough to meet its needs. A jazz combo is an excellent illustration of distributed leadership. To operate without a leader is not really as foreign to our experience as the word is to our vocabulary. The difference between a leaderless and a led group lies in the locus of authority — in one it is concentrated in a single individual who has special status in the group, in the other it is shared by many persons of equal status. Both leaderless groups and those with a designated leader, however, may, or may not, have effective leader*ship*.

[2] Franklyn S. Haiman, "Concepts of Leadership," *Quarterly Journal of Speech* (October, 1953), p. 321.

The "leadershipless group," on the other hand, is an anarchy. Without leadership there is no rapport among the members, no effective communication, no cooperative thinking, in fact, no group. When this occurs, and it sometimes does, it is because no one takes the initiative or has the skills to supply the functions of leadership. If this is the case, the group will not be improved automatically by naming someone leader. If no one knows how to resolve conflicts, prepare an agenda, make decisions, or deal with problem members, no gavel will confer that talent upon him. Many groups repeat this mistake: At the first sign of failure or inefficiency they set up a cry for a leader, not realizing that it is not the lack of a leader that is causing their trouble, but the fact that they lack the skills necessary to conduct a successful meeting. The results of being without leadership are described by Lewin, Lippitt, and White in their studies of autocratic, democratic, and laissez-faire leaders.[3] Under laissez-faire conditions groups were far less effectively organized, were less efficient, and less satisfying to the members. There was a much higher percentage of irrelevant communication within the group, more outright aggression, loss of interest, and more task failures which led members, in some instances, to destroy their own work and the work of others.

Advantages of the Single Leader

Centralized leadership, the most familiar pattern, has not survived for so long a time without having many advantages. To begin with, having an officially recognized leader satisfies the desire for a figurehead, someone to look up to. In this sense naming a chairman fulfills both a functional and symbolic purpose. Sociologists recognize this factor when they note how frequently someone is elected leader who not only meets the requirements of office, but who has sufficient glamor to serve as a sort of substitute father-image. One of the strongest arguments for the English monarchy is that the King and Queen serve as a living embodiment of the values of the British people. This need for a symbol, for someone who represents and embodies the group spirit, may be present even in the small group.

Also, the members of an organization know more clearly where they stand when there is a recognized leader. If everyone is

[3] See, for example, White and Lippitt, *op. cit.*

responsible for leadership this may mean that no one is really responsible. The fluid, unstructured relations in the leaderless group are confusing. Members do not know what is expected of them. Berkowitz, who studied the behavior of college students in experimental situations and executives in business and industry, found, among other things, that group members seemed to want a designated leader and reacted negatively to those who competed with that person for leadership.[4] Knowing where one stands may improve communication because committee members will know what channels exist and will use them with some regularity. External details such as arranging for meetings, preparing reports, scheduling activities, can be handled most efficiently if someone is unmistakably in charge. When decisions are necessary, people will know to whom to look.

There are real advantages, too, in a division of labor. Why not have the most skillful member of a group do the leading and let the rest concentrate on what they can do well? The principle of specialization has worked well in industry and has led to great efficiency and economy of effort. No one interested in winning ball games would substitute a guard for quarterback, or a third baseman as pitcher. The effectiveness of any committee would seem to be enhanced by putting an experienced and well qualified leader in the position where he can do the most good.

It is true that appointing a leader means some concentration of authority. But is this necessarily bad? With one person in charge group discipline should be easier to maintain. When the leader states a consensus, regulates participation, or rules irrelevant talk out of order, there will be no long, drawn-out argument, or bickering, over his action. Of course, the conformity that is achieved may be only on the surface, but at least order is preserved. Even in self-governing organizations, such as college dormitories, it is often necessary to make some*one* finally responsible for maintaining rules and regulations. When everyone is a part-time cop, friendships are constantly strained. It is sometimes important, too, to be able to fix responsibility for action. A corporation must be able to hold someone accountable for the failure of its policies. If changes in a factory lead to higher profits, administrative officials want to reward the person most responsible. If a school board

[4] Leonard Berkowitz, "Sharing Leadership in Small, Decision-Making Groups," in Hare, Borgatta, and Bales, *op. cit.*

makes a decision outside its legitimate authority, citizens must be able to criticize or remove the offending person from office. And, if no one is leader, who will act as spokesman for the group, announce their decisions, publicize their activities, or represent them before affiliated organizations?

Furthermore, a designated leader who takes his job seriously can act impartially in any crisis that develops. A certain "distance" helps the leader to keep his perspective. A chairman may be able to detect, more easily than others, when the group is getting off the track or when hidden motives are obstructing its operation. Instead of being drawn into conflicts as a partisan he is able to function as an arbitrator or referee. There is some danger, of course, that under a cloak of impartiality he may abuse his power by throwing his weight on the side he favors, frankly or subtly. If this happens the consequences may be disastrous, for his influence is disproportionate to that of other members because of the authority of his position. If he abuses his power he can do far more harm than good. If not, he may assist the group by helping people to be more objective, by separating essentials from nonessentials, and by acting judiciously on disputed points.

Some argue that procedural decisions are of little importance in a group. The really vital decisions have to do with the topic under discussion; the way in which the group operates, within limits, is a matter of little consequence. Hence procedural responsibilities may as well be turned over to some individual in the group to permit the rest to concentrate on the problem at hand. If the leader takes himself too seriously or abuses his position the group can depose him or reject his control. (This applies, of course, only when the group elects its own leader.)

Those who favor an elected or appointed leader feel that it is the most productive, most efficient, and most satisfying way to conduct group meetings.

Advantages of the Leaderless Group

Before reaching any conclusion about the locus of leadership, one ought to examine the principal arguments in favor of the leaderless group idea. The leaderless group, first of all, draws upon the total leadership talent of the group. The motive behind appointing a committee of any sort is that several heads are better than one. If it is true that through discussion more information, more experience, and more inventiveness are brought to bear on the *substantive* problem before the group, will this principle not hold true also for the *procedural* problems of the group? By having a number of alternative leads to choose among, by discussing their merits, by deciding democratically, the group will be able to function better than it would under the wisest control of a single person. In view of what we know about the effects of hidden agenda upon the course of a discussion, for example, it is clear that the technical problems of working together cannot be dismissed as of less concern than the objective problem before the group. Too sharp a distinction between the external and internal tasks seems unjustified.

Sharing in the leadership of a group will also lead to greater involvement in its deliberations. As each person assumes more responsibility he will attach greater importance to the group and his own role in it. Chairmen of committees usually take the work of a group more seriously than do other members because of the larger role they have in it. Giving greater influence to committee personnel may increase their stake in the outcome of the deliberations.

Since appointing or electing a leader leads to specialization of roles it reduces the contribution this person may make as an ordinary participant. To act as chairman requires that one maintain a certain "apartness" — if not to symbolize the difference in status, at least to remain impartial and objective when crises arise. This has the effect of sterilizing the leader and taking him out of circulation. It usually deprives a group of the opinions of its most informed and valuable member. But if everyone shares the responsibility of leadership, no one will be kept from contributing vital information or worth-while points of view.

Furthermore, it has been found that leaders who cannot participate fully in a discussion are less satisfied with decisions reached by the group. In a study of supervisory and participant leaders by Paul Hare, for example, "the supervisory leaders who were specifically told to stay out of the discussion had little chance to influence the group. They tend to have the least agreement with the group ranking after discussion."[5] The leaderless group,

[5] Paul Hare, "Small Group Discussions with Participatory and Supervisory Leadership," in Hare, Borgatta, and Bales, *op. cit.* p. 558.

therefore, makes for better participation *and* better leadership.

Avoidance of specialization of roles may also increase a group's survival power. The military platoon in which all authority for decisions is assigned to one member does not develop the leadership resources for dealing with emergencies when that person is lost as a battle casualty or replaced through re-assignment. The committee that becomes dependent upon its chairman will most readily fall into chaos when he is absent or fails to function.

In addition, barriers to communication multiply as status differences become established. Wide differences in standing have been found to impede the flow of information. Criticism is stifled. Information is withheld or distorted in order to please, or to influence in some other way, the high status members of an organization. Ideas are cut off because of fear of disapproval.

> If the indications of the few experimental runs that have been made to date are any guide, both occurrence and utilization of insight will be found to drop rapidly as centrality is more and more highly localized. In one group, the individual to whom the necessary insight occurred was "ordered" by the emergent leader to "forget it." Losses of productive potential, in this way, are probably very common in most working groups, and must be enormous in society at large.[6]

Under these conditions people create unofficial, private channels for the sharing of their feelings, as in the case of the office grapevine, and these channels obviate the natural ones. The motive for distorting or choking off ideas, however, is lacking in the leaderless group. Morale is likely to be improved because group members can now talk freely and frankly with each other.

The leaderless group, according to its advocates, is healthier for people because self-discipline is more effective in the long run than discipline through external authorities. As Robert Bales has found in his studies of small group interaction, any member who takes over task leadership is likely to arouse hostility toward himself. When leadership functions are shared, people are more inclined to regulate their own behavior. This reduces the need for group restraints and makes people less disposed to use someone as a scapegoat for their own shortcomings.

Finally, the leaderless group offers the maximum opportunity

[6] Alex Bavelas, "Communication Patterns in Task Oriented Groups," in Cartwright and Zander, *op. cit.*

for its members to develop their own skills of leadership. The group is stronger because, first, at any point of decision there will be more alternatives available to it and, second, because the group is no longer dependent upon a single member. In military terms, "Every soldier carries a marshal's baton in his knapsack." The leaderless group, in short, is likely to be more flexible, more resilient, and more resourceful.

The Leader in Reserve

There are, as was mentioned earlier, other positions between the extremes of the leaderless group and the group under a single, officially recognized leader. Any number of persons can divide up the functions of leadership. Another idea is that of the "leader in reserve." In this case, even though someone is formally designated to lead the group he functions only as he is needed. He acts as a kind of balance wheel. If the group is sufficiently involved he will do nothing to stimulate it. If it is moving forward, he will refrain from directing its thinking. If a reasonably constructive climate prevails, he will not interfere. He will sometimes hesitate to exert leadership, even when the group is in trouble, in order to allow participants a chance to develop their own solutions to the problem before he helps out. But if committee members become too partisan, and are doing nothing themselves to correct it, he may try to bring about more objectivity. If the discussion is too abstract, he will try to make it more concrete and meaningful. If the group is lost and wasting precious time he may try to clarify its objectives and suggest a new direction. In all cases, however, he acts only if the difficulty is serious enough to threaten group morale or efficiency and if the group members themselves are not successfully coping with the problem.

Situational Considerations

Which of the various plans for providing leadership is adopted depends not only upon the merits of the arguments for each of them, but also upon a number of factors in the group context. A British psychologist describes this as the "Law of the Total Situation."

> In so far as a man contributes to the collective leadership function . . . he will realise that the ultimate authority and true sanction for leadership at every point where it is exercised, resides — not in the individual, however dominant, strong or efficient he may be — but in the "total situation" and in the demands of that situation, i.e., the Law of the Total Situation. It is the situation that creates the imperative, not the individual. To the extent that the individual is aware of that imperative, is able to make others aware of it, is able to make them willing to serve it: to the extent that he is able to release collective capacities and emotional attitudes that may be related fruitfully to the solution of the group's problems: to that extent he is exercising leadership.[7]

An informed decision regarding the locus of leadership cannot be made without appraising the setting in which leadership will be given.

People, for one thing, usually expect to have a leader. Almost the first question to be asked by appointees to a committee is, "Who is chairman?" It makes things so much simpler to know where the authority lies, to whom to turn for advice, on whom to place the responsibility for success or failure. In large part this simply reflects the culture in which we have been nurtured. We are used to having leaders. A decision to act differently may have to be explained or justified, even when it is a wise decision. In addition, many people are not mature enough — or think they are not mature enough — to break out of the leader-follower mold. They are difficult to convince that they can function in any other way. At least they think they never have. The prospect of controlling their own impulses, of sharing responsibility with others, of having to develop new skills, is disquieting to say the least.

> To teach . . . people to be subservient to authority is relatively easy. To teach them to achieve the maturity of self-directed responsibility is much more difficult. . . . The development of free men requires more intelligence, more patience, more faith in human beings. No one can be forced to be free. Men can only be invited and encouraged to accept the responsibility of freedom.[8]

[7] H. Harris, *The Group Approach to Leadership Testing* (Routledge and Kegan Paul, 1949), p. 258.

[8] William Biddle, *The Cultivation of Community Leaders* (Harper, 1953), p. 58.

As Erich Fromm reminds us, the reaction of many people upon being accorded an opportunity for self-direction is to "escape from freedom."

Then there may be very real practical obstacles which must be considered. As Bales has found, there is a tendency toward greater "formality of authority" as the group grows older, as its size increases, as the members become more heterogeneous in background, as the complexity of the task mounts.[9] Social conversations normally do not have leaders because there is no pressing need to unite in action. A small committee of close friends may work well without a chairman because many of the problems of leadership — competition for the floor, communication breakdowns, the need to summarize diverse ideas — do not appear. As a committee grows in size diffused leadership becomes more and more difficult, and finally impossible. The locus of leadership must also be consistent with environmental pressures surrounding the decisions. A sinking ship, a burning theatre, a military rout, are situations that call for a single, powerful figure. By the same token we should remember that we spend very little of our lives on sinking ships or in burning theatres, and any decrease in the pressure for decisions should favor more diffused leadership as a way of preparing for future emergencies. But, as the task becomes more complicated, and as differences in knowledge and competence increase, centralized leadership becomes more attractive and more justified.

It is out of the interaction among such factors as individual needs of members, the character of the task, the size of the group, and external pressures, that the decision will have to be made to concentrate or diffuse leadership responsibilities.

Philosophies of Leadership

The second question we posed at the outset of this chapter concerned *how* leadership functions should be exercised in a discussion group. How should one regulate participation? What method should one follow in planning an agenda? What is the best way to handle conflict? As we have seen throughout this book, the question of method and philosophy are inextricably bound together. One cannot decide intelligently upon a course of action without examining the assumptions underlying the alterna-

[9] Bales, *Interaction Process Analysis*, p. 176.

tives and without making some evaluation of the consequences of choosing one technique over another. There are many ways to Rome, and many ways to lead. One can command, persuade, suggest, or psychologically manipulate. Broadly speaking, however, there are two main philosophies or styles of leadership — autocratic and democratic — and most of the others are subtle variations on these two.

The kind of influence we exert on other people reflects a whole body of assumptions we make about the nature of man. When we order others about, or use social pressure to accomplish our purpose, we reveal implicitly a concept which holds men to be in need of direction. When we recoil from manipulating others we usually do so, we say, because it violates their integrity. These two competing sets of assumptions, or philosophies, have inspired many of the conflicts we have known in history — in politics, religion, and education.

The autocratic style

One view holds that man is basically irrational. Most of what passes for good sense in human affairs is in actuality only a mask for the real motives under the surface. Human beings are not very creative or original, except for an occasional superman, a genius, who stands out above most of the other members of the human race. Man is also selfish and self-centered. Control through rules and regulations is necessary to keep one man from abusing another. Men are children and need to be told what to do. Since they are so irresponsible, ways must be found to insure that they will carry out their assigned functions, and rewards and punishments are instituted for this reason. Stated so boldly, of course, most of us would reject this philosophy. But it is the underlying premise in many of the great writings of the past and present. Plato, Machiavelli, Carlyle, Nietzsche, are all part of this stream of thought. Hitler's Third Reich was built upon this structure. But it has been best expressed, within the democratic community, by Alexander Hamilton.

> Take mankind as they are, and what are they governed by? Their passions. There may be in every government a few choice spirits, who may act from more worthy motives. One great error is that we suppose mankind more honest than they are. . . .

> All communities divide themselves into the few, and the many. The first are the rich and well-born, the other the mass of the people. The voice of the people has been said to be the voice of God; and, however generally this maxim has been quoted and believed, it is not true to fact. The people are turbulent and changing; they seldom judge or determine right. Give, therefore, to the first class a distinct, permanent share in the government.
>
> . . . The ancient democracies, in which the people themselves deliberated, never possessed one feature of good government. Their very character was tyranny; their figure deformity. When they assembled, the field of debate presented an ungovernable mob, not only incapable of deliberation, but prepared for every enormity.[10]

One can readily extrapolate the leadership principles that would derive from these premises. If man, in general, is uncreative, those who are inventive should be elevated to positions of authority. If man is untrustworthy and undependable, restrictions must be set up to limit his conduct. If the ordinary man lacks vision, then leaders — wise and able ones to be sure — must be selected who can direct the energies of the mass of men. Given this philosophy one wonders what the autocrat is doing in a discussion at all. Probably if he had his way he would not resort to democratic procedures. But in a democratic culture, where a modicum of representation and participation is the accepted pattern, the autocrat frequently finds himself in a discussion. Therefore it becomes necessary for him to express his philosophy through subtle or sometimes not so subtle attempts to manipulate the group.

The democratic style

The opposite view holds that man is basically humane and rational in his impulses. He is capable of sound judgment and can be trusted, in the long run, to rise above petty desires and act judiciously in the crises that confront him. He has a potential for original thought that is repeatedly demonstrated not only in the arts, but in science, engineering, medicine, and government. Man can be trusted to put the welfare of others above his own selfish and temporary advantage. When he acts irrationally or irresponsibly it is because his natural impulses have been dis-

[10] James Truslow Adams (ed.), *Hamiltonian Principles* (Little, Brown, 1928), pp. 31–37.

torted by society; he has been crippled because of being manipulated, deprived, coerced, or used by others. We may shrink back also from this oversimplified assertion of the democratic faith. But it, too, has its supporters, not the least of whom was Thomas Jefferson.

> Men by their constitution are naturally divided into two parties. Those who fear and distrust the people. . . . Those who identify themselves with the people, have confidence in them, cherish and consider them as the most honest and safe . . . depository of the public interest.
>
> We both consider the people as our children. . . . But you love them as infants whom you are afraid to trust without nurses; and I as adults whom I freely leave to self-government.
>
> Sometimes it is said that a man cannot be trusted with the government of himself. Can he, then, be trusted with the government of others? Or have we found angels in the form of kings to govern him?
>
> I know of no safe depository of the ultimate powers of society but the people themselves.[11]

The leadership growing out of this philosophy would encourage the maximum in self-expression. It would be facilitative rather than restrictive. Those in positions of authority would diffuse and share their responsibility with all those participating in the decision. Since people are capable of self-determination, any attempt to coerce them, physically or psychologically, is both immoral and impractical. Manipulation only leads to counteraggressiveness, resistance, and apathy. The democratic leader, in keeping with the Jeffersonian tradition, is a member of the group, equal in status to every other member, responsible only, as is every participant, to assist in, but not determine unilaterally, the procedure to be followed.

A Resolution of the Dilemma

"The animosity between the two men," said Judge Learned Hand of Hamilton and Jefferson, "was well founded and inevitable.

[11] Saul Padover (ed.), *Thomas Jefferson on Democracy* (Appleton-Century, 1939), pp. 150, 163, 24, 162.

They represented, and we are right still to take them as our most shining examples, of two theories of human society; that which demands external control, and that which insists upon the opportunity for self-expression."[12] Choosing between these alternatives, however, is difficult, for there is much in human experience to support both positions. Men do rise to great heights when it is expected of them. They can be exceedingly creative. They are often reasonable and fair in dealing with one another. But they can be vicious and destructive at times. Power is sought solely to exploit others. In the absence of controls, people are capable of abusing and deceiving each other. James Truslow Adams, in preparing Hamilton's work for publication, came to this conclusion concerning the two men we have sampled so briefly:

> It may be that without a vision men shall die. It is no less true that, without hard practical sense, they shall also die. Without Jefferson the new nation might have lost its soul. Without Hamilton it would assuredly have been killed in body.[13]

There is another way of looking at this dilemma. This view is that man is both of these things: that constructive and destructive impulses lie side by side within us. At one and the same time we are potentially reasonable and unreasonable, responsible and irresponsible. The problem, therefore, is improperly phrased. The question is not what *is* man — an unanswerable one — but what is man capable of doing? And on this we find widespread agreement. Hamiltonian and Jeffersonian will each admit that man acts wisely *and* foolishly, altruistically *and* selfishly, maturely *and* immaturely. The issue then becomes one of discovering the social conditions that are most likely to elicit creative, cooperative, and reasonable responses, rather than their opposites.

Social scientists are coming around to a similar conclusion. Psychiatrists say that any of us can become mentally ill if the conditions are conducive to it, and sociologists have shifted their attention away from the criminal as a person and toward the environmental determinants of deviant behavior. "We know," says Boodin, "that a man manifests different characteristics and reacts differently in different group situations as truly as an atom

[12] Learned Hand, *The Spirit of Liberty* (Knopf, 1952), p. 68.
[13] Adams, *op. cit.*, p. xvii.

behaves differently in different molecular groups."[14] This can readily be illustrated. Let the reader recall a number of groups in which he has participated recently. Was he the *same* person in each of them? Probably not. At one meeting he may have been argumentative and uncompromising, at another open-minded and cooperative. In some groups he may have been excited and talkative, but in others quiet and withdrawn. Sometimes we are impelled to act foolishly; on other occasions we are the epitome of sobriety. The addition of a new member to a group, or a change in the tactics of the leader, can trigger off antisocial behavior latent in everyone. Leadership can "bring out" manipulative tendencies in people, or encourage them to respect one another.

It is on this basis that we would reject autocratic leadership as a technique of influence in the discussion group, for it is inconsistent with the goals of such a group. Autocratic control tends to erect status barriers which interfere with the frank discussion of controversial issues. It distorts the thinking of group members and leads to the acceptance of ideas, not on merit, but on the basis of who sponsors them. It discourages people from exercising their own initiative. It complicates the process of communication, impeding the free flow of information and opinion. It stifles individuality and makes it difficult for people to explore and resolve their differences objectively. Domination leads to the passive acceptance of the leader's ideas which converts a truly deliberative process into a hollow and pointless ritual.

Autocratic and Democratic Control Compared

The difference between autocratic and democratic influence in the face-to-face discussion group can be made more concrete if we examine how each style would affect the exercise of leadership functions in the areas specified in the last chapter. In view of the fact that earlier we indicated that leadership might rest in one or all members of a group we shall henceforth discuss the autocratic and democratic *person* rather than limit ourselves to the autocratic and democratic *leader*. Everyone exerts some influence in a group, whether officially designated leader or not, and everyone should be aware of the character of his influence.

[14] J. Boodin, *The Social Mind* (Macmillan, 1939), p. 17.

Influence in the area of creative and critical thinking

The autocratic person is likely, whenever it is expedient, to avoid announcing the purpose of the meeting in advance, either because he feels it is "not the business" of others to know, or because he can more easily control the meeting with this exclusive knowledge. Armed with a private agenda, he is the only one who can prepare adequately for the meeting. And the man who is best informed can often dictate decisions. In contrast, democratic behavior in the area of planning would require that everyone be equally informed as to the purpose of the group so they can all study the problem from their own vantage point and come prepared to consult and act. Any conflict over goals would be cleared up at the outset of the meeting so that everyone could contribute to reaching them.

Or, to act autocratically may mean that a person will make up his mind about the topic prior to a meeting and then use the meeting time only to secure support for his predetermined decision. This, of course, changes discussion from a cooperative investigation into a rhetorical device for manipulating people. Frequently it is just that. Discussion creates a democratic façade that deludes people into believing that because they have been given a chance to speak they have actually participated in decision-making. Sir Winston Churchill, in response to a reporter's charge that he was an autocrat, is said to have replied, "I'm not an autocrat. I simply believe that after due discussion my cabinet ministers ought to agree with me." Democratic behavior does not mean that a person must come to a meeting without any opinions, an intellectual virgin. The alternative to a closed mind is not an empty, but an open, mind. A person disposed to act democratically will have convictions, will explain and defend them with every fact and legitimate argument at his disposal, but he will not resort to stratagem, subterfuge, or manipulation to win his point. He will refrain from exploiting social pressures to maneuver others into agreeing with him.

The autocratically inclined person, when he stimulates others to think, will have an ulterior motive in mind. He is seldom interested in ideas *per se* but in those ideas that will advance his own purpose. He may introduce issues with prejudicial statements that prevent people from viewing them objectively.[15] He may use whatever status or sanctions are at his disposal to win converts. The threat of a pay cut, the loss of certain privileges, or the disapproval of others are weapons he does not hesitate to use in the conference room. One low-status member we once observed won his point repeatedly by threatening that "the administration is very much opposed to this." Since he was the only one who claimed to have a private line to the source of power, his statements, regardless of their inaccuracy, had a devastating effect upon the decisions that were reached. The autocrat who asks questions and poses new issues is not so interested in enlarging the freedom of others to think for themselves as he is in subtly directing their minds toward a foregone conclusion. The democratically inclined person, on the other hand, is more genuinely interested in ideas themselves. His questions are intended to "open up" new avenues of thought, to explore glossed-over possibilities, to encourage speculation. He will criticize the ideas of others, and expect his own opinions to be subjected to the same sort of scrutiny. He may even supply arguments and facts in support of an opposing point of view. On occasion he may step in to counteract status-conscious remarks and get an issue resolved on its merits, for he is less interested in winning arguments than he is in finding the truth.

Influence in procedural matters

The difference between autocratic and democratic influence is most clearly seen in the control of procedure. A meeting that is organized openly and collaboratively stands in sharp contrast to one in which choices are limited, or in which no provision is made for alternative procedural arrangements.

Framing the agenda is the first, and one of the most critical, leadership decisions. The specific topics to be considered, and the order assigned to them, can greatly affect the outcome of the meeting. A person who wishes to dominate the discussion is

[15] This technique is pointed up in a cartoon which appeared in the *New Yorker* magazine some years ago. It pictured a scoutmaster, surrounded by his young charges, standing beside a short-order wagon on the edge of a woods. He was saying, "All right men. Are we going to eat here or should we go to all the work of scrounging around for wood to build a fire with?"

likely to prepare an agenda privately, rather than publicly, and may not afford others an opportunity to amend or revise it. In some cases he may not provide any opening at all for a discussion of group procedure. Because of his status, or his superior knowledge, he regards this matter as his personal prerogative. Democratic group members who wish to contribute to, but not dominate, the planning of a meeting will refrain from imposing their own pre-arranged plan upon the group. Or, if they prepare a draft of an agenda they will invite others to amend, rewrite, or discard the plan if it seems wise to do so. A participant who wishes to avoid infringing upon the freedom of others will suggest a plan for the group to follow but will make it clear that it is not to be adopted simply because he has taken the trouble to prepare it, or because it is the path of least resistance.

Opening a meeting will often bring out the autocratic and democratic tendencies in group members. The person who starts a discussion by arbitrarily stating, "First we will take up the cost figures" or "Where do you all stand on the honor system?" does not encourage or even permit others to have a voice in organizing group thinking. On the other hand, the person who opens a meeting by asking, "How should we go about discussing this problem?" or "Do any of you have ideas on how we should proceed?" does invite others to participate in planning. Even more helpful, and as democratic, is the person who raises the question of procedure and also offers several alternative plans himself. His action not only alerts others to the leadership problem they face but makes a contribution to its solution without cutting off those who may have better suggestions.

One of the most difficult problems in the management of discussion is to keep the group moving from point to point without stalling somewhere or getting off on unnecessary tangents. Group thinking is managed autocratically when someone stops discussion of an issue by announcing, "That's irrelevant!" or "We're off the track!" (Some caution must be exercised in interpreting these phrases, since vocal inflection and emphasis can greatly change the meaning. An extremely democratic person, as well as an autocrat, might say "We're off the track"—but the former would mean, "In my opinion, we're off the track" and the latter would mean, "We *are* off the track." The speaker's past behavior and general attitude will have to be considered as a clue to his present intention.) Anytime the group is suddenly catapulted into a new issue without knowing how it got there, it is probable that someone led it there arbitrarily. The person, however, who asks, "How does this tie in with our topic?" alerts the group to the problem of relevance and asks for clarification without redirecting attention to a new point. The question of relevance is a particularly knotty one because it is so difficult, even for experts in group work, to agree on what is relevant and what is not. This fact alone should make arbitrary leadership in this area suspect.

Summaries must be made and agreements verbalized before the work of a group can be terminated. Autocratic influence, in this area, means that the ideas discussed in the group will be filtered and edited to suit the person who summarizes them. Certain opinions will be repeated accurately, others forgotten, still others reworded in an effort to bring them into line with those of the speaker. Sometimes the sentiments of individual members, or the underlying attitude of the whole group, will be completely overlooked. Or a person may cover up his distortions through his artful use of language. We must be careful, however, not to conclude too quickly that a summarizer is autocratic. It is difficult to phrase a good summary and many of the abuses are due to lack of skill, not intent. Some idea of the motive of the speaker may be obtained from his readiness to invite revisions in his statements or to qualify the conclusions he draws. It may then be clear that accuracy, not manipulation, is intended.

Sometimes the factor of time is used to control the direction and depth of group thinking. The autocratic person may allow the group to consume most of its time on minor points, and then inform them that only twenty minutes remain in which to reach a conclusion. Under democratic direction the group would be made fully aware of its time limits and how they will affect the discussion. Perhaps some short cuts might be indicated. If this is not done, there is the danger that someone will use the lack of time to bludgeon others into approving or disapproving of ideas simply because the deadline demands it.

Whenever a member slows a group down, or speeds it up, or directs it this way or that, and does so without obtaining the free consent of the participants he is exercising arbitrary and autocratic control.

Influence in the area of interpersonal relations

Autocratic influence in regulating participation can take many forms. Those who monopolize a conversation are, by the very act of talking so much, forcing others to remain silent. When active members, on the other hand, insist that nonparticipants express an opinion, they also prevent noncontributors from choosing to stay out of the discussion. A remark such as "We ought to hear from everyone on this," democratic as it sounds, is actually quite coercive. There are also indirect — nonverbal — methods of controlling participation. Turning away while someone is speaking, snickering, gesturing approval or disapproval, are all attempts to impose certain habits of communication on others. Even the nonparticipant (verbally) is sometimes guilty of autocratic behavior in this area.

Is it possible to bring about better communication in a group and still do it democratically? It may be difficult, but it is possible. When a person communicates effectively himself — listens empathically, avoids interrupting, speaks to the entire group, expresses himself frankly — he encourages but does not force others to imitate him. Or when some member becomes aware of communication barriers in the group and brings them to the attention of the rest of the members he makes it possible to discuss the difficulty openly without imposing his standards on others. It is possible, also, to ask another for his opinion without putting him on the spot or compelling him to answer. For example, one might simply say "Joe, do you have anything further to add?" rather than "What's your opinion, Joe?"

When we turn to democratic and autocratic influence in other areas of interpersonal relations, climate-making in particular, we are dealing with a much more subtle and perplexing topic. How can we describe in words the coercive or permissive human personality? Feelings of warmth and acceptance, or of coldness and rejection, are conveyed very largely by nonverbal symbolization. The way we dress says something to others. Our gestures and posture communicate our personality. Just as a formal arrangement of magazines on a coffee table says, "Do not touch," so the wrinkling of a brow, the tightening of lines about the mouth, or the nervous drawing in of a breath may say, "Let's not talk so frankly. I am getting uncomfortable." Conversely, a quieting pause or a look of acceptance may establish rapport and understanding.

Interpersonal attitudes are also communicated verbally, however. Adriza Stampar, one of the founders of the World Health Organization, is said to have run its meetings with a "unanimity complex." He would conclude discussion by saying, "If you have confidence in your chairman you will adopt this item," or "I would be the most unhappy man in the world if the assembly rejected this proposal." [16] Lord Barbason, wartime Minister of Aircraft Production in Britain, described Churchill's treatment of his cabinet ministers as "unbearable." "He behaved as if he were a bully schoolmaster. Everyone, in his opinion, was a half-wit; and if anyone said anything, he was jumped on and snubbed." [17] "Compulsive democracy" is the term used by one executive to describe the Hollywood studios of Walt Disney. "The lowliest ink-girl calls Walt by his first name. 'If we didn't,' says one employee, 'we'd get fired.' " [18]

The climate in any group is a product of many remarks from the most trivial to the most serious. The person, on a hot day, who tells everyone to "Take off your coats" forces everyone to conform, including the person who suspects his shirt is embarrassingly wilted, while the question, "Do you want to take off your coats?" is noncoercive (especially when it comes from a low-status person). A discussion of housing may be forced to a personal level if someone belligerently announces what his house cost, implicitly demanding that others be as confidence-sharing as he is. A liberal or conservative pall can be thrown over a meeting by a "tsk, tsk" or hollow laugh. An arched eyebrow or sly dig can be used by professional Religionists, Capitalists, Artists, Harvard Graduates, Scientists, or Atheists, to announce "Danger, Conformists at Work!" The list of ways in which we influence interpersonal relations is endless, but the principle is clear — any attitude, action, or statement that makes it difficult for others to respond spontaneously and autonomously is not democratic.

Democratic influence seems consistent with the ends of discussion because it coordinates without coercing, because it organizes without restricting, because it promotes rapport rather than

[16] *Time* (July 7, 1955), p. 69.
[17] *New York Times* (September 23, 1956), p. 19.
[18] *Time* (December 27, 1954), p. 44.

alienation, because it encourages constructive rather than destructive criticism; in short, because it preserves the group while respecting the individuality of every member.

Nondirective Leadership

We noted earlier that influence in a group is a product both of status and function. So far, in our description of autocratic and democratic styles, we have tried to isolate the functions of leadership (the acts of coordinating) from the leader (the person who holds a position of influence). However, people are often assigned to a post of leadership. What then? Can they avoid being autocratic when position and function are combined? Even a democratic suggestion in one of the areas we have described is likely to be uncritically accepted when it is a reasonable move by someone in authority. Teachers, for example, will find sometimes that a class will force them into a highly influential role by their own passivity or eager acquiescence.

One solution to this problem is found in what has been termed "nondirective" leadership. (See Chapter 10.) This method, which derives from nondirective counseling procedures, is one in which the therapist refrains from controlling, advising, or directing the client. He does this for a number of reasons: first, he recognizes the tremendous influence he has over the client because of his *position and training;* secondly, he does not want to *coerce other persons* into living by his standards; third, he believes that every person has within himself the potential for becoming *autonomous and mature* if given time and support. Note the close parallel between these assumptions of the nondirective therapist and the person who wishes to lead a discussion group democratically![19] Both have high-status positions. Both may have profound influence if they choose to use their power. The democratic leader, like the therapist, however, also wants his "clients" to become less dependent upon him and more able to assume responsibility for directing their own activities.

An officially designated leader, by following in the footsteps

[19] In some ways the name "nondirective" is a misnomer. Whatever we do in any human relationship, even if it is remaining silent, influences other people. Perhaps in recognition of this Rogers himself now refers to his approach as "client-centered" rather than "nondirective."

of the nondirective therapist, can work toward sharing his leadership responsibilities with the members of his committee and cultivate in them the skills they need. In spite of his position he can refrain from offering direction at critical junctures in the life of the group. He can withhold leadership, sometimes letting the group flounder, so that participants will develop their own motives for leading. On some occasions he may alert the group to its problems but refuse to solve them. On other occasions he will offer so many alternatives, in response to their requests for help, that they will still have to make their own decisions.

He will not, however, default from leadership. Laissez-faire and nondirective leadership are different breeds altogether. The laissez-faire leader does nothing at all, either because he does not know what to do, or because he does not care. The nondirective leader works hard at his job. He listens intently to what is being said. He tries to understand what people are saying to one another — both consciously and unconsciously. He will try to reflect back to the group what he believes they are feeling so they will become more sensitive to their own impulses. As one of the patients in a group psychotherapeutic session remarks in the book *Fortunate Strangers,* "there's a great deal of difference between do-it-yourself and a relationship in which another person says, in effect, 'Try it and I will help you explore the unknown and yourself.' "[20]

Experimental Leadership

We have described a number of approaches to leadership. Some people favor a strong, central group leader; others support a central leader only if he operates democratically. There are those who believe in nondirective leadership, and those who prefer the leaderless group. We are unwilling to support any one of these to the exclusion of the others because such a decision would fail to take into account the specific situational variables and the unique context in which leadership is always exercised. (It would also reflect on the character of our own leadership!) A leisurely conversation calls for one kind of leadership, a crisis demands a very different sort. A large group cannot operate successfully

[20] Cornelius Beukenkamp, Jr., *Fortunate Strangers* (Grove Press, 1958), p. 125.

with the same degree of freedom as a small one. A single meeting attended by strangers presents different problems and opportunities than a series of meetings between close friends or colleagues.

To the readers of this book we would propose something we can best describe as "experimental leadership." Each person should try out different methods of influencing others and determine for himself which is most deeply satisfying. How we influence others is so much a product of our personal needs, our sensitivity to others, our acceptance of diversity, our skills in interacting, that it would be a mistake to force people to conform to a single mold. What we believe should be the general *direction* of this experimentation should nevertheless be clear. The aim, it seems to us, should be toward a wider sharing of leadership responsibility, toward a more permissive relationship with other people, toward greater individuality and spontaneity, toward autonomy and self-direction. The reason is self-evident — a democratic relationship is more likely to fulfill the conditions for healthy discussion and contribute to the maximum growth and maturity of the individual.

Scientist and laymen alike agree on the general importance of leadership in our culture. In this chapter several questions concerning the locus and style of that leadership have been explored.

When leadership is defined as a series of functions performed in a group it is possible to divide the responsibility for these services in many ways. One can elect a single leader, a team of leaders, or have everyone participate in running meetings. The central leader stands at one end of the continuum, the leaderless group at the other. The latter, however, is not to be confused with a leadershipless group in which anarchy prevails because no one coordinates the efforts of group members.

By concentrating authority in the hands of a single person the group may benefit from specialization of roles, channels of communication may be better established, responsibility for success or failure can be fixed, the short-run efficiency of the group can be increased, and the leader, because of his status, may be able to act more impartially. The leaderless group, on the other hand, utilizes the total resources of the members, leads to higher involvement in the task, cultivates skills that may be needed at other times, diminishes status differences, and increases the survival potential of the group. Midway between these concepts is that of the "leader in reserve" who has the status of a leader but who uses his authority with discretion. He refrains from directing the group except when it is in danger of disintegrating or failing to meet its obligations. Situational factors, such as the expectations of the members, the size of the group, the complexity of the task, and the pressure of time, must be weighed in any decision to diffuse or concentrate authority in a group.

Most of the possible methods of leading a group are outgrowths of the democratic or autocratic philosophies. The former emphasizes that man is basically good, rational, just, and these attributes are corrupted when he is coerced or controlled by others. The latter assumes that the bulk of men are not reasonable nor virtuous and that society must regulate their behavior in the public interest. It is evident from history that man is capable of acting both stupidly or sensibly, constructively or destructively. What man is like, in a given circumstance, is a reflection of the social pressures of that moment and the potential within him. Democratic control seems best designed both to secure the ends of discussion and to elicit the most mature behavior from men.

Each member of a group, whether leader in name or not, influences other members in the areas of critical and creative thinking, procedural matters, and interpersonal relations. One can behave so as to force others to conform in these areas, or so that each person is free to act as he wishes. Nondirective leadership is another approach that is open to the person who has been appointed leader of a group but who wants to use his position to cultivate the leadership skills of the rest of the group. "Experimental leadership," in which one tries out various kinds of roles and adapts them to the specific circumstances, is one way of developing flexibility of leadership. It seems clear, however, that the general direction should be toward more democratic and more diffused control since these are conducive to group effectiveness and individual maturity.

RECOMMENDED READINGS

Adorno, T. W., Else Frenkel-Brunswik, D. J. Levinson, and R. N. Sanford. *The Authoritarian Personality.* Harper and Brothers, 1950.

Argyris, Chris. *Executive Leadership.* Harper and Brothers, 1953.

Gordon, Thomas. *Group-Centered Leadership.* Houghton Mifflin Company, 1955.

Haiman, Franklyn S. *Group Leadership and Democratic Action.* Houghton Mifflin Company, 1951.

———. "Man, Not Superman," *Adult Leadership* (March, 1953).

———. "Concepts of Leadership," *Quarterly Journal of Speech* (October, 1953).

Part Five

DISCUSSION IN THE MODERN WORLD

Chapter Fifteen

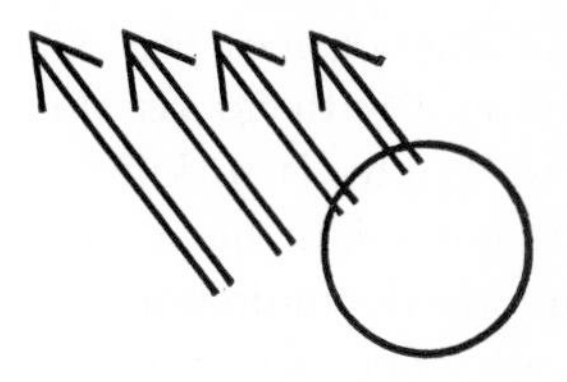

The Uses and Abuses of Discussion

We have asked our readers to follow us through fourteen chapters of exposition regarding the philosophy and methods of group discussion without having confronted the basic question: Why discuss at all? Why take the time and trouble to call a group together when one person can handle matters so much more quickly and easily by himself? We have deliberately postponed our consideration of the merits and shortcomings of discussion until this point because we felt the reader would be in a stronger position to appraise the pros and cons after becoming better acquainted with the process being evaluated. But now it is time to face the critics, who incidentally have become extremely vocal in recent years. In fact it is currently as fashionable to criticize group discussion as it used to be to advocate it.

The Charges Against Group Discussion

The most prominent arguments against discussion follow two major lines. The first is that groups are overrated and overused as instruments for solving problems, making decisions, or working out ideas. The second is that group discussion — or "groupthink" as William H. Whyte calls it — is producing a society of bland conformists for whom togetherness is the main goal in life. Let us examine each of these propositions in more detail.

The critics argue, first, that group discussion is overrated and overused. Mr. Whyte, for example, in his book, *The Organization Man*, expresses the view that the American business world is group-ridden; that conferences are called incessantly, frequently for no good reason and with no visible results. About all they succeed in doing, feels Whyte, is to kill the spark of initiative and creativity that individuals might have, and reduce all problem-solving to the lowest common denominator. He is joined in this view by Charles Kettering, a former official of the General Motors Company, who is reported to have remarked that if you want to kill an idea the best way is to give it to a committee. Then, too, there is the old saw that the explanation for the grotesqueness of the camel is that it was created by a committee.

Not only in the world of commerce but in academic circles as well, there are those who complain of the ever-growing pervasiveness of group discussion. The critics of progressive trends seem to feel that no small part of the blame for the alleged watering-down of education can be attributed to those teachers who have abandoned their traditional authoritative roles in favor of a greater degree of student participation.

The thesis that the growing interest in group activities is part of a cultural trend toward conformity and a loss of individuality is most vividly developed in David Riesman's *The Lonely Crowd*. Mr. Riesman portrays middle-class urban America as a nation of "other-directed" people, each man carrying a highly sensitive radar set designed to pick up cues from his contemporaries which guide his thoughts and actions. Some critics even suggest that we, in America, are but a short step from the brainwashing processes cultivated, largely through the use of group discussion, by the Chinese Communists. "Beware of the social engineers," warns William Whyte, who, under the guise of "democratic discussion," have forged a powerful new weapon for the domination of men's minds.

Where there is so much heated expression of views receiving such widespread popular support (both *The Lonely Crowd* and *The Organization Man* have been top-selling volumes) there must be some provocation. Has group discussion been used or abused in ways that would justify the charges leveled against it? Is it, indeed, a process which naturally lends itself to such abuse? What, if any, values does it possess? And are they sufficient to warrant our promoting it as a method of learning and decision-making?

An Appraisal of Discussion

In answering these questions we feel it necessary to respond in guarded terms. This is not a simple black-and-white issue, and one cannot talk about it intelligently without specifying conditions and qualifications. Still, we do not want to evade our responsibilities or to hide our enthusiasm for discussion. We do propose to support the view that *in general,* and *under most circumstances,* group discussion is a valuable method for conducting human affairs. More specifically, we believe that under most circumstances it is better as a decision-making method than the determination of policy by one man or by a small elite. We believe that under most circumstances it is better as an educational tool than lectures, films, or other one-way means of communication. We believe that under most circumstances it is a more effective vehicle for developing and evaluating solutions to problems than is solitary cogitation.

First let us make clear why we are unwilling to claim the superiority of discussion in *all* circumstances. Although we would maintain that two heads are *generally* better than one, it depends whose heads one is talking about. We would expect an Albert Einstein, working alone, for example, to outperform five average physicists working in a group discussion. We would expect a straight "A" student who listens to a lecture by the most interesting professor on campus to learn more than he would if he were to engage in a discussion on the same topic with a group of "D" students.

Yet are such comparisons a fair test of the discussion method? If we are to compare discussion to other means of problem-solving and of learning we must keep the conditions under which the comparisons are made equal. In place of the foregoing illustrations, perhaps we ought to ask, "Would a discussion group of average physicists in which Einstein was a participant do better than Einstein working alone?" Or, "Does an 'A' student learn more listening to the lecture of a leading professor than he would if he were to discuss the same subject with that same professor?"

But are even these questions fairly phrased? After all, it stands to reason that five men working on a problem for an hour ought to be able to accomplish more than one man working the same length of time, inasmuch as five man-hours are being devoted to the issue rather than one. If the only advantage of discussion is to pile on more man-hours of labor, the participants might just as well work separately. To demonstrate the superiority of group discussion it is necessary that something be gained from the process of interaction *per se*. That is, we must be able to show that the five men do better working as a group than the same five would do, in the same amount of time, working alone.

With these preliminary cautions in mind, let us turn to an examination of the discussion process to determine what values may be gained from its uses, and to note at the same time its limitations and the possibilities for its abuse. Why do we feel that under most circumstances discussion is a superior method of operation, and with what qualifications or exceptions do we advance these assertions?

Discussion makes it possible to bring to a topic a wide variety of information, attitudes, insights, and talents.

It is not without good reason that the cliché, "Two heads are better than one," has been so often repeated. One can cite personal experience and the testimony of others, as well as experimental evidence, to document the proposition that many problems can be solved more effectively through the interplay of several minds than by people working alone. When discussion does not take place, costly errors can be made. We know of one company which invested a large sum of money in new space for its office — complete with new desks, new telephone lines, and other modern equipment. The arrangement of the new office had been placed in the hands of efficiency experts, who did not take the trouble to consult the women who actually worked at the desks. The entire plan eventually had to be scrapped and the office rearranged at considerable expense, because one detail had been overlooked. The new placement of telephones made it impossible for the secretaries to carry out a well-established office custom — reaching over and taking each other's calls when one of them stepped out of the office.

This may seem a rather obvious oversight, but in a complicated world, where problems take on so many dimensions, even the most intelligent individuals find it difficult to encompass all aspects by themselves. Whether it be a question in medicine, business, government, or military operations, responsible people have found that they must bring together specialists of all kinds to contribute their insights and talents to the solution of problems. Policies for our national military establishment, for example, have been formulated for the past several years by a *Joint* Chiefs of Staff. In the realm of big business there are probably few major decisions that are made without drawing upon the advice of a multitude of interested parties. In the field of entertainment, the production of the Dinah Shore Chevy Show on television has been described by the *New York Times* as "creation by committee."

We need not rely on casual observation alone, however, to demonstrate that discussion, by its utilization of a variety of insights, can increase problem-solving effectiveness. An experiment was recently conducted in which comparisons were made between persons working individually on problems in logical reasoning and persons working in groups. All conditions, such as time and personnel, were held equal. It was found that group solutions as a result of discussion were distinctly superior to those of the *best* individual member of the group when working alone. They were also superior to group solutions which were arrived at merely by combining individual judgments via majority vote. This latter finding indicates that it is not just the additional number of persons which accounts for the improvement in decisions, but the interaction itself.[1]

It is therefore not true, as John Steinbeck asserts in *East of Eden,* that "nothing was ever created by two men." If what critics like Steinbeck mean is that there is no such thing as a "group mind" and that ideas cannot be generated in the ether between individuals we would have to agree. Ideas can only come from people. The issue is whether more and better ideas come from then when they are involved in interacting with others than when cogitating in solitude. On this ground, as we have seen, the Steinbeck generalization is fallacious.

Qualifying conditions

Yet we are not prepared to go to the opposite extreme and maintain that group thinking is always superior to that of an in-

[1] Dean C. Barnlund, "Comparative Study of Individual, Majority and Group Judgment," *Journal of Abnormal and Social Psychology* (January, 1959).

dividual. There are a number of qualifications that need to be made.

First, we cannot expect discussion to produce a variety of insights from a group of people who are so much alike in backgrounds, abilities, interests, and opinions that they largely duplicate each other's views. For discussion to be worth while there must be at least some degree of heterogeneity among the participants. In an experiment conducted by Jenness, "Groups were formed either to have great or little heterogeneity of original opinion. A greater increase in individual accuracy was found when the group contained a relatively large range of opinion."[2] After reviewing this and two other related investigations, Kelley and Thibaut conclude that "The preceding three studies suggest the possibility that in some instances the failure of groups to achieve any greater accuracy than individuals may be attributable to extreme homogeneity of opinion in the groups."[3]

On the other hand, too *much* heterogeneity can also negate the effectiveness of group action. If there is a wide divergence of attitudes among the members, and insufficient unity in goals or values, there may be repeated deadlocks. The following comment, for instance, has been published regarding the operation of the Theatre Guild:

> "We gave up the committee method of producing," Mr. Langner explains, "because there was too much talking and not enough work getting done. Time was wasted debating and arguing every little point. Playwrights went crazy waiting for a decision on a script or waiting for suggestions for re-writing. Elmer Rice used to call it the Death Watch. You had to get unanimity among six different people, all of them with strong and different opinions."[4]

One wonders if in this particular case the difficulty was really a lack of common goals, or if it may have been an instance of inadequate skill in group collaboration. Nevertheless there are cases where discussion does break down because of insufficient agreement on purpose or because the participants fail to perceive com-

[2] Harold H. Kelley and John W. Thibaut, "Experimental Studies of Group Problem Solving and Process," in Gardner Lindzey (ed.), *Handbook of Social Psychology,* Volume II (Addison-Wesley, 1954), p. 771.

[3] *Ibid.*

[4] Maurice Zolotow, *New York Times,* (May 11, 1959), Section 2, p. 1.

mon interests which they actually may have. A closely related circumstance which also militates against successful discussion exists when the participants come to the meeting as instructed delegates from another group and are permitted little or no flexibility in discovering common ground. This is often exemplified in labor-management negotiations and, even more strikingly, in the many international conferences which have been held between East and West.

Discussion may also go awry because of too great a gap in knowledge among the participants. Unless the members of a group are somewhat equally well-informed and of relatively comparable intelligence, the result will either be a conversation dominated by the most able (which becomes a monologue rather than a discussion) or a meeting in which the more capable people are pulled down to the level of the weakest contributors.

Finally, the value of interaction can be lost if a group is too large for unrestricted communication to take place. In order for discussion to be most fruitful, the group must be small. Some experts place the maximum as low as eight, although our experience would indicate that as many as fifteen or twenty skilled participants can work together effectively on a discussion basis. Even with larger groups it is possible to organize meetings to provide at least some degree of two-way communication and thus to derive at least partial benefit from the variety of people present. Panel discussions in which a cross-section of the audience comes forward to talk informally with each other in front of the rest of the group, or meetings in which a large gathering of people is subdivided into smaller units which talk for a while and later report their ideas to the general assemblage, are but two possibilities for large group interaction. Nevertheless it must be recognized that as a group increases in size beyond fifteen or twenty, the optimum values of discussion cannot be expected.

Participants in a discussion can check each other's thinking processes.

"Men are never so likely to settle a question rightly as when they discuss it freely," said Lord Macaulay. This observation was probably based upon the realization that when others check on us we are more likely to catch our mistakes than if we have to rely entirely on our own processes of self-examination. It was undoubtedly an awareness of this principle which motivated the Australian tribesmen who declined to cooperate with an anthropologist who wished to give them I.Q. tests. They could not understand why he insisted on each individual taking the test separately. To them it seemed more sensible to discuss the questions and give him group answers, since this was the way they always solved their problems.

On this point, too, there is considerable supporting experimental evidence. We quote directly from the "Comparative Study of Individual, Majority and Group Judgment" cited previously:

> Knowledge that one's opinions were to be shared publicly made group members more cautious and deliberate in their own thinking. The necessity of explaining a conclusion forced many students to be more self-critical. Errors that might have been committed privately were checked before they were communicated to others.
>
> Groups had greater critical resources than individuals working alone. . . . Even the poorest members contributed significantly to the quality of the group product. Remarks that went no deeper than "I don't understand" or "That's absurd" often saved the group from error by forcing them to justify their opinions and in so doing disprove their own conclusions.
>
> A more objective view of the problem resulted from competition between the private prejudices of group members. The test arguments were stated in loaded terms designed to make the choices between conclusions as difficult as possible. Each individual, however, brought a different set of values to his group. When arguments were stated so they appealed to persons of one persuasion, those in opposition were anxious to detect their error. In this way, liberals counteracted conservatives, Republicans offset Democrats, and "independents" guarded against critical lapses on the part of fraternity members. Groups were forced to become more objective, and this, of course, increased their chances of drawing valid conclusions.[5]

Shaw also has reported similar findings:

> Individuals and groups of four worked on a number of problems. When compared on speed of performance, the data were inconsistent; but not so when compared on accuracy. The groups produced a substantially greater percentage of correct solutions to the

[5] Barnlund, pp. 58–59.

problems. Observation of the group process revealed on one problem, for example, that although twice as many correct as incorrect suggestions were made, the groups rejected five times as many incorrect as correct suggestions. Further, the initiator rejected only one-third as many of his own incorrect suggestions as did other members of the group. Shaw comments: ". . . one point of group supremacy is the rejection of incorrect ideas that escape the notice of the individual when working alone." [6]

Qualifying conditions

To argue that discussion produces gains in critical thinking presumes a discussion *at its best.* But we must not overlook the fact that there are certain kinds of group situations where critical facilities are lowered rather than heightened. We have in mind meetings where a kind of mob psychology pervades the atmosphere, or where social pressures are brought to bear against anyone who dares express a point of view which differs from the prejudices of the majority. We have already referred to experimental studies such as those of Asch and Schachter demonstrating the pressures toward conformity that groups tend to exert upon minority members. The Barnlund study also revealed that one of the factors that accounted for the majority of group errors during the experiment "was that group members agreed immediately and unanimously upon the wrong answer to the problem. Further discussion of the issue was then considered unnecessary and wasteful." [7] This is the phenomenon that Jenness and Allport refer to as the "impression of universality." [8] It is one of the factors that explains the success of Communist brainwashing.

Although evidence indicates that these pressures for conformity are a natural and common aspect of the group process, we cannot conclude that they are inevitable. On the contrary, there is also considerable evidence, as we have indicated, that discussion can raise the level of critical thinking of the individuals involved. Perhaps the answer to this dilemma is to be found in still another investigation which demonstrated that people derive considerable

[6] Reported by Kelley and Thibaut, *op. cit.*, p. 740.

[7] Barnlund, p. 59.

[8] A. Jenness, "The Role of Discussion in Changing Opinion regarding a Matter of Fact," *Journal of Abnormal and Social Psychology* (October–December, 1932).

satisfaction from discussions in which "deindividuation" (defined as the inability to recall who said what) occurs.[9] In interpreting their findings, the experimenters conclude that groups probably provide two different sorts of satisfactions for their members. On the one hand, if a group is to have a more stable quality than the "momentary and evanescent existence of crowds," opportunities must be available for recognition of members on an individual basis. On the other hand, important satisfactions are apparently derived by members "getting lost" in the group. "Groups which succeed in being very attractive to their members probably provide both types of situations on different occasions." [10]

Another doubt which the critics raise is whether group discussion is really necessary in order to insure that the errors of individuals will be checked. They argue that in the area of governmental decision-making, for example, the same value is achieved by the functioning of an opposition political party which serves to keep the "ins" on their toes. Although we would admit that sniping from the sidelines often has a salutary effect upon decision-makers, we would maintain that in general it is better to bring the parties together in face-to-face contact. How much more profitable would it be, for instance, if our presidential candidates, instead of making separate speeches to separate audiences and evading each other's arguments, were to appear on the same platform and discuss these topics with one another? Perhaps it is a desire to avoid the vital issues which has prevented a revival of the Lincoln-Douglas tradition.

A shortcoming of discussion which we find more convincing is that there may be a limit to the objectivity which can reasonably be expected or asked of people. Where deeply vested personal interests are involved it may well be that discussion should give way to majority vote or arbitration from above. Although a few employers have experimented with the idea of putting competing candidates for a job together in a room and letting them discuss and decide which one is best qualified to be hired, perhaps this places an unfair emotional strain on all involved. The same would be true of allowing a class of students to discuss and decide upon the grades

[9] Leon Festinger, A. Pepitone, and Theodore M. Newcomb, "Some Consequences of Deindividuation in a Group," in Hare, Borgatta, and Bales, *op. cit.*

[10] *Ibid.*, p. 292.

which should be given to each member of the group. Referring again to the Theatre Guild experience:

> Professional jealousy also made the committee set-up impractical. Mr. Moeller would naturally want the first choice of plays to direct, Mr. Simonson would want to design the best plays. This alienated other designers and directors who were not on the billboard. "Everybody wanted to protect his own interests," Mr. Langner says.[11]

Finally, there may be some topics upon which certain individuals do not care to be objective and to have their thinking examined critically by others. They may prefer to decide the matter for themselves on the basis of faith or intuition rather than rational thought. We would argue that this is every man's privilege *so long as* his decisions affect only himself and nobody else. However, in this closely interrelated world there are relatively few problems that fit this description. Most questions do affect more than one person, and when they do we would maintain that private logic is inappropriate. If people are to make decisions which involve other human beings they should be expected to subject themselves to the crossfire of critical discussion.

Discussion creates greater motivation, interest, and involvement in learning and in decision-making.

Every one of us has probably had the experience of feeling that we can stay with a job much longer, and work harder, if we have company. The social satisfactions derived from interacting with other people seem to make the task less onerous. Sometimes a job which is considered quite boring when undertaken alone can become fun when done with others. Likewise those who have sat in classes conducted by the discussion method have surely noticed how much more quickly the time goes by than when listening to a lecture. This is due to the fact that there are many more sources of stimulation and human interest in a discussion — a variety which even the most outstanding lecturer would have difficulty in matching. In the Barnlund experiment it was found that subjects

> concentrated more intently on the assigned problems after being appointed to a group than they did when solving the problems individually. Group members found themselves more and more deeply

[11] Zolotow, *loc. cit.*

involved as they proposed, and were forced to defend, their ideas. Participants identified with their own groups to such a degree that when some members became fatigued, others urged them to continue working.[12]

One can cite other studies which have demonstrated that where there is greater interaction in a group there is higher morale and deeper personal involvement among the participants.[13] But the point is so clearly supported by everyday human experience that elaborate proof hardly seems necessary.

In this value of discussion lies one of the answers to the critics who charge that nothing is ever created by a group. If we understand that a group consists of nothing more than individual human beings, it is clear that if they are creative when alone there is no reason to assume that they cannot continue to be creative, and perhaps even more so, when exposed to the stimulation of other people. Indeed, we could name some individuals who had never known what it was to do truly creative thinking until they were prodded into it by group interaction.

Qualifying conditions

Still, we will agree that, *for certain kinds of work,* interaction with others may be more of a distraction than a productively motivating force. Although students can frequently gain much from studying together for an examination which will involve questions asking for relationships and interpretations, they would probably do better to prepare by themselves if it is to be the type of test which calls for the memorization of lists of terms.

A rather enlightening experiment was conducted a number of years ago by Thorndike, comparing group and individual effectiveness in solving crossword puzzles and in constructing crossword puzzles. He found that "groups showed a greater superiority in solving the puzzle than in constructing it."[14] Kelley and Thibaut comment on this finding as follows:

> . . . the puzzle construction task has some very interesting properties. It requires reaching decisions on early phases which can only be validated subsequently as the task nears completion. An individual

[12] Barnlund, p. 58.

[13] For instance, Bavelas, *op. cit.*; and Murray Horowitz, "The Recall of Interrupted Group Tasks: An Experimental Study of Individual Motivation in Relation to Group Goals," reported by Kelley and Thibaut, *op. cit.*

[14] Kelley and Thibaut, *op. cit.*, p. 760.

> working alone will hit upon an approach and follow it out consistently. But in a group, a beginning suggested by one member must be accepted pretty much on faith by the others. He is little able to justify it without elaborate discussion which would virtually constitute a complete solution in itself. Since several persons will have initial hunches as to how to begin, they are likely to continue developing them. These developments most probably will result in independent solutions with little or no interchangeability of parts.[15]

With this kind of task, it would seem that it is better for an individual to follow through uninterruptedly on a lead, even if it is a poor one, than to have to stop to defend his initial premise. Although a group might do well at outlining a paragraph in a report, only an individual, working at least momentarily by himself, could construct an intelligible sentence. We would not oppose other group members suggesting revisions in the sentence, but they ought first to let somebody formulate a tentative statement which they can then improve.

There are other considerations, in addition to the nature of the task, which might nullify the normal motivating power of group discussion. Man needs solitude as well as comradeship, and often some of us do not get enough of the former. Thus, rather than enjoying work on a problem with others we might find it more attractive to do it alone. Individual temperament is another variable. It may be that people like John Steinbeck, who assert that groups are poor vehicles for creative endeavor, are simply expressing their own temperamental aversion to working creatively with others. *For them* it might well be true that "nothing was ever created by two men." This does not make the generalization valid for all people.

Lastly, people sometimes feel less responsible for solving a problem, and hence less involved, when working with others than when working alone. They take the attitude in a group that "somebody else will do it" and play a passive role themselves. If they had to do the job alone they would not be able to shunt it off on someone else. In other words, buck passing rather than greater interest might result from some discussion situations.

Discussion provides a safety valve for emotional tensions.

The release of tension is a rather self-evident value of group discussion. Human beings inevitably build up emotional strains,

[15] *Ibid.*

and find some relief in being able to air their feelings with others. Even if they are not able to eliminate the cause of their frustration, it helps just to tell somebody how they feel about it. It is probable that a good portion of the benefit derived from group psychotherapy lies in the opportunity to share one's hates, fears, and anxieties with fellow patients. To the extent that members of every group, even though highly task-oriented, inject personal concerns into a discussion, that meeting will provide some of the values we are here considering.

Qualifying conditions

It is quite possible, however, for a group to indulge so heavily in catharsis that the participants no longer use it as a safety valve for tensions but rather for wallowing in preoccupation with self. Sessions in which hypochondriacs sit around evening after evening complaining to each other of their ailments serve no real therapeutic purpose, as evidenced by the fact that the participants never seem to get enough of this kind of discussion. If anything constructive were happening the tensions would be sufficiently "bled off" so that the group could turn its attention to other matters. Some of the training programs in group dynamics which rely heavily on group self-analysis have been accused of this kind of emotional indulgence, and unkindly labeled the "cesspool school of group dynamics." Although a good deal of this criticism reveals a lack of understanding of the purposes of the programs being attacked, some of it appears to be quite justified.

Discussion produces more internalization of decisions and of learning.

One of the most basic problems confronted by any society — from the family to the nation — is that of securing understanding and acceptance of social norms and policies from all of the members of the group. Perhaps the most significant claim we can make for the superiority of discussion over one-way communication lies in its accomplishments in this area. When members of a group have an opportunity to participate in decision-making processes they feel more identified with decisions, understand them more fully, and are more apt to support and abide by them than if policies are handed down to them ready-made from above. By the same token, in Learning Groups the members are more likely to master ideas which they have had a chance to discuss than if they are simply exposed to information from an expert.

These generalizations have repeatedly been tested and found valid in a wide variety of experiments, not only in the psychologists' laboratories, but in real-life settings as well. Among the better known pieces of research are the work of Bavelas,[16] Coch and French,[17] Levine and Butler,[18] and Lewin.[19] Bavelas, for instance, found that the production of sewing machine operators increased from 60 to almost 90 units per hour as a result of a group decision to increase output, whereas work groups which did not participate in that decision failed to change at all. Coch and French experimented with three different procedures of decision-making regarding a conversion to new work methods in a factory — no participation, participation through representatives, and total participation by all persons to be affected by the changes. The investigators discovered that with each degree of increase in participation, the effectiveness of the change was markedly improved. Lewin's experiments demonstrated the superiority of discussion over lectures in bringing about modification in the meat-using habits of American housewives during World War II. Levine and Butler summarized their own work as follows:

> A formal lecture method was compared with group decision in inducing 29 supervisors of 395 factory workers to overcome their biased performance ratings. The results showed that only the group of supervisors involved in group decision improved in their ratings. The lecture group did not change. . . .[20]

A number of explanations have been advanced for the greater effectiveness of discussion in producing support for decisions. The reader may recall the observation quoted in our first chapter from the Renaissance philosopher, Marsiglio of Padua, to the effect that the citizen in a democracy is more likely to obey a law of his

16 Reported in Kelley and Thibaut, *op. cit.*, pp. 755–756.

17 *Ibid.*, p. 756.

18 Jacob Levine and John Butler, "Lecture vs. Group Decision in Changing Behavior," in Cartwright and Zander, *op. cit.*

19 Kurt Lewin, "Studies in Group Decision," in Cartwright and Zander, *op. cit.*

20 Levine and Butler, *op. cit.*, p. 286.

society "because he himself seems to have imposed it upon himself and, therefore, cannot complain against it." Modern psychology adds some additional insight:

> One possibility is that a participation procedure increases the likelihood that a goal will be set which is congruent with individual goals. That this is not the whole story, however, is indicated by the fact that initial preferences are sometimes set aside in favor of the group goal. Another possibility is that because of the discussion involved in setting the goal, members are more likely to have adequate knowledge of the goal and of its value to themselves and to the group, as well as a realistic view of its attainability. A somewhat different explanation would be that a positive evaluation of the goal is derived from hearing that other group members value it. Thus, if the goal is definitely desired by some members and this becomes apparent through the discussion, their associates may either change their judgments of the goal or work toward it simply as a means of helping their friends.[21]

We would suggest the additional possibility that involvement in decision-making has a maturing effect on the participant's sense of responsibility. We recall the experience of a camp director who, upon becoming weary of the complaints from his eight- and nine-year-olds about the swimming, boating, tennis, and baseball schedule, placed the entire problem of mapping out a timetable for the use of the camp's limited facilities in the youngsters' hands. Through this experience in group decision-making the campers discovered how complex it was to figure out a plan in which everyone would be given a fair and equal chance at the various facilities, and they were thenceforth much more tolerant of not being able to do exactly what they wanted to do when they wanted to do it.

An interesting point offered by Marquis, Guetzkow, and Heyns should be noted here in passing. They

> provide data which suggest that the *possibility* of participation is more important than whether or not the person actually participates. In a series of studies of decision-making conferences they found that member satisfaction with the meeting and the decisions reached does not correlate with amount of overt participation but is related to whether or not the member feels he has an opportunity to say what he wanted to during the meeting.[22]

[21] Kelley and Thibaut, *op. cit.*, p. 757.
[22] *Ibid.*

Whether it is true, *in general,* that "silent participation" is as effective in producing support for social decisions as active verbal involvement is a question which requires further investigation. In Learning Groups, at least, there is some reason to believe that it is the act of participation itself which gives discussion the advantage over lectures. Two studies of Bos, reported by Kelley and Thibaut, for example, suggest that

> the very act of formulating an opinion or idea for communication to the group leads to a sharpening and refining of the idea. . . . In both experiments children in pairs were substantially more accurate than as individuals. Part of this superiority Bos credits to the resistance offered to vague ideas by the demands of communication.[23]

Whatever the many reasons may be, it is clear from the research in this field that discussion does produce greater internalization of information and of group norms and policies than one-way communication. In recognition of this point psychiatrists have long since given up trying to bring about changed behavior by telling patients what to do about their problems. Instead they attempt, in conference, to help them work matters out for themselves. Here also lies the answer to those business executives, organization presidents, and others, who grieve about the tremendous amount of time consumed — or wasted, as they usually put it — in meetings. What they fail to realize is the even greater amount of time spent, in the absence of discussion, attempting to secure understanding and acceptance of policies from those who must act upon them. If the one-way communicator knew how little of his message was getting across with the meanings he intended, he might be more willing to take the time to engage in discussion. If the executive who issues orders were to count up the hours devoted to selling, supervising, and enforcing his policies down the line he would find that it might have saved time to have held a discussion in the first place. Furthermore, many administrators seem quite naïve about the extent to which their arbitrary decisions are ignored when they are not around.

Qualifying conditions

Although most of the critics of group discussion will readily admit its superior effectiveness in producing change in the participants,

[23] *Ibid.,* pp. 743–744.

they find this very value to be a cause of considerable alarm. We must confess that, to some extent at least, we share their concern. They point out that since discussion is so penetrating in its influence it can become a powerful weapon of the hidden persuader. Shrewd manipulators of ideas and of people may pervert the discussion process in such a way that the participants think they are making decisions for themselves when in fact the outcome has been predetermined. Hence, the ideas which they internalize and make so very much their own have been imposed upon them without their knowing it. If we can rely upon reports which have come out of China and out of the Korean prison camps, this is precisely what happens in Communist brainwashing. One wonders, too, how many business conferences or classroom discussions in our own country are *pseudo*-discussions in which the leaders cleverly guide the group to their own foregone conclusions.

Yet we certainly cannot condemn discussion itself for this abuse of its purposes, and retreat, as William H. Whyte would apparently have us do, to the alternative of rugged individualism. Rather we must see to it that ever-increasing numbers of people are trained in group dynamics so they will be able to detect this kind of perversion when it is attempted. There is no inherent danger in the fact that a group decision is effectively internalized—*so long as* those affected have truly had an opportunity to participate in the formulation of the decision, and so long as that decision remains open to further exploration and review.

Another cause for concern in this area has been that, in an effort to gain sufficient group consensus for internalization to take place, the quality of decisions tends to be watered down to the lowest common denominator. In other words, in our eagerness to achieve unanimous or nearly unanimous agreement we may compromise important principles, adopt plans with no teeth in them, or settle for policies whose only virtue is that they offend no one. We have mixed feelings about this line of attack. One can argue, in rebuttal, that it is more important for a decision to be acceptable to the people who must implement it than that it possess somebody's abstract notion of high quality. A plan or policy is not much good, even though it may be the "intelligent thing to do," if it cannot be carried into action. By watering it down to the point where those affected by it can understand it, and at least accommodate themselves to it, if not actively support it, more has been gained than by constructing a "perfect" or "ideal" solution whose only existence is on a piece of paper.

But having said all this, we are almost immediately disposed to contradict ourselves. The decision of the United States Supreme Court on school desegregation, or any other civil liberties issue for that matter, immediately comes to mind. Should the Supreme Court, instead of ruling as it did, have compromised with the attitudes of the average southerner? Should the justices have discussed the problem with the attorneys for the South until a mutually satisfactory arrangement had been achieved? Or was there an important principle here which had to be enunciated, albeit unilaterally, regardless of whether some people liked it and would abide by it or not. We are inclined to the latter view. We might wish that something had been done years earlier, through the processes of discussion, to bring about a climate of opinion in which mutually satisfactory plans of gradual desegregation could have been achieved. (We are not suggesting that this was the responsibility of the Court.) But, having arrived at the place we found ourselves in 1954, it is our belief that the Supreme Court had to do what it did. As Peter Viereck has pointed out:

> The concept of civil liberties is aristocratic. It bravely defies majority rule. . . . Guarding the Bill of Rights even against majorities and even *against the people's will,* the American Constitution performs an aristocratic function.[24]

We would support Viereck's statement only after adding that even the Constitution and the Bill of Rights can and ought to be changed by the people if, after thorough deliberation and via due process of law, they wish to do so. In other words, we condone autocratic action and the abandonment of discussion only as a temporary corrective to mob thinking, not as a normally recommended procedure.

Lastly, in response to the assertion of discussion's value as a vehicle for effective internalization, some have argued that sufficient understanding and support can be achieved in a group without discussion. In fact it has been said that an unusual charismatic

[24] Peter Viereck, *The Shame and Glory of the Intellectuals* (Beacon Press, 1953), p. 220.

leader, such as an Adolf Hitler, Franklin D. Roosevelt, Winston Churchill, or John L. Lewis can gather even more support through one-way communication than can be won through the best of group discussions. Certainly the existence of these examples cannot be denied. Outstanding organization leaders, in all walks of life, succeed in rallying impressive support and loyalty from their followers, who appear to commit themselves rather wholeheartedly to the causes being advocated. Likewise, we can probably all cite instances of an exceptionally vivid lecture or series of talks which have had great influence upon us, just as we can think of discussions which have had no influence at all.

In order to make fair comparisons between one- and two-way communication on this score, however, we must know something of the other conditions under which the understanding or support are achieved. It may be that during crisis circumstances, such as those which confronted Franklin D. Roosevelt in 1933, where the need for action and the attitudes of the public were rather clear, a leader is allowed, even expected, to make unilateral decisions in which he is then supported. Or if a leader, such as Hitler, is skillful enough to detect latent fears and hostilities in a people and to give them expression and direction, he may secure formidable backing. Also, if a leader is satisfied merely to obtain behavioral conformity, has enough physical or economic power to impose it, and does not care how people feel and think, one-way communication may accomplish his purposes.

On the other hand, it should be recognized that a following achieved through coercion or the power of a personality, rather than through discussion and an understanding of the issues, tends to be an ephemeral thing. Loyalty is to the leader rather than to the cause, and when he is gone or when people become disenchanted with him, the organization, if it is an Action Group, is likely to disintegrate and the cause be forgotten. In a learning situation, this kind of reverence for a teacher, though it may and frequently has produced skilled actors, writers, or musicians, more typically develops second-rate imitators of the teacher's style rather than creative human beings. In short, where there is little or no opportunity for the development of self-direction one cannot count on the changes which are induced in people to last for very long. This brings us directly to the final value of discussion.

Discussion develops the abilities and creative potential of the members of a group.

Not least among the advantages of discussion is what it does for the individuals who participate in it, and thus indirectly for the group as well. By taking an active part in the decision-making or learning processes which affect them, people are able to exercise and develop whatever creative potentialities they may have. Undoubtedly in recognition of this principle many parents and teachers encourage young people who are a bit shy or withdrawn to join in group activities at school or in the community. The assumption here is that this experience will help draw them out as individuals — certainly not that it will intensify their tendencies toward conformity. The experience of interacting with others is not only immensely satisfying to the individual, but aids the group as well. Other members are able to benefit from the greater riches which are uncovered. Leadership talents which might otherwise have remained latent are elicited and encouraged. In fact, one of the nation's largest farm equipment manufacturers discovered, quite as an accidental by-product of a discussion program which it introduced throughout the company, that this was one of the best means it had ever found for identifying future leaders. Contrary to what many of the critics have asserted, discussion, when properly conceived and conducted, provides a stimulus and an arena for the testing of new ideas and for the expression of emerging leadership. Rather than stifling individuality, it can provide fertile soil for the fuller unfolding of human personality.

Qualifying conditions

But note that we have said "discussion, properly conceived and conducted." Groups can, and some groups do, suppress individuality and creativity. They are not only anti-leader, but anti-leadership as well. We have already observed how great the pressures toward conformity in a group can be, particularly when such a high value is placed on maintaining friendly relations that anyone who is "different" is cut down to size. Genius, as well as more modest forms of creativity, are discouraged, and mediocrity rides triumphant. Anyone who has come up through an American high school or college knows what the social pressures are against being "too smart," or violating the norm of the "gentleman's C."

We would merely repeat again that the kind of atmosphere in which this sort of thing happens is not an inevitable result of group discussion. It can, and in fact is more likely to, occur in a group where real discussion does not take place. Furthermore, even when it does come about as a result of discussion, we need to recognize that, to some extent at least, the frustrating of genius may be necessary to the survival of a group or society. Although we would not want to advocate this as a desirable goal, we are forced to admit that the creative individual is of little value either to himself or to society if he is *completely* out of tune — hence out of communication — with his fellow men. He can fulfill himself as a human being only if he is able to establish relationships with others. If this means cramping his style somewhat by having to adapt to certain norms, or slowing him down some while others try to catch up it may be worth the cost. So long as he is not *always* having to adjust to other people, it may do him good once in a while to come to grips with human reality. Thus, although the current move in our schools to segregate gifted children and give them a chance to speed ahead is much needed and long overdue, it can also be carried too far. Exceptional students ought, in at least some of their classes, to remain with those who are not so bright, just so they know how the "other half" live and do not lose their sense of rapport or ability to communicate with them.

What is more, we should not be too quick to assume that "fast people" can learn nothing from slow ones. The teacher, for example, who employs discussion in the classroom is not necessarily pulled down to the level of his students. Not only should he and will he do some pulling up, but the pulling by the students is not always downward. After many years of teaching by discussion we still find ourselves learning a great deal from the members of our classes. We can also assert, with unlimited confidence, that for the overwhelming bulk of students, the discussions we have observed have been a stimulant, not a depressant, to creative individuality.

All of the arguments presented throughout this chapter in favor of or against group discussion seem to turn ultimately on the question of what kind of discussion and what kind of group atmosphere one is talking about. Where the group is composed of excessively homogeneous or heterogeneous people; where there are wide gaps in knowledge between the participants; where the group is too large for unrestricted communication; where group pressures toward conformity are strong; where personal interests are irreconcilable; where the nature of the problem requires uninterrupted concentration; where periods of privacy are too rare; where self-indulgence is rampant; where manipulators remain hidden; or where basic and valuable principles are compromised — under such conditions there is good reason to fear that group discussion will do more harm than good. To this extent we can be grateful to the critics for pointing up the dangers of "groupthink."

On the other hand, where both common purpose and divergent backgrounds are present; where individual differences are respected and encouraged; where the solving of the problem can benefit (as most can) from the interplay of many minds; where the participants can, with good reason, trust one another; and where they are willing and able to converse rationally — under these conditions group discussion provides many values. It makes it possible to bring to a topic a wider variety of information, attitudes, insights and talents. Participants can check each other's thinking processes. There is greater motivation, interest and involvement in learning and in decision-making. Discussion provides a safety valve for emotional tensions. It also produces more internalization of decisions and of learning. Finally, it develops the abilities and creative potential of the members of a group.

It would seem reasonable then that, in response to the critics, we should not agree to abandon discussion or reduce our interest in it — a course of action which would be impossible in view of the forces discussed in Chapter 1. Rather we should move in the opposite direction — namely, to learn as much as we can about the process so that we may encourage its use where appropriate, discourage it where inappropriate, and attempt to promote the kinds of group norms which will highlight the values of discussion and minimize its abuses.

RECOMMENDED READINGS

Benne, Kenneth. "Democratic Ethics and Social Engineering," *Progressive Education* (May, 1949).

Coyle, Grace. *Group Experience and Democratic Values.* Woman's Press, 1947.

Haiman, Franklyn S. "Groupthink or Group Thinking," *Adult Leadership* (March, 1953).

Hunter, Edward. *Brainwashing in Red China.* The Vanguard Press, 1951.

Whyte, William H. "Groupthink," *Fortune* (January, 1952).

——— "The Social Engineers," *Fortune* (March, 1952).

——— *The Organization Man.* Doubleday & Company, Inc., 1956.

Chapter Sixteen

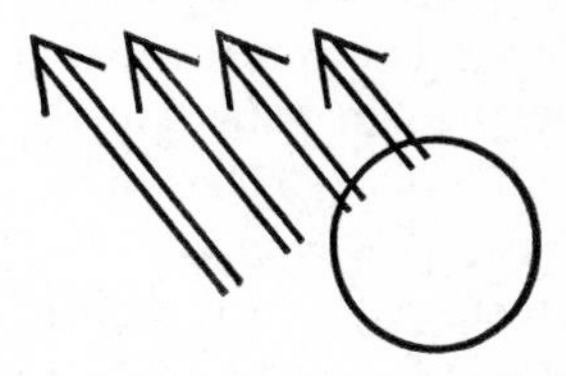

Discussion in Contemporary Life

THE PERISHABILITY OF HUMAN INSTITUTIONS, particularly democratic ones, is an inescapable fact of life. All claims to the contrary notwithstanding, our rights as citizens are not "inalienable." They were bought for us, and are preserved by mortal men, not gods. Our methods of governing ourselves, of determining public policy, hinge precariously upon the ability of each generation to adapt these procedures to the needs of their age.

The assumptions underlying the democratic philosophy, for that is what they are, have repeatedly been disputed. Nevertheless, we have made a choice. Our decision rests upon certain truths that we hold to be "self-evident." Among them is a belief, and a hope, that the safest repository of power is the private citizen, that all authority must ultimately derive from him. Furthermore, that with a modicum of education, and access to sources of information, the voter is able to inform himself on public problems, and will do so. We hold, also, that intelligent participation in government by the electorate will produce the wisest decisions and will elicit the widest public support for them. Finally, we have developed means consistent with this philosophy — discussion, debate, persuasion — as techniques for translating the diverse motives of men into united action.

In every age there have been those who questioned the validity of these assumptions. Critics have claimed that self-government is an illusion, or that it is an undesirable ideal. Some have argued that men are so obviously unequal in their talents that it would be better to rely on "philosopher-kings," "divine monarchs," "great men," or "heroes" to conduct the affairs of less talented and gifted human beings. The controversy goes on, even today. George Kennan, former Russian expert in the Department of State, states the problem in this way: "One of the recurring problems of a democratic society in a complex and changing era is to adapt and perfect its techniques to the changing social scene. Is America, or for that matter any free nation, capable of doing that?"

The leading contemporary critics, however, take a somewhat different approach than their predecessors. They no longer favor government by an elite, the disenfranchisement of voters, or destruction of human liberty. They argue, rather, that democracy if it is to survive must be redesigned and modified to keep pace with the problems of this "age of anxiety." They question, for example, whether a free economy can compete with those in which every material resource is mobilized in the national interest. Will individualistic societies prevail against those able to cultivate and exploit any human resource? Are governments which rely on public opinion capable of eliciting the personal sacrifices required from nations exerting world leadership? Can the slow, somewhat tedious, processes of democracy outperform the speedy, secret, and opportunistic methods of the dictatorships?

None of these loyal and conscientious critics deserves more serious study than Walter Lippmann. In his early books, such as *Public Opinion* and *The Phantom Public,* as well as more recently in *The Public Philosophy,* he has argued that democratic methods must be revised to cope successfully with the problems of the contemporary world. The crises of today demand a strong central government that is free to act speedily and vigorously without having to wait upon the slow tide of public opinion. The average citizen upon whom public policy depends, Lippmann argues, is now in the position of a "deaf spectator" who knows he is watching something "out there" that vitally concerns him, but which he is unable to grasp or form an intelligent opinion about. The ordinary man cannot keep abreast of such a fast-moving and complicated environment.

> As a private citizen he does not know for certain what is going on, or who is doing it, or where he is being carried. No newspaper reports his environment so that he can grasp it; no school has taught him how to imagine it; his ideals, often, do not fit with it; listening to speeches, uttering opinions, and voting do not, he finds, enable him to govern it. He lives in a world which he cannot see, does not understand and is unable to direct.[1]

Survival, according to Lippmann, in a world of cold wars, space travel, and nuclear tests, requires some basic alterations in our conception and practice of democracy.

The problem, as Lippmann sees it, lies in our placing far too much confidence in the interest and intelligence of the man in the street. In expecting voters, who have no direct acquaintance with public problems, and are unable to obtain or understand technical data, to participate in and direct their own affairs we have set up an impossible democratic ideal for this age.

> I think it is a false ideal. I do not mean an undesirable ideal. I mean an unattainable ideal, bad only in the sense that it is bad for a fat man to try to be a ballet dancer. An ideal should express the true possibilities of its subject. When it does not it perverts the true possibilities. The ideal of the omnicompetent, sovereign citizen is, in my opinion, such a false ideal. It is unattainable. The pursuit of it is misleading. The failure to achieve it has produced the current disenchantment.[2]

As a result of pursuing this unattainable and impractical ideal there has been a "functional derangement" of the relations between citizenry and government. The voter has acquired power which he cannot use intelligently to guide national policy and the government has surrendered authority which it rightfully must have in order to act. The proper roles of citizen and government have to be redefined. Lippmann suggests this new line of demarcation:

> The answer cannot be simple. But for a rough beginning let us say that the people are able to give and to withhold their consent to being governed — their consent to what the government asks of them, proposes to them, and has done in the conduct of their affairs. They can elect a government. They can remove it. They

[1] Walter Lippmann, *The Phantom Public* (Harcourt, Brace, 1925), pp. 13–14.

[2] *Ibid*, pp. 38–39.

can approve or disapprove its performance. But they cannot administer the government. They cannot themselves perform. They cannot normally initiate and propose the necessary legislation. A mass cannot govern.[3]

The objections to self-government, then, are twofold: (1) Survival demands some restrictions on popular rule in order to make democracy more efficient and effective in coping with the complex issues of the twentieth century. (2) Democracy in a large scale modern political state can be, at best, only a democracy of consent, not of participation.

The democratic "revisionists," although few in number, are men of stature whose opinions cannot be lightly shrugged off. Fortunately (in our opinion), their views are openly challenged by many equally expert and interested authorities. Thus the issue is a highly debatable one, and any informed decision as to whether the present situation calls for an extension or limitation of participation in public affairs should rest upon a careful analysis of current social and political trends. Before removing the citizen from his role as a possible governing agent and committing him to one of referee we should review the changes in our country that have led Lippmann and others to reject a democracy of participation. In considering these trends we would like both to test their force as antidemocratic influences and examine the counteractive tendencies that exist, or are available. Many of the changes that have taken place — in transportation, communication, technology, finance — have altered the conditions of decision-making. But is it true, as Lippmann claims, that "the problems that vex democracy seem to be unmanageable by democratic methods"?

Emergency Decisions

One of the developments of recent years that strikes directly at the foundation of democratic processes is the trend toward increased dependence on what can be called emergency decisions. The slower methods of discussion are unsuited to solving crisis situations. When social problems are undetected until the last moment, when there is not sufficient time to investigate, when relevant data cannot be gathered, or when environmental pressures prevent the careful study of alternative courses of action, not only

[3] Walter Lippmann, *The Public Philosophy* (Mentor, 1955), p. 19.

democracy, *but rationality itself*, becomes impossible. Yet there is no escaping the fact that we live in a push-button world. A riot in South Africa, a shift in world markets, a political realignment in the Middle East, the launching of an ICBM — these can change the course of world affairs overnight. "Brinkmanship," the art of crisis diplomacy, rules out cooperative deliberation.

The growing reliance on emergency decisions is not limited to world politics. Our personal lives have also been affected. Families are peremptorily transferred from one part of the country to another to carry out corporate plans. In the course of a few days dozens of family decisions must be made concerning living quarters, schools, furniture, personal commitments. In industry, a manufacturer changes his product slightly or reduces his cost by introducing a technological change and his competitors must retool or redesign their product within weeks. In a matter of months quiet farmland is converted into a new and busy community and suddenly schools, fire departments, and police protection are needed. Each of these emergencies creates a demand for action, immediate action. People insist, when threatened by catastrophic change, that "somebody ought to do something about this." That "something" does not often carry a democratic connotation; it is usually a request for the police, the National Guard, the expert, or anyone to "step in and take over." A temporary hiatus in democratic procedures is rationalized on the grounds of a "clear and present danger." Talk is decried, action sanctified.

At first glance these crises, and the climate they create, seem to constitute a force that would inevitably and inexorably undermine democratic institutions. But there are counteractive forces and there are alternatives.

The number and intensity of crises in this modern age is directly traceable to the increased interdependence and crowding together of people brought about through improvements in our methods of transportation and communication. But these improvements also increase our incentive and facilities for cooperative decision-making. We can get together more quickly and more easily to consult with one another. Face-to-face meetings can be called in the space of a few hours anywhere in the country; telephone conferences can be arranged in a few minutes. Information reaches us in greater quantity and with greater speed. The instruments that bind us together more closely, that create emergencies, can also be used to dispel them.

Many of the crises that frighten us are also of our own making. They are only "problems" on which we have defaulted. Recognition of this fact is greatly retarded, even among the leaders of democratic nations.

> As Mr. Eisenhower sees it, you do not decide until "the event reaches you," and then you act — you send the paratroopers to Little Rock, you send the Marines to Lebanon, you send the Seventh Fleet to Quemoy.[4]

The idea of waiting for events to overwhelm you before preparing to meet them is a questionable stance for any democratic leader to assume. Today there are new problems on the horizon — the population explosion, the depletion of natural resources, the control of land and air traffic, increasing racial tensions, rising nationalism — all of which are incipient emergencies. The Council on Foreign Relations, a private, nonpartisan organization in New York City made up of many leading figures in our country, has as its aim, for example, "to study the problems before they become issues." Too often it is our own inertia and lack of foresight, not the crisis, that forces a short-circuiting of democratic methods.

Emergencies often play into the hands of those who want to get their own way. The naked use of power is generally frowned upon in our society, but this moral stricture is removed when action is desperately called for. So a political figure, a company president, or a parent may find it serves his purpose to let events get out of hand so he can justify arbitrary decisions about them at a later date. Sometimes, of course, leaders are not really aware of doing this. They are simply uninformed about the conditions required for democratic decision-making. They will be counteracted only when citizens, children, students, workers, realize that one of the costs of self-government is to take an interest in problems and demand discussion of them long before they have become too critical to talk about.

Secrecy and Censorship

It is often assumed that security — for an individual or a nation — is best guaranteed by withholding from others critical facts concerning present actions or future plans. Those who are informed

[4] Walter Lippmann, "Mystification as a Tactic for Dealing with Emergencies," *The Seattle Times* (September 2, 1958), p. 12.

about any matter have a natural advantage in making decisions over those who must act in ignorance of the facts. This is most obvious in the case of military decisions. A nation hopes to protect itself from attack by keeping the enemy in the dark regarding its current military strength, the development of new weapons, or the present deployment of its forces. A successful invasion cannot be launched without this information. In foreign affairs it seems equally desirable, on occasion, to cloak diplomatic maneuvers in secrecy. Negotiations about new trade agreements, economic aid, or military alignments, if conducted in the open, might have an upsetting effect upon the world in general and defeat the very purpose behind them.

Groups that are in competition with each other, such as labor and management, also dislike divulging information about their financial positions. Each wants to keep the other in ignorance so that its position will appear the stronger. Companies try to prevent "leaks" concerning new models and new products so they may get a head start on their competitors.

Personal injustice or injury may be cited as justification for secrecy in other instances. A congressional hearing conducted before television cameras may permit citizens to observe the operations of government but the publicity may ruin the reputations of innocent people. The disciplinary committee on a university campus may refuse to announce the names of students who appear before it and the sentences they are given because it will add unfairly to their punishment. Parents may not want to discuss finances in front of Johnny, either because they feel it is not important for him to know or out of fear that he will spread the information indiscriminately around the neighborhood.

Secrecy and censorship when practiced in the interest of security, competition, or privacy, however, if carried to extremes, constitute a threat to democratic processes. Some idea of the current seriousness of this problem on the national level can be gained from facts reported by the freedom of information committee of Sigma Delta Chi, a society of professional journalists.

> In 1953, congressional committees held 1,357 secret meetings from which both press and public were barred and wherein the restraint of public opinion was missing and political privilege ruled supreme. This was 44 pct. of the 3,105 congressional committee meetings held in 1953.
>
> These 1,357 secret congressional meetings dealt with such important

> matters of the American people's business as appropriations, expenditures, taxes, drouth relief, foreign aid, disposal of surplus farm products, financing of the Korean war, investigation of waste in government, tariffs, public housing, immigration, and virtually every matter before congress.[5]

They conclude by saying that if this trend continues there will be "little contrast between the secret Communist government of Soviet Russia and the secret executive government of an American school board, city council, or congressional committee. Each does the people's business behind locked doors without the restraint of public opinion . . . and then each issues a propaganda statement to the people." [6]

The stamping of "secret" on an ever-widening circle of public affairs destroys the means of popular government. As we saw in the opening chapter of this book, the equalization of knowledge through universal education has been one of the major forces that has made democracy and discussion possible. Control of information, in most situations, is tantamount to control itself. The person, group, or agency without critical facts is at the mercy of those who have them. The efficiency expert who refuses to divulge his data is free to manipulate employees as he pleases. The husband who deprives his wife of knowledge of their financial affairs forces her into a subordinate role in family decisions. Government agencies which abuse the citizen's right to know are difficult to criticize, reform, or abolish.

Even more dangerous is the fact, not widely appreciated, that secrecy is self-defeating; it blinds everyone, not just the person from whom the fact was intended to be concealed. What is kept from an enemy or competitor is also kept from one's colleagues and friends. A Herblock cartoon makes this point very cryptically. It pictures two scientists trying to use a microscope in the dark. It is obviously impossible to make any discoveries under these conditions but one says to the other, "If we put in a light bulb, some spy might be able to see what we're doing." Limitations on the ability to communicate freely are nondiscriminatory in nature — they hurt everyone.

During the decade following World War II a series of presiden-

[5] Charles Roos, "Government by Secrecy," *The Denver Post* (August 22, 1954), p. 4.

[6] *Ibid.*

tial envoys was sent to study the situation in China, but each filed a confidential report with the President and their observations and recommendations were not revealed to the public until long after the nationalists had been thoroughly defeated. This sort of censorship, as E. B. White notes, is inimicable to the health of a popular government.

> Even within a political unit such as ours, where a free press is fundamental to our society, the right to know stops abruptly at the threshold of the State Department. We have never, as citizens of a republic, enjoyed the right to know what goes on in that difficult region where national government ends and the international poker game begins.[7]

One wonders if the actions of our government would have been any less effective in coping with the Chinese revolution if Americans had been better informed of conditions there, or if the issues had been debated in public forums.

It has taken a United Nations investigation, according to Norman Cousins, for example, to inform the American public about its own nuclear testing program carried out under the jurisdiction of the Atomic Energy Commission.

> Every bit of vital information concerning the real dangers in testing had to be dredged out of the A.E.C. None was volunteered. The accidents in the Pacific Ocean involving the Marshall Islanders and the Japanese fishermen, both groups of which were far outside the designated danger zone; the release of radioactive Strontium and other elements as a by-product of nuclear explosions; the serious miscalculation with respect to the detection of the Nevada test — all were not disclosed in the first instance by the A.E.C. but from outside the A.E.C.[8]

In Congress, Representative John E. Moss, assailing the hush-hush policies of federal agencies, has called attention to the fact that security measures have prevented scientists in one branch of the government from consulting with those in other branches working on the same problem, and that basic research data, open to discovery by anyone, has not been freely distributed. The urge to withhold information has led to a variety of abuses, from stamping

[7] E. B. White, *The Wild Flag* (Houghton Mifflin, 1946), pp. 56–57.
[8] Norman Cousins, "Beyond the Beginning," *Saturday Review* (September 6, 1958), p. 24.

as "secret" English translations of publicly available Russian reports to refusing to release figures on the cost of congressional junkets abroad. Bureaucratic secrecy, according to Moss, has reached new and dangerous heights.

Government by secrecy is not, and cannot be democratic. But the current trend toward the control of information, however strong it may appear, is reversible. It is true there are areas where secrecy is unquestionably needed. It would be foolhardy to announce the exact placement and strength of our military forces to the world. It is unnecessary to share production techniques for the manufacture of military weapons with potential enemies. There are occasions when secret talks between foreign ministers are justified.

Perhaps the first step that needs to be taken is to define more clearly the areas where information may be legitimately withheld. The question must be asked again and again whether the facts being suppressed will not hurt the censor more than the censored. Critical information, in some cases, would be more valuable in the hands of the citizens of a nation than withheld from an enemy. Failure to publicize a community problem, in the interest of "good public relations," fails to educate citizens for meeting future crises. A campus disciplinary committee that refuses to make its actions public keeps the students in ignorance about the seriousness of rules infractions. As has been pointed out by many before us, history is full of instances where politicians, operating behind closed doors, have not acted wisely or in the public interest. But it is difficult to find a single case where an informed public harmed or destroyed itself.

Other remedies may be needed. An investigation of current censorship practices in the various branches of government by a nonpartisan committee might lead to new regulations for controlling the withholding of information. The present procedures encourage censorship. No one, to our knowledge, has ever been thrown in jail for overclassifying a report or document. So if an official is in doubt he tends to "play it safe." But it would seem as serious a crime to foster ignorance in a free society as it is to reveal secrets to an enemy. Laws are needed that will correct this unbalance in emphasis and give as much attention to ways of distributing vital facts as to ways of suppressing them.

There are signs of corrective action being initiated. Citizens, in some communities, are objecting to city councils and school boards that conduct their business in executive sessions behind closed doors. The press and public seem far more alert to the dangers of censorship than they were a few years ago. Government secrecy is much more widely criticized. A majority of the United States senators who replied to the Sigma Delta Chi report favored more open meetings and less secrecy in the running of government. As more and more people are willing to assert and insist upon their right to know, secrecy as an obstacle to discussion can be greatly minimized.

Centralization of Power

The symbol of democracy has long been the town meeting where banker, clerk, housewife, and bus driver have gathered to talk over such problems as enlarging the school, putting in new curbstones, improving the local water supply, or replacing fire equipment. The town meeting is a lovely symbol, but one, unfortunately, that scarcely corresponds to the kind of democracy most of us know in the twentieth century. Very few of us have ever witnessed — much less participated in — a town meeting.

Our problems today, the really important ones at least, are almost never matters of local concern. The village militia has given way to a national defense effort involving millions of men and billions of dollars. The individual farmer who once decided how he would plant his own acreage now participates in a federal crop control program. Social welfare measures for a large and aging population have become necessary on a national scale. Regional programs for flood control and hydroelectric power have proven essential as private business has become inadequate for carrying out these purposes.

This trend is duplicated in the field of commerce. The old-fashioned grocery shop has been taken over by the chain store or converted into a supermarket that is part of a national retail organization. And these units not only sell groceries, as did their predecessors, but they produce goods, distribute them, and fix their prices.

In education, the country school and small community college are being squeezed out of their share in the educational program of the nation by consolidated schools and large state universities.

Fewer and fewer of our problems in this day and age lend themselves to solution within the framework of the town meeting. As Woodrow Wilson was aware:

> Yesterday and ever since history began, men were related to one another as individuals. . . . To-day the everyday relationships of men are largely with great impersonal concerns, with organizations, not with individuals. Now this is nothing short of a new social age, a new age of human relationships, a new stage-setting for the drama of life.[9]

Do these changes in industry, education, and government, therefore, spell the end of participation in decision-making by the private citizen? At first glance it would seem so. How else can our defenses be mobilized, commerce regulated, crops controlled, or foreign aid administered, except by taking authority away from the individual and placing it in the hands of national and international governing bodies?

But what has actually happened? To begin with, the increase in the size of organizations has not always or inevitably reduced the scope of authority of the individual in them. As Harlan Cleveland points out:

> The result of bigness is actually a diffusion of the decision-making and decision-influencing process far beyond the wildest dreams of those worshippers at the shrine of Louis Brandeis, who wanted to keep power diffused by keeping the units of society small.[10]

As we grow to rely on one another more heavily there is, in many large-scale organizations, more dependence upon techniques that permit reciprocal influence — more, not less, conferring through discussion.

The individual has also counteracted the trend toward centralization by joining with others in groups designed to increase his control over social problems. He joins a labor union, a cooperative, a fraternal organization, or a farmer's alliance. Meanwhile others are taking part in manufacturer's associations, joining political parties, or participating in professional organizations of one sort or another. These interest groups, in attempting to secure mass support, use

[9] Woodrow Wilson, "The New Freedom," as quoted in John Dewey, *The Public and Its Problems* (Gateway Books, 1946), p. 96.

[10] Harlan Cleveland, "Dinosaurs and Personal Freedom," *Saturday Review* (February 28, 1959), p. 13.

their resources to advertise their arguments, educate the citizenry, and inform public officials. Although it has been necessary to enact laws to prevent abuse of their power they have, in large part, acted in responsible ways.

This change in the channels of influence in democracy has brought with it a number of advantages. In the group to which he belongs the ordinary citizen has not only gained back some of the power he formerly exercised over his own affairs but, in addition, has enlarged his influence over the affairs of persons far removed from his own doorstep. A professor may once have been able to speak directly to his colleagues and change their vote on academic matters on his local campus but now, through the American Association of University Professors, he can not only look over the shoulder of his own administration but is able to defend academic freedom or advance college standards throughout the nation. The average labor union member would hardly consider returning to the "good old days" when he could talk personally to his boss but when his influence over company policy was practically nil. Today, by uniting with his fellow workers, he has profoundly improved his own standard of living, protected himself against all sorts of abuses and injustices, and affected national economic policies as well. What farmer would exchange the protection against flood, drought, and glutted markets which his modern status has brought him, for the privilege of being his own boss with all the natural and economic hazards of fifty years ago? Minority groups in America made very little progress toward economic or political equality until they were able to organize into groups such as the National Association for the Advancement of Colored People, The Anti-Defamation League, and so on. Few students would trade the weight of their voice in university policies of today for the close personal contact, but microscopic influence, they had over campus life a generation ago. Over-all, it would seem that the individual has gained, not lost, in the battle for control of his own destiny.

To be sure, the growth of powerful self-interest groups is not without its dangers. Attempts to influence government policy and public opinion by organizations such as the American Legion, the American Bar Association, the Chamber of Commerce, the American Medical Association, and various unions and professional groups, are desirable only if their stands have been reached democratically with full opportunity for all members to have a voice in policy-making. Some of the interest groups that have arisen have been notorious for the way in which they are controlled by a powerful inner circle. Some unions allow the rank and file to vote, but carefully selected professionals choose what shall be voted upon. The table of organization of some professional groups is such that it guarantees that authority will rest in a close-knit clique of officials with power to act as they choose.

A slender book bearing the intriguing title, *A Little Democracy Is a Dangerous Thing,* appeared shortly after World War II.[11] Its author argued that much remains to be done to insure that democracy does not remain a parochial concept which applies only to the conduct of our political life, but that it extend to all our social relations. The challenge of the modern "organization age" to which Woodrow Wilson alluded is to apply democratic methods to an ever-widening circle of "nonpolitical" activities.

In the last decade something has been done, particularly in industry, to implement this goal. Douglas MacGregor, for example, spells out four ways in which management is revising its concepts of administration to bring about greater democracy in industry: decentralization, job enlargement (increasing job significance), worker participation in management, and self-evaluation.[12] The first of these, decentralization, has already been put into practice by such large corporations as Sears and Roebuck and Standard Oil of New Jersey. Companies like General Mills, Ansul Chemical, and General Electric have experimented with giving workers greater responsibility for planning, making decisions, and evaluating their own performance.

This does not mean that control of industry should be turned over entirely to the workers, homes run by the children, or schools by the students.

> As a matter of fact this is not democracy, because democracy means the participation of all who are involved in a situation, each in proportion to his ability. A democracy will never be achieved until parents and children learn how to live and work together. Student government will never be effective until it is a government of students

[11] Charles W. Ferguson, *A Little Democracy Is a Dangerous Thing* (Association Press, 1948).

[12] Douglas MacGregor, "Adventure in Thought and Action," *Proceedings of the Fiftieth Anniversary Convocation of the School of Industrial Management,* (Massachusetts Institute of Technology, April 9, 1957).

> and teachers working cooperatively. Industrial democracy will never achieve its real possibilities until capital and labor are working together to make of industry a real enterprise. Democracy will never reach its goal in municipal, state, and national life until some method is developed by which the people may really share with the representatives they have chosen in the working out of problems of government. Group thinking, a technique for democratic participation, involves the sharing of all, each according to his ability.[13]

For the individual this means having a voice in determining those matters which affect him intimately and on which he is informed. For the group it means capitalizing on the total potential of its members in the interest of successful performance and survival.

Mass Communication

The development of mass media of communication during the past four decades would seem to be an important contribution to democratic processes. Information can now be transmitted from one part of the globe to another in a matter of seconds, enabling the remotest citizen to keep abreast of current events. Television, with its ability to bring us face-to-face with events taking place in Warsaw and Washington, should make us less dependent upon the word of self-appointed authorities. The mass media constitute a powerful and unparalleled educational agency for overcoming the illiteracy, ignorance, superstition, and prejudice which hobble democratic processes. The multiplication of channels of communication should expose citizens to wider and more diverse points of view thus encouraging people to think for themselves. But any citizen of today knows that his television screen, newspaper, and radio have not fulfilled this promise.

The last ten years have been disappointing ones as far as the mass media are concerned. Television, with its great potential for educational and cultural improvement, has become almost solely an agency for entertainment. Even this has usually been at the lowest possible level. While it is true that the Federal Communications Commission has provided some two hundred and fifty channels for educational uses, only thirty-five have actually been used. The obligation to stockholders and advertisers has apparently driven the television industry out of the business of informing and educating

[13] Elliott, *op. cit.*, pp. 15–16.

the public or of providing a forum for the discussion of social problems.

A free press is usually regarded as the final bulwark of democracy. But this is true only if freedom of the press stimulates the flow of information and encourages the expression of diverse opinion. Only twenty years ago forty-two of our leading metropolitan centers had competing newspapers which represented a variety of editorial viewpoints. This number has since declined to twenty-four and in many two- and three-newspaper cities the difference in the political and economic views of the papers that remain in business is negligible. Our leading news magazines, although each has a wide national circulation, mirror essentially the same moderately conservative values.

Radio and television have done little to offset this trend. The five-minute newscast, which seems to have become a sort of compulsive fixation, really informs no one. This "censorship by time" lets the listener know what is happening without explaining why it is happening, what it means, or how it may affect the course of human events. As the listener or viewer turns from one network to another in the hope of obtaining a variety of reports and interpretations of the news, he gets the impression — and it is an accurate one for the most part — of hearing the same phonograph record played over and over. What passes for news gathering and news editing turns out to consist of tearing the same story in the same words (gathered by United Press, Associated Press, or International News Service) from rented teletype outlets across the nation. The danger should be obvious. When fact and opinion are turned out with the same uniformity as automated engines, democracy will atrophy from lack of nourishment.

Fortunately, there are some signs of change, and some oases of maturity which might be cultivated within the communications industry. The press and public have benefited greatly from the appearance of the newspaper columnist, an authority who is given almost complete freedom to write as he pleases about a wide range of political and economic questions. It would be difficult to name very many newspapers of several decades ago that would open their pages at one time to the freewheeling and conflicting views of a Dorothy Thompson, a Walter Lippmann, and a Marquis Childs.

Television and radio have occasionally realized their promise as an educational influence. Programs such as "Meet the Press" and

"Face the Nation" have done much to stimulate interest in public affairs. The broadcasting and televising of Senate hearings and of United Nations debates have suggested a new role for the mass media. Millions of citizens were able to look over the shoulders of their delegates to the Security Council during debates on the Arab-Israeli conflict, the Suez crisis, and the Hungarian Revolution. Discussion programs such as "The Great Challenge" and "Small World," which have brought together experts from all over the globe, have shown that television can be intellectual without being academic. The present fight to free the networks from purely objective reporting of news, when departures are clearly labeled as editorial comment, is a sign of growing maturity. Nor need we shrink back, in a free society, from establishing a competitive government-owned network, if necessary, to bring about reforms in the present media and to inform and educate in the public interest.

Specialization

A democratic society, based on the idea that men shall rule themselves, is also threatened by the increased specialization of modern life. The issues of a few generations ago were, for the most part, concrete, uncomplicated, and familiar. The average farmer, storekeeper, or artisan was well prepared to dispose of community problems since common sense, supported by a modest amount of information, was sufficient. But each advance in science, education, and technology has resulted, as the saying goes, in our knowing "more and more about less and less." The ideal of the "renaissance man" — the person who was able to master all the arts and sciences — has long since been relegated to the ashcan. Where men were once generalists, now everyone is a specialist. The farmer must rely upon the work of the expert in soils, genetics, chemistry, and conservation. The general practitioner in medicine is being replaced by the internal specialist, surgeon, orthopedist, gynecologist, dermatologist, obstetrician, and so on. Human behavior, which was once the province of the philosopher, is now divided up among psychologists, sociologists, political scientists, and psychiatrists. And each of these, in turn, has given birth to still more specialisms.

Where does all of this leave the ordinary citizen who wishes to inform himself and act with intelligence on public affairs? Will he be able to cope with this complicated and fragmented universe? Consider some of the public issues he faces: Will fall-out lead to genetic changes? Should we prepare for "brush-fire" wars or for an atomic global war? Should the financial system be manipulated to control inflation and, if so, how? What proportion of the federal budget should be assigned to national defense, foreign aid, or welfare measures? Should the government do anything about the expanding population? This has led many critics to wonder if democratic techniques are adequate to meet this challenge.

Part of the answer has already been suggested. Our modern age demands an intensification of efforts to inform and educate the citizen for living in a complicated environment. The man in the street must not only be supplied with more information and better information but he must be taught to sift and evaluate it as well. He must be part generalist as well as part specialist.

Paradoxically, however, it is the very increase in specialization so widely decried as a threat to citizen participation in public affairs that has made cooperative deliberation more inevitable than ever. When each of us knows "more and more about less and less" it is impossible to arrive at any sort of informed decision without collaborating. It would be the height of folly to build an atomic submarine, institute a program of slum clearance, support the economies of undeveloped nations, or manipulate the financial system without relying on the opinions of many persons. A community cannot integrate its schools, change its tax structure, introduce a city manager system, or alter even its traffic regulations without some guidance from specialists. And nearly all of us are specialists in something.

This means there will be more consulting, more conferring, more deliberating together — more democracy — not less. But it also indicates some new directions in training for democratic participation. There is the problem of knowing when authoritative opinion is needed and where to obtain it. Can we revise our own curriculum, or will we benefit from the help of authorities? Do we know enough to decentralize operations in our plant, or should we seek advice? If so, what kind of advice do we need, and from whom? There is the question, too, of weighing the judgments of different sorts of experts. Should the pathologist or surgeon have the most to say about this operation? Should the military expert or economist determine defense plans? And, finally, there is the problem of what to do if the experts within a specialized field disagree with each other. All our physicists do not have the same opinion of the dangers of Strontium 90; all our political scientists do not see eye to eye on proportional representation; all our psychologists do not speak with a single voice on matters of family discipline.

But limiting democracy because of the growth of specialization seems ill-calculated to meet the challenge. The larger and more complicated our problems become, the more they lend themselves to cooperative deliberation. In fact, no other method of making decisions seems so inherently suited to the problems of our day.

Apathy

The last, and most important, threat to democratic institutions comes, not from the existence of hostile foreign states or even from antidemocratic forces latent in our own society, but from the personal attitudes of the private citizen. The danger is not external so much as it is internal.

> A democratic nation faces its greatest danger not when it is up against a frightening concentration of force but when the people of that nation become detached from their government, when they fail to make their will known, when they convince themselves they are helpless to take part in the big decisions that have to be made, when they fail to get the necessary information, when they fail to communicate with one another, when they separate themselves from their ideals.[14]

Democratic privileges seem less in danger of being destroyed through violence than of being surrendered because of boredom and indifference on the part of the average citizen.

As our population multiplies the voter sees himself less and less as an instrument of government, and more and more as a victim of it. "Government," according to Ferguson, "is something that is done to us, not something in which we have a creative part. Citizenship is largely a matter of paying taxes, getting licenses, standing in line, avoiding penalties, filling out forms."[15] Soon the ordinary person, whose share of the collective responsibility is

[14] Norman Cousins, "Reflections on the Brink," *Saturday Review* (September 20, 1958), p. 28.

[15] Ferguson, *op. cit.*, p. 12.

1/250,000 part of his city government or 1/170,000,000 part of his national government, stops regarding public agencies as an extension of himself through which he can create the kind of society he wants, and begins to see them as unfriendly and uncontrollable competitors in his struggle for self-aggrandizement.

The growing indifference toward government is illustrated in its most prosaic form by Richard Rovere. He describes a family traveling along a bumpy suburban road. Suddenly someone asks, "When will they *ever* fix these roads?" Rovere then subjects this question to a lengthy analysis, part of which goes as follows:

> Observe that the stress, a register of exasperation, is on the "ever." It could as well be on "when" or "will" or "fix" or "roads." It is unlikely, in my family or in yours, to be on "they." Yet notice how natural and right, how colloquially authentic, the unaccented "they" sounds.
>
> Everyone knows what is meant by "they" in this context. It means the people who run things, the man in charge, the wheels, the system, the power elite, the powers that be. But we never, in our anger, stress the pronoun, for this would raise awkward questions of identity. If someone said, "When will *they* ever fix these roads?" someone else would say, "Who's *they*?"[16]

It might also prove embarrassing to emphasize "they" for it would remind someone that "we" was a more accurate term, and then "we" might have to do something about it besides complain.

Much of the disinterest in the problems of our day is of our leaders' making. Empty and platitudinous speeches do little to encourage an interest in public affairs. Political debates in which the leading candidates studiously avoid any reference to vital issues are hardly designed to stimulate serious thought. The surrender of our political campaigns to the advertising agencies of Madison Avenue is one of the most serious blows suffered by popular governments in recent years. From the long ballot, containing the names of hundreds of candidates for insignificant public offices (which makes it impossible for the average man to vote intelligently), to the outmoded machinery of the national convention, democracy is needlessly encumbered and prostituted.

The picture, however, is not a hopeless one by any means. The

[16] Richard Rovere, "The Easy Chair," *Harper's Magazine* (September, 1956), p. 11.

conditions that give rise to apathy can, and are, being altered. In part the citizen's sense of impotence is an illusion, and he needs to be made aware of this. While he represents a smaller and smaller fraction of the total population in a mathematical sense, his influence over social problems has, on the whole, increased as we have seen through the numerous and powerful organizations to which he belongs. By participating in religious organizations, school committees, professional groups, community clubs, unions, political action committees, and management associations, to name only a few, he can play a larger role than ever in the determination of social policy.

Fundamental changes which are already occurring in the field of politics illustrate how this potential may be released. No nostalgia for the good old days will obscure the fact that politics in the past was often under the control of ward heelers, precinct captains, political appointees, and party professionals. All sorts of devices from gerrymandering to ballot box stuffing reduced the citizen's control over his own affairs. Often an "invisible government" actually determined public policy. But the extension of the franchise, political redistricting, the use of voting machines, and better supervision of elections have corrected many of the abuses which corrupted democracy in earlier days. None of them is as encouraging, however, as the growth of interest in politics on the part of the ordinary voter.

> Since 1952 each major election campaign has been marked by the appearance of "citizens for . . ." clubs dedicated to some particular candidate. In much of the country the old party professionals, so skilled in translating favors into votes, are being challenged by amateurs who have been forming their own political clubs to agitate "the issues" at a highly literate level.[17]

In some cases these amateurs have wrested control from party hacks while in other cases they have brought about major reforms in the practices of old-line political parties. In either event, they have stimulated wide community interest in public problems and have brought thousands into an active role in the political life of the country.

Also, the degree to which a society is democratic cannot be

[17] Samuel Lubell, "Amateurs Replace Pros at Polls," *Saturday Review* (June 6, 1959), p. 21.

measured solely by the extent to which voters participate in public elections. The total number of opportunities for creative participation in *all* facets of the life of a community is an equally important index. In this sense we are clearly becoming more democratic than before. The business tycoon of a few generations ago would hardly comprehend, much less approve, the degree to which companies have diffused managerial responsibility. Labor unions have given workers, in many instances, more to say about the conditions of their work. Discipline in the home, once the exclusive prerogative of the male, has become less despotic and more widely shared by all members of the family. Community organizations of various sorts, from the Parent-Teacher Association to the Welfare Board, have given citizens a larger voice in local affairs.

Much remains to be done nonetheless. Indifference and cynicism are still widespread. A sense of responsibility, or concern, for public problems will be engendered only by reaching a larger portion of our population and giving them a more important part to play in the management of public affairs. "No government will be successful," according to Follett, "which does not rest on the individual, and no government has yet found the individual."

> We have outgrown our political system. We must face this frankly. We had, first, government by law, second, government by parties and big business, and all the time some sort of fiction of the "consent of the governed" which we said meant democracy. But we have never had government by the people. The third step is to be the development of machinery by which the fundamental ideas of the people can be got at and embodied; further, by which we can grow fundamental ideas; further still, by which we can prepare the soil in which fundamental ideas can grow.[18]

Democracy, as Follett points out, is not a matter of sending men to a ballot box; it rests in giving them a significant and active part in creating common purposes and programs.

Two lines of action for achieving this goal can be tentatively suggested at this point. The first is that democratic control needs to be extended and its appropriateness tested in solving a wider variety of human problems outside as well as within government. Each time we fail to solve a problem through discussion or debate we force reliance upon authoritarian modes of control. Every

[18] Follett, *The New State*, p. 174.

failure reinforces old patterns of dictation and leaves us more dependent, more subject to manipulation, and more apathetic about managing our own affairs. Second, we need to cultivate the talents required for democratic processes. Discussion is often discarded in favor of other ways of reaching decisions not because it is unsuitable but because people do not have the skills necessary to make it work. People follow an ideal only to the extent that they understand and are capable of following it.

> The mere furnishing of sound information or excellent advice does not seem in practice to secure the character results that are desired. If a human being is to be honest or to have good will or to be reliable, he will be so only as he has worked out this way of action in situation after situation until it becomes a habit of life. An ideal can be effective in life as a whole only in proportion to the variety of situations in which it is actually applied.[19]

Skills of cooperative deliberation cannot be acquired automatically or easily. No amount of lecturing or reading about the democratic philosophy or the rights of man can substitute for actual experience in the methods of democratic decision-making. To live democratically with one's fellow man requires a certain attitude toward people and a commitment to certain values. But skill is also indispensable, for democracy is, most of all, a *way* of life. And the discussion group is its laboratory. It is our hope that this book may help to awaken in some a sense of the problems and possibilities of democratic action.

We return now to our initial question: Is our form of government outmoded? Can democracy survive the stresses and strains of this modern age? Should we continue to seek to achieve a "participant-democracy" in which every citizen contributes to the limit of his ability in the management of his own affairs? Or should we, as Lippmann suggests, settle for a "spectator-democracy" in which voters, by means of ballots, referee, but do not engage in, public affairs?

It is our conviction that democracy is not outmoded, that popular rule is still the strongest, most flexible, most resilient — and most satisfying — form of government known to man. It is true that life in this complicated and interdependent era goes on at a faster pace,

[19] Elliott, *op. cit.*, pp. 5–6.

that secrecy will have to prevail in some areas of public affairs, that governments will be asked to do more and more, and that these added functions may lead to continued centralization of authority. But even in some places where centralization has exerted a stronger influence than here — in England, Sweden, and Denmark — it has not led to any loss of personal freedom or stifling of individual initiative. As Robert Hutchins reminds us, it is not the government that governs least, but the government that governs best, that should be our ideal. The problem of secrecy, too, is a difficult one but not an unmanageable one if attacked with an appreciation of all the considerations it involves. Citizens and public officials also may have to become more sensitive to incipient problems and be prepared to assume responsibility for them earlier to avoid their developing into crises which force undemocratic solutions.

But there are many compensating factors. All the social forces which we cited in the opening chapter of this book — the raising of educational standards, the growing respect for the rational-scientific method, the equalization of political and economic power — promote the democratic management of our affairs. The mass media of communication can enable a modern state to collect and diffuse a greater amount of information than was ever possible before. The increased complexity of public problems, instead of limiting democratic participation, has had almost the opposite effect — it has made consultation and wider communication about public questions absolutely essential.

The most serious and unpredictable factor in the balancing of forces that promote or restrict democratic participation is the attitude of the average citizen. If he chooses to reject responsibility for the management of his own affairs when it is proffered him, or fails to develop the intellectual and interpersonal skills that discussion requires, then democratic institutions are doomed. If, on the other hand, he takes advantage of such opportunities to share in decision-making and, as a result, cultivates the talents needed to become self-governing, then democracy can be extended into many new areas of human endeavor.

Ultimately, then, the future of democracy rests on solving the problem of apathy. As we have seen earlier, however, callous and passive people are that way largely because they feel cut off from a vital role in the life of their community, because they feel they have no effective voice in managing their own affairs. The solution, then, is not to reduce still further their role in solving public problems. Instead it is to increase their influence so they will discover some of the rewards and satisfactions that come from democratic participation.

To settle for a "democracy of consent" in place of a "democracy of participation," as Lippmann suggests, is to surrender to an impractical ideal, as well as an unworthy one. The voter is to be relegated to a seat on the sidelines. He is not to govern, or attempt to govern. Periodically he will be asked, through an election, to approve or disapprove of what is happening to him. He can remove those officials who displease him, and allow others to continue to manage his affairs. And just how is he to decide who is to remain in the game, and who is to be replaced? How shall he determine when his representatives are acting in his best interests? Should he vote for a candidate who favors fixed parity prices or flexible ones? for an official who has supported free trade or protective tariffs? for someone who believes in the United Nations or in "going it alone?" Obviously the only rational way to judge the performance of his representatives is to understand the issues. To judge on any other basis is to introduce irrelevant criteria. Imagine turning over the direction of a football team, a symphony orchestra, or a repertory theatre to a group of laymen who periodically and superficially pass judgment on the quality of the end product and whether it pleases them or not without any knowledge of athletics, music, or drama. To act as a referee demands some knowledge of the game. Consent without understanding is nothing but acquiescence. Decisions must be informed ones if any group or society is to survive and the best way to become informed about the seriousness and complexity of problems is to be encouraged to investigate them and to participate in their final disposition.

If we believe in self-determination we should busy ourselves, not with renouncing our rights under a façade of government by consent, but with learning how to master the art of ruling ourselves through the process of discussion. We would say, along with Gerald Johnson:

> Let us make the wager, then, with stout hearts and quiet minds. At least we can console ourselves with the knowledge that it is a

great experiment. If it succeeds, if one nation in this world attains such political maturity that every man will have even a little skill in the use of leadership, and a fair ability to avoid its abuse, the effect will be tremendous beyond comprehension. It may, indeed, confound philosophy by bringing into existence the condition that Plato deemed impossible, the nation where "political greatness and wisdom meet in one," though philosophers had not become kings, nor kings philosophers.[20]

To make the gamble pay off successfully will demand moral courage, intellectual responsibility, infinite patience, and interpersonal skills of a high order. But as one of the earliest of civilization's democratic citizens, Pericles, wrote: "We differ from other states in regarding the man who holds aloof from public office not as 'quiet' but as useless; we decide or debate, carefully and in person, all matters of policy, holding, not that words and deeds go ill together, but that acts are foredoomed to failure when undertaken undiscussed."

[20] Gerald W. Johnson, "The Use and Abuse of Leadership," *Saturday Review* (July 5, 1958), p. 31.

RECOMMENDED READING

Dewey, John. *The Public and Its Problems.* Gateway Books, 1946.

Ferguson, Charles. *A Little Democracy is a Dangerous Thing.* Association Press, 1948.

Lippmann, Walter. *The Public Philosophy.* Mentor Books, 1955.

Russell, Bertrand. *Authority and the Individual.* Simon & Schuster, Inc., 1949.

Smith, T. V., and Lindeman, E. C. *The Democratic Way of Life.* Mentor Books, 1951.

Appendices

LEARNING TO DISCUSS

Appendix A

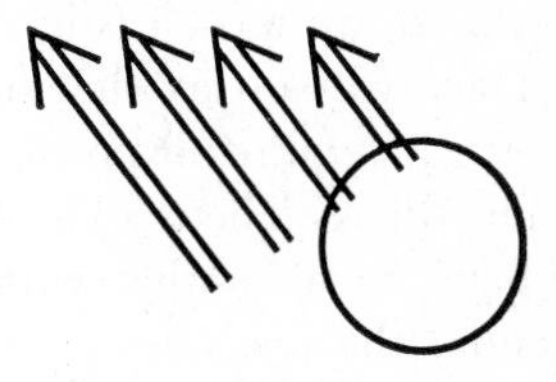

A Philosophy and Method of Change

How does one go about teaching or learning the art of group discussion? Is it enough for a student to read a book such as this one, perhaps pass an examination on it, and then store it on the library shelf? Will this improve his understanding and skills of group participation and group leadership? Or would he be better off forgetting about the books and getting as much practice as he can in actual discussion? To answer questions such as these we must first recognize that there are several possible kinds of learning that an individual can experience, and that the methods for achieving each type are quite different. All learning is essentially change, but one can change in many ways.

Intellectual Learning

The first, and perhaps most commonly accepted interpretation of the word "learning," can be described as *change in the amount of information or knowledge that the learner possesses.* In other words, it is learning *about* things and people in the world around us. This is the kind of change that usually is associated with studying a subject in school, reading books, listening to others talk, and observing our environment. It is a predominantly intellectual process, and that is why formal education is so often thought of as the "cultivation of the mind." Intellectual learning involves, in large measure, the acquisition of a broader vocabulary, since new concepts or ideas are most easily assimilated when we have names for them. Thus we can say that intellectual learning is basically a verbal process; it requires exposure to and acquisition of new terms as well as new ideas. The reader of this book, for instance, may not previously have been familiar with such concepts as group norms, hidden agenda, the leaderless group, and so on. It is difficult to imagine how he could have learned *about* these matters without having names for them.

Skills Learning

A second kind of learning has to do with *change in the learner's skills* — that is, in his ability to perform certain acts, be it bowling, cooking, driving a car, painting a picture, or exerting leadership in a discussion. Learning, in this sense, has to do with the development of the student's motor skills or of his techniques of manipulating tools, words, or even people. The process through which change of this kind is brought about is often called training rather than education (though some people use the words synonymously), since it usually involves considerable practice, and can also be a relatively "blind" sort of learning. That is to say, behavioral skills can be developed without much involvement of one's conscious thought processes, since it is often simply a matter of mastering new habit patterns. Just as dogs are trained to beg or heel, so people can be trained to drive a car, hit a baseball, or knit a sweater.

To be sure, many complex human skills such as operating the controls of an automated factory, analyzing an argument, or summarizing a discussion require more than blind training. Intellectual learning must also take place if the activity is to be carried out successfully. Yet the fact that one can gain proficiency in so many skills without much accompanying mental activity is what has led the proponents of the so-called "liberal arts" in education to scorn the "mere training" offered in vocational, professional, or skills courses, and to suggest that this work is not worthy of academic credit. Too often these critics fail to see the distinction between a course in basket-weaving, typing, penmanship, or voice and diction, on the one hand, and surgery, English composition, teaching, or discussion and debate, on the other. All involve the performance of skills, but only those at the first extreme can be accomplished simply through imitation and practice. At the latter extreme the learner must understand the whys and wherefores behind what he is "trained" to do, or he will develop only stereotyped patterns of behavior which are too inflexible to be adapted to the variety of unique situations which he must be prepared to confront.

Emotional Learning

A third type of learning is that which involves *change in the student's attitudes, feelings, or values.* Some of us like to refer to this inelegantly, but expressively, as "gut learning." Although the general semanticist shies away from making a separation between "mind" and "emotion" and reminds us, quite properly, that there can be no "mental" activity without "emotional" activity, and vice versa, nevertheless one can make a rough distinction between learning which is *predominantly* verbal in nature, and that which affects the entire nervous system. Anyone who has worked with people who have emotional problems knows that it is one thing to help an individual gain intellectual insight to the point where he can talk about himself rather perceptively, and quite another thing to help him *feel* different. Many people have experienced this distinction in the realm of race relations, where they may understand, "intellectually," that prejudice is foolish, and yet they still *feel* prejudiced. In other words, they have learned, at the verbal level, that racial prejudice makes no sense, but they have not learned it in their "bones."

By the same token, it is quite possible for emotional learning to take place with relatively little conscious awareness of what is happening on the part of the learner. Traumatic experiences which are repressed in the unconscious, but which nevertheless profoundly affect a person's attitudes, are one kind of illustration. Courses in which a common student reaction is, "I know I've learned a lot, but I can't tell you what it is" are another. In short, the change which takes place comes about primarily through direct experience, and to the extent that the learning has not been intellectualized, hence verbalized, it is incommunicable. As Louis Armstrong is reported to have said of the appreciation of jazz, "If you have to ask, you'll never find out."

The debate in educational circles over intellectual versus emotional learning is at least as vehement, if not more so, as that between intellectual and skills learning. There are those, for example, who heatedly condemn the extent to which our public schools have "gone soft" by moving in the direction of teaching for "life adjustment" rather than for "discipline of the mind." Likewise, at the level of higher education, there are those who argue that it is not the business of a college or university to change people's values, but only to expose them to information. On the other hand, there are teachers who feel that there is not much point in a course in race relations, political philosophy, economic policy, or group discussion which affects nobody's attitudes. The first school of thought charges the second with indoctrination. The second charges the first with sterility. Both charges are in most cases probably unfounded, since we suspect that it is only poor courses which deserve these labels, and we are confident that a good teacher, regardless of which school of thought he leans toward, is one who will provide some degree of balance for his students.

Learning at All Three Levels

Having explored the various kinds of learning to which a student can be exposed we return again to the question: How should one learn to discuss? And, like typical integrationists, the authors reply, "we like all three ways." We believe that for education in group discussion to be effective the intellect, the feelings, and the actual behavior of the student must become involved in the process. None of the three kinds of learning alone, nor any two of them in combination, are sufficient to produce the results we regard as most ideal.

To emphasize intellectual learning at the expense of the others, we feel, is to run the risk of leaving the student with only a change in his vocabulary, plus perhaps an increased ability to observe discussions analytically. Although we would not want to deprecate the latter achievement, it has obvious limitations. Without any increase in the learner's emotional sensitivity to people or any new behavior patterns to accompany his greater intellectual understanding, he has become neither a better participant nor a more effective leader. Even his analyses may be warped by virtue of his missing some of the subtle interactions which cannot be detected from a position of emotional detachment.

A strong emphasis on skills training, though appropriate for learning to operate a drill press, is grossly inadequate when it comes to the complex interactions of human relationships. There are too many people who think that effective communication with others can be reduced to a set of simple formulae or bag of tricks. We have seen the sad effects of this kind of training in discussion — the participant who launches forth on an eloquent summary when no summary is needed or wanted by the group, or the leader who graciously asks all the members for their opinions when it is painfully obvious that he is not the least bit interested in them or their opinions. True skill in discussion, although it does take practice, can occur only when one has learned to think his way through each new situation in creative and adaptive ways. It requires intellectual understanding and emotional sensitivity as well as verbal skills. It cannot come about through the learning of stereotyped patterns of behavior. That is why the authors, throughout this book, have tried to avoid offering any single answers or pat rules for dealing with the kinds of problems that occur in discussion groups. Rather we have attempted to make the reader aware of the issues, and a variety of possible solutions, so that in each situation which he encounters he will be able to evaluate and choose for himself.

Emotional change, by itself, is also a limited kind of experience. We have already seen that the individual whose learning is too heavily weighted in this direction is unable to communicate his understanding to others, except perhaps by his own example. Operating by hunch, he is also less able than the "intellectual" person to engage in self-analysis and self-correction, because he lacks the mental tools with which to do so. Finally, it is frequently possible for a person to have the "right" attitudes about a situation and still not be able to act effectively due to lack of practice. We conclude, therefore, that the most successful kind of learning for the student of discussion is that which takes place at all three levels of change which we have described. Thus he may attain a higher degree of behavior skill, based upon emotional responsiveness and guided by an informed intelligence.

The next question is how to achieve such a combination. It cannot come simply from reading about discussion or listening to lectures on the subject, for these are primarily, though not exclusively, intellectual experiences. Nor can it result from practicing the skills of discussion in exercises which are arranged, guided, and evaluated solely by an instructor, for this makes insufficient allowance for the development of the student's own creative standards. It comes too close to "mere training." On the other hand, participation alone, even if it be in a multitude of discussion groups and even though it provide a wealth of satisfying emotional experiences, does not constitute the most effective kind of learning *unless* some provision is made for the analysis of those experiences. A combination of the three levels *can* be achieved in a learning situation wherein teacher and student, working together, create opportunities for the practice of discussion skills, and where these experiences are collaboratively analyzed and evaluated, using whatever useful concepts have been derived from readings or other authoritative presentations. In our chapter on the uses and abuses of discussion we found that knowledge is most effectively internalized when discussion and group decision-making are employed. This principle is valid for learning about discussion as well as any other subject. It is for this reason that we urge both teachers and students to join together in directing the learning process. It is for the same reason that we have included a section on "Learning to Discuss" in this textbook, accessible to both student and teacher, rather than publishing it separately as an instructor's manual.

Methods for Learning to Discuss

Having outlined in broad terms the philosophy we feel should underlie any process of learning to discuss, we now turn to some of the specific methods by which these goals may be achieved. We shall cite four possible patterns which are representative of some of the best current practices, and which may be employed separately or in various combinations. There may be other worthy alternatives now in use or yet to be developed, but these four are ones which our own experience recommends.

Lecture-discussion method

This pattern for teaching and learning discussion is the one most widely employed in college and university courses. The instructor presents occasional lectures on topics such as those which have been dealt with in the various chapters of this book. The remainder of class time is devoted to practice discussions among the students on subjects of current political, economic, or social affairs, followed by critical analysis and evaluation utilizing some of the tools for that purpose which are described in Appendix B. In the lecture-discussion method, the teacher plays essentially two roles. As occasional lecturer he provides the students with theoretical (or verbal) tools which may be used to analyze and better understand group interaction. As an observer of the practice sessions he provides group members with feedback which they can use in evaluating their discussions. He also helps to stimulate analysis with leading questions. Sometimes the instructor participates in discussions, and frequently students take over the responsibilities of observing and of instigating evaluation.

The subject matter for discussion is usually selected by the participants, with or without guidance from the teacher. Topics are such that they make some intellectual demands upon the student in the way of preparatory research. (See Appendix C for some of the forms this preparation may take.) Ideally the topics should also be such that the learner can become emotionally involved in them. It may be that both of these objectives cannot be obtained with one topic — in which case a variety of subjects, some doing the first job and others the second, is advisable. A sequence of subjects such as, "What should be our foreign policy with regard to Communist China?" "Should we discourage interracial dating?" and "What can be done to improve student government on our campus?" would provide such a balance. It will be noted that the topics for these discussions are stated as general questions, in contrast to the case approach which will be discussed shortly.

Role-playing

Although the use of role-playing is becoming increasingly popular in the formal classroom, it has had its greatest application in various kinds of short courses for adults. Under this method of learning, students participate in spontaneous, simulated discussions in which each member acts out the role of some individual whom he has chosen or been assigned to represent. The group may pretend that it is the local Board of Education, the executive committee of a civic organization, or the staff of a business concern. Individual participants may attempt to portray the behavior of apathetic or overaggressive people; they may enact the role of mediators; or they may create and try to deal with hidden agenda, autocratic leadership, highly emotional conflict, or decision-making under deadline conditions.

Role-playing may be employed for two somewhat different purposes. First, as a demonstration, the instructor may set up a scene by briefing each of the members in such a way that some procedural or interpersonal problem is illustrated which is common to discussion groups. This is a vivid and emotionally involving way of calling the attention of students to an important issue, such as group disorganization; having them experience it, at least vicariously; and providing a concrete episode which all have observed and can analyze together. Here, the evaluative discussion which follows the demonstration is more important than the role-playing itself, which can be done rather ineptly and still provide a useful springboard for analysis.

The other use of role-playing is for the purpose of providing the learner with an opportunity to practice certain discussion skills. For instance, if it is desired to develop ability to resolve differences, an imaginary conflict situation can be set up, and the student asked to do his best to help the parties to the dispute to find an agreement. Or, if initiating discussion and stimulating thinking are the skills in need of practice, an apathetic group setting can be enacted in which the student attempts to arouse interest. As in the case of role-playing for demonstration purposes, this kind of scene is also analyzed and evaluated. But, in contrast to demonstrations, the hope here is that learning will come about not only from the post-role-playing discussion, but that also the scene itself will be enacted realistically enough that effective skills practice can be achieved.

It is at this point that some of the critics of role-playing raise objections. They feel it is impossible to derive useful practice from mock sessions which, no matter how well acted, are bound to be somewhat artificial. Although it is often true that role-playing exercises do fail for this reason (and the teacher cannot always predict or control this), we have also found them to be exceedingly helpful. In the first place, the same kind of objection that is raised against role-playing can also be leveled against any educational program, because no two situations are ever exactly alike and there is always the problem of transfer of learning from one setting to another. If students are made aware of this, and seek to discover basic principles of operation rather than specific patterns of behavior which they can literally transfer *in toto,* then the artificiality of role-playing is no more of a handicap than any other off-the-job educational program. Also, the student must be sufficiently flexible and imaginative to overlook minor flaws of amateur acting and focus his attention on the elements of reality that are present. These there will always be, inasmuch as the participants in role-playing are never able completely to divorce themselves from the parts they are playing. They become somewhat identified with their roles and, as a result, bits of real human interaction emerge out of the scene.

A number of role-playing exercises which are helpful in developing discussion skills are presented in Appendix C.

Case method

The case method is often used in conjunction with the lecture-discussion approach, and actually adds only one new element. The practice discussions in which students participate center around a concrete case rather than a generally phrased topical question. Instead of discussing "What should be done about juvenile delinquency in our community?" the group might discuss (after having been given the facts in a case) "What should Joe do about his delinquent son?" In either event the discussion is followed by analysis and evaluation.

Cases may be prepared in advance by the instructor or written and submitted by the students out of their own personal experiences. They may have to do with an incident or problem in such fields as politics, business, civil liberties, and psychology, or they may be examples of breakdowns in group or interpersonal communication. Usually the participants do no research other than to read and think about the facts in the case.

The advantage of the case method over the use of general topics is that there seems to be less difficulty in developing involvement in the subject among the participants — a problem that is always troublesome in any educational endeavor. The concreteness of a specific human situation is more easily gotten ahold of by a group, and besides, say the advocates of the case method, this is the way discussion topics arise in real life. There are, however, good counterarguments. First, it is not true that groups in real life always start their work with a case. As we saw in Chapter 4, often discussion will not take place until a number of events have occurred which finally become generalized into a major problem. Furthermore, while it is true that broad topics sometimes permit participants to escape into vague generalities, case discussions tend to suffer from the complaint that "we don't have enough facts." And no matter how many more facts are included in the original story, there are always those who insist that the problem cannot be solved "until we know more." It is our feeling that both the case method and the general topic approach each have their values and limitations, and that a rounded program might well consist of both techniques. We have included some sample cases for discussion in Appendix C.

Laboratory method

The basic idea of the laboratory method of training in group processes was first developed, so far as we are aware, at the National Training Laboratories summer sessions in Bethel, Maine. In this approach, the students come together in a small group (ideally about fifteen) with an instructor (or trainer, as he is called at Bethel — unfortunately, perhaps) who proceeds to play a highly nondirective leadership role. He may outline, in general terms, the purpose of the course and of his intended role in it, and then ask the group to take over the responsibility of planning its own procedures. The instructor also acts as an observer who stimulates the group to analyze its own processes as it struggles to organize itself and carry on whatever discussion it has chosen to undertake. So far as the teacher is concerned it is of secondary importance whether the group engages in substantive discussion (i.e., politics, religion, etc.) or spends all its time on procedural matters. The reason for this attitude is that, after all, procedure (broadly defined) is the substance of an educational program in discussion. Furthermore, regardless of what the members of the group talk about, interaction takes place, some kind of atmosphere and structure develop, and these matters can then be subjected to further analysis and evaluation. The advocates of the laboratory approach maintain that this is group behavior "in the raw" and that the way for a student to *feel* as well as *understand* group processes is to participate in the birth and early growing pains of a new group which has no superstructure imposed upon it from without.

Ordinarily, the discussion meetings are supplemented by occasional "theory sessions" (in the form of lectures, films, demonstrations, etc.) in which instructors provide the students with concepts which may help them to understand what is happening in their laboratory groups. This experience may be further supplemented with suggested reading materials about group behavior.

Part of the argument which has raged among the experts over the merit of the laboratory method is, we feel, based upon a misunderstanding. A number of its critics, perhaps with some justification based upon their personal experiences, feel that the nondirective guidance which is provided by the instructor is intended as a model for leadership in all situations — either in real life decision-making groups or in learning groups where the content is something other than discussion. It is true that many of the people who teach with the laboratory method do believe that the leadership commonly provided in most learning and decision-making groups could be considerably more nondirective than it now is. It does not necessarily follow, however, that the instructor intends the very specialized kind of behavior he exercises in the laboratory setting to serve as an example for other situations. On the contrary, it seems to us that a knowledgeable teacher who uses the laboratory method would be well aware that the kind of floundering for leadership and intense self-consciousness that characterize laboratory sessions would be quite inappropriate in a group whose goals were something other than learning about small group behavior.

We would repeat once again that the four educational methods described here are not mutually exclusive. One can employ them in various combinations and to various degrees. So far as we are concerned, the matter of most importance is that an educational program in discussion somehow contain these elements:

1. An opportunity for the learner to participate in group discussions.

2. An opportunity for the learner to analyze and evaluate the group behavior in which he has participated.

3. An opportunity for the learner to become acquainted with

ideas for conceptualizing and verbalizing what takes place in a discussion.

4. An opportunity for the learner to become emotionally involved in the learning process and to help control its direction.

RECOMMENDED READINGS

"Can Leadership Training be Liberal Education?" *Adult Leadership* (June, 1953).

Cantor, Nathaniel. *The Dynamics of Learning.* Foster and Stewart, 1946.

Lippitt, Ronald, Jeanne Watson, and Bruce Westley. *The Dynamics of Planned Change.* Harcourt, Brace and Company, 1958.

Appendix B

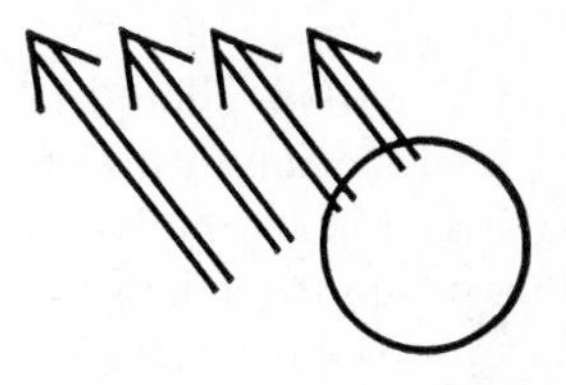

Evaluating Discussion

"EXPERIENCING" AND "LEARNING" can be differentiated on the grounds that the latter always involves some sort of evaluation. Things happen to us every moment of our lives. Sometimes we learn from these experiences, particularly if they are shocking enough to jar our complacency or if we become curious about them for one reason or another. Generally, however, we associate learning with some sort of planned experience in which there is a conscious effort to dissect what has happened, why it has happened in a particular way, and what can be done to prevent or encourage certain features of it from occurring again.

One may go to the golf links with some regularity, but hitting a golf ball over and over again does not automatically improve one's stroke. Nor does writing one essay after another, practicing at the piano, investing repeatedly in the stock market, or chairing a number of committees guarantee that one will cultivate writing talent or musical ability, accumulate a fortune, or develop skills of leadership. As many have pointed out, the old axiom that "practice makes perfect" needs to be revised to read "practice makes permanent." Repeating the same mistakes over and over only makes our errors habitual.

Learning, therefore, requires assessing our experiences. So far in this book we have described a number of problems that any group is likely to encounter in the course of working together. Most of these — organizing a meeting, handling information, resolving conflicts, or dealing with problem members — can be handled in a variety of ways. In one way or another the group must finally check on the suitability of the measures it adopted in dealing with task and interpersonal problems so that it may determine which methods should be continued and which dropped in the future. This means utilizing some sort of feedback. Used in this context, feedback simply refers to reviewing the past actions of the group to find out how they advanced or retarded progress toward the group's goals. Through the intelligent use of feedback a group can reinforce patterns of interaction that increase its effectiveness or modify norms that interfere with its operation.[1]

Unstructured Evaluation

Often busy executives, harassed government officials, department chairmen, and lay leaders of community organizations ask what can be done to improve the functioning of committees under their direction when there are no training facilities available, when a lengthy educational program is impossible, or when elaborate techniques are out of the question. There are many committee chairmen who will admit their meetings could be improved but who cannot afford to hire a special consultant in human relations. To them we would say that one of the easiest ways for people to learn how to work together more effectively is for a group periodically to take "time out" to study its own operations. An objective analysis, even without an expert, can heighten people's sensitivity to unnoticed aspects of group process and stimulate the development of interpersonal skills. It is quite possible for a group literally to "pull itself up by its own bootstraps." This technique — of unstructured evaluation or free feedback — is not, however,

[1] In this appendix we shall concentrate on methods of "selective feedback" in which only details that seem significant are discussed, in contrast to "complete feedback" in which an unedited record is made of the entire meeting. In the latter instance a transcript is prepared from shorthand notes, or a tape recording is played back, and the group reviews its entire interaction. This record will probably contain a number of episodes which can then be diagnosed and evaluated. While this method has some advantages in the classroom it is so time-consuming as to be impractical in most group situations.

limited to unsophisticated groups which cannot afford the time or do not have the skill required by more elaborate methods. Any group, even the most mature, will profit by studying its own past actions in this manner.

Timing

When should a group discuss its own processes? Is it best to set aside a definite period of time, say at the beginning or end of its meetings, or should a group discuss its actions whenever something goes sour that deserves attention? Should evaluation become a formal part of the group's agenda, or should it occur spontaneously?

One of the arguments in favor of setting aside a regular period for group self-analysis is that it insures that some evaluation will be made. When analysis is left to chance it is easy to gloss over, rationalize away, or suppress evidence of malfunctioning. Some people feel awkward about bringing incipient problems to the attention of their colleagues for fear they will appear hypercritical of others. When one becomes aware of an instance of social pressure, of failure to communicate effectively, of exclusion, or of disorganization, it is tempting to believe that it was just a temporary matter and will not occur again, or that the trouble will disappear without calling attention to it. Regular periods of assessment have been built into business procedures for precisely this reason. Leaving evaluation to chance often means that an employee never learns what his assets are, or in what he is deficient, until too late. If we are to learn from experience it might be wise to provide for regular inspection of all human relationships in the home, classroom, office, and conference room.

Another argument in favor of a systematic review of past performance is that it is likely to be more objective. In the heat of an emotional crisis or at a moment of intense conflict a group will have considerable difficulty trying to look dispassionately at its own internal processes. One of the reasons why discipline so often fails is that it is attempted when parent and child, student and teacher, or supervisor and worker are so emotionally upset that reason cannot possibly prevail. Anxiety and stress tend to make people defensive. We hang on to old ways of evaluating ourselves to maintain our self-respect. If a group analyzes itself after the regular business has been disposed of, however, the members should be able to look at themselves more calmly and be less defensive about changing their habitual behavior patterns.

Setting aside a regular period for evaluation, however, has its limitations. Like any prescribed routine it can easily deteriorate into an empty ritual. To delay analysis also makes it more difficult to talk accurately about events in the life of the group. Committee members may find that postponing evaluation to a prearranged time turns the analysis into an argument over what actually happened earlier, what people meant by what they said or did, and how it affected subsequent relationships. Like the mental patient, a group may have trouble dredging up experiences in the past and members may become discouraged in laboriously retracing their steps to misunderstandings that have long since been forgotten.

Another reason for discussing problems as they arise during meetings is that they can become more serious if not dealt with immediately. A doctor does not wait to cure a patient until he is critically ill; he begins treatment as soon as the first symptoms are noticed. Similarly it is held that a group suffering from an unrealistic agenda, interpersonal friction, or from problems in communication should not wait until these produce a complete breakdown before they are corrected. The longer they fester, the more serious they become, and the more difficult to eradicate. A group, like a husband or wife who believe in clearing up misunderstandings before retiring for the night, may prevent its differences from becoming so complicated that they can never be discussed quietly and reasonably. Also, the members of a committee will be more highly motivated to analyze their own interactions just after something has gone wrong. Participants will be more interested in talking about communications after a misunderstanding has occurred, and will be more concerned with methods of handling conflict after they have had trouble settling a dispute. Later on the investigation of these crises may seem like an academic exercise.

So far we may have given the impression that the group should analyze only its mistakes. While we are often more interested in these because they are so irritating to us personally, it is important that desirable attitudes and actions also be recognized. Successful actions — an effective job of planning an agenda, the improving of the psychological climate in the group, the extension of participation to more members, the successful resolution of a conflict, increasing objectivity toward the problem, greater frankness in communication — all need to be reviewed. To discuss the successful solving of some problem in group relations may be even more instructive than a diagnosis of errors, and may contribute as well to the general morale of the group. Reinforcing constructive acts is as important as criticizing unconstructive behavior.

Both spontaneous and routine evaluation have been used widely and with considerable success. Each will have to be judged in terms of the social context in which it is to be employed. Perhaps this suggests that the evaluation procedures themselves should be subjected to scrutiny through feedback!

Content

A period of self-analysis, whether occurring spontaneously or provided for at the beginning or end of a meeting, is relatively simple to conduct. Anyone in the group can initiate a "discussion of the discussion" by referring to some past action which seemed significantly related to the performance of the group. A person who feels the meeting was poorly organized may question whether or not the agenda was clear and logical. Someone else may comment on the extent of apathy in the group and probe its causes. A minor detail, such as the arrangement of the chairs or the accessibility of the meeting place, may be brought up. Some of the participants may be interested in talking about the locus and character of the leadership. Others may want to delve into the norms of the group and their possible negative effect upon the attitudes members have toward each other. Participants may want to discuss how well or how poorly informed they are and what, if anything, should be done about it. During this conversation the group may skip from the most mundane mechanical detail, such as the possible advantage of using a blackboard to record their progress, to the most intimate personal reaction. Any of the topics touched upon throughout this book might come up during a period of unstructured evaluation.

It is important that this period of analysis be handled as objectively as possible, and that people talk as frankly as they can about their impulses and reactions. This is an opportunity for people to let their hair down and share their doubts, fears, and expectations for the group. It is perfectly apparent that all of us do think and talk about the groups to which we belong. Why not, instead of having this come out in surreptitious conversations on the way home or in private telephone conversations, provide for a frank exchange of these reactions as a part of the discussion itself? There will be less chance for distortion because faulty or biased private interpretations can be corrected on the spot. Also, the group as a whole will profit from the sharing of evaluations. As people talk about their own impulses and reactions they are likely to become more critical of themselves and more highly motivated to improve their behavior. A few minutes of evaluation can clear channels of communication, dissipate antagonisms, correct inappropriate procedures, and increase motivation for working more effectively in the future.

Structured Evaluation

In some settings it is preferable not to leave the group self-analysis to the whims and curiosities of the participants, for they may fail to talk about the truly critical incidents in their discussion. Instead the evaluation period is structured by gathering certain kinds of data about the group and using these facts as a guide in the "discussion of the discussion." There are a number of ways of doing this.

Post-Meeting Reaction Sheets

Many situations are far too threatening to expect people to speak with frankness and objectivity about their reaction to the procedures that have been followed in a meeting. Groups in which autocratic figures dominate, in which great personal competition exists, in which there are wide status differences, or where ulterior motives are operating, are not healthy settings in which to analyze the behavior of individual members. Groups of relative strangers, or people who are working together for the first time, may feel justifiably embarrassed at revealing their personal feelings toward each other. The members of a faculty or the supervisors in a plant who have seldom been consulted before will be somewhat timid about engaging in a free-for-all discussion of the strong and weak points of the first committee on which they have ever served. Yet it is groups like these that are often most seriously in need of looking critically at their own relationships.

One of the least offensive and most helpful devices for bringing out member reactions to a discussion is the Post-Meeting Reaction Sheet. It consists simply of a written questionnaire designed to elicit comments from the members of a committee on critical aspects of their relationships. Sometimes the PMR focuses on substantive issues — the planning of the agenda, the quality of ideas, the extent of information, the handling of conflict, or the practicality of decisions. Or it may concentrate on interpersonal matters — the climate of the group, the leadership, the manipulation of social pressures, or problems of participation. Normally it includes items evaluating both the task and emotional areas. The questionnaire is filled out anonymously by each individual at the conclusion of a meeting or series of meetings. Its anonymity protects people who may have strong feelings about the conduct of the group but who are afraid to express themselves publicly because of possible repercussions outside the meeting. The results obtained from administering the questionnaire are reported to the group (perhaps on a dittoed sheet, or posted on a blackboard) and serve as a guide for reviewing and evaluating current practices. The objective and anonymous nature of the data makes the diagnosis far less personal but still provides members with vital information about their own performance. An illustrative Post-Meeting Reaction Sheet is provided below.

REACTION SHEET

Instructions: Simply check the point on each of these scales that represents your honest opinion. Do not sign your name.

1. How satisfied are you with the conclusions or decisions reached?

Very Satisfied	Moderately Satisfied	Very Dissatisfied

2. How productive was this discussion in terms of new ideas?

Very Valuable	Moderately Valuable	Waste of Time

3. How orderly and systematic was the group in its overall approach?

Too Regulated	Just Right	Too Chaotic

4. Was the atmosphere of the group conducive to effective communication?

Too Cooperative	Just Right	Too Competitive

5. Is the responsibility for leadership properly distributed?

Too Concentrated	Just Right	Too Diffused

6. How do you feel about the character of our leadership?

Too Autocratic	Just Right	Too Laissez-faire

There is nothing sacred about the particular items that appear on a Post-Meeting Reaction Sheet. Any question can be included that will provide insight into the attitudes of individuals in the group. It is, in short, one of the simplest, most flexible, and least threatening instruments for ascertaining the degree to which a group is living up to the expectations and needs of its members. The data obtained from it can provide a firm foundation of fact on which to base any changes in procedure.

The use of group observers

Another way of obtaining information about significant episodes in the group meeting and structuring the evaluation is to appoint observers. These people, who usually sit outside the circle of actual participants, do not take any part in the discussion itself but record, as carefully as possible, any interactions that seem to influence the effectiveness of the group. The main reason for appointing official observers, rather than depending on the members of the group for procedural feedback, is that observers are in a better position to give an objective report of what happens. Someone deeply involved in a conflict is hardly in a position, at the same time, to take detailed notes or give an unbiased picture of what actually occurred. This should not be interpreted to mean that participants are absolved of responsibility for being sensitive to procedural problems and bringing them to the attention of the group. We would only caution that a member of the group who participates may be too close to what is happening to see it in proper perspective and thus may exaggerate or minimize its importance.

Although a single observer may be sufficient to do an adequate job, many groups will find that it is better to appoint at least two people to take notes on different aspects of the discussion process; one to concentrate on the problem-solving aspects — the quality of thinking, the handling of evidence, the testing of ideas — and another on the interpersonal aspects — the psychological climate, the character of the leadership, the nature of hidden agenda.

The observer who is responsible for evaluating the group's ability to think collectively should be able to report on some of the following matters.

(1) Were the members of the group clear as to the type of problem they were dealing with (perception, diagnosis, attitude, or action)? Did it appear to be clearly defined and limited?
(2) Was the problem investigated in a logical and systematic way considering the topic and purpose of the group? If not, why not?
(3) At what points did digressions occur? How serious were they? Who was responsible for them? How did the group recover?
(4) Was an atmosphere of inquiry and objectivity maintained toward the problem? If not, were the lapses serious and were they justified?
(5) Was sufficient information brought to bear on the problem? Were facts tested for reliability? Was good use made of the information available in the group?
(6) Did the members of the group place too little or too much reliance on authorities? If authorities were used, were they adequately evaluated?
(7) Was the problem adequately diagnosed — i.e., were its causes gone into broadly and deeply enough or was the analysis superficial and oversimplified?
(8) Did the group reason logically? Any failure to do so? When, if ever, did the group resort to prejudice, name-calling, or exhortation as a substitute for thinking?
(9) How creative was the group in finding a wide range of hypotheses or solutions? Was sufficient consideration given to explanations or solutions which were unusual or unorthodox?
(10) Did the group periodically summarize its conclusions so that the participants knew what had been covered and what issues remained to be settled?

(11) Did the group make use of its findings in earlier stages of its deliberations when considering possible decisions?
(12) Was a sufficiently persistent effort made to explore, pursue, and attempt to resolve significant conflicts in points of view?
(13) Do you think that the final decisions reflected the best thinking of which this group was capable?

The observer who is responsible for reporting on the psychological and interpersonal conditions in the group should be able to give data on some of the following items.

(1) In what kind of psychological atmosphere did this group work? Did it seem to be overly cooperative? Overly competitive? Too rigid and formal? Too anarchic?
(2) Was sympathetic consideration given to all contributions? If not, why not?
(3) Was there evidence of social pressure being exerted against any member of the group? If so, was it justified?
(4) Did there appear to be any hidden agenda in this meeting? Should it have been brought out into the open or not?
(5) Did all the members of the group have an equal *opportunity* to participate? Did the group make the best use of its resources?
(6) Were there any significant breakdowns in communication? Were participants sufficiently sensitive to language barriers?
(7) At what point did interpersonal tension exist? Why? What brought it about? How was it released?
(8) Did you notice any members who continuously performed certain functions or played such roles as "harmonizer," "obstructionist," or "initiator"?
(9) Did the leadership of the group rest in one individual, or was it shared by many members of the group?
(10) Was the leadership autocratic or democratic in character? Was it consistent with the demands of the situation?
(11) Do you believe that the members of the group were satisfied with their decisions? Satisfied with their own contribution to the group?

The observer reports

After gathering their data, what role should the observers then play in the evaluation of the meeting? One way to help the group would be simply to give an objective report on the course of the discussion. The observers might indicate from their notes, for example, how the meeting was opened, what issues were discussed, how conflicts were settled, what decisions were, or were not, made, who exerted leadership, and so on. They would refrain from offering any diagnosis of why these things happened as they did, or from making suggestions as to new procedures they would recommend. These matters would be left in the hands of the participants.

The observers, on the other hand, might not limit themselves to an objective description of the meeting, but offer interpretations of why certain things happened as well. After noting a serious unbalance in participation, an observer might suggest that this appeared to be a result of social pressure, lack of information, or a reflection on the leadership of the group. Gross deviations from the original plan for the meeting might be related to the failure to give everyone a voice in formulating the agenda, unresolved differences in the goals of group members, or lack of clarity in stating the final plan. Having witnessed the discussion from a different vantage point than the actual participants, the observer is often in a position to offer helpful explanations for the behavior of the group. Yet there is some danger in this approach. Observers may find that their explanations — no matter how compelling they seem from outside the group — do not square with the perceptions of the participants themselves. Argument may then ensue over the "real" meaning and motives behind some incident. Yet if a diagnosis is offered with some caution and humility it will often be found that an outside observer can pick up clues to which group members themselves are almost entirely blind.

The final possibility is to combine description and interpretation with evaluation. In this case the observers assess what appears to them to have been the strong and weak points of the discussion. During the analysis period the observers may compliment the group for its frankness in handling a tense situation, for probing so thoroughly into a basic conflict in values, for its rigor in testing certain ideas. Or they may criticize the leadership, blame certain members for their lack of preparation, or take the group to task for its failure to organize and discipline its thinking. Evaluation of this type, coming from outside the group, is often difficult for hardworking committee members to take graciously. But it sometimes focuses attention sharply on critical procedural matters and often may express what members of the group secretly feel to be the case but are afraid to state so boldly.

Selecting observers

Should an ordinary member of the group or a specialist in human relations be designated to serve as observer and to lead the period of analysis? At first glance it would seem natural to choose an expert whenever possible. Being specially trained for the job he would be more likely to pick out the significant action of group members. He should be better equipped to offer explanations of the motives which find expression in apathy, dominance, monopolization, or overaggressiveness. Further, his experience should prepare him to make valuable recommendations for improving the performance of the group.

While, on the whole, these arguments are convincing, they leave out several factors. The consultant, for one thing, is usually an outsider and this complicates his relationship with the group. His observations and especially his evaluations may not be taken seriously (internalized) by the participants because they feel he does not really understand them, or because he misinterprets what happened. (In much the same way that children and students sometimes reject the advice of parents and teachers.) Group norms may exist of which he has no knowledge, and some patterns of interaction, both verbal and nonverbal — gestures, griping, kidding — may serve a different function than those to which the observer is accustomed. (The anthropologist has found that the role of "participant observer" of a foreign culture is a difficult one to maintain. The observer must become involved in the society to understand it, but if he becomes too involved he loses the ability to assess objectively.) Also, the group may become dependent upon the expert in an even more serious way than they are on their own leader. To the extent that they abdicate responsibility for analyzing and assessing their own behavior they will not develop standards of judgment of their own. When the expert leaves, they may be no better off than before he assisted them.

An alternative method of providing for feedback is to rotate the job of observer among the members of a group. There is much to be said for this solution. Serving as an observer is one of the most effective ways of training people for more sensitive participation. To step out of the role of participant and into the role of critic often leads to important insights into social relationships. The change in perspective allows people to look behind the scenes and to appreciate why the group operates as it does. Observers often comment that their temporary isolation from the group has led them to see themselves in a different light and to understand better some of the motives that dictate their behavior. Yet using a member of the group as observer does sterilize that person and deprives the group of his knowledge and skills. As teachers and consultants know, it is also easy to misevaluate other people's actions, even when you have known them for a long time. Sometimes, too, the ordinary member of a group is not sufficiently sensitive or sophisticated to recognize symptoms of mature or immature behavior. It is possible, of course, to combine the talents of expert and layman, teacher and student, by having both act in the capacity of observer at the same time.

Additional Descriptive and Evaluative Instruments

There are a number of additional tools that can be used to isolate and evaluate specific aspects of group behavior. Most of these instruments are devices which enable the user to get more objective information about the elusive and transient interactions that occur in discussion.

Interaction analysis

Some methods of analyzing the flow of discussion have already been suggested in previous pages. It is possible to keep a record of the quantity of participation by preparing an interaction diagram like the one described in Chapter 12. An observer simply draws lines on a diagram of the group, connecting individuals who communicate with one another. Intersecting bars indicate the frequency with which a particular channel has been used in the discussion. Lines drawn from each participant away from the group represent remarks addressed to the group as a whole. Inspection of such a chart by the group will reveal whether or not communication is unbalanced, which members are staying out of the discussion, who is monopolizing the conversation, and so on.

Another way of analyzing a discussion is to keep a list of the various ideas talked about during the meeting. This record may suggest that the group is not sufficiently organized, that members do not clearly understand their goals, or that the agenda is illogically put together. If the group jumps randomly from one issue to another, or periodically comes back to the same issue, this may mean that the agenda was never really understood or accepted, or that it is inappropriate in view of other situational factors.

More detailed information concerning a discussion may be obtained by categorizing every contribution to the discussion and then analyzing the significance of shifts in the frequency of each type of interaction, or noting the characteristic roles played by various members of the group. An instrument of this type is suggested below.

PARTICIPATION RECORD[2]

Category of Interaction	*Name or Number of Participant*					Totals
1. Expresses support, releases tension.						
2. Agrees or accepts conclusion.						
3. Gives information.						
4. Gives opinion or idea.						
5. Gives argument, reasons.						
6. Defines or clarifies remark.						
7. Offers procedural help.						
8. Asks for procedural help.						
9. Asks for clarification.						
10. Answers argument, refutes, criticizes.						
11. Asks for opinion.						
12. Asks for information.						
13. Disagrees, objects, blocks.						
14. Expresses antagonism, tension.						
Totals						

[2] This interaction chart is based on an instrument described by Bales in his *Interaction Process Analysis*.

The leadership rating scale

Since leadership is such an important ingredient in the life of a group, various attempts have been made to construct devices for describing or evaluating it. One of these instruments is the *Barnlund-Haiman Leadership Rating Scale.*[3]

Barnlund-Haiman Leadership Rating Scale[4]

Instructions: This rating scale may be used to evaluate leadership in groups with or without official leaders. In the latter case (the leaderless group) use part A of each item only. When evaluating the actions of an official leader use parts A and B of each item on the scale.

INFLUENCE IN PROCEDURE

INITIATING DISCUSSION

A. 3	2	1	0	1	2	3
Group needed more help in getting started			Group got right amount of help			Group needed less help in getting started

B. The quality of the introductory remarks was:

Excellent	Good	Adequate	Fair	Poor

ORGANIZING GROUP THINKING

A. 3	2	1	0	1	2	3
Group needed more direction in thinking			Group got right amount of help			Group needed less direction in thinking

B. If and when attempts were made to organize group thinking they were:

Excellent	Good	Adequate	Fair	Poor

[3] This is a revised form of the original *Barnlund-Haiman Leader Rating Scale* which was developed as a research instrument at Northwestern University and was first published in Franklyn Haiman, *Group Leadership and Democratic Action,* Appendix A.

[4] This scale may be reproduced without permission of the publisher or authors provided that it is reproduced in full, with the title *Barnlund-Haiman Leadership Rating Scale,* and that it is used only for educational purposes by nonprofit organizations. Permission must be obtained for other purposes.

CLARIFYING COMMUNICATION

A. 3 2 1 0 1 2 3

Group needed more help in clarifying communication	Group got right amount of help	Group needed less help in clarifying communication

B. If and when attempts were made to clarify communication they were:

Excellent	Good	Adequate	Fair	Poor

SUMMARIZING AND VERBALIZING AGREEMENTS

A. 3 2 1 0 1 2 3

Group needed more help in summarizing and verbalizing agreements	Group got right amount of help	Group needed less help in summarizing and verbalizing agreements

B. If and when attempts were made to summarize and verbalize agreements they were:

Excellent	Good	Adequate	Fair	Poor

RESOLVING CONFLICT

A. 3 2 1 0 1 2 3

Group needed more help in resolving conflict	Group got right amount of help	Group needed less help in resolving conflict

B. If and when attempts were made to resolve conflict they were:

Excellent	Good	Adequate	Fair	Poor

INFLUENCE IN CREATIVE AND CRITICAL THINKING

STIMULATING CREATIVE THINKING

A. 3 2 1 0 1 2 3

Group needed more stimulation in creative thinking	Group got right amount of help	Group needed less stimulation in creative thinking

B. If and when attempts were made to stimulate ideas they were:

Excellent	Good	Adequate	Fair	Poor

ENCOURAGING CRITICISM

A. 3 2 1 0 1 2 3

Group needed more encouragement to be critical	Group got right amount of help	Group needed less encouragement to be critical

B. If and when attempts were made to encourage criticism they were:

Excellent	Good	Adequate	Fair	Poor

BALANCING ABSTRACT AND CONCRETE THOUGHT

A. 3 2 1 0 1 2 3

Group needed to be more concrete	Group achieved proper balance	Group needed to be more abstract

B. If and when attempts were made to balance abstract and concrete thought they were:

Excellent	Good	Adequate	Fair	Poor

INFLUENCE IN INTERPERSONAL RELATIONS

CLIMATE-MAKING

A. 3 2 1 0 1 2 3

Group needed more help in securing a permissive atmosphere	Group got right amount of help	Group needed less help in securing a permissive atmosphere

B. If and when attempts were made to establish a permissive atmosphere they were:

Excellent	Good	Adequate	Fair	Poor

REGULATING PARTICIPATION

A. 3 2 1 0 1 2 3

Group needed more regulation of participation	Group got right amount of help	Group needed less regulation of participation

B. If and when attempts were made to regulate participation they were:

Excellent	Good	Adequate	Fair	Poor

OVER-ALL LEADERSHIP

A. 3	2	1	0	1	2	3
Group needed more control		Group got right amount of control			Group needed less control	

B. If and when attempts were made to control the group they were:

Excellent	Good	Adequate	Fair	Poor

The scale is based on the assumption that leadership must always be evaluated in terms of its appropriateness in a given setting. This means that factors such as the size of the group, the nature of the problem, the purpose of the group, and the time available must be taken into consideration in evaluating leadership behavior. It is possible for the same action to receive different ratings in two groups because of differences in the context in which the action is taken. Further it is assumed that democratic leadership is the goal and that deviations from this norm must be a result of situational pressures.

The scale permits an observer to make two independent judgments about each of the functions of leadership. The first (A) reveals to what extent members of a group (or an official leader) were sensitive to the needs of the group. It is a ratio between the amount of control the group needed and the amount actually supplied. Thus a group is as bad off because it is too tightly controlled as when it is too loosely controlled. To provide leadership in resolving conflict or regulating participation when these are not needed is as serious as failing to recognize the need for more control of participation or more help in resolving conflict. Thus, the first rating in each category is concerned with responsiveness to the need for leadership in a given social context.

The second judgment (B) is a measure of the quality of the leadership provided. Was a particular suggestion valuable in organizing the group, establishing a better climate, or resolving conflict? Did the leader in question summarize effectively, or did the summary hopelessly confuse or distort the issue? Was an attempt to clear away barriers to communication successful or did it complicate matters still further? These two aspects of leadership—sensitivity to group needs and skill—are of course interrelated, but a separate rating will reveal in which specific area the group is having the most trouble.

The light board

One of the most difficult of all group dimensions to measure is the emotional tone of a group and the relative strength or weakness of individual reactions to events that occur. Posture, language, and facial expression give clues to the intensity of personal response, but these indicators are consciously controlled by some people (the poker player is a notable example) and in other cases the outward signs are sometimes misleading.

One way of plotting the reaction profile of a group of people is to make use of an electronic device called the light board which will give a continuous record of individual responses to the ideas that are exchanged during a discussion. The light board consists of a set of switches (one for each person in the group) which are wired to a control bank of relays. Each relay activates a red or green pilot light depending on the position of the switch. When a member of a group reacts negatively (because of fear, anger, embarrassment, antagonism) he moves the switch to the "red" position. When he reacts positively (because of support, agreement, satisfaction) the switch is moved to the "green" position. From the bank of lights one can determine at a glance the emotional climate of the group.

Although primarily a research tool, the light board has diagnostic and educational uses as well. Ordinarily the board is located out of sight of the participants and used by experts to analyze some facet of interpersonal relationships. But a group of committee members, by placing the board in its own view, can use it to detect internal problems of various sorts. Whenever a given number of red lights are on, the group can agree to stop and analyze its own procedure to discover what is causing the negative reaction of so many members. Or it can be used as a sort of continuous ballot by having people indicate their approval or disapproval of each new idea that is proposed and discussed. It is one more way of obtaining additional objective information about a group. We should add that it can also make a group so self-conscious that it may disrupt their proceedings. For this reason we do not recommend it for group self-analysis except in unusual circumstances.

Sociogram

The sociogram, or chart of interpersonal attraction and repulsion, is another possible tool for group analysis. Participants are asked to fill out ballots which contain the following sorts of questions:

> What three members of this group would you most like to have as committee chairman? Least like to have?
> What three members of this group do you find most difficult to understand? Least difficult to understand?

A diagram is then constructed in which arrows are used to indicate who is attracted to or repelled by whom.

This is explosive information and is ordinarily not made indiscriminately available to all members of a group. In fact, it is intended primarily for research purposes, like the light board, and should be employed for group self-analysis only with the utmost discretion.

If learning, rather than experiencing, is the objective of a group, it is important to conduct some sort of evaluation of group interaction. An unstructured evaluation — feedback which is not organized around any particular set of data or topics — can be accomplished by setting aside a period for group introspection at the beginning or the end of meetings or by analyzing episodes whenever someone in the group is moved to do so. An evaluation can be structured, on the other hand, by collecting specific information through the use of Post-Meeting Reaction Sheets, group observers, interaction analysis, rating scales, or sociograms, and using these records as a basis for evaluating performance. In any case, the unexamined and unevaluated social experience is not likely to improve either the individual or the group to which he belongs.

RECOMMENDED READINGS

Howell, William, and Donald K. Smith. *Discussion.* Macmillan Company, 1956.

Torrance, E. P., "Methods of Conducting Critiques of Group Problem Solving Performances," in Paul Hare, Edgar Borgatta, and Robert Bales, *Small Groups.* Alfred A. Knopf, Inc., 1955.

Appendix C

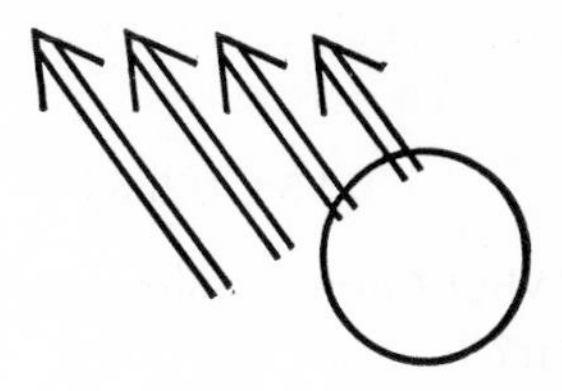

Exercises in Discussion

THERE ARE MANY PRACTICAL WAYS of learning how to discuss. In Appendix A some of these methods were evaluated. Here it is our purpose to give specific directions on how to prepare for topical and book discussions, how to set up and conduct role-playing scenes, and how to use case materials in discussion. Illustrative cases and sample role-playing scenes which have been used with some success by the authors are included.

Preparation for Topical Discussions

Preparation for practice discussions on topics of current affairs ordinarily consists of asking the participants to investigate the problem as thoroughly as they can in the time available to them before the discussion takes place. They should read about the topic in a wide variety of sources and, wherever appropriate, be encouraged also to do interviewing, make field trips, etc.

In credit-bearing academic courses in discussion there are at least two ways in which the student's preparation can be recorded and evaluated. The first is the discussion outline method; the second consists of note cards and a quiz.

Sample discussion outline

After choosing the topic, "What Changes Should be Made in the Status-of-Forces Agreements?" the members of this group (Fall, 1957) were asked to read as widely as they could on the subject and submit outlines such as the one which follows.

DISCUSSION OUTLINE

Problem: What Changes Should be Made in the "Status of Forces" Agreements? *

I. *Clarification of the problem*

A. "Status of forces" agreements will be interpreted as international laws requiring the following:

1. That the U.S. shall have the right to exercise legal jurisdiction over members of the U.S. Armed Forces in foreign countries in relation to offenses arising out of any act or omission done in the performance of official duty. (22)
2. That the host nation shall have jurisdiction in all other cases. (22)
3. That a joint committee consisting of representatives of both nations shall decide the issue of jurisdiction in cases in question. (22)
4. That members of the U.S. Military Forces being tried in foreign courts shall have the following rights:
   a. Prompt trial. (23)
   b. Right to be informed of the charges. (23)
   c. Right to confront witnesses. (23)
   d. Right to communicate with U.S. authorities. (23)
   e. Right to free trial, court costs and legal fees being paid by the U.S. government. (23)
5. That U.S. authorities shall be allowed to perform the following acts for imprisoned U.S. servicemen:
   a. Inspect the prison. (20)
   b. Provide medical care if necessary. (20)
   c. Supply extra food and personal items. (20)

* This is based on a student outline submitted by Dennis R. Hunt.

6. That in the event the accused would be denied rights he would enjoy in the U.S., the host state must give sympathetic consideration to the U.S. request that jurisdiction be waived. (22)

B. The term "official duty" as used is not meant to include all acts of members of the Armed Forces and civilian components during periods on duty, but is meant to apply only to acts which are required to be performed. (14)

C. This problem will include consideration of U.S. jurisdictional agreements with the following nations:

1. North Atlantic Treaty Organization nations: Belgium, Canada, Denmark, France, Greece, Iceland, Italy, Luxembourg, Netherlands, Norway, Portugal, United Kingdom, Turkey, Germany. (3)
2. Nations enjoying such jurisdictional rights by virtue of executive agreements: Azores, Bermuda, Cuba, Egypt, French Morocco, Spain, Malta, West Indies, Philippine Islands, Panama, Saudi Arabia. (1)

II. *Fact-finding*

A. Legal aspects of the problem.

1. The State Department holds that sovereign nations have always had jurisdiction over individuals accused of offenses within their boundaries, whether soldier or civilian. The "Status of Forces" agreements modify this jurisdiction and give U.S. servicemen abroad special protection. (20)
2. Schooner Exchange *vs.* McFadden (Supreme Court ruling, John Marshall, 1811): Military personnel passing through or stationed in a foreign nation by agreement of the sovereign authority of that nation are not subject to the laws of the host nation. (3)
3. Coleman *vs.* Tennessee (Supreme Court, 1867): A foreign army permitted to march through a friendly country or to be stationed in it by permission has exemption from civil and criminal justice of the place. (3)
4. Casa Blanca Case (Permanent Court of Arbitration, The Hague, 1909): The exclusive jurisdiction of the officers and military tribunal of a nation over its own troops is recognized. (3)
5. U.S. Manual of Courts Martial: Under international law,

jurisdiction over members of the Armed Forces of the U.S. or other sovereign nations who commit offenses in the territory of a friendly state in which the visiting armed force is by consent quartered or in passage, remains in the visiting sovereign. (14)

B. Results of the present program.
   1. Foreign nations have waived jurisdiction in 67% of the cases coming under the agreements. (10)
   2. 4,437 cases in all have been tried in foreign courts. (10)
   3. Charges have been dropped in 330 cases. (10)
   4. While 286 have been given sentences of confinement by foreign powers, 108 of these have been suspended. (10)
   5. The length of terms of confinement is as follows: 1 year, 11 confined; 1–2 years, 10 confined; 2–3 years, 13 confined; 3–4 years, 12 confined; over 5 years, 7 confined. (10)
   6. Types of crimes committed by servicemen now in foreign jails: robbery and larceny, 40 imprisoned; rape and sex crimes, 13; murder and manslaughter, 6; negligent homicide, 3; traffic offenses, 3; aggravated assault and related offenses, 2; passing worthless checks, 1. (10)
   7. U.S. servicemen receive the same prison treatment as do nationals. (3)

III. *Discovery of possible causes of the problem*
   A. Dissatisfaction of foreign nations with "Status of Forces" agreements.
   B. Dissatisfaction of the United States with "Status of Forces" agreements.

IV. *Evaluation of alleged causes of the problem*
   A. Dissatisfaction of foreign governments is illustrated in the recent riots in Taipei, Formosa, against the U.S. Embassy as a result of the court martial of a U.S. soldier for a civil crime. (15)
   B. Dissatisfaction of the United States with "Status of Forces" agreements.
      1. The trial of Army Specialist Third Class William S. Girard for manslaughter in the shooting of a 46-year-old Japanese woman has provoked controversy. The Supreme Court ruled that the case should be tried in Japan. Girard was found guilty but his sentence of three years at hard labor was suspended.

2. It is claimed that servicemen are not given democratic treatment by foreign nations.
   a. Foreign legal systems often include the levying of excessive bail, presumption of guilt, unreasonable search, admission of hearsay evidence, and no right of petition. (7)
   b. Foreign governments sometimes do not provide for public trials, trial by jury, protection from double jeopardy, protection from self-incrimination, right of appeal, protection against the use of force and duress. (3)
   c. Only England and Canada have a system of justice that resembles our own.
3. It is alleged that servicemen are often subject to unusual punishment such as death for killing a cow in India, hand amputated for stealing in the Middle East, or death for manslaughter in France. (7)
4. Legislative reaction.
   a. The Bow Resolution (H.R. 16) is designed to revise "Status of Forces" agreements or withdraw from foreign alliances. (3)
   b. The Gross Resolution (H.R. 236) provides that men stationed abroad should be completely informed of the legal status they have in foreign nations. (4)

V. *Discovery of possible solutions to the problem*
   A. Sentences imposed by foreign courts to be served in U.S. military prisons.
   B. U.S. constitutional rights be upheld in foreign courts.
   C. Obtain immunity for servicemen from foreign laws not observed in the U.S.
   D. Explain to soldiers their rights in foreign nations.
   E. Demand complete U.S. jurisdiction over American servicemen abroad.

VI. *Evaluation of possible solutions to the problem*
   A. Sentences served in U.S. prisons.
      1. Advantages:
         a. Servicemen would not have to endure bad prison conditions abroad.
         b. Would relieve foreign governments of the cost of imprisoning Americans.

2. Disadvantages:
   a. This might not be acceptable to foreign governments who want this jurisdiction.
   b. Danger of alienating friendly governments.

B. Protection of constitutional rights.
1. Advantages:
   a. Would insure justice for American servicemen according to their own standards.
   b. Might contribute to spreading American ideals of justice.
2. Disadvantages:
   a. Probably unacceptable to foreign governments.
   b. Impractical because of differences in educational levels and in concepts of justice.

C. Immunity from foreign laws
1. Advantages:
   a. Servicemen would feel they were judged more fairly.
2. Disadvantages:
   a. Also unacceptable to foreign governments for they have long felt they have a right to enforce their own laws.
   b. Foreign peoples feel strongly that servicemen stationed in their countries should abide by laws and customs of the country they are visiting.

D. Explanation of legal rights abroad.
1. Advantages:
   a. Fewer violations.
   b. Less occasions for generating anti-American feeling abroad.
   c. Better relations with allies.
2. No disadvantages.

E. Complete U.S. jurisdiction over Americans abroad.
1. Advantages:
   a. Assure fair trials and maximum of justice.
   b. Free servicemen from prosecution under unusual foreign laws.
   c. Prevent U.S. servicemen from enduring substandard prison conditions.
2. Disadvantages:

a. Likely to be unsatisfactory to foreign governments.
b. Will contribute to anti-American world opinion.

BIBLIOGRAPHY

American Mercury — *Reference Number*

"American Servicemen Abroad" (January, 1956) (1)

"Why Put G.I.'s in Foreign Jails?" (April, 1956) (2)

Hearings of the U.S. House Committee on Foreign Affairs (July, 1955, to February, 1956)

"Testimony of Congressman Bow" (3)

"Testimony of Congressman Varys" (4)

"Testimony of Congressman Jackson" (5)

"Testimony of Congressman Lanham" (6)

"Testimony of Congressman Dorn" (7)

"Testimony of Mr. Downer (V.F.W. legal aid)" (8)

"Testimony of Wilbur Brucker (U.S. Army legal aid)" (9)

"Charts from Department of Defense" (10)

Life

"Girard and the Larger Problem" (June 17, 1957) (11)

"New Story" (July 22, 1957) (12)

London Daily Express (September 10, 1955) (13)

Manual of Courts Martial (U.S. Army) (14)

Nation

"G.I.'s and Asian Justice" (June 15, 1957)

Text by Carlos Romulos (Philippine Islands) (15)

Statement by Congressman Rayburn (Speaker, House of Representatives) (16)

New Republic

"The Case of Girard" (July 15, 1957) (17)

Newsweek

May 27, 1957 (18)

March 19, 1956 (19)

U.S. Department of State Bulletin

"A Statement by the Under Secretary of State Concerning the Status-of-Forces Agreements" (August 1, 1955) (20)

"State Department Views on the Status-of-Forces Agreements" (July 29, 1957) (21)

"The Supreme Court Upholds the Girard Decision" (July 29, 1957) (22)

"The Secretary of Defense and the Secretary of State Review the Girard Case" (June 24, 1957) (23)

Sample note cards and quiz

After choosing the topic, "What should be the United States Policy in Berlin?" the members of this group (Spring, 1959) were asked to read as widely as they could on the subject and submit a series of note cards such as the following:

Current situation in Berlin

"In a decade, 3,000,000 of East Germany's subjects have fled into West Berlin, including in recent months the cream of its technical and professional ranks most needed to carry out Communist plans. Berlin may be an inconvenient outpost for the West to supply, but for the East it is an embarrassing magnet.'

Time (December 1, 1958), p. 20.

Causes of present crisis

Kennan believes that the major reason for the Soviet Union's desire to get the West out of Berlin is that effective domination of Eastern Europe requires that "every possibility and hope of an alternative be denied the subject people. So long as a free Berlin exists, this denial cannot be exerted against the people of Eastern Germany."

He also points out that continued frustration over Berlin weakens the belief of Eastern Europeans in the "unalterable success of Communist principles."

George F. Kennan, Former U. S. Ambassador to the U.S.S.R and former head of State Department Policy Planning Staff, "Disengagement Revisited," *Foreign Affairs* (January, 1959), p. 187.

On the day preceding the discussion, the students' packets of note cards were turned into the instructor and the following quiz was given to determine how well informed the participants were on the subject:

(1) Why does our present position in Berlin seem to disturb the Russians so much?
(2) What threat, short of force, do the Russians hold over the heads of the western powers in pushing us toward a modification of our present stand on Berlin?
(3) Describe the plan for reunification of Germany which the western powers have presented to the Russians at Geneva.
(4) What proposal has Russia made regarding Berlin's future?
(5) Briefly describe the city of Berlin on the following points:
  a. Relative population of eastern and western sectors.
  b. Comparison of the economies of the two sectors.

Book Discussions

Another method of preparing for a practice discussion is to ask the participants to decide on a provocative book or essay which they will all read and then discuss. It is sometimes useful to ask the members of the group to write out their personal reactions to the author's ideas so that they will come to the discussion having already formulated some tentative thoughts on the subject. We have found the following books and essays useful for these purposes.

Erich Fromm, *Psychoanalysis and Religion.*
Eric Hoffer, *The True Believer.*
Robert Hutchins, *Conflict in Education.*
Aldous Huxley, *Brave New World.*
Niccolò Machiavelli, *The Prince.*
Karl Marx and Friedrich Engels, *The Communist Manifesto.*
John Stuart Mill, *Essay On Liberty.*
Bertrand Russell, *Authority and the Individual.*
Henry D. Thoreau, *On Civil Disobedience.*

Role-Playing

This section contains a number of role-playing scenes which may be used either for demonstration purposes or for skills practice. In each instance, a general description of the situation is provided, along with specific briefings for the participants.[1]

[1] For further information on the handling of role-playing see Alan F. Klein,

The first step in setting up a role-playing exercise is to read aloud to both audience and participants the description of the general situation. Those who have been selected, or who have volunteered, to play parts may then be given their individual briefings, assuming that this has not already been done in advance.

For those scenes in which a leader is to practice dealing with a problem situation in the group, the person playing that role should be sent out of the room while the other participants are briefed. It is frequently helpful to send another person with him who can later sit at his elbow and view the situation as he sees it. This "alter ego" or consultant may serve several purposes. He may pass notes of advice to the leader. The scene may occasionally be interrupted so that the leader can confer privately with his consultant, or so that the consultant and leader can trade places. Lastly, having an alter ego at his side may give the leader the moral support he needs in order to feel less on the spot than if he were alone, and thus to be more willing to experiment with his role.

Ordinarily, the members of an audience who are watching a role-playing scene are given only a description of the general situation and are asked not to look at the specific briefings of the participants. In this way they can view the scene from the vantage point of an objective observer and thus be given an opportunity for practice in analysis. However, if it is particularly desired that they observe from other perspectives, they can be referred to some or all of the participant briefings. Another possibility is for one segment of the audience to identify with each participant by looking at his briefing only.

In most exercises it is important that the participants be informed only of their own roles and not read the briefings of other members of their group. The "School Board Meeting" (Scene 1, below) is an exception to this rule, for here only the leader need be kept uninformed, since the other role-players are cooperating in a deliberate attempt to create problems for the chairman.

Multiple role-playing, such as in the "Staff Meeting of the XYZ Toy Manufacturing Company" (Scene 3, below), is a technique in which several small groups within the class enact the same

---

Role Playing (Association Press, 1956). For both instruction and sample scenes (in an industrial setting) see Norman R. F. Maier, Allen R. Solem, and Ayesha A. Maier, *Supervisory and Executive Development* (Wiley, 1957).

scene in different parts of the room simultaneously, a procedure which provides an opportunity for more people to obtain skills practice. It also makes it possible later for the total group to compare what happened in the various sub-groups. When multiple role-playing is employed it is useful, before the actual scenes are enacted, for each of the participants to meet for a short while with those playing the same role in the other sub-groups to talk over their part and get warmed up to it.

Scene 1. School Board Meeting. A Problem of Hidden Agenda.

General situation

Centerville, a town of 100,000 in the Midwest, has some industry and a heterogeneous population of various religious, racial, and nationality groups. There are several grade schools, three junior high schools, and one high school.

Mr. Jason, the Superintendent of Schools, has been on the job in Centerville for three years. It is now Spring and his contract is expiring. The Board of Education has been discussing for several weeks whether or not Mr. Jason's contract should be renewed. A decision has to be made at this meeting of the Board, since he must be given adequate notice if he is to be released.

There is a great deal of controversy over the issue of retaining Mr. Jason. The major questions over which the controversy seems to have been raging are three:

1. *Progressive education.* Some people in the community feel that Mr. Jason has gone much too far in bringing so-called progressive methods of education into the schools. It is asserted that not enough attention is given to the fundamentals of "reading, writing, and arithmetic" and that a lot of time is devoted to "social adjustment" and discussion of controversial social and political issues which children are not adequately prepared to talk about. Other people feel that the most up-to-date knowledge about the psychology of learning is being employed, and that children should be informed on questions such as the United Nations, racial prejudice, etc.

2. *Administrative abilities.* Complaints have been voiced by some teachers, principally the older, more conservative ones, that

Mr. Jason's methods of dealing with his staff leave much to be desired. They complain of the amount of extra time they are expected to devote to various kinds of faculty committees, and they feel that those teachers who try to maintain high standards and discipline are discriminated against when it comes to promotions, favorable teaching assignments, etc. Other teachers seem to feel that Mr. Jason is a dynamic administrator who is simply trying to inject more democracy into the running of the schools.

3. *Off-the-job activities.* Many members of the community are disturbed at the off-the-job activities of Mr. Jason. He is an active member of the local chapters of the Americans for Democratic Action and the American Civil Liberties Union, and, when asked to give speeches before groups such as the Rotary and other service clubs, often delves into controversial political and social issues, such as advocating the elimination of racial and religious barriers in the community. Many people feel that the superintendent of schools should remain a more impartial figure. Others feel that it is not only his right but his duty as a private citizen to engage in whatever activities off the job he sees fit to.

Specific briefings

The *chairman of the school board* (and an alter ego) should be sent out of the room after the entire group has been given the information contained above in the description of the general situation.

Four to six participants should be chosen as *school board members.* Each one may choose and describe to the other participants and the audience his own role in the community—for example: a businessman with two children in elementary school, a housewife with a daughter in senior high school, etc.

At least two members of the board should be instructed to be pro-Jason and two anti-Jason. The others may represent varying degrees in between. The board members should then be instructed that there is a hidden agenda in this situation. The arguments about Mr. Jason outlined in the general briefing are only the surface issues. The real bone of contention is that Mr. Jason seems to have allowed, if not indirectly encouraged, social intermingling (e.g., dancing, dating, etc.) of racial and religious groups at the high school. The anti-Jason forces are much disturbed about this. The pro-Jason forces are not. However, this racial issue has never been openly aired at the board meetings, inasmuch as none of the members wishes publicly to reveal his personal prejudices. Any allusions to the real issue are veiled and indirect.

When the chairman is brought back into the room he should be informed of the roles in the community which each of the board members has chosen. The meeting is then called to order to take up the question of the renewal of Mr. Jason's contract.

Scene 2. Labor Union Executive Council. A Problem of Apathy.

General situation

This is a meeting of the officers of Local 123. This local has been troubled in the past two or three years by an almost total lack of interest in union affairs on the part of the general membership. It has gotten to the point where practically no one but the officers and a few other loyal souls come out to union meetings, and there is practically no understanding among the men about union problems. They are doing pretty well economically and do not seem to realize the potential danger of being complacent about some of the social, economic, and political problems that the union ought to be working on for the future. Also, there seems to be a growing attitude in the general public that there is not much democracy in the way labor unions are being run, and the officers of Local 123 would like to do something to improve their union in this respect, too. You cannot have democracy if people do not come to meetings.

The purpose of this meeting of the officers is to talk over this general problem and see if they can figure out something to do about it.

Specific briefings

Union Local President

Role for *Union Local President.* You are president of Local 123. You have held this office for several years, having been re-elected without opposition the last two times you were up. You feel that there are not many people in the world who have the get-up-and-go to assume responsibilities in an organization, and have found that the best way to get things done is to do them yourself. Even the other officers in your local are better at talking than working, so you have just taken union matters pretty much into your own hands. When problems needed to be solved, or decisions made for the organization, you have worked them out yourself. You feel that the men in the union have confidence in you and have been satisfied with your leadership, or they would not have kept re-electing you to office. You are disturbed, however, that so many members take such an irresponsible attitude toward union problems, because you know you cannot have a strong union without the wholehearted support of the members. You have got to figure out some way to get cooperation in the programs and policies you have worked out for them.

Secretary-Treasurer

Role for *Secretary-Treasurer.* You are secretary-treasurer of Local 123. You have held this office for several years, having been re-elected without opposition the last two times you were up. You have worked closely with the president over these years, and feel that he has done an excellent job. He is a real "idea man" and a vigorous leader. You feel that the people in the union do not truly appreciate the tremendous amount of work he does for them. They just take him for granted. You are not too disturbed about the fact that the interest in union affairs on the part of the general membership has been somewhat lacking. What difference does it make as long as things get done? And the president has certainly proved himself capable of handling things very efficiently and in the best interests of the men.

Executive Committee Member #1

Role for *Executive Committee Member* #1. You have been a member of the executive committee for a number of years and are pretty well satisfied with the way things have been going. The president is a capable leader and you have been glad to support him right down the line. He has good ideas, and is willing to do the work to put them into effect. With him in charge there really is not much you have to worry about. The Local would be pretty hard up if they lost him. You are a little concerned, however, by the fact that the members of the union do not seem as loyal to the group, or as interested, as they did several years ago. You do not quite understand why this is so. They seem to like the way things are being run — at least they keep re-electing their officers — and yet they do not come out to meetings or show much enthusiasm for supporting the policies and projects worked out by the president. Maybe somehow the union could be made more important to them.

Executive Committee Member #2

Role for *Executive Committee Member #2.* You are pretty fed up with the way this organization has been run for the past few years, but it is difficult, if not impossible, to say anything about this. The president and secretary-treasurer, who have been running things for a long time, seem to enjoy the confidence of the general membership and keep getting re-elected all the time. Also, they do their jobs efficiently, so there is no real agitation for a change. Anyone who spoke up against them would really get the cold shoulder. However, it is your feeling that in spite of the president's great efficiency and big ideas, he is himself one of the main causes of the difficulty the union is now having in maintaining the interest and support of its members. He seems to have the attitude that no one but himself has any brains or sense of responsibility, so he keeps all the power he can to himself and never seeks anybody else's ideas or help. No wonder people lose interest. Even though you are an officer you have practically lost interest yourself in coming to meetings. What's the point? Nobody cares what you think, so it is kind of useless to bother. And you suspect that this explains the complacency of a lot of the members. Why should they come to meetings just to sit around and listen to the president making long speeches? He does not need them. However, you feel that this is a dangerous atmosphere for the health of the organization, and that if something doesn't happen soon, the union will be on its last legs.

Executive Committee Member #3

Role for *Executive Committee Member #3.* You are a young man and relatively new to the executive committee. You think that unions are one of the most important things to which a person can devote his time, and you are extremely eager to work hard for the organization. As yet you have not been given a chance to do very much. The president seems to have things pretty much well in control, and although you would like to volunteer to take on some responsibilities you have not yet seen much of an opportunity. You feel that this problem of getting more interest and support from the general membership is very important, and that perhaps there are others like yourself who would like to do something for the group but do not quite know how to go about it. Maybe if they were given more chance to speak up at meetings and express their ideas on things, or were appointed to committees to work on various projects, they would show more enthusiasm. Now they can just sit back passively because everything is being taken care of for them. They may think this is okay now, but what happens to the organization if something were to happen to the clique now running things. Nobody else would know how to take over.

Scene 3. Staff Meeting of XYZ Toy Manufacturing Company. A Problem of Resolving Differences. (Multiple Role-Playing)

General situation

The executive officers of the XYZ Toy Manufacturing Company are meeting to try to come to a decision on a problem that has been under study for several months and has caused tempers to flare on all sides: to wit, shall the Personnel Division set up a program of counseling for employees on personal problems, hiring a small team of full-time professional psychologists to do this work. There are 10,000 employees in the company, about 70 per cent of them in various aspects of production, and the remainder in clerical, sales, and administrative positions.

Specific briefings

The President of the Company

The president of the company, who is chairing the meeting, has no strong convictions on the subject under discussion. He is more interested in finding what seems to be the most sensible solution to the problem, giving all viewpoints as much satisfaction as possible, and doing what is best in the long run for the company.

The Vice-President in Charge of Administrative Services

The vice-president in charge of administrative services is an old-timer, but a fairly flexible person who is open to new ideas when he thinks they are good. He is not entirely sold on the counseling plan but is quite interested in it. Everything he knows about it thus far leads him to feel favorable toward it, and he tends to think it is at least worth a try.

The Vice-President in Charge of Production

The vice-president in charge of production is also an old-timer, and one who takes a dim view of "all this new-fangled psychological stuff." He thinks that the company has no responsibility for the personal lives and problems of its employees and that nothing should be done to distract them from their work.

The Director of Personnel

The *director of personnel* is an extremely progressive man who goes in for all the latest management ideas in a big way. He is vigorously pushing this plan and feels it will be the biggest step forward that the company has ever taken.

The Treasurer

The *treasurer* of the company is interested in the dollar sign above all. He does not want to spend money for anything which does not show promise of visible, material returns. He tends to feel that the counseling plan is an expensive luxury that a profit-making organization cannot afford.

Scene 4. Campus Committee on Discriminatory Clauses. A Problem of Resolving Differences.

General situation

Early in the fall a resolution was brought before the Student Governing Board of Midwestern University proposing that fraternal organizations be given five years in which to remove all clauses from their constitutions which deny membership to any student on racial or religious grounds. Ever since the introduction of this motion the campus has been wracked with controversy over the merits and demerits of the idea. Campus organizations have taken sides, student religious bodies have announced their stands, faculty groups have issued pronouncements on the matter. A great deal of ill feeling has been generated among students, faculty, and administration. Even more serious is the fact that the controversy has been given wide publicity and the excellent reputation of the school is being jeopardized among its alumni and supporters.

Though generally believing in staying out of such matters, the administration has felt it necessary to try to assist in calming the conflict. The President, therefore, has asked the Dean of Students to intervene and arrange an informal meeting between the leading spokesmen of the various interested groups to try to achieve some agreement. It would be desirable, if possible, to issue a joint statement that would relax some of the tension on the campus and reduce the harmful publicity the University is receiving in the press.

The Dean has called a meeting in his (or her) office to discuss the fraternal clauses and the furor they have generated. The following persons will be present at this meeting.

Specific briefings

The Dean (of Men or Women)

The Dean (of Men or Women). You recognize that no matter what your personal feelings may be about discriminatory clauses, it is essential for the good of the University to bring about some sort of resolution, even if temporary, in this controversy. Four persons representing a cross section of opinion and interest have been asked to attend the meeting and you are hopeful that some compromise can be worked out. If a joint statement can be formulated at this meeting and publicized properly it would have a very beneficial and quieting effect both on and off the campus.

Alumna

Alumna. As a former student and sorority member you are convinced of the necessity of maintaining restrictions on membership in social organizations. As a fund-raiser for the University you are sure that the furor on the campus will hurt it financially. This sort of thing would never have come up while you were on the campus and you are worried lest the school acquire a reputation of being "leftist."

Fraternity President

Fraternity President. You are a fraternity president and have opposed the lifting of discriminatory clauses from fraternal constitutions. You believe, sincerely, that discrimination is unreasonable but believe that a student's social life is a private matter. You fail to see how eliminating racial and religious clauses from fraternity constitutions will stop people from discriminating anyway. Also, there seem to be some practical difficulties in getting the national organizations to change their constitutions.

Sorority President

Sorority President. You are a sorority president. While you believe that discrimination will be practiced in spite of the elimination of restrictive clauses, you do see substantial merit in the arguments against them. As a matter of fact your sorority (one of the few on campus) has never had such a provision in its constitution and things have worked out very well. On a few occasions minority group members have been elected, but there has been no "taking over" of the sorority by any racial or religious group. At least the elimination of this barrier leaves the door open for fraternities and sororities to choose their members as they please.

Independent

Independent. You are an independent, an active leader in campus affairs, and president of one of the largest men's dormitories. You have led the fight against discrimination in university housing, admissions, and scholarship grants. You cannot understand why a university should give tacit approval, through its leasing of fraternity and sorority houses, to any sort of undemocratic principle. In your opinion everyone has a right to choose his own friends, but barriers such as discriminatory clauses do not really permit this freedom of choice.

Case Method

In using the case method the members of a group should decide whether to write up original cases from their own experience or rely on those prepared by experts and available in casebooks of various types.[2] If the group decides to prepare its own cases, each member should be instructed to select a specific episode which he believes is significant and write an objective and impartial description of it. All relevant facts, background information, and as much verbatim material as can be remembered or obtained from records, should be included. Writers should be careful to avoid coloring their account in such a way as to prejudice readers of the case in favor of a particular conclusion. Copies of the best cases are then circulated and, after allowing time for study, are discussed.

Preparation for this type of discussion may be handled in several ways. Sometimes a case is handed out just before the meeting and members are given only enough time to read it before the discussion begins. Usually, however, the case is distributed well in advance of the discussion, and participants are expected to study it and, in some instances, to write an analysis of it. A written appraisal tends, sometimes, to make people less flexible and more defensive about their own opinions, but it does have the advantage of insuring that everyone will have given the case some serious thought.

A case discussion often opens up with a general and open-ended question such as, "What do you see in this episode that is interesting or significant?" Eventually the group will ferret out the critical facts, probe the causes, test conflicting opinions about the motives and behavior of the principal figures, suggest and evaluate possible courses of action. Groups will usually find that a realistic case description forces them to maintain a healthy balance between

[2] For further instructions on the handling of case discussions see Kenneth R. Andrews, *The Case Method of Teaching Human Relations and Administration* (Harvard University Press, 1955). Those interested in using cases extensively in discussion training will find a number of excellent casebooks available: F. K. Berrien and Wendell Bash, *Human Relations: Comments and Cases* (Harpers, 1951); John T. Dunlop and James J. Healy, *Collective Bargaining: Principles and Cases* (Richard D. Irwin, 1953); Franklin E. Folts, *Introduction to Industrial Management* (McGraw-Hill, 1954); Irving Lee, *Customs and Crises in Communication* (Harpers, 1954.) Harvard University also maintains an excellent collection of cases on a wide variety of industrial problems.

theorizing and abstracting on one hand and fact-finding on the other.

A variety of sample cases follows.

The Gundelachs

Mr. and Mrs. Gundelach are Unitarians. They do not go to church regularly, and are very much opposed to any kind of dogma, ritual, or authority when it comes to religion. Their son, Al, who is sixteen years old and a very intelligent, sensitive boy, goes off to college. Near the end of his freshman year he writes a long letter to his parents explaining that during the year he has come under the influence of a group of friends, who are Catholic, and a very dynamic and wonderful priest who is their Catholic chaplain on campus. He has been to many of their meetings and is now convinced that he would like to become a Catholic. He asks his parents' permission. If you were Mr. and Mrs. Gundelach what would you do?

Discipline for Political Affiliation[3]

A. Article XXIV, Section 1, of the constitution adopted in 1946 by the International Association of Machinists provides:

> Any member or members of any district or local lodge circulating or causing in any manner to be circulated any false or malicious statement reflecting on the private or public conduct, or falsely or maliciously attacking the character, impugning the motives, or questioning the integrity of any officer of the Grand Lodge, or officer or member of any local lodge, shall be deemed guilty of conduct unbecoming a member and subject to fine or expulsion, or both.

In 1948 charges of "conduct unbecoming a union member" were filed by a member of Lodge 122 against Hector Duff. The local trial committee found him guilty as charged, but by vote of the membership meeting, the report of the trial committee was set aside, and Duff was ruled not guilty. The complainant then appealed the decision of the Lodge to the International Executive Council.

International President Brown reviewed the evidence as pre-

[3] John T. Dunlop and James J. Healy, *Collective Bargaining: Principles and Cases* (Richard D. Irwin, 1953), pp. 225–26. Reprinted by permission.

sented in the transcript of the trial. The evidence implied that Duff was a communist. This implication was based on a newspaper clipping of the *Toronto Globe and Mail* captioned "T.L.C. Turns Down Move to Bar Communists from Union Positions." The clipping went on to report that "Machinist Duff told the delegates he has 'been a Communist for fifteen years, and I am proud of it.'"

Since President Brown considered the possibility that Duff may have been misquoted, he wrote him to give him an opportunity to deny or admit the newspaper quotation. Duff replied, "In reference to your letter . . . and the quotation from the *Toronto Globe and Mail,* I want to say, I did say what I am quoted as having said. I am convinced that communists make very good trade unionists. Having sailed the North Atlantic Convoy routes for close to three years, I think I have earned a right to have a democratic opinion in a democratic country." On the basis of this reply, President Brown reversed the decision of the Lodge, whereupon Duff appealed to the Committee on Appeals and Grievances of the 1948 Convention.

The Committee convened to consider the appeal, but Duff neither appeared to defend himself nor did he submit a brief on his behalf. Since Duff failed to produce any evidence that he was not a communist, the Committee recommended to the Convention that the decision of the Executive Council be sustained. By vote of the Convention the report of the Committee was accepted, and Duff's expulsion was ordered.

Guidance Director [4]

Robert Thorpe, Superintendent of Schools in the small city of Wachusetts; John Turrell, Principal of the Wachusetts High School; Edward Ray, Guidance Director of the Wachusetts Schools; and Henry Walters, Executive Director of the Chamber of Commerce, were seated around the conference table in the Superintendent's office.

Henry Walters of the Chamber was talking, "Let me brief you all up-to-date. Two months ago, the Chamber sponsored a Senior Industry Visitation Day during which all seniors in the high school

[4] Daniel E. Griffiths, *Human Relations in School Administration* (Appleton-Century-Crofts, Inc., 1956). Reprinted by permission.

visited the local industries. Before that day, a committee of industrialists arranged to feed these 200 seniors and 20 teachers after the visits to industries. It was agreed that an evaluation would be made of the visits."

"May I interrupt?" Edward Ray said. "I would like to point out that at no time was I invited to participate in this Senior Visitation Day although I am Director of Guidance, and vocational placement is part of my job as well as directing young people into jobs in local industry. I just want that in the record."

"All right," Walters admitted. "Then just yesterday, there appeared in the paper an article headlined as follows: 'Seniors Don't Want to Work in Local Industries.' This article originated from the Guidance Office.

"The very next day, Ronald Jones, of the Jones Shoes Company, came to see me. He was raging. He claimed the article was a terrible blow to local industry. He blamed me for the article."

"Let me interrupt again," Edward Ray said. "I had all seniors answer a questionnaire which included such questions as 'Would you like to work in local industries?' 'If so, which ones?' Now, no senior said he wanted to work in Jones Shoe Company. It's a well-known fact that Jones is a labor baiter and pays below the prevailing wage and has threatened to close shop if the union organizes in his factory. When the questionaire was completed, I mimeographed it and sent it to each industry which had seniors in their plants. How this information got to the newspapers, I don't know."

"Well, Jones, after accusing me of sending it to the papers, has accused you, Mr. Ray. Now this morning, he has resigned from the Chamber of Commerce, the Rotary, and as chairman of the new school building committee and permanent scholarship committee; isn't that right, Mr. Thorpe?"

The superintendent sighed and said, "That's right. As you know, Ray, Jones is highly influential in town. He can block the construction of a new school. He can prevent more seniors from getting scholarship aid. He's a heavy contributor to the Chamber of Commerce. Now, Mr. Turrell and I have talked this thing over and we have decided you've got to go down there and apologize to Jones and tell him the article was a mistake and that your students misunderstood the questionnaire and that they really want to work in his factory."

Edward Ray jumped up. "I won't apologize because there is something else about this you haven't heard. Jones called me up on the phone and told me he was going to get me fired; that I was ruining the city of Wachusetts; that there were a lot of educators he didn't like and I was one of them; and that I'd better get wise to myself or I'd be looking for a new vocation as he had power throughout the state."

John Turrell spoke up then, "But he also told us that you insulted him over the phone."

"I didn't insult him," Ray said. "I just told him the truth. That I was never invited to participate in the preliminary planning, but that you and Mr. Thorpe had. I also told him it wasn't my fault the boys didn't wear ties. I told him I had suggested that they should but Mr. Turrell overruled me. I told him I hadn't sent that material to the newspaper and that I was not his servant and he had no right to threaten me, especially when he doesn't even live in our city, and sends his children to private schools."

Henry Walters of the Chamber spoke up. "But he feels he's been insulted and he's badly hurt. Something's got to be done, or else he'll sabotage the Chamber of Commerce, at least the industrial division."

Edward Ray spoke up again. "I'm going to say something else while it's necessary for me to defend myself. It is this. Ronald Jones is sore because the Babbit brothers who run the Babbit Electronic Company are taking his help away from him, his prestige, his power in the city; and another thing, when Jones' daughter wanted a job teaching here last year, the school committee turned her down. He's just taking his venom out on me. Isn't that right, Mr. Walters?"

The Chamber of Commerce man reluctantly nodded his head. "Yes. All is not sweetness in the Chamber. Jones and the Babbits have been fighting now for some time. That was going on long before we had this Visitation Day. They don't get along at all. Understand, I'm not blaming anybody. I just want to know what can be done to make Jones change his mind, rejoin the Chamber, get back on the scholarship committee and the new school committee."

Mr. Thorpe, the Superintendent, said, "I can't see anything else but for Mr. Ray to visit him and apologize."

"If I go visit him," said Ray, "I'll only tell him a few more things, like what he did to my uncle one time, and it'll be worse than before."

Mr. Turrell, the Principal said, "Write him a letter, explaining why the students don't want to work there, or rather why they didn't say they wanted to work there."

"They don't want to work there," Ray said, "simply because it's a sweat shop, the pay is low, and conditions are poor all round. Besides that, the old man Jones is always losing his temper, throwing things around, and acting like a baby, like he did over this."

"But the point is," Mr. Thorpe repeated, "he'll block construction of the school. I know him. He's that type. He's got a lot of people who'll follow him, not because they like him, but because he's important. He'll be a focal point around which the opposition can gather in enough strength to ruin our plans."

"But I'm not going to get down on my knees and humble myself in front of a great big overgrown b——, when I did nothing wrong, except reveal some of the truth. What you're asking me to do is sacrifice a principle of mine just to kow-tow to him. And if I do what will happen? He'll be expecting the school system, like everybody in town, to give in to him every time he desires to go against somebody else. I can't see that."

Mr. Turrell said, "I'll go see him and apologize."

Henry Walters said, "It won't do. He's got to have an apology from Edward Ray or nobody. I spoke with him before I came over here and that's what he told me."

"But I've got nothing to apologize about," Ray said.

"And he wants a statement in the local newspaper that the questions were misunderstood and no reflection on the Jones business was intended."

"I refuse," Ray said.

"I'll have to bring this matter up before the school committee," Mr. Thorpe warned.

"Bring it," Ray snapped. "I'll tell them what happened."

Mr. Walters said, "I know exactly how you feel, Mr. Ray. But there's more involved than your feelings toward some abstract principles. You better think it over. But he's got to have an apology before tomorrow night or he'll never return to any of his positions. I'm going now."

Arno Annello, Machinist [5]

The standards department of the Schoonway Machine Company recommended that Arno Annello, who operated a battery of automatic gear-cutting machines, be discharged for failure to attain required minimum production as set by the standards department. The foreman in whose department Annello was employed objected to the recommendation. The matter was placed before the production manager for final decision.

Arno Annello came to this country from Finland. He had received the equivalent of a grade-school education in his native land but had practically no knowledge of the English language. He secured a job as a floor cleaner in the Schoonway plant. He showed himself to be industrious and thorough, and the foreman of the milling and gear-cutting department became interested in him. One day he suggested to one of Annello's friends that the floor sweeper should apply for a better job. When Annello heard this, he signified his desire to become an operative of the automatic sharpening machines. These machines were used to sharpen the teeth of cutters after the cutters were otherwise finished. They were automatic in operation, and with proper setup there was very little danger of spoiling the work. The foreman or an experienced assistant personally supervised each setup. The operative inserted and removed the work, started and stopped the machines, and dressed the emery wheels when necessary. He operated from four to eight machines, depending on the character of the work.

When a vacancy occurred in the department, the foreman decided to give Annello a chance, and obtained his transfer (on trial) from the cleaning department. Over a period of several months, Annello, with the assistance of the foreman, became proficient in operating the machines, and he was given a permanent job. For the next two years Annello showed steady improvement. He became known in the department as a first-class operative of automatic cutter-sharpening machines and finally developed into a skilled machine setter. While he improved as a machinist, Annello showed no aptitude in mastering the English language, and any extended or involved conversation had to be handled through an interpreter. The foreman, however, believed that Annello had the

[5] By permission from *Introduction to Industrial Management,* by Franklin E. Folts. Copyright 1954. McGraw-Hill Book Company, Inc.

makings of a first-class machinist and was willing to put up with this inconvenience.

The company decided to install a new battery of gear-cutting machines for milling the teeth in cutters, and the foreman was confronted with the task of getting additional operatives to run these machines. The work of operating the automatic gear-cutting machines required considerably more skill than was necessary to run automatic cutter-sharpening machines. The machine attendant had to set up the indexing mechanism for the cutter blank, set the tooth-milling cutter at the correct distance off the center line of the blank, see that the cutter was properly sharpened, and set the machine for the correct stroke. The machine fed and indexed automatically, but considerable care was necessary on the part of the operative to keep the indexing at exactly the proper adjustment. The foreman approached Annello with the suggestion that he prepare himself to work on the new machines. Annello was highly pleased and put in all his spare time trying to familiarize himself with the work. He succeeded so well that by the time the machines were finally installed the foreman felt that Annello was sufficiently qualified and gave him a place on the new battery. Here Annello worked along with the other workmen, all of whom had been trained at one time or another by the foreman. He appeared to do average work and was well liked by the other men.

The standards department of the Schoonway Machine Company decided to institute a series of studies relative to the operations of gear-cutting machines for milling teeth in cutters. After the routine research had been made, the standards engineers announced the minimum amount of output which a worker must attain in order to be considered efficient. No bonus could be earned until this standard was exceeded.

During the period in which the studies were made, Annello was nervous. He appeared unable to keep his machine in proper adjustment. The pieces which he turned out were inferior in quality, and the total number gradually fell below the point at which the minimum standard was finally set. Engineers from the standards department, knowing that Annello was a protégé of the foreman, sought to ascertain the cause of his trouble, but he was unable to make an intelligible explanation. They warned him of the seriousness of the situation. For several days there was no change. Then, at the suggestion of the foreman, time-study men retimed Annello, in an endeavor to find the cause of his failure. His showing was worse than ever. The engineers began to question whether or not he had the native ability to do the work. The head of the standards department expressed that doubt to the foreman. The foreman insisted that Annello was a first-class workman. The standards department believed that the foreman was prejudiced because he did not object when they suggested that Joseph Smith be discharged. Smith had been employed on the new battery for about the same length of time as Annello and his output was not so low.

With their watches concealed in their pockets so as not to arouse Annello's suspicion, the time-study men clocked him for a third time. Still he showed no improvement. After that, the standards department became insistent that Annello be discharged. The foreman was obdurate, and the standards department appealed to the production manager for a final decision. The latter listened to the recommendations of the standards department and to the objections which the foreman raised, and then made a ruling that at the end of one week the standards department was to make another clocking of Annello's work. If it still was unsatisfactory, the foreman was to be given an additional week in which he could take any measures he chose in attempting to bring the machinist's work up to standard. If he failed to do this within the allotted period, Annello was to be fired for inability to attain the minimum standard.

At the end of the first week the new timings were made. Annello showed no improvement. When the foreman received this information, he went to Annello accompanied by a friend of the latter's, who acted as interpreter. The foreman told the machinist that his work was coming along well and that he had no need to fear the time-study men, that they would bother him no more. He said he would see to it personally that nothing happened to Annello and that as long as he tried his best he always could have a job with the Schoonway Machine Company. Annello thanked the foreman profusely and said that he always tried to do his best. The next morning he appeared at work smiling and happy. His output for the day was just at the minimum standard, but the quality was excellent. The next day his output increased. At the end of the week he was earning a good bonus. Six months later the standards department, as well as the foreman, rated him as the best worker on the automatic gear-cutting machines.

The Roberts Machine Company [6]

It was customary for the Sales Department of the Roberts Machine Company to meet for dinner about every other month. A hotel private dining room was engaged and after dinner a business meeting was conducted by Gordon Swift, Sales Manager. Present at the October meeting in 1957 were Swift, Al Rockland, Assistant Sales Manager, and ten salesmen of the department, six of whom had more than fifteen years of service with Roberts. Also present was James Jacobs, Sales Manager of Electro-Products, Inc., manufacturers of electrical components for home appliances. Jacobs, a personal friend of Swift's and known to most of the men, had been invited to observe the meeting. Swift had previously accepted a similar invitation from Jacobs.

The agendum for the meeting was the consideration of a new method for communicating product information to Roberts' dealers. The new technique was a phonograph record to accompany the firm's catalog. The catalog-record idea was for the dealer, in his own shop or home, to play the record as he leafed through the Roberts catalog. Swift felt the pictures and written words of the catalog alone could not communicate as adequately as the record and catalog combined. The record, in his words, "added another dimension to product communication."

Swift opened the meeting by explaining the purpose of the catalog-record technique and asked the salesmen to play the role of the dealer as they listened to the record. The salesmen leafed through the catalog as the record called their attention to certain aspects about the products.

When the record ended, Swift asked for comments about the technique. Most of the men contributed to the informal discussion which followed. Mr. Jacobs did not participate.

Various pros and cons of the technique were discussed but the majority of the men seemed to agree that the catalog-record idea was basically a good one. Most of them approved of the method as a way of communicating to the dealer in two media, visually and aurally, simultaneously. A few, however, wondered if it might be

[6] William V. Haney, Northwestern University School of Business, Copyright 1958. Reprinted by permission. All names and organizational designations have been disguised. Northwestern University cases are reports of concrete events and behavior, prepared for class discussion. They are not intended as examples of "good" or "bad" administrative or technical practices.

too difficult for a man to listen, look at pictures, and read at the same time.

There was some disagreement as to whose voice should appear on the record. Several felt a professional announcer should do the job while the majority preferred that Mr. Swift be the narrator. They suggested that his voice would add a note of warmth and make the process seem more personal than the usual media such as catalogs, pamphlets, newsletters, etc.

Some thought the record offered a special advantage in increasing the accuracy of the communication. They said the emphasis and inflection of the narrator's voice on certain words would help to convey information more precisely than would the written word alone. One man wondered if the average dealer would have the facilities for playing the record but others felt almost every home had a 78 rpm record-player these days.

About thirty minutes after the discussion began, one of the younger salesmen, Ed Knoll, commented: "As long as we're talking about dealer communication, I think we could capitalize on the visual communication angle, too. I wonder if we couldn't take some film clips of several of our machines in action."

There was an audible groan from several of the men. The next person to speak referred to another topic and the subject of film clips never arose again.

Jacobs was somewhat puzzled about the apparent apathy and even negative reaction to the film clip idea. While it was not strictly relevant to the catalog-record technique, it did appear to Jacobs that the idea had potential value for Roberts' over-all sales program. The Roberts machines were intricate; a motion picture of them in action could convey what words and still pictures could not possibly communicate. Moreover, Jacobs had always considered Knoll as a bright, hard-working young man who had expressed sincere interest in Roberts during his three years with the firm. But Jacobs remained silent and the meeting continued for another hour.

Eventually, Swift said: "Well, gentlemen, I think we've kicked this around long enough and I certainly appreciate your comments. Al and I will get our heads together next week and we'll let you know whether or not we decide to go ahead with the catalog-record idea.

"But right now, I'd like to hear what our friend, Jim Jacobs, has to say about the performance we put on for him. He's been sitting here soaking it all in. Any reactions, Jim?"

"You're right, Gordon, I have been soaking it all in, which is a bit unusual for me. I'm ordinarily running the show rather than watching it — and I certainly appreciate your invitation. I'd like to do this more often.

"Now, if you don't mind, Gordon, I wonder if I could impose upon you and your men for about three minutes."

"Go right ahead, Jim. Got something cooked up?"

"Well, in a way. You men all know how enthusiastic Gordon is on the subject of communication. And most of you know that I'm pretty much the same way myself. As a matter of fact Gordon and I have spent hours at a time talking about the problems of communication in a business and heaven only knows we've got them in our plant — and in my own department, too. Now, there was one point in this meeting that particularly interested me. Do you all recall that remark of Ed Knoll's about film clips? Well, I wonder if you'd oblige me by writing a short sentence or two about your reaction to Ed's comment. Don't bother to sign your name."

Each man wrote a brief note and passed it to Jacobs who said: "Thank you very much, gentlemen. You might be interested in what I'm up to. Frankly, it's just a little 'experiment' I thought of while I was sitting with my ears open for a change instead of my mouth. I really don't know what to expect from it.

"But Gordon is giving me a lift home so I imagine you'll be getting the results through him."

"Fine, Jim," Swift replied. "This might be interesting at that. And now, unless anyone has anything else to add, let's adjourn the meeting."

Swift began speaking with two or three of the salesmen at the door while the others were collecting their papers and getting into their coats. Jacobs called Knoll over and said: "Ed, I wonder if you would tell me just what you had in mind with that film clip idea?"

"Well, Mr. Jacobs, I thought we could shoot a short film on our own — probably wouldn't run more than ten or fifteen dollars. I have a 16mm camera and if the company would buy the film and me rig up a few lights — "

"Were you suggesting that the film would be coordinated with the record?"

"Oh, no — it would be entirely apart from the catalog and record. It would be just another way of communicating with our dealers and their customers, too. Our machines are too big, too expensive, and there are too many models for our dealers to stock them. The film would be a way of communicating the actual operation of our machines."

Jacobs thanked Knoll and went over to Swift who was waiting to drive him home. As they rode Jacobs read the statements aloud. There were eleven of them:

"COST! ! !" [7]

"Oh, no! Not the movie boys again!"

"That isn't the kind of thing we can afford to do now."

"Coupled with the record and preview of the catalog the film would be a sharp idea."

"Necessity of having a projector and screen besides a phonograph — too much apparatus."

"Completely irrelevant in terms of a critique of the record idea."

"The idea is for catalogs and records to be sent out and heard. If they are going to show movies you don't need catalogs."

"Vision with the record sounded like a good idea."

"A sound film would be better than a film with a separate record."

"Book, voice, and pictures — too much to observe."

"That's all we need — another unusable film!"

[7] Jacobs discovered from Swift that the Roberts Co. had a very unpleasant and costly experience with a product film prepared by a film production firm. The film had cost $7500 and for various reasons had never been used.

AUTHOR INDEX

SUBJECT INDEX

FGHIJ—R—73210/698765